Irish Family and Local History

Robert Blatchford

and

Elizabeth Blatchford

The Irish Family & Local History Handbook 2

ISBN: 978 0 9552399 7 7

Published by
Robert Blatchford Publishing Ltd
33 Nursery Road, Nether Poppleton YORK, YO26 6NN U.K.
T: +44 1904 332638
E: sales@ genealogical.ie sales@genealogical.co.uk
W: www.genealogical.ie www.genealogical.co.uk

The Irish Family & Local History Handbook 2 **Published February 2013** **ISBN 978 0 9552399 7 7**

Design, layout and typesetting by Robert Blatchford Publishing Ltd

Printed and bound by
Charlesworth Press, Flanshaw Way, Flanshaw Lane, Wakefield WF2 9LP U.K.
T: +44 (0) 1924 204 830 E: info @charlesworth.com W: www.charlesworth.com

About the Editors & Publishers

Robert Blatchford LL.B (Hons)
is a law graduate of The University of Hull, England. He is a member of The Society of Genealogists as well as Cleveland, The City of York, Devon, Dyfed, Glamorgan, Somerset & Dorset & Gwent Family History Societies. He is a former Chairman of The City of York FHS and former Vice Chairman of the North East Group of Family History Societies. He has undertaken research in England, Wales, Scotland, Belgium and France as well as in Ireland, Australia and the United States. He has edited and published all of the thirteen issues of *The Family and Local History Handbook*, *The Family and Local History Handbook 1- 10* Data CD containing issues 1 - 10 of the Handbook in pdf format. *The Family and Local History Handbook Omnibus 1 - 13* Data DVD was published in 2012 containing issues 1 - 13 of the Handbook in pdf format. He has also published *Herbert Chapman on Football* - a facsimile.

Elizabeth Blatchford
has been involved in genealogy and family history for over 25 years. She is a member of several family and local history societies. Elizabeth has been involved with this publication since its inception and has assisted with the editing of several editions. Elizabeth took early retirement from Local Government. She now owns a successful Training and Consultancy business in Health & Social Care. Elizabeth is also fully involved in the editing of *The Family and Local History Handbook* and with her four grandchildren and her cat, Alfie!

Going to Mass

contents

7	Editorial	
8	Researching Irish Ancestors	Dr William Roulston
21	The Certificate of Irish Heritage	John Hamrock
25	The Irish Family History Foundation	Karel Kiely M.A.
31	The Distress in Ireland - The Illustrated London News - March 13, 1880	
32	The National Library of Ireland	
37	Irish DNA Atlas	Dr. Gianpiero Cavalleri & Michael Merrigan MA, FGSI
42	The Sad Side	Joseph O'Neill
44	Upon Your Honour Sir! Duelling in Ireland 1750-1820	Stephen Wade
49	The General Valuation of Rateable Property in Ireland	Mary P McConnon M.A.
59	John (Count) McCormack (The Peerless Irish Tenor)	Brian Parnaby
62	The Irish in Wales	Beryl Evans M.A.
66	The National Archives of Ireland	Aideen M. Ireland
69	The National Museum of Ireland	
70	Dublin City Archives	
73	The Genealogy Advisory Service at National Archives of Ireland & National Library of Ireland	
75	The Irish in London	Emma Jolly
79	The Petty Session Order Books	Ross Weldon
85	British Parliamentary Papers relating to Ireland	Dr William Roulston
97	The Spanish Civil War 1936 – 1939	Joseph O'Neill
99	From Gibraltar to Belfast	Chris Paton
103	The Public Record Office of Northern Ireland	Dr Ann McVeigh
109	From the Mixer to the Modem - the Irish Navvy in Britain	Joseph O'Neill
113	A Lawless Outrage: Abductions in Eighteenth Century Ireland	Stephen Wade
117	Attempt at Abduction at Tipperary - Illustrated London News 8th July 1854	Fred Feather
118	Seeking Irish Ancestors in South Africa	Rosemary Dixon-Smith
123	Harry Furniss : Illustrator	Fred Feather
125	The Origin of the Species	Fiona Fitzsimons
132	Roman Catholic Parish Registers	Mary McConnon M.A.

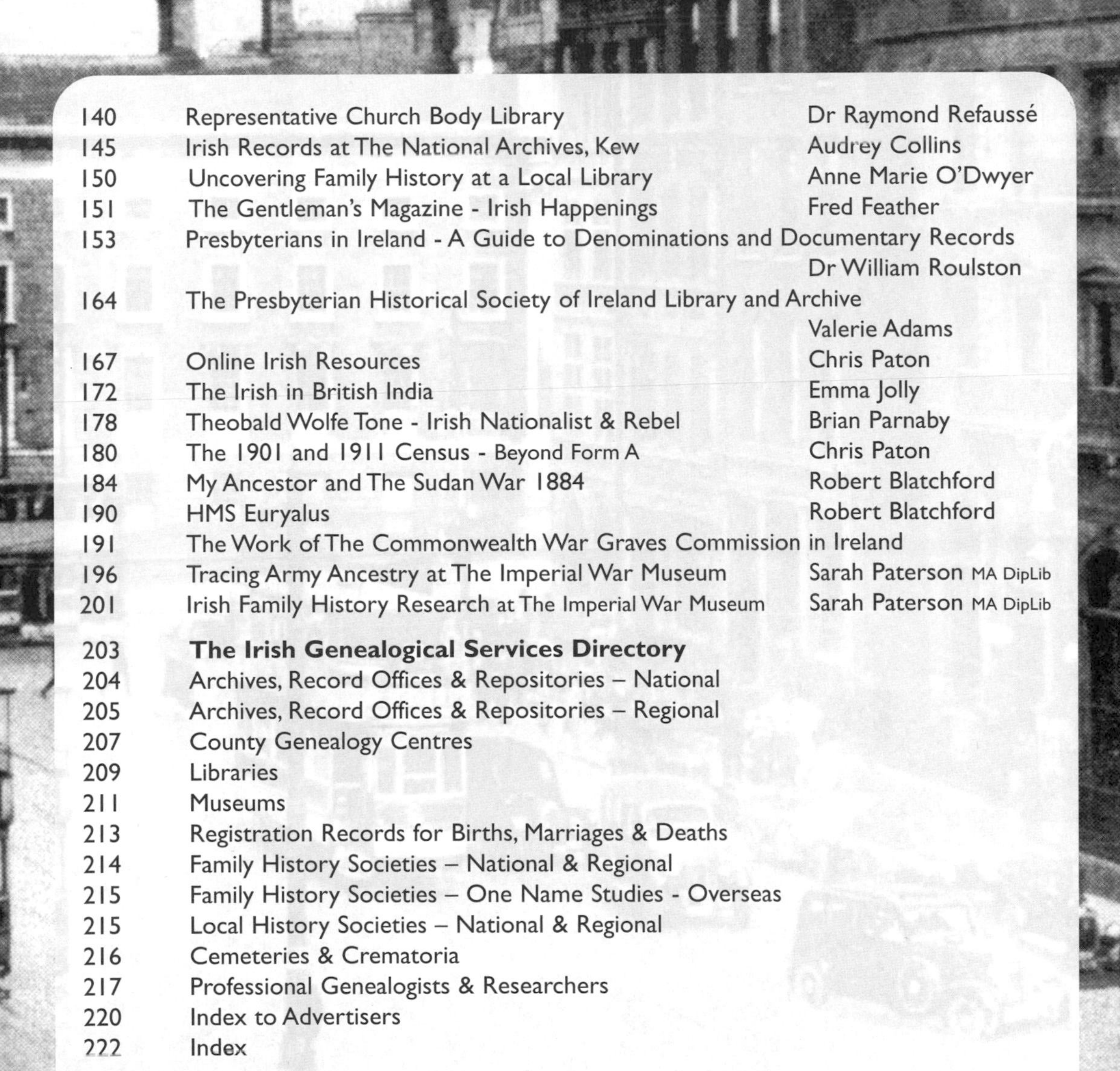

140	Representative Church Body Library	Dr Raymond Refaussé
145	Irish Records at The National Archives, Kew	Audrey Collins
150	Uncovering Family History at a Local Library	Anne Marie O'Dwyer
151	The Gentleman's Magazine - Irish Happenings	Fred Feather
153	Presbyterians in Ireland - A Guide to Denominations and Documentary Records	Dr William Roulston
164	The Presbyterian Historical Society of Ireland Library and Archive	Valerie Adams
167	Online Irish Resources	Chris Paton
172	The Irish in British India	Emma Jolly
178	Theobald Wolfe Tone - Irish Nationalist & Rebel	Brian Parnaby
180	The 1901 and 1911 Census - Beyond Form A	Chris Paton
184	My Ancestor and The Sudan War 1884	Robert Blatchford
190	HMS Euryalus	Robert Blatchford
191	The Work of The Commonwealth War Graves Commission in Ireland	
196	Tracing Army Ancestry at The Imperial War Museum	Sarah Paterson MA DipLib
201	Irish Family History Research at The Imperial War Museum	Sarah Paterson MA DipLib
203	**The Irish Genealogical Services Directory**	
204	Archives, Record Offices & Repositories – National	
205	Archives, Record Offices & Repositories – Regional	
207	County Genealogy Centres	
209	Libraries	
211	Museums	
213	Registration Records for Births, Marriages & Deaths	
214	Family History Societies – National & Regional	
215	Family History Societies – One Name Studies - Overseas	
215	Local History Societies – National & Regional	
216	Cemeteries & Crematoria	
217	Professional Genealogists & Researchers	
220	Index to Advertisers	
222	Index	

Editorial

Welcome to *The Irish Family and Local History Handbook 2* in which we have tried to provide a wide range of new and interesting topics which stand alone and contain original and unpublished material. As in our first issue this *Handbook* is relevant to the whole of Ireland and has been created to help people research their Irish ancestry encompassing both the north and the south. There are a few articles included from the first issue which have been revised and updated by their authors.

The Irish Family and Local History Handbook 2 provides essential guidance for the beginner as well as the experienced researcher and with the first issue creates a wealth of material for the reader and is intended to be an essential companion to research whether it is by using the extensive material in libraries, archives and museums or from the internet.

We hope *The Irish Family and Local History Handbook 2* becomes an indispensable tool for your Irish research. The listings in *The Irish Genealogical Services Directory* section have been checked and updated.

The magazine reviews for the first issue were very encouraging. *Your Family History* magazine said it was *'Like a giant and most expensive hamper . . . overflowing with delight and information' 'created with a view to assisting family historians be they beginners . . . or the long term experienced.'* The magazine concluded by commenting that it was *'the best £10 worth on the market today.'*

The Internet serves us well but we must raise a cautionary note again. There is a vast array of information available to us through the Internet and care should be taken when using unverified data found there as it can easily lead us astray. Always remember when dealing with any information that nothing should be taken for granted and where possible original documentation should be checked.

It is important that our descendants are able to rely upon the accuracy of our researches and by following this advice you will create a family history that will become an heirloom.

We are again grateful to all our authors for their expertise and willingness to contribute to each issue.

We hope that you, our readers, again enjoy this dedicated Ireland second issue as much as our first one.

Robert & Elizabeth Blatchford

Researching Irish Ancestors

An Introduction to the Sources and Archives

William Roulston

Ulster Historical Foundation

Interest in researching Irish ancestors has never been greater. Given Ireland's history of emigration, it is hardly surprising to find that around the world tens of millions of people have family connections with the island. Much of this interest comes from the USA, Canada, Australia and New Zealand. Many people in Britain also have an Irish connection and I am no longer surprised at the extraordinary number of individuals who want to quiz me on how to trace Irish ancestors when I am giving talks in England and Scotland. This article provides a basic introduction to researching Irish ancestors. It highlights what the major sources are and where they can be found. For a fuller look at Irish genealogy the reader should refer to some of the books noted below. Prior to 1922 Ireland was under one jurisdiction and so where I refer to Ireland I mean the entire island. Where I am referring specifically to Northern Ireland or the Republic of Ireland I will try to make this clear.

Some Background Information

Exploding a myth

A popular misconception about researching Irish ancestors is that it is a fruitless exercise because so many records were destroyed. There is no denying that the loss of so many records in the destruction of the Public Record Office, Dublin, in 1922 was a catastrophe as far as historical and genealogical research is concerned. However, since 1922 the work of archivists to gather records of historical importance has resulted in a vast amount of material being available for the genealogical researcher to peruse. In addition there are other repositories in Ireland where the collections have survived virtually intact, as well as categories of records now available that were not in the Public Record Office in 1922 and so escaped destruction.

Three main categories of record were destroyed in 1922:

- Virtually all census returns, 1821-51
- The registers from over 1,000 Church of Ireland parishes
- Virtually all original wills probated before 1900

Many other records, including records relating to government and the courts, were also lost. However, not destroyed in 1922 were the registers from some 600 Church of Ireland parishes as well as church records for all the other denominations in Ireland. Neither were official records of births, deaths and marriages destroyed.

Getting Started

As is the case anywhere, the best way for someone to begin researching their ancestry is within their own family. In nearly every family there is at least one member with an encyclopaedic knowledge of who married who and how many children they had and where they lived etc., etc. Collect as much information as possible on names, dates and places relating to your family; write it down and begin to plot out the skeleton of a family tree. Occasionally wrong information may be given, yet it is surprising just how often an elderly person's reminiscences prove to be an accurate recollection of the facts. A family Bible is another possible source

Four Courts, Dublin

Bank of Ireland, Dublin

of information on your ancestors. Gathering this information before you visit the archives can save a great deal of time. Once you find out what you do know you will then be aware of the gaps and will have a clearer idea of what you should be looking for.

What's in a name?

In carrying out research in Ireland, or anywhere for that matter, it is important to take into consideration all possible variant spellings of a name. Frequently the O and Mc or Mac prefix will be dropped. For example, a Sarah McElhatton of County Tyrone became Sarah Hatton when she moved to the north of England in the late nineteenth century. Names can also change slightly. Two examples of changes between Ireland and Scotland that I have encountered are Mooney to Moodie and McMahon to Maughan. Often names were changed slightly to remove some of the 'Irishness' about them and to allow newcomers to better assimilate into the host population.

The Internet

The internet has transformed genealogy around the world and Ireland is no exception. To list all the websites that deal with Irish genealogy would be impossible as they seem to be increasing almost by the day. A website providing a fairly comprehensive listing of internet sites relating to Irish genealogy is www.cyndislist.com/ireland.htm. Some websites focus on a particular county or district and contain extensive lists of digitised sources, while others concentrate on a particular family. It must be remembered that many Irish sources are not yet available online and currently available only through a visit to the relevant archives. Most of the main archives in Ireland now have a website and these are listed below along with other contact details.

Sources for the History of Irish Civilisation

When initially starting out on Irish family history research, it is a good idea to consult the multi-volume guides to sources compiled under the editorship of Richard Hayes. *Manuscript Sources for the History of Irish Civilisation* (Boston: G. K. Hall, 1965) includes four volumes on persons, two each on subjects, places and dates, and a single volume containing a list of manuscripts. Places are arranged alphabetically within counties. Estate records and maps are also listed by county. Five years later there appeared *Sources for the History of Irish Civilisation: Articles in Irish Periodicals* (Boston: G. K. Hall, 1970). This included five volumes on persons, three on subjects and a single volume covering places and dates. After a further nine years there appeared the *First Supplement, 1965–75* (Boston: G. K. Hall, 1979) in three volumes. Copies of Hayes's guides are available

Grafton Street, Dublin

in many libraries and repositories across Ireland and beyond. The information in these volumes is now available online as the 'Sources' database on the website of the National Library (http://sources.nli.ie). This comprises over 180,000 catalogue records for Irish manuscripts as well as articles in Irish periodicals.

Books

Numerous books on Irish genealogy have been written. Probably the best general guide is John Grenham's *Tracing your Irish Ancestors* (2012), now in its fourth edition. Another useful guide is *Tracing Irish Ancestors* by Máire Mac Conghail and Paul Gorry (1997). Other volumes deal more closely with a specific area, period or theme. Ian Maxwell's *Tracing your ancestors in Northern Ireland* (1997) is primarily concerned with records in the Public Record Office of Northern Ireland. He is also the author of two county guides published by the Ulster Historical Foundation: *Researching Armagh Ancestors* (2000) and *Researching Down Ancestors* (2004). Genealogical guides for counties Cork, Donegal, Dublin, Kerry, Limerick and Mayo have been published by Flyleaf Press. William Roulston's *Researching Scots-Irish Ancestors: the essential genealogical guide to early modern Ulster, 1600-1800* (Belfast, 2005) provides a comprehensive overview of sources for studying family history in the seventeenth and eighteenth centuries, including a summary listing of sources for virtually every parish in Ulster for this era.

Administrative divisions

The main units of administration in Ireland are:

Barony

A unit used in Ireland between the sixteenth and nineteenth centuries for administrative (census, taxation, and legal) purposes. Often drawn on pre-existing Gaelic divisions, baronies consisted of large groupings of townlands within a county. The 1891 census was the last to use the barony as an administrative unit.

County

There are 32 counties in Ireland, six of which are now in Northern Ireland. The county system as a form of territorial division was introduced into Ireland shortly after the Norman conquest in the late twelfth century. The creation of counties or shires was gradual, however, and the present arrangement of county boundaries was not finalised in Ulster until the early seventeenth century. In 1898 local councils based on county divisions were created. County councils remain the principal administrative body of local government in the Republic of Ireland but were abolished in Northern Ireland in 1973.

Parish

This territorial division refers to both civil and ecclesiastical units. Civil parishes largely follow the pattern that was established in medieval times. Ecclesiastical parishes do not always coincide with civil parish boundaries, however. Following the Reformation in the sixteenth century, the Church of Ireland more or less maintained the pre-Reformation arrangement. Church of Ireland parishes are, therefore, largely coterminous with civil parishes. When the Catholic Church began its institutional re-emergence in the late eighteenth and nineteenth centuries, it constructed a new network of parishes which did not necessarily follow the civil parish network.

Poor Law Union

Under the Irish Poor Law Act of 1838 commissioners were empowered to *'unite so many townlands as they think fit to be a union for the relief of the destitute poor.'* A Union was a group of parishes usually centred on a market town, where a workhouse might be built, with parishes and townlands as subdivisions. Rates, land based taxes, were collected within these areas for maintenance to the poor. They were named after a large town. The same districts later became used as General Register Districts.

Province

Provinces are composed of groups of counties. There are four provinces in Ireland: Ulster in the north, Leinster in the east, Munster in the south, and Connacht or Connaught in the west.

Townland

This is the smallest administrative territorial unit in Ireland, varying in size from a single acre to over 7,000 acres. Originating in the older Gaelic dispensation, townlands were used as the basis of leases in the estate system, and subsequently to assess valuations and tithes in the eighteenth and nineteenth centuries. They survive as important markers of local identity.

The Archives

The most important archival repositories in the Republic of Ireland are the National Archives of Ireland, the National Library of Ireland and the General Register Office; in Northern Ireland they are the Public Record Office of Northern Ireland and the General Register Office of Northern Ireland. An indispensable book is *Guide to Irish Libraries, Archives and Genealogical Centres* by Robert K. O'Neill (2nd edition, 2006) which provides contact details, as well as summary information on collections held by the main archives in Ireland.

The abbreviations used in this article for the main archives are:

- GROI – General Register Office of Ireland
- GRONI – General Register Office of Northern Ireland
- NAI – National Archives of Ireland
- NLI – National Library of Ireland
- PRONI – Public Record Office of Northern Ireland

Civil Registration

Civil registers of births, marriages and deaths provide basic family history information. However, their usefulness for the genealogist will depend on the period being researched. Civil or state registration of all births, deaths and marriages began in Ireland on 1 January 1864. Non-Catholic marriages, including those conducted in a government registry office, were required in law to be registered from 1 April 1845. Civil registration followed the administrative divisions created by the Poor

High Street, Belfast

Law Act of 1838. Under this act the country had been divided into over 130 Poor Law Unions. The Poor Law Unions were subdivided into dispensary districts, each with its own medical officer. Under civil registration the area covered by a Poor Law Union was used as the basis of each superintendent registrar's district, while the dispensary districts corresponded to the registrar's districts. In some cases the medical officer also served as the registrar. In overall charge of registration was the Registrar General in Dublin. Certified copies of all registers compiled locally were sent to his office and, from these, master indexes covering the whole of Ireland were produced.

Birth Certificates

Birth certificates record the date and place of birth of the child. Normally the name of the child is also given, but in some cases only the sex is given, i.e. the child had not been given a name by the time the birth was registered. The name and residence of the father is given. Usually this will be the same as the place of birth of the child, but in some cases it will show that the father was working abroad or in another part of Ireland when the child was born. The father's occupation is also given. The mother's maiden name is provided as well as her first name. Finally, the name and address of the informant is given, together with his or her qualification to sign. This will usually be the father or mother or someone present at the birth, such as a midwife or even the child's grandmother.

Marriage Certificates

Civil records of marriage normally give fuller information than birth and death certificates, and are the most useful of civil records. Information on the individuals getting married includes their name, age, status, and occupation. The names and occupations of their fathers are also given. The church, the officiating minister and the witnesses to the ceremony are named. In most cases the exact age of the parties is not given, and the entry will simply read 'full age' (i.e. over 21) or 'minor' (i.e. under 21). If the father of one of the parties was no longer living, this may be indicated in the marriage certificate by the word 'deceased' or by leaving the space blank, but in many cases it is not.

Death Certificates

Civil records of death in Ireland are rather uninformative in comparison to other countries. The name of the deceased is given together with the date, place and cause of death, marital status, the age at death, and occupation. The name and address of the informant is also given. Usually this is the person present at the time of the death; this may be a close family member.

The Indexes

Indexes to civil marriages 1845–63 are hand-written, but thereafter all indexes are printed. From 1864 to 1877 indexes for births, marriages and deaths consist of a single yearly volume covering the whole of Ireland. From 1878 the annual indexes are arranged on a quarterly basis. In each index the surnames will be arranged alphabetically, followed by the first names. The name of the superintendent registrar's district is also given, followed by the volume number and page number of the master copies of the registers in Dublin. In the indexes to deaths the age of the deceased will be provided. When using the indexes it is important to bear in mind possible variations of the name being researched. In the birth indexes an unnamed child will appear as *'male'* or *'female'* after the surname.

The General Register Office of Ireland

The administrative headquarters of the General Register Office in the Republic of Ireland is now in Roscommon, but there is a research facility open to members of the public in the Irish Life Centre, Lower Abbey Street, Dublin. The GROI holds master copies of births, death and marriages for all of Ireland up to 1921 and thereafter for the Republic of Ireland only.

General Register Office of Northern Ireland

The General Register Office of Northern Ireland (GRONI) has records of births, marriages and deaths for the six counties that now make up Northern Ireland. At GRONI it is possible for members of the public to book an index search (with verification of entries by staff) or an assisted search which allows for a general search of records for any period of years and any number of entries.

FamilySearch Record Search

In 2009 the website FamilySearch (www.familysearch.org) made available online civil registration indexes for Ireland 1845-1958. Rather than searching the indexes in Belfast or Dublin genealogists can now search a single name index of births, deaths and marriages for the period 1845-1921 with additional indexes for the Republic of Ireland after 1922.

The FamilySearch website also hosts the International Genealogical Index (IGI). The IGI contains information on family history drawn from a variety of sources and is always worth consulting for it may provide clues as to the place of origin of an ancestor. Very usefully it includes abstracts of civil births in Ireland from 1864 to 1880, giving the exact date of birth, child's and parents' names and a location which can vary from the townland to the county. It is also possible to search by parents' names which can be a good way of finding additional siblings.

Irish Family History Foundation

The Irish Family History Foundation is the co-ordinating body for a network of county genealogy centres on the island of Ireland. The databases on its website (www.rootsireland.ie) comprise the largest online collection of Irish civil records and church records. The records available cover most counties in Ireland, though the comprehensiveness of the coverage varies from county to county, with some being better for civil records and others stronger on church records. The indexes to the databases are free, but the records themselves can be purchased on a pay-per-view basis. The Advanced Search facility provides more options in searching for ancestors and in narrowing down the entries most likely to be of interest.

Church Records

Prior to the commencement of civil registration the main sources of family history information are church registers. PRONI has a vast collection of microfilms and photostat copies of church records, as well as some original material, relating to nearly all denominations in the province of Ulster. Family historians should consult PRONI's *Guide to Church Records* for more information. The National Library of Ireland has microfilms of over 1,000 sets of Roman Catholic registers for the whole of Ireland (John Grenham's *Tracing your Irish Ancestors* (2012) includes a listing for every county in Ireland. The Representative Church Body Library in Dublin has many Church of Ireland records both in original form and as microfilms. The Presbyterian Historical Society in Belfast has a few Presbyterian records that are not available elsewhere.

Denominations

The single largest denomination in Ireland is the Roman Catholic Church. Following the Reformation in Ireland the Catholic Church went through a lengthy period when its activities were severely curtailed. The Penal Laws were a series of enactments of the late seventeenth and early eighteenth centuries designed to remove the rights of Catholics to public office and to careers in certain professions. In spite of the Penal Laws, Catholic priests and bishops operated freely in most areas. During the eighteenth century the Catholic Church was able to set up diocesan and parochial structures. It is important for family historians to bear in mind that Roman Catholic parishes generally do not conform to civil

Christ Church Cathedral, Dublin

parishes. Many Roman Catholic parishes have more than one church. Sometimes only one register was kept for the entire parish, but at other times each church had its own registers.

The Church of Ireland is the largest Protestant denomination on the island of Ireland. Until 1870 it was the established or state church and enjoyed various privileges in consequence of this. The Church of Ireland was required to keep proper records of baptisms, marriages and burials from 1634, but very few registers survive from the seventeenth century. In general, however, the records of the Church of Ireland start much earlier than those of other Protestant denominations and of the Roman Catholic Church. The Church of Ireland is organised into parishes which in general conform to civil parishes. In 1922 over 1,000 Church of Ireland registers were lost in Dublin in the destruction of the Public Record Office of Ireland.

Presbyterianism came to Ireland from Scotland in the early seventeenth century. It did not become an organised denomination until the second half of the seventeenth century, however. The distribution of Presbyterian churches in Ulster is generally a reflection of the pattern of Scottish settlement in the province. As well as the main Presbyterian Church in Ireland there are two smaller historic denominations, the Non-Subscribing Presbyterian Church and the Reformed Presbyterian Church.

Methodism emerged in Ireland in the eighteenth century as a result of John Wesley's many visits to the island. To begin with the majority of Methodists belonged to the Established Church and they remained members of their own local churches. Therefore they continued to go to the parish church for the administration of marriages, burials and baptisms. In 1816 a split developed between the Primitive Wesleyan Methodists, who retained their links with the Established Church, and the Wesleyan Methodists, who allowed their ministers to administer baptisms.

The information found in church records can be categorised as follows:

Baptismal Registers

The basic information provided in a baptismal register is the name of the child, the name of the father and the date of baptism. The mother's name will usually be given as will a specific location. The occupation of the father and the date of birth of the child may also be provided. Roman Catholic registers will normally give the names of the sponsors of the child.

Marriage Registers

Prior to the standardisation of marriage registers after 1845 for non-Catholics and 1864 for Catholics, these will give in their simplest form the date of the marriage and the names of the bride and groom. The residence and the name of the father of each party are often provided. The names of the witnesses may also be given.

Burial Registers

Burial registers can be fairly uninformative, with the name of the deceased, the date of burial and occasionally the occupation and age at death given. The deaths of children will usually include the name of the father, while the burial of a wife may include her husband's name. Many Catholic 'burial' registers are actually registers recording payments made at the funeral of the deceased.

Vestry Minute Books

Vestry minute books record the deliberations of the parish vestry and will be found, where they survive, with the Church of Ireland records for a particular parish. The role of the vestry included the upkeep of the Church of Ireland church, the maintenance of roads in the parish and the care of the destitute and abandoned children. The money to pay for these things was raised through a cess or tax on the land in the parish. Vestry minute books are a rich source of information on life in a parish in

Queenstown, Cork reverted to its Irish name Cobh in 1922

bygone times. Occasionally they will include a list of the names of the parishioners drawn up for taxation purposes.

Online Access to Church Records

Mention has already been made of the online availability of Irish church records on the website of the Irish Family History Foundation (www.rootsireland.ie). As previously noted, the comprehensiveness of the coverage varies from county to county. The majority of Irish Catholic registers have been indexed, but many Protestant church records have yet to be digitised. The website Irish Genealogy (www.irishgenealogy.ie) hosts a free database of church records for selected areas, including Church of Ireland records for the city of Dublin and Roman Catholic records for the diocese of Kerry. Church records are available on many other websites, sometimes on a restricted basis and on other occasions for free. See Bready Ancestry (www.breadyancestry.com) for what has been digitised for one corner of County Tyrone.

Gravestone Inscriptions

The value of gravestone inscriptions for ancestral research has long been recognised. The discovery of a single gravestone may provide more information on the history of a family than could otherwise be gleaned from hours of searching through documentary sources. A visit to the graveyard in which your ancestors are buried is, therefore, an essential part of compiling your family tree. Discovering the graveyard in which your ancestors are buried is not necessarily straightforward. They may be buried in the graveyard adjoining the church to which your family belongs. Alternatively they may be buried in a graveyard no longer in use or adjoining another church. Burial registers kept by a church are one way of finding the place of burial, but as was explained above, these have limitations and do not survive for every graveyard. In many of the older graveyards it is not unusual to find all denominations buried.

The information recorded on a gravestone varies considerably. Some gravestones will record the dates of death of several generations of one family. Others may simply record the family surname. In most graveyards there will be at least one gravestone that has an overseas connection, recording the name of a family member who had died abroad. Ages of death on gravestones should be treated with some caution as they are often guesses or have been rounded up. Nonetheless they provide a basis for working out the year of birth which can be useful when it comes to looking for a birth certificate or record of baptism.

The recordings from many graveyards have been published in local historical or genealogical journals or books. Many websites with also host gravestone inscriptions from burial grounds across Ireland. John Grenham's *Tracing your Irish ancestors* provides a good guide to what has appeared in print and also what is available online.

Census Records

The first census was held in Ireland in 1821 and thereafter every ten years until 1911. Unfortunately, the earliest census that survives in its entirety for the whole of Ireland is the 1901 census. Census returns 1821-51 were almost entirely lost in 1922 in the destruction of the Public Record Office in Dublin. Census returns 1861-91 were completely destroyed by government order, many pulped as scrap paper during the First World War.

1901 Census

On 31st March 1901, a census was taken of the whole island of Ireland. The information in the census is listed under the following headings: name; relationship to the head of the household; religion; literacy; occupation; age; marital status; county of birth (or country if born outside Ireland); and ability to speak English or Irish.

1911 Census

The 1911 census was taken on 1st April of that year and contains additional information including the number of years a wife had been married, the number of children born alive and the number still living.

1901 and 1911 Census Online

Census returns from both 1901 and 1911 are now available online thanks to a joint initiative between the National Archives of Ireland and Library and Archives Canada (**www.census.nationalarchives.ie**).

1821 - 51 Census Survivals

Portions of census returns 1821-51 do survive for certain areas. For example, returns for over a dozen parishes survive for County Cavan for 1821. For County Londonderry an abstract of the 1831 census is available which provides the name of every head of household

Irish Village

as well as numerical information on the composition of the household. All or parts of a number of parishes in County Antrim survive from 1851.

Old Age Pension Claims

It is worth checking the old age pension search forms, as they contain extracts from the 1841 and 1851 censuses, the originals of which were almost completely destroyed. The old age pension was introduced on 1 January 1909 for those over seventy years of age. For many born before 1864, when the state registration of births began in Ireland, it was necessary to pay for a search to be made of the 1841 and 1851 censuses in order to prove their entitlement to the pension. The forms submitted by the claimants include such information as the names of parents, location at the time of the 1841 or 1851 census, and age at the time of the claim and during the relevant census year.

Individual application forms completed by or on behalf of the applicant are known as 'green forms'. The green forms are held at the National Archives, Dublin, under reference CEN/S/8. Another form of evidence related to the old age pension returns are 'form 37s', which were submitted by local pensions offices. These include the applicant's name, stated age, parents' names and address at the time of the census. Two volumes, one covering Northern Ireland and the other the Republic of Ireland, based mainly on surviving old age pension claims were compiled by Josephine Masterson of Indianapolis, USA, and published as *Ireland: 1841/1851 Census Abstracts*.

Records Relating to the Occupation of Land
The Primary or Griffith's Valuation 1848–64

The 1848–64 valuation gives a complete list of occupiers of land, tenements and houses. This Primary Valuation of Ireland, better known as Griffith's Valuation after the Commissioner of Valuation, Sir Richard Griffith, is arranged by county, within counties by Poor Law Union division, and within Unions by parish. It includes the following information: the name of the townland; the name of the householder or leaseholder; the name of the person from whom the property was leased; a description of the property; its acreage; and finally the valuation of the land and buildings. Griffith's Valuation is of particular interest to anyone wishing to trace their family tree, due to the fact that so little of the nineteenth century census returns has survived.

A set of the bound and printed version is available at PRONI and NLI while partial or complete sets can also be found in libraries across Ireland. These volumes are arranged by Poor Law Union within counties, and then into parishes and townlands. There is an index at the front of each volume which enables searchers to identify the page or pages in which a specific townland may be found. The valuer's annotated set of Ordnance Survey maps showing the location of every property is available at PRONI for Northern Ireland and at the Valuation Office in Dublin. These enable a researcher to identify the exact location of the house in which an ancestor may have lived.

In the recent years a number of free indexes

to the information contained in Griffith's Valuation have been made available online. The most useful of these websites is www.askaboutireland.ie which provides a free search facility. You can search by surname and/or first name or limit your search by county or parish. Not only does the website include scanned images of the original printed version of Griffith's Valuation, it also includes the annotated valuation maps which allow you to pinpoint the precise location of every property in Ireland at that time.

Valuation Revision Books, from c.1864

The manuscript valuation books were updated on a regular basis. The so-called 'cancelled books' consist of manuscript notebooks kept by the valuation office and updated to take account of changes in tenure. When a change of occupancy occurred, the name of the lessee or householder was crossed off and the new owner's name written above it, while the year was noted on the right-hand side of the page. Different-coloured ink was often used to differentiate between years with a key at the start of each book to indicate which colour went with each year.

The years in which changes in occupancy took place help to establish significant dates in family history, such as dates of death, sale or emigration. On rare occasions there can even be a comment to the effect that a family had emigrated or that an individual had died. Changes in the valuation of buildings can indicate when a new house was built or when the existing one was abandoned. By the early years of the twentieth century most of the occupiers of land had become landowners, thanks to a series of land purchase acts. This explains the initials L.A.P. (Land Act Purchase) that may be found stamped on an entry in the revision lists. In Northern Ireland valuation revision books are available in PRONI and for the Republic of Ireland they may be consulted in the Valuation Office in Dublin.

Tithe Valuation

In 1823 the Composition Act was passed which stipulated that henceforth all tithes due to the Established Church, the Church of Ireland, were to be paid in money rather than in kind as they previously could have been. This necessitated a complete valuation of all tithable land in Ireland, the results of which are contained in manuscript form in the tithe applotment books arranged by parish. The tithe applotment books contain the name of the tithe-payer, the size of his farm and the amount of tithe he paid. Copies of the tithe applotment books for Northern Ireland are available in the PRONI and for the Republic of Ireland in the National Archives of Ireland.

Landed Estate Records

Until the early part of the twentieth century, most of the land in Ireland was possessed by landowners whose estates ranged in size from 1,000 acres or less to, in some cases, over 100,000. Nearly all of the farmers in Ireland were tenants on such estates. The records generated by the management of landed estates are a major source of genealogical information. The best collection of Irish estate papers is housed in the Public Record Office of Northern Ireland. A two-volume *Guide to Landed Estate Papers*, covering the six counties of Northern Ireland, is available for consultation in the Public Search Room. It is arranged by county with the estate collections listed alphabetically according to the name of the landowning family. PRONI also holds estate collections from other counties in Ireland, notably Donegal and Monaghan. For several of the larger estates there are excellent records. In the Republic of Ireland the best collection of estate papers is in the National Library.

Some categories of estate papers are more useful to genealogists than others. Title deeds are concerned with the legal ownership of an estate, and are generally of limited value to genealogists. The same can be said of mortgages. Wills and marriage settlements usually refer only to the members of the landowner's family. However, rentals, leases, lease books, maps and correspondence can all be extremely useful to those searching for their ancestors within landed estate records.

Wills and Testamentary Papers

Prior to 1858 the Church of Ireland was responsible for administering all testamentary affairs. Ecclesiastical or Consistorial Courts in each diocese were responsible for granting probate and conferring on the executors the power to administer the estate. Each court was responsible for wills and administrations in its own diocese. However, when the estate included property worth more than £5 in another diocese, responsibility for the will or administration passed to the Prerogative Court under the authority of the Archbishop of Armagh.

Unfortunately, nearly all original wills probated before 1858 were destroyed in Dublin in 1922. However, indexes to these destroyed wills do exist. In the absence of a will

Patrick Street, Cork

letters of administration were sometimes granted. These were usually issued to close family members. The original administration bonds were also destroyed in Dublin in 1922, but index volumes for dioceses are available. On the PRONI website (www.proni.gov.uk) it is possible to search many of the diocesan will and administration bond indexes for the north of Ireland under its Name Search facility.

From 1858-99 transcripts of original wills are available at the Public Record Office of Northern Ireland for the district registries of Armagh, Belfast and Londonderry. From 1900 onwards original wills for Northern Ireland can be read at the Public Record Office of Northern Ireland and for the Republic of Ireland at the National Archives.

The PRONI website now includes a database of entries from the printed will calendars relating to the three district probate registries of Armagh, Belfast and Londonderry covering the period 1858-1943. Over 90,000 digitised images of entries from the transcript will books covering the period 1858-1900 are now available online, making it possible to read the actual contents of wills from that period.

Early Sources

The further one goes back in time the more difficult it becomes to discover precise details about family history. Sources specific to the seventeenth and eighteenth centuries are rarely more than lists of names, sometimes arranged by townland and parish. They will usually not provide information on family relationships, and because they almost always give the name of the head of the household nearly all of the names will be those of men. Occasionally two men with the same name will be found in the one townland and may be distinguished with the words, *'senior'* and *'junior,'* in which case it is reasonable to infer that they are father and son. At the same time, despite their limitations sources from the seventeenth and eighteenth centuries are useful if they can be used to demonstrate that a particular name occurred in a parish or townland at a certain date.

The principal sources from this period are listed below. In several cases the originals were destroyed in 1922, but transcripts survive. For more information on early sources for the province of Ulster and where they can be accessed refer to William Roulston, *Researching Scots-Irish Ancestors* (Belfast, 2005). Some of them are searchable online at www.ancestryireland.com/scotsinulster and the PRONI Name Search database www.proni.gov.uk

Fiants of the Tudor Sovereigns 1521–1603

Fiants were a documentary series unique to Ireland. These documents preceded the issue of royal grants. When Irish chiefs were granted pardons under *the 'surrender and regrant'* policy they often listed scores of members of their extended families as well as gallowglasses (mercenary soldiers), horsemen and yeomen, husbandmen, tenants and even, on occasion, cottiers. Individuals were identified with their full names, often with specific locations. Originally published as appendices in the steady stream of annual reports published by the Public Record Office of Ireland in the years 1875–90 (Reports nos 11–13, 15–18 of the Deputy Keeper of the Public Records of Ireland), they were reprinted in four volumes, including a comprehensive index, for the years 1521–1603 by Edmund Burke in 1994.

Hearth Money Rolls, 1660s

In the 1660s the government introduced a tax on hearths as a means of raising revenue. The returns, arranged by parish and usually with townland locations, list the names of all householders paying this tax survive for half the counties in Ireland with coverage most complete in Ulster (in full or in part for all counties except Down).

The *'Census of Protestant Householders'* 1740

What has generally been termed a 'census of Protestant householders' was compiled in 1740. The returns were made by the collectors of the hearth money and it has, therefore, been suggested that this 'census' is actually a hearth money roll and for some areas includes Catholics as well. It is no more than a list of names arranged by county, barony and parish and, reflecting its supervision by the inspector responsible for collecting hearth money, it is occasionally divided into 'walks'. Some parishes are also divided into townlands.

The Religious Census of 1766

In March and April 1766, Church of Ireland rectors were instructed by the government to compile complete returns of all householders in their respective parishes, showing their religion, as between Church of Ireland (Episcopalian), Roman Catholic (termed 'Papists' in the returns) and Presbyterians (or Dissenters), and giving an account of any Roman Catholic clergy active in their area. Some of the more diligent rectors listed every townland and every household, but many drew up only numerical totals of the population.

Petition of Protestant Dissenters, 1775

The Petition of Protestant Dissenters is a list of names of Dissenters on either a parish or a congregational basis which were submitted to the government in October and November 1775. Most of them relate to the province of Ulster.

The Flaxgrowers' List, 1796

In 1796 as part of a government initiative to encourage the linen industry in Ireland, free spinning wheels or looms were granted to farmers who planted a certain acreage of their holdings with flax. The names of over 56,000 recipients of these awards have survived in printed form arranged by county and parish. A photocopy of the original volume is available in PRONI.

Archives and Libraries

The following is a list of the most important archives and libraries in Ireland. Note: it is vitally important that you make contact prior to your visit to ensure that the institution in question is open. Some of the archives and libraries listed here are only open at certain times or have restrictions on who can access them.

GENERAL REGISTER OFFICE OF NORTHERN IRELAND, Oxford House, 49/55 Chichester Street. Belfast, BT1 4HL T: + 44 (0)28 9025 2000 E: gro.nisra@dfpni.gov.uk (Birth, Death and Marriage Certificate Enquiries)
W: www.groni.gov.uk

GENERAL REGISTER OFFICE OF IRELAND (Administrative Headquarters) , Convent Road, , Roscommon, Ireland T: +353 (0)90 6632900 W: www.groireland.ie

GENERAL REGISTER OFFICE OF IRELAND (Public Research Room), Irish Life Centre, Lower Abbey Street, Dublin 1, Ireland

LINEN HALL LIBRARY , 17 Donegall Square North, Belfast, BT1 5GD T: +44 (0) 28 9032 1707 E: info@linenhall.com W: www.linenhall.com/Home/home.html

PUBLIC RECORD OFFICE OF NORTHERN IRELAND, 2 Titanic Boulevard, Belfast, BT3 9HQ E: proni@gov.uk W: www.proni.gov.uk

NATIONAL ARCHIVES OF IRELAND, Bishop Street Dublin 8 T: (01) 407 2300 E: mail@nationalarchives.ie W: www.nationalarchives.ie

NATIONAL LIBRARY OF IRELAND, Kildare Street, Dublin 2 T: +353 (1) 603 0200 E: info@nli.ie W: www.nli.ie

William Roulston is Research Director of the Ulster Historical Foundation.
He is the author of a number of publications including *Researching Scots - Irish Ancestors: the essential genealogical guide to early modern Ulster, 1600-1800* (2005).
He holds a PhD in Archaeology from Queen's University, Belfast, and has worked on several radio and television projects including research for *Who Do You Think You Are?*

Ulster Historical Foundation is an entirely self-funded educational non-profit organisation.

Our aim is to encourage an interest in the history of the province of Ulster, promote a positive image of Northern Ireland overseas, strengthen the links between Ireland and those of Ulster descent and to broaden access to historical documents and records for Irish and Scots-Irish genealogy.

If you need genealogical advice, would like to commission research or want more information on our other services, please contact us using the details below.

☎ (0)28 9066 1988

✉ enquiry@uhf.org.uk

f facebook.com/UlsterHistoricalFoundation

or visit www.ancestryireland.com

BOOK PUBLISHING

We are a leading publisher of quality historical, educational and genealogical books and have produced over 200 titles to date. You can find our bookstore online at **booksireland.org.uk**

FAMILY RECORDS

We have over 2 million records including Birth, Marriage & Death records, Gravestone Inscriptions, Street Directories and much more available on our website.

CLASSES & TOURS

Throughout the year we run a variety of classes, tours and activity holidays across Ulster, our most popular being our annual genealogy Summer School which runs in June.

BECOME A MEMBER

To access a range of specialist resources and services as well as discounts on all of our titles, visit ancestryireland.com/index.php?guild

The Certificate of Irish Heritage

John Hamrock

The Irish Nation cherishes its special affinity with people of Irish ancestry living abroad who share its cultural identity and heritage,

Constitution of Ireland - Article 2

The idea for the Certificate of Irish Heritage came out of the Global Irish Economic Forum held in September 2009 at Farmleigh House in Phoenix Park, formerly one of the Dublin residences of the Guinness family, and now an official guest house of the Irish Nation. This event brought together international figures of business, government and culture from Ireland and the Irish Diaspora to generate ideas for leading the country out of recession and to bring leverage support of the emigrant network after the fall of the Celtic Tiger. Some speakers at the forum were critical of the fact that there had been no attempt to reach out to the 70 million people of Irish descent who wanted to be part of the Diaspora, but who were unable to qualify for Irish citizenship by not having a parent or grandparent born in Ireland.

CERTIFICATE OF IRISH HERITAGE

The Official Certificate from the Government of Ireland

The Certificate of Irish Heritage provides recognition of the recipient's ancestry by the Government of Ireland. It offers no legal benefits or rights, but it is a beautiful item which honours the recipient's ancestor(s) and symbolises their connection to Ireland. While the Certificate was created to recognise those of Irish descent, it is not available to those born in Ireland.

A person of at least 18 years of age can qualify for a Certificate if they have an ancestor who was born in Ireland and it can be acquired for you or as a gift for a family member, a colleague, or a friend. Adults can also purchase Certificates for children under the age of 18. The Certificate of Irish Heritage is issued on behalf of the Irish Government by the Minister of Foreign Affairs who currently is also the Tánaiste or Deputy Prime Minister. The official web site is www.heritagecertificate.ie The Certificate of Irish Heritage is operated by FEXCO on behalf of the Irish Department of Foreign Affairs and Trade.

There are three designs available, in English, Gaelic and Spanish. The lettering is hand drawn by renowned Master Scribe and calligrapher, Tim O'Neill.

Celtic Knot – this Certificate uses a simple Celtic Knot motif reminiscent of the beautiful Celtic art seen in the famous Book of Kells and Durrow.

Emigrant Ship – for many people the ship is an emotional evocation of the hazardous journey that their ancestors made.

The West of Ireland – many people identify with the landscape design as it represents the place where their ancestors came from.

The Irish Government has an ongoing programme of Certificate presentations. Recipients have included President Bill Clinton, William Clay Ford, Jr., and NYC Fire-fighter Joseph Hunter (awarded posthumously who died at the World Trade Center on 9/11 and presented to his family, the very first recipient of the Certificate).

There is also a Presentation Programme which provides Certificates of Irish Heritage as a presentation gift for organizations worldwide, to honour or recognise a person of Irish descent. For the honoree, it is both unique and personal, speaking to their family history and their connection to Ireland. It is available to eligible organisations worldwide including Irish associations and societies, Irish Genealogy associations and societies, professional, philanthropic, sporting, cultural and educational bodies with an Irish connection, and also State agencies.

The application process is an online process so

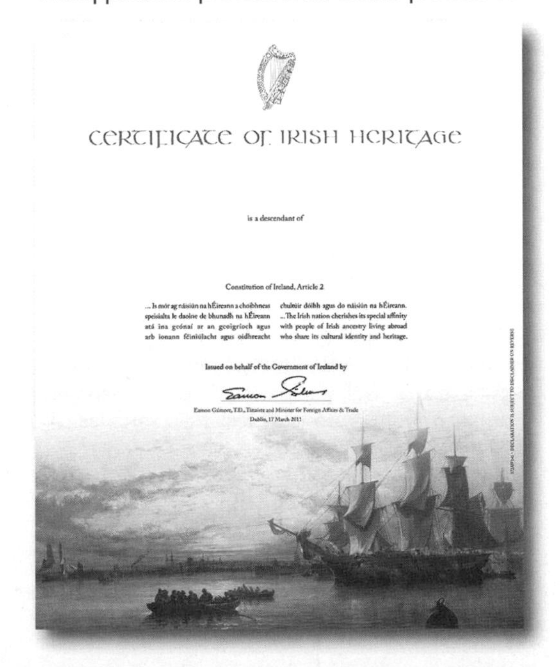

CERTIFICATE OF IRISH HERITAGE

is a descendant of

Constitution of Ireland, Article 2

... Is mór ag náisiún na hÉireann a choibhneas speisialta le daoine de bhunadh na hÉireann atá ina gcónaí ar an gcoigríoch agus arb ionann féiniúlacht agus oidhreacht chultúir dóibh agus do náisiún na hÉireann.

... The Irish nation cherishes its special affinity with people of Irish ancestry living abroad who share its cultural identity and heritage.

Issued on behalf of the Government of Ireland by

Eamon Gilmore, T.D., Tánaiste and Minister for Foreign Affairs & Trade

Dublin, 17 March 2011

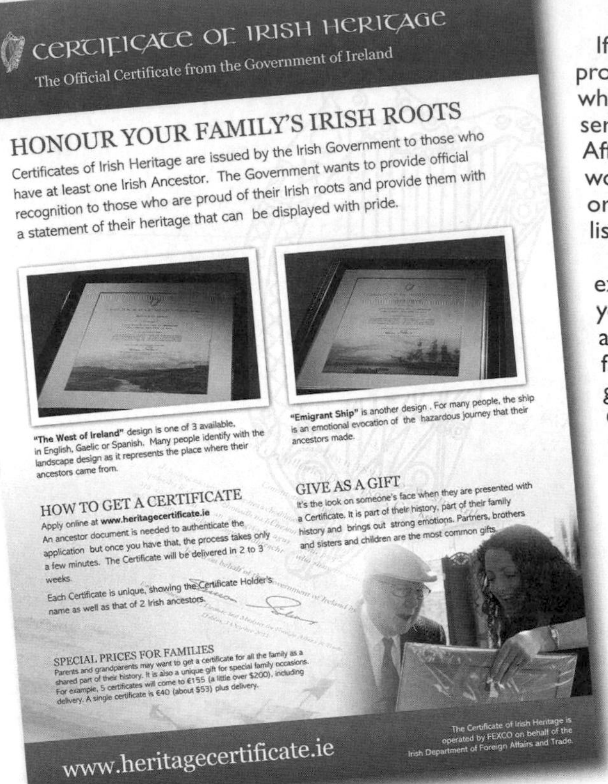

if you have difficulties accessing a computer, you will need to seek help from a family member or friend, or through your local library. In cases of severe or unusual difficulty you can contact the Customer Service Team at help@heritagecertificate.ie

The price of the first Certificate on an order is €40.00, plus delivery costs and Value Added Tax, where applicable. Second and subsequent certificates on an order cost €29.00. If you would like to purchase the Certificate in a frame, the cost of a frame is an additional €60.00 plus delivery costs and Value Added Tax. This includes the frame itself, the secure positioning of the Certificate in the frame and the professional packaging for secure delivery.

As part of the application process, you will need to provide an "ancestor document" which identifies the recipient's ancestor as Irish or as being born in Ireland. FEXCO, the programme administrator, will accept an ancestor document from any country, not just Ireland. Examples of the types of documents they accept include:

- census record
- birth certificate
- marriage certificate
- death certificate
- passenger manifest

Many of these ancestor documents are available online.

If you need help to find a document, FEXCO provides the option of contacting them directly where they have a free document finding service. Alternatively, FEXCO has a list of Affiliated Genealogists. Yet another alternative would be to do the document search yourself or to hire a genealogist not on their affiliated list.

The www.heritagecertificate.ie website is an excellent source of information about building your family tree and about finding your Irish ancestors or the Irish ancestors of other family members or friends. It has helpful guides and templates, such as Line of Descent Chart which you can download from the site to allow you to record the name, date and place of birth, marriage or death of your ancestors.

There is practical genealogical advice such as initially talking to members of your family, particularly older relatives who may be able to provide you with crucial pieces of information such as names, dates and places.

The web site also advises that the next step is to try and source a relevant supporting document. Any such document which you submit with your application must give the place of birth of your Ancestor as Ireland, or a place within Ireland, or refer to your Ancestor's nationality as Irish.

Before searching online resources, you or a member of your family may have old family documents. There may well be, for example, an old baptismal certificate, birth certificate or marriage certificate which you could scan and submit with your application.

If you have been unable to locate an original document in your family's records, you will need to find your supporting document from historical records available to the public. The significant availability of historical documents having been digistised and placed online for you to search means that there are many records available for obtaining the Certificate of Irishness.

Many of Ireland's records have not yet been digitised and so depending on when your Ancestor left Ireland, records from the country where your Ancestor settled will be more relevant.

If you are visiting Ireland, particularly Dublin, you are advised to visit the General Register Office Research Room at the Irish Life Centre, The National Archives of Ireland on Bishop Street, and both the Main Reading Room and the Manuscript Reading Room of the National Library of Ireland. Both the National Archives of Ireland and the National Library of Ireland offer a genealogy advisory service free of charge and can help to provide access to documents not available

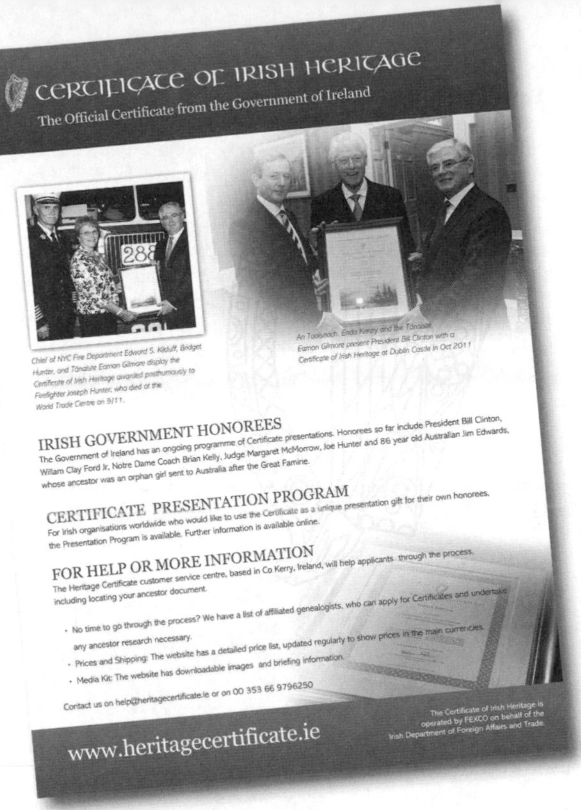

online which would support your application.

If you have been actively researching your Irish family history where genealogy and family history is your hobby, you may find that you have discovered an ancestral connection to Ireland, and have copies of documents which link your Ancestor to Ireland. Providing the document gives the name of your Ancestor and their place of birth as Ireland (or a place in Ireland) or nationality as Irish, you can submit a scanned copy or digital image with your application.

If you hold an Irish passport and were born to an Irish born parent, you should provide a scanned copy of your Irish born parent's birth certificate. If one of your grandparents was born in Ireland and your birth details have been entered in the Foreign Births Register (FBR), you would have provided documentation in relation to your grandparent. This document can be submitted with your application for a Certificate of Irish Heritage.

If you are entitled to, but have not claimed an Irish Passport, there is a section of the website for help in finding a supporting document which links your Ancestor to Ireland.

If you cannot locate an ancestor document, the Certificate of Irish Heritage customer service team can help you with all aspects of the process, and for a limited time will be able to carry out a document search for you. You also have the option to appoint an affiliated professional genealogist to do the entire application on your behalf.

Alternatively, you can complete an Affidavit, the form which can be obtained from the web site, which provides the information the Certificate of Ireland programme needs and which should sworn in the presence of a Notary Public, Commissioner of Oaths or other person authorised to take affidavits or administer oaths.

Opportunity for Professional Genealogists

If you are a professional genealogist, you can apply to join the Certificate of Irish Heritage's Genealogist Affiliation programme. The programme is designed to provide those who wish to apply for a Certificate of Irish Heritage with the opportunity to engage a professional genealogist to assist with the application process, whilst enabling the professional genealogist to include the Certificate of Irish Heritage in his or her own suite of products.

Members are required to:

• Actively promote the Certificate of Irish Heritage as part of their services

• Ensure applications completed adhere to the eligibility requirements and application criteria set out in this website

• Membership is open to professional genealogists.

It should be noted that the Certificate of Irish Heritage is not a party to any research or service agreements entered into between consumers and affiliated genealogists, and consequently is not responsible for the terms or outcome of any such agreement. Additionally, FEXCO reserves at its absolute discretion the right to terminate the affiliation of any genealogist who brings the good name or reputation of the Certificate of Irish Heritage, FEXCO or the Irish Government into disrepute.

Emigrant Online
NEWS FOR THE GLOBAL IRISH COMMUNITY

The Irish Emigrant - Articles

First Certificate of Irish Heritage goes to fallen FDNY hero

On a visit to New York last week to speak at the 66th United Nations General Assembly, Tánaiste and Minister for Foreign Affairs and Trade, Eamon Gilmore T.D., used the opportunity to present the first Certificate of Irish Heritage to the family of Joseph (Joe) Hunter, a New York fireman who lost his life in the 9/11 attacks.

The Certificate of Irish Heritage aims to recognise those of Irish lineage in an official way, giving greater expression to the sense of Irish identity felt by many around the world who might not otherwise be able to do so.

Joe Hunter was born in New York in 1970, the son of Bridget [who hails from Co. Galway] and Joseph Hunter. At 18 he joined the South Hempstead Fire Department as a volunteer, and in 1996 he was accepted into the New York Fire Department (FDNY) as a member of Squad 288 in Maspeth, Queens.

Chief of the NYC Fire Department Edward S. Kilduff, Bridget Hunter and Tánaiste Eamon Gilmore display the Certificate of Irish Heritage at a recent ceremony.

The ceremony at the firehouse of Squad 288 was attended by the Hunter family, former colleagues of Joe's, and FDNY chief Edward S. Kilduff. Presenting the certificate to Joe's mother Bridget, the Tánaiste spoke of the longstanding bonds between Irish emigrants and the emergency responders.

"Generations of Irish have been proud and privileged to serve with New York's finest - in the Fire Department, the NYPD, and other emergency services," he said. "We in Ireland felt the pain and loss of all Americans in the obscenity of 9/11 but we felt a particular pain in our hearts for those brave men and women of Irish heritage who lost their lives on that day."

After receiving the award, Mrs. Hunter said it would have been an extremely proud day for her son. "Joseph was very proud of his Irish roots and in continuing the brave and selfless tradition of service given by the Irish to the FDNY," she said. "He would have been very honoured to receive the first Certificate."

The Tánaiste confirmed that applications for the new Certificate of Heritage can be submitted online from the end of this month at ***certificateheritage.ie***. Applications are open to persons who were *not* born on the island of Ireland and who can provide appropriate supporting documentation connecting them to an individual Irish ancestor.

The benefits of memberships to the Genealogist Affiliate programme are:

- Individual listing in the Affiliated Genealogists section of the website, including contact details, link to your website, your photograph or logo, a short paragraph outlining your services and areas of expertise
- Earn commission on Certificate of Irish Heritage sales
- Use of Affiliate Genealogist Certificate of Irish Heritage branded logos on your website and printed materials
- A unique log-in to the Certificate of Irish Heritage application website enabling you to complete applications on behalf of your client

About FEXCO

Established in 1981, FEXCO - www.fexco.com - is Ireland's most successful privately owned financial services company. FEXCO today employs 1500 people across its operations in Ireland, the UK, the USA, Asia Pacific, the Middle East and Australia. Over its thirty year history FEXCO, has been a pioneer and innovator in the broad arenas of Global Payments, Foreign Exchange, Tourism Related Financial Services, Transaction Processing, Managed Services and Business Process Outsourcing.

The Irish Family History Foundation

Karel Kiely M.A.

The Irish Family History Foundation is the largest provider of family history research services in Ireland. It has a network of 33 county genealogy centres covering 30 of 32 counties on the island of Ireland. The majority of the centres have made their records available to search and purchase online at www.rootsireland.ie

The sources that have been computerized include church and civil records of baptisms, births, marriages and deaths; Griffith's Valuation, the Tithe Applotment Books, the 1901 and 1911 census returns, ships' passenger lists and gravestone inscriptions. A unique Standard Surname function allows users to search across all variants of a surname. There are currently over 19 million records available on the website but further records are added on a regular basis.

How do I start to trace an Irish ancestor?

Trying to find a particular person in the millions of Irish records can be daunting. A name or surname is not enough. You need to compile as much information as possible before you start searching databases in order to have the best possible chance of locating your ancestors. It is also easier to focus on one or two individuals initially as you gain experience in doing research.

Ideally, you should start your research where you know the ancestor spent the last years of their lives. Where did they have their family and who were they? Where and when did they die? Can you find a death notice or obituary in the local newspapers? Check census returns in Ireland or in the country the ancestor emigrated to in order to establish a county of birth in Ireland.

If you are searching for ancestors that left Ireland you will need to see if you can find out where they married and what information is recorded on their marriage record. Where were their children born//baptized? Can you find other Irish people living in the same town and where were they from?

You need to start with the most recent information you have on your ancestor, in your ancestor's home county or country, and go back from location to location retracing the ancestor's footsteps. If your ancestor emigrated from Ireland do not start your research in Ireland. It is also important not to skip generations.

Try to learn the following before using the databases:

Check List

- Name and name variations
- Age
- Occupation
- Religion
- Parents' names and approximate ages
- Spouse's name
- Siblings' Names
- Possible associates

How do I find out where my ancestor came from in Ireland?

This is often the hardest question to answer when searching for an Irish ancestor. Locating the COUNTY of origin is the central and essential key to tracing any emigrant line in Ireland. Start looking where the person ended their life and move backwards from there. Things to look for are memorial cards, family bibles, letters, naturalization records, obituaries and gravestones; church records that may record where they were baptized or married; any record that might include their birthplace or place of origin. In sources outside Ireland, particularly census records, the birthplace will be given as Ireland but a county, parish, or even townland may be given in some sources.

If the ancestor emigrated there may also be clues amongst the records pertaining to anyone who may have emigrated with them including siblings, relatives or neighbours from Ireland.

When did my ancestor leave Ireland?

It is useful to try to establish the age of someone when they emigrated. If they were very young they may have been with their parents or other siblings. If they were older they may have already been married and travelling with a spouse and perhaps even children born in Ireland.

The year of emigration can be checked with particular events in Irish history as different groups migrated at different times from particular locations. If you can learn when your ancestor left Ireland it may point to a particular location in Ireland.

You may be able to establish the ship, date and port of arrival and can then look for the passenger list for a particular voyage. This can provide information about whether they traveled with family members, neighbours or friends.

If your ancestors did not leave Ireland you will still need to follow the same steps, working back from the present, generation by generation.

You will need to know a first name and surname. Remember there may be variations of the spelling of a surname. At a minimum you will need to have an idea of a possible year of birth, marriage or death, and place of origin in Ireland. It is important to know the religious denomination; it is helpful if you can learn any of the following - their parents' names/parents' birth years; spouse's name/birth year; any other family members; an occupation.

There are many people who do not have a county or parish of origin for their Irish ancestor. This means that a search can be impossible in some cases if the surname is very common; however, it can still be possible for some people to locate their Irish ancestor because of an unusual first name or because a combination of a husband's name and a wife's name reduces the likely possibilities. The Online Research System of rootsireland.ie offers you the ability to search across all the participating counties' records or to select one or more counties to limit/extend your searches.

Problems you may encounter

If your ancestor was born or married before 1820 in Ireland it will be difficult to locate records. Many Catholic parishes did not begin to keep records until around this time. The start dates of parishes vary from county to county. Church of Ireland (Anglican) parishes can be available from a much earlier date; sadly, however, a lot of these records were lost during the Irish Civil War.

Sometimes a name and a date have too many possible matching records on a database. A county genealogist may be able to assist by pinpointing the occurrence of a surname in a particular parish or location within a parish.

You may locate only part of a family if some

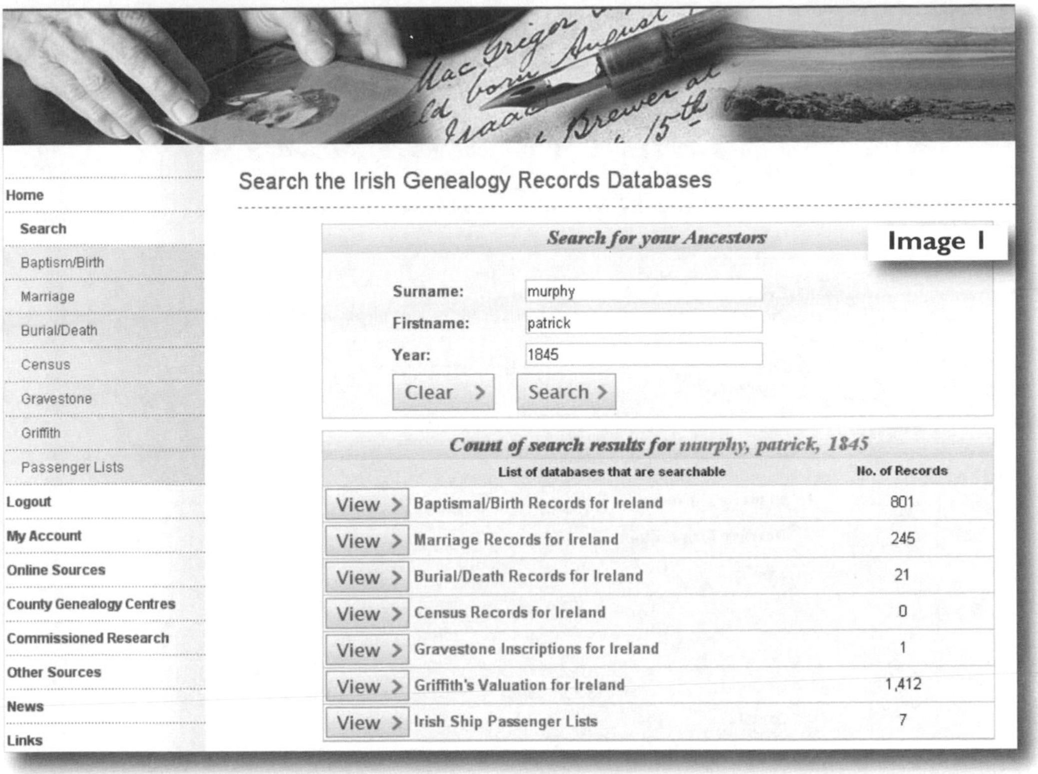

	List of databases that are searchable	No. of Records
View >	Baptismal/Birth Records for Ireland	801
View >	Marriage Records for Ireland	245
View >	Burial/Death Records for Ireland	21
View >	Census Records for Ireland	0
View >	Gravestone Inscriptions for Ireland	1
View >	Griffith's Valuation for Ireland	1,412
View >	Irish Ship Passenger Lists	7

family members were married or baptized before record keeping commenced in the parish. Please consider looking for siblings of your ancestor; your direct ancestor may not be recorded, but you may be able to pinpoint a townland or parish by looking for other members.

Original parish records can be inaccurate; there may be omissions, gaps, mixing up of names, incorrect dates, torn or damaged pages etc.

Before you start to search on the website please take some time to look at the HELP seciton of the website.

First Names

The recording of first names can vary from record to record, e.g. Elizabeth, Betty, Lizzie, Maryanne, Mary Anne, Patrick or Pat. Our website has a FIRST NAMES listing for guidance which has been compiled from the variants we have found recorded in the original sources. Remember the wild card search facility can used, e.g. PAT% or %LIZ%.

On some records one or more of the parents' first names may not have been recorded in the original source, may have been illegible or been recorded incorrectly by the priest. It was also less common to record the surname of the mother on baptismal records. It may be recorded on one child's baptism but not on a subsequent baptism. Please be flexible in searching.

Surname Variants

Because of the variation in the spelling of many surnames, it is useful for a researcher to be able to search for a range of spellings of a surname by the input of one surname only. Thus a search for the surname Smith will find all the records for Smith, Smyth, Smythe, and possibly another half a dozen variants. The main problem with this facility is not in its implementation in software, but in the choice of surnames that belong to each Standard Surname. The list may be too long: for example if Smyth includes surnames such as Smitters, Smithies, Sixsmith, McSmyth and Smithson, Smithdale, Smithwick, and many others, then the recall (meaning the coverage of possible options) will be very full. The list of results may be so large that you cannot find what you need, i.e. the precision of your search may be too low to be useful.

When performing a Standard Surname search on www.rootsireland.ie the search criteria displayed at the top of the search results includes the "surname (plus variants)". Click on this to view all surname variations that are being matched for your search.

We recommend that you first try the Standard Surname index to find what you are

Baptismal/Birth Records for Ireland

117 matches for the search criteria: **murphy (plus variants) patrick 1840-1850**

First Page (1 Credit) | Next Page (1 Credit) | End Page (1 Credit)

Page: 1 of 12

Click on the buttons above to view a page of search results.

Standard Search

Record Type* : Baptismal/Birth Records for Ireland

Surname* : murphy

First Name : patrick

Father's Surname:

Father's First Name : john

Mother's Surname:

Mother's First Name :

Year* : 1845 +/- 5 years

Counties : ☐ Select all

☐ Antrim	☐ Armagh	☐ Cavan
☐ Cork	☐ Derry	☐ Donegal
☐ Down	☐ Dublin	☐ Fermanagh
☐ Galway	☐ Kildare	☐ Kilkenny
☐ Laois	☐ Leitrim	☐ Limerick
☐ Longford	☐ Louth	☐ Mayo
☐ Meath	☐ Monaghan	☐ Offaly
☐ Roscommon	☐ Sligo	☐ Tipperary
☐ Tyrone	☐ Waterford	☐ Westmeath
☐ Wexford	☐ Wicklow	

Surname Match* : Standard Surname Index

Clear > Search >

Image 2

looking for and, if too many results are returned, then select Exact Match to reduce the number of hits. Simply select the desired Surname Match option at the bottom of the Search Box.

Note that there are no standard first names used in the searches on the website. First names searches are always done as a wild card search, e.g. the first name of Mar% will return matches for Mary, Maria, etc. but if you enter Mary, variants such as Maria will not be returned.

It was also less common to record the surname of the mother on baptismal records. It may be recorded on one child's baptism but not on a subsequent baptism.

What information can I expect to find in the records?

The various types of records on the rootsireland.ie database may not contain information in all of the record fields. The records have been transcribed directly from the original Parish registers and Civil records in Ireland. Unfortunately, there were no template information fields when the various clergy were recording information in the parish registers, although Catholic parish registers did become more formalized in the late 19th century. Some records are very detailed while others contain a minimum amount of information. In some instances the writing in the registers may be illegible or faded, or registers have been damaged. The original data also contains errors and omissions. Some data may have information restrictions as per individual agreements between IFHF centres and the local clergy, i.e. some comments/remarks recorded within the record are withheld. The cost to view a record is the same regardless of the information that it may contain. You can see samples of the various types of records on the website. The website does not contain images of original sources.

There are differences between parish records

Baptismal/Birth Records for Ireland

4 matches for the search criteria: **murphy (plus variants) patrick 1840-1850**

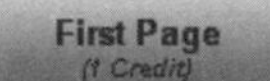

Page: 1 of 1

Click on the buttons above to view a page of search results.

Standard Search

Record Type* : Baptismal/Birth Records for Ireland

Surname* : murphy

First Name : patrick

Father's Surname:

Father's First Name : john

Mother's Surname:

Mother's First Name : mary

Year* : 1845 +/- 5 years

Counties : ☐ Select all

☐ Antrim	☐ Armagh	☐ Cavan
☑ Cork	☐ Derry	☐ Donegal
☐ Down	☐ Dublin	☐ Fermanagh
☐ Galway	☐ Kildare	☐ Kilkenny
☐ Laois	☐ Leitrim	☐ Limerick
☐ Longford	☐ Louth	☐ Mayo
☐ Meath	☐ Monaghan	☐ Offaly
☐ Roscommon	☐ Sligo	☐ Tipperary
☐ Tyrone	☐ Waterford	☐ Westmeath
☐ Wexford	☐ Wicklow	

Surname Match* : Standard Surname Index

Clear > Search >

Baptismal/Birth Records for Ireland

4 matches for the search criteria: **murphy (plus variants) patrick 1840-1850**

Page: 1 of 1

Click on the buttons above to view a page of search results.

Action	Cost	Source	Surname	First Name	Year	County	
View >	25 credits	Church Baptism	Murphy	Patrick	1845	Co. Cork	
View >	25 credits	Church Baptism	Murphy	Patrick	1844	Co. Cork	
View >	25 credits	Church Baptism	Murphy	Patrick	1842	Co. Cork	
View >	25 credits	Church Baptism	Murphy	Patrick	1849	Co. Cork	

Standard Search

Record Type* : Baptismal/Birth Records for Ireland

Surname* : murphy

Image 3

and civil records:

A church baptismal or marriage record is a record entered by the priest in his parish register. These can vary widely in content. Catholic and Church of Ireland (Anglican) parish records also vary in the information that they contain.

A civil record is a state record. The civil records usually contain more information than the church records; for instance a civil marriage record will contain the bride and groom's parents' names, addresses and occupations, whereas the church record will only sometimes contain the fathers' names and less often the mothers' of each party. A civil birth record will contain the occupation of the child's father while this is rare in Catholic Church baptismal records but more common in Protestant records.

A civil death record will state the cause of death and the name of the informant of the death whereas a Church of Ireland burial record will usually not have that information. A civil death record does not state the graveyard in which the person is buried.

The last thing to look at before you start to search on the site is the listing of Online Sources. This will let you see what exactly is available for each county with records online.

The start and end date of parish records is given for each parish and any gaps in registers are noted. Please take the time to look at these listings as it could save you a lot of time if you are looking for something that is not yet online or does not cover the time period in which you are looking.

How to use the Rootsireland.ie Search Facility

To make full use of the search facility it is possible to narrow your search by entering as much detail as you can before having to use credits to view the results. This example will take you through the process. You will need to purchase credits to use the website and view records.

1. I want to find some Baptismal information on Patrick Murphy born/baptized around 1845. By completing the basic search form I can see that quite a large number of records would be returned for that basic search criteria:

See Image 1

2. By clicking the *'View'* button I will be brought to the Search Results page where I can narrow my results further before having to use any credits as searching through 801 records is unrealistic.

3. By entering the Father's First Name as John I have narrowed my search to 117 matches (but this is still too many):

See Image 2

4. I can do this as many times as I want without using any credits. In the example below I have entered the Mother's Name as Mary and limited the results to show only County Cork records that gives me 4 possible results. As this is all the information I have I will choose to view those Search Results and use 1 credit:

5. Viewing the Search Results has given me 4 possible entries and I can now decide which record I would like to view. The cost of the record is displayed in credits and if I have already purchased a record previously the search table will display *'Already Purchased'*:

See Image 3

Based on the example of a search for a Patrick Murphy I have refined my search using common first names and surnames whilst looking in a mid- nineteenth century timeframe when most parishes were keeping records.

The county genealogy centres also offer a commissioned research service for those who do not want to carry out their own research. You can contact the county centres directly to speak to a local genealogist and to commission research.

The Distress in Ireland

The Illustrated London News - March 13, 1880

The fisheries along the western shores of Ireland are next in importance to the cultivation of the land, as means of subsistence for the distressed population. Our Special Artist lately in Connemara furnishes the sketch of a fisherman's hut, which appears among the Engravings in this Number of our Journal. The total number of men and boys employed in all the deep-sea and coast fisheries of Ireland is about 21,000, with nearly six thousand vessels. Twenty years ago, in 1860, there were nearly 56,000 persons so employed, and about 13,500 vessels.

In former periods there was a large measure of Government assistance to this industry. The amount of grants and loans from the Treasury, to support Irish fisheries, between 1821 and 1864, was not less than £234,000, of which £197,000 was expended on piers and harbours.

The Board of Works are even now authorised to lend money for the building, purchase, or repairs of fishing-boats, of houses and sheds for curing fish, and for nets or other fishing gear; but in the year 1878 the applications for such loans came to only £11,808, half of which sum was granted on loan. The value of all the fish exported from Ireland to England in 1878, was estimated at £924,000, of which the salmon represents £418,000, herrings £241,000, mackerel, £97,000, and cod £166,000, besides oysters, crabs, and lobsters. But the herring fishery is chiefly in St. George's Channel, and is shared by Cornishmen, Manxmen, Scotchmen, and other people of Great Britain.

The Galway deep-sea fisheries have sadly declined, and this occasions much distress, not only in Connemara, the maritime district north of Galway Bay, but all round the coasts of Mayo, Sligo, and Donegal, and in the numerous small islands. The sufferings of the poor islanders, at Inisboffin, Inisturk, Clare Island, Achill, and other places, have been very severe; and H.M.S. Goshawk, gun-boat, has been cruising about there, with an officer of the Local Government Board, and with stores of meal and other comforts, to visit and relieve the famishing people.

The general progress of the efforts by voluntary contributions to mitigate this great calamity in the West of Ireland continues without relaxation. The Duchess of Marlborough's Fund was reported last Monday to have reached £80,000, and the Dublin Mansion House Fund is £102,000, half of which has been expended. The Committee of the Duchess of Marlborough's Fund have laid out £30,000 in seed potatoes. Arrangements for the distribution of the *New York Herald* Fund are now completed.

Editor's Note:

The values today would be: £924,000 = £389 million (€496 million) : £418,000 = £176 million (€224.5 million) : £80,000 = £33.5 million (€42.7 million)

The National Library of Ireland

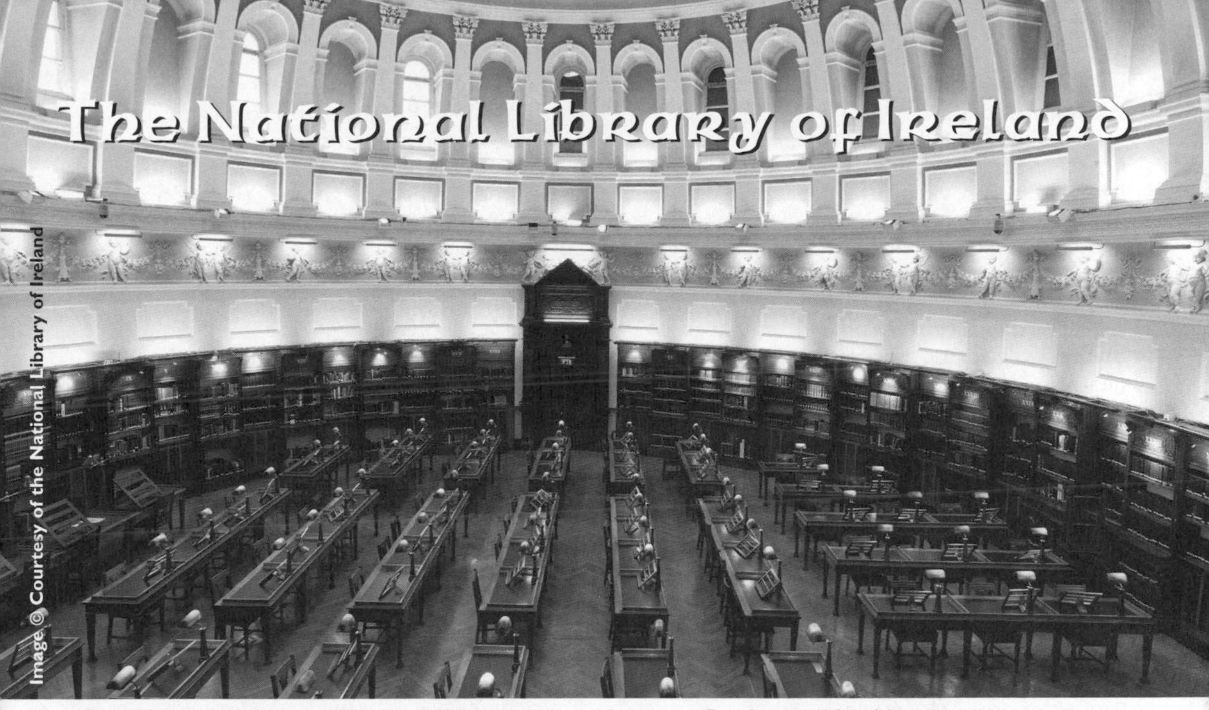

Image © Courtesy of the National Library of Ireland

The National Library of Ireland derives its origins from the Library of the Royal Dublin Society, founded in 1731. In 1877 a substantial portion of the Royal Dublin Society library was purchased by the State and the new National Library of Ireland was established.

The National Library of Ireland was established by the Dublin Science and Art Museum Act, 1877, which provided that the bulk of the collections in the possession of the Royal Dublin Society, should be vested in the then Department of Science and Art for the benefit of the public and of the Society, and for the purposes of the Act.

An Agreement of 1881 provided that the Library should operate under the superintendence of a Council of twelve Trustees, eight of whom were appointed by the Society and four by the Government; this Agreement also conferred on the Trustees the duty of appointing the officers of the Library. This historic arrangement ended with the establishment of the National Library of Ireland as an autonomous cultural institution on 3rd May 2005 under the National Cultural Institutions Act, 1997.

Situated in Kildare Street, Dublin, the Library aims to collect, preserve, promote and make accessible materials on or relating to Ireland, whether published in Ireland or abroad, together with a supporting reference collection. The Library's current collection of some eight million items constitutes probably the most outstanding collection of Irish documentary material in the world, an invaluable representation of Irish history and heritage. Books, serial publications, newspapers, manuscripts, maps, photographs, official publications, prints, drawings and ephemera make up the bulk of the collections.

The National Library is open, free of charge, to all those who wish to consult the collections. A Reader's Ticket is necessary in order to consult most categories of material.

The Library does not lend books and reading is done in the various reading rooms. There is also a copying service and it is possible to get photocopies and photographs, of most items in the collections. The Library has an ongoing programme of exhibitions.

The Office of the Chief Herald in Kildare Street, and the Photographic Archive in Temple Bar are all part of the National Library.

The National Library has long been one of the key centres for family history research in Ireland. In recognition of this the Library's Genealogy Service - an expert service staffed by experienced Library staff - is designed with the specific needs of family history researchers in mind.. Visitors to the Genealogy Service are offered expert advice on their research together with access to reference material and finding aids. Information leaflets, including a series on family history research in the Library, are readily available.

While the Genealogy Service is of particular value to first-time researchers, the Library also encourages more experienced family history researchers to continue to use the facilities for next-step advice from the Library staff there.

The records most used by family history researchers in the National Library fall under the following headings:

Parish Records

For most family history researchers parish registers are the earliest direct source of family information, providing clear evidence of links between one generation and another (via baptismal registers) and one family and another (via marriage registers). They are particularly important for any information they provide for the period before the commencement of civil or State registration of all births, marriages and deaths in 1864.

The National Library holds microfilm copies of almost all Roman Catholic parish registers up to circa 1880. Most of the registers begin in the period 1810-1830 but some - particularly in counties along the western seaboard - begin somewhat later. In a number of counties in the province of Leinster registers begin in the 1780-1790s, while in the cities the start dates may be as early as 1760. The microfilms of the parish registers area available on self-service access in the Genealogy Microfilm Reading Room, opposite the Advisory Service. A comprehensive listing of the Library's holdings may be found on the NLI website.

Land Valuation Records

The *Tithe Applotment Books* and *Griffith's Valuation* are nineteenth-century property valuation records which are much used by family history researchers providing, if only in part, a substitute for the loss of almost all nineteenth-century census records for Ireland .

The Tithe Applotment Books

The *Tithe Applotment Books* were compiled between 1823 and 1838 as a survey of titheable land in each parish. (They do not cover cities or towns). In general, the information contained in the *Tithe Books* is as follows: name of occupier; name of townland; acreage; classification of land; amount of tithe due.

The *Tithe Applotment Books* are available on self-service access **microfilm** in the National Library of Ireland. A guide to the Tithe Applotment Books on film is available in the Reading Room and in the Genealogy Room. The originals of the *Tithe Applotment Books* are held at the National Archives, Bishop Street, Dublin 8.

The Primary Valuation of Ireland (Griffith's Valuation)

The *Primary Valuation of Ireland* or *Griffith's Valuation* - carried out between 1848 and 1864 - is an important Census Substitute. It provides the only detailed guide to where people lived in mid-nineteenth century Ireland and to the property they possessed.

It is arranged by county and, within each county, by Poor Law Union. Each Poor Law Union is divided into electoral divisions, parishes (Civil Parishes) and townlands.

The *Valuation* contains the following information in respect of each townland or street: map reference number (location of the holding on the first edition six-inch Ordnance Survey maps); names of occupiers of holdings; names of immediate lessors (the person from whom the holding was leased); descriptions of tenements (holding) eg, "House, offices and land" ; area (in Acres, Roods and Perches) of each holding; valuation of buildings, land, etc. with Total Annual Valuation of each holding

Griffith's Valuation is available online at **www.askaboutireland.ie** and www.irishorigins.com

The county by county Index of Surnames, a listing of the surnames recorded in Griffith's Valuation and the Tithe Books, continues to be a much-used source. The Index of Surnames acts as a valuable aid to pinpointing relevant parishes and parish records, and to understanding the distribution of particular surnames in parishes throughout the country.

Trade and Social Directories

The National Library has extensive holdings of Dublin, provincial and countrywide trade and social directories. The first of the Dublin directories dates from 1751. Dublin directories, which steadily expanded in scope over the years, continue in publication up to the present time. While the earliest of the provincial directories - *Ferrar's Directory of Limerick* - dates from 1769, the nineteenth century saw the widespread publication of such directories. The nineteenth-century also saw the publication of countrywide directories such as *Pigot's Commercial Directory of Ireland* (1820 and 1824) and *Slater's Directories* (1846, 1856, 1870, 1881 and 1894), all of which may be consulted in the Library. To find out if the Library holds a printed directory for the area relevant to your research, check the Online Catalogue.

Newspapers

The National Library has the largest newspaper collection in Ireland, with complete files of many local as well as national newspapers. In newspapers, the bulk of information relevant to genealogical research occurs in the form of advertisements and biographical notices (of birth, death or marriage). As there are few indexes available, relevant family information can be difficult to locate. As with the trade and social directories, newspaper information tends to be exclusive of the majority of the population: most births, marriages and deaths went unannounced and daily life continued without advertisement or report. Nonetheless, while direct family

Image © Courtesy of the National Library of Ireland

information may not be available, newspapers are rich in context and provide a sense of the community and times in which particular ancestors lived. A small number of newspapers have been digitised and are available to access online in the National Library.
Information on the Library's newspaper holdings is available in the newspaper database on the NLI website.

Manuscripts Records

The main components of the Library's manuscripts collections are Gaelic manuscripts, landed estates archives, maps, political material and literary papers. Of these, it is the archives of the former landed estates that are of particular interest to family history researchers. Among the more notable of these archives held by the Library are Castletown (Co. Laois), Clements (Cos. Leitrim and Donegal), Clonbrock (Co. Galway), Coolattin (Co. Wicklow), De Vesci (Co. Laois), Doneraile (Co. Cork), Headford (Co. Meath), Inchiquin (Co. Clare), Lismore (Co. Waterford), Monteagle (Co. Limerick), O'Hara (Co. Sligo), Ormond (Cos. Tipperary and Kilkenny), Powerscourt (Co. Wicklow), Prior-Wandesforde (Co. Kilkenny), Sarsfield (Co. Cork) and Wicklow (Co. Wicklow). Estate archives contain the records of the administration of estates by landlords and their agents, and generally include leases, rentals, accounts, correspondence and maps, mostly dating from the eighteenth and nineteenth centuries. Also of interest to family history researchers in the Department of Manuscripts are a number of collections of wills and will abstracts.

Information on the various estate collections as well as other manuscripts items of interest to family historians is available on the Library's online catalogue and Sources database, both of which are available on the NLI website. For those intent on searching for relevant estate material, the expert advice from the Library's Genealogy Service will be of assistance in pinpointing who the relevant landowner might have been.

Maps

The Library's map collections comprise some 150,000 maps and include cartographic materials ranging from a 12th century coloured sketch map of Europe to the most recent Ordnance Survey maps. Special collections include the Down Survey maps (18th century copies of 17th century originals), 18th century estate maps - including the collection of surveyors Brownrigg, Longfield and Murray, maps commissioned by the County Grand Juries (late 18th -19th century) and Ordnance Survey maps (1830s onwards).

Both printed and manuscript maps are listed in the online catalogue and Sources database.

Other Sources

Other sources regularly consulted by family history researchers in the National Library include many printed family histories, often compiled and published for private circulation by individuals who have researched their own family history. It should also be noted that publications of local history societies from around the country often contain valuable transcripts of local sources, including gravestone inscriptions, freeholders lists, etc.

Other relevant material in the Library's collections include the annual printed *Army Lists, Navy Lists, Royal Irish Constabulary (RIC)* publications including the annual *RIC Directories*, the *1796 Spinning Wheel Premium Entitlement List* (microfiche) and various other records of trades and professions, as well as a comprehensive series of *Registers of Electors*. Also, as research progresses, the appendices to nineteenth-century *Parliamentary Reports* may prove useful.

You will, most likely, reach a stage in your research when it will be impossible to find direct family information from the available records. While this may be disheartening remember that your ancestors lived as part of a community and that to understand something more of their lives and circumstances it is always rewarding to research the history of their locality. There are a multitude of sources for local history research in the National Library.

The Library's photographic collections - held at the Photographic Archive in Meeting House Square, Dublin 2 - may also be of interest. Collections acquired from various commercial photographic studios such as Poole (Waterford and surrounding counties) and Wynne (Castlebar) include studio portraits and an unparalleled collection of topographical images of Ireland. Over 35,000 images from the Library's photographic collections have been digitised and are available online at www.nli.ie.Exhibitions and publications: Exhibitions are held in both the main Library building and in the Photographic Archive.

Admission to the National Library of Ireland: For Genealogy (microfilms) and Newspaper research, passes - which may be obtained in the main Library building - are required. Other readers must apply for a Readers Ticket (for which proof of identity is necessary).

Genealogy Advisory Service

The Genealogy Advisory Service is available free of charge to all personal callers to the Library who wish to research their family history in Ireland. No appointment is necessary. For first time researchers this Service is an ideal starting point, allowing them the opportunity to discuss their research with experienced Library staff, and ready access to important finding aids. More experienced family historians are also welcome to avail of the Service if they need assistance with on-going research.

The National Library does not offer a research service. If you wish to commission someone to carry out research on your behalf a list of researchers - private individuals and organisations - who have indicated a willingness to undertake family history research on a professional, fee-paying basis, can be downloaded from the Library website.

Library Opening Hours:

Main Reading Room, Main Building, Kildare Street, Dublin Mon - Wed: 9.30am - 7.45pm; Thurs & Fri: 9.30am - 4.45pm; Saturday: 9.30am - 12.45pm

Genealogy Advisory Service Mon - Fri: 9.30am - 4.45pm

Manuscripts Reading Room 2/3 Kildare Street, Dublin Mon - Wed: 9.30am - 7.45pm; Thurs & Fri: 9.30am - 4.45pm; Saturday: 9.30am - 12.45pm

Photographic Archive Reading Room, Meeting House Square, Temple Bar, Dublin 2 Mon - Sat: 10am - 4.45pm; Sunday: 12pm - 4.45pm

Contact details:
National Library of Ireland, Kildare Street, Dublin 2 T: +353 1 603 02 00 F: +353 1 661 25 23 E: info@nli.ie W: www.nli.ie

THE NATIONAL LIBRARY, DUBLIN.

Irish DNA Atlas

Dr. Gianpiero Cavalleri & Michael Merrigan MA FGSI

Background to the project

A major new All-Ireland project was launched at the very successful ***'Back To Our Past'*** show at the RDS in Dublin in October 2011 by the **Genealogical Society of Ireland** and the **Royal College of Surgeons in Ireland**.

Over the past decade or so genealogists from around the world have become increasingly intrigued by the possibilities afforded through the scientific advances in genetic genealogy to augment or confirm our traditional record based research. Therefore, it is no wonder that media interest was high with much quality radio and newspaper coverage in Ireland when the ***'Irish DNA Atlas Project'*** was launched at the RDS.

What is DNA, and what can it tell us about the history of Ireland?

Deoxyribonucleic acid (DNA) is helical strip of sugars (the deoxyribose part) protecting a series of nitrogen-rich chemicals (the nucleic acids) which code for proteins, the building blocks of life. We describe the nucleic acids as a series of letters – A, T, C and G – and the arrangement of these letters allows for diversity in life. Humans carry around 3 billion letters in their DNA, and collectively we refer to this our 'genome.' These 3 billion letters are arranged across forty-six thread-like structures called chromosomes, with one set of twenty-three inherited from the mother and the other from the father. Arranged along these chromosomes are genes which code for specific proteins. With each generation changes are introduced to our DNA (mutations), this diversity in our DNA contributes to the diversity we see in a population, those differences we see in height, eye, hair and skin colours, blood type etc., all inherited, at least in part, from our parents and ultimately from our ancestors.

By studying the distribution of genetic changes (mutations) in individuals, we can use DNA to inform on the history of a population. Three broad approaches are currently available to genetic ancestry studies and these differ based on the section of DNA that is being studied.

They are

1. Y chromosome
2. mitochondrial DNA (mtDNA)
3. whole genome.

These three general approaches are complementary and have strengths and weaknesses.

Men carry a Y chromosome which is inherited from their father and their father's father before them in an unbroken line through the generations very much like an inherited surname. This makes the Y chromosome ideal for tracing the patrilineal journey through the consistencies and, critically, the small changes that occur in the chromosome with every generation.

There are many different types of Y chromosomes and just like a surname, they can be typical of a region or associated with particular historical groups which have different origins, e.g. Norse, Pictish, Anglo-Saxon, Irish, etc. Except unlike surnames, Y chromosomes extend back to the dawn of humanity in Africa! Reading the Y chromosome code of an individual can tell us about the patrilineal ancestry of that person or the region from which they come.

Mitochondrial DNA is a section of DNA carried by both men and women but inherited, in a similarly *'unbroken'* line, from their mother and their mother's mother before them. Just like a Y chromosome there are many different types of mtDNA and they can be typical of a region or historical group. Again, just like the Y chromosome they can tell us about the ancestry of a person or a particular population but from the maternal aspect. The difference is that the mtDNA explores the historical maternal line as opposed to the paternal line with the Y chromosome. The Y chromosome and mtDNA are invaluable in that they provide a wealth of information on two branches of our family tree, but of course there are many more branches (and ancestors) not represented by these subsections of our DNA.

Whole genome approaches look at the nature of the code across *all* of our DNA. This approach is very good for providing a broad picture of ancestry, for example your DNA looks 50% Irish, 25% French, 25% Italian. Indeed, in theory it's possible to resolve down to the level of a region (Kerry vs Donegal, as opposed to simply *'Ireland'*.) But this approach cannot however, provide the resolution that the Y chromosome or mtDNA does for their particular lineages.

The ***Irish DNA Atlas Project*** team will apply a combination of the above approaches to explore the broad history of the Irish population, particular regions within Ireland, and/or distinct groups of Irish. As an island population on the edge of Europe, Ireland has a rich cultural heritage that is the product of a continual series of migrations since ancient times to modern. By characterizing the nature of these migrations, The ***'Irish DNA Atlas'*** will provide valuable information on settlement patterns across the island of Ireland – from our first farmers to the plantations of sixteenth and seventeenth centuries. Understanding and preserving this history enriches our culture. It's important to assemble 'the Atlas' now as ever improving transport results in greater mobility, thus the historical structure of the regional populations of Ireland become harder to trace. Although historical records and archaeological studies have uncovered many wonderful aspects of Irish history, there are many questions left unanswered. It's important to appreciate that the demographic history of a population can impact on the health of the current day people. For example, Ireland has the highest incidence of cystic fibrosis in the world. This condition is entirely determined by genetics, one or more ancient migrations carried this condition to Ireland. The project is therefore not only concerned with the movements and interrelationships of population groups, it also has a valuable contribution to make to the study of the health of the people of Ireland.

In this way, geneticists can begin to realise the potential of the Irish genome as a resource for understanding our past. For example geneticists will be able to characterise the structure of the Irish population at a genetic level – characterising signals of migration (e.g. Celts, Vikings, Normans etc). Also, from a genealogical and historical perspective, genetics can be used to determine whether there was a single or indeed, multiple origins for certain Irish surnames which appear to be similar but do not document origin narratives of surnames like O'Connor which has, in fact, several different origins as indicated by the separate septs of O'Connor Kerry, O'Connor Faly, O'Connor Sligo and, of course, the family of the first President of the Genealogical Society of Ireland, Denis O Conor Don.

The much less documented surnames such as Merrigan (Irish: *Ó Muireagáin*) have, for example, many different areas of origin based on the early nineteenth century records ranging from east Co. Cork, Co. Waterford, south Co. Kilkenny, Co. Tipperary, north Co. Wexford, Co. Wicklow, Co. Longford, Co. Roscommon and, of course, with the migration to Dublin in the mid nineteenth century, the capital city and county have many Merrigan families of presumably diverse origins. Is Merrigan a single surname or, in fact, does it represent many different origins possibly linked to the larger septs in each area?

Surnames such as Walsh (Irish: *Breathnach* meaning 'Welshman'), which, is amongst the most common of Irish surnames and is found in all areas of the country, especially, in the south east where it is frequently rendered as Welsh, is generally associated with the Cambro-Norman invasion of Ireland in the late twelfth-century. However, given the geographic spread of this surname throughout the country far beyond the areas of settlement of the Cambro-Normans, is it reasonable to assume that all persons of this surname have a Cambro-

Launch of the Irish DNA Atlas Project
from left, Rory Stanley, FGSI, GSI President; Dr. Gianpiero Cavalleri, RCSI; Pádraic Ingoldsby, MGSI, GSI Cathaoirleach and Séamus O'Reilly, FGSI, GSI Irish DNA Atlas Project Coordinator

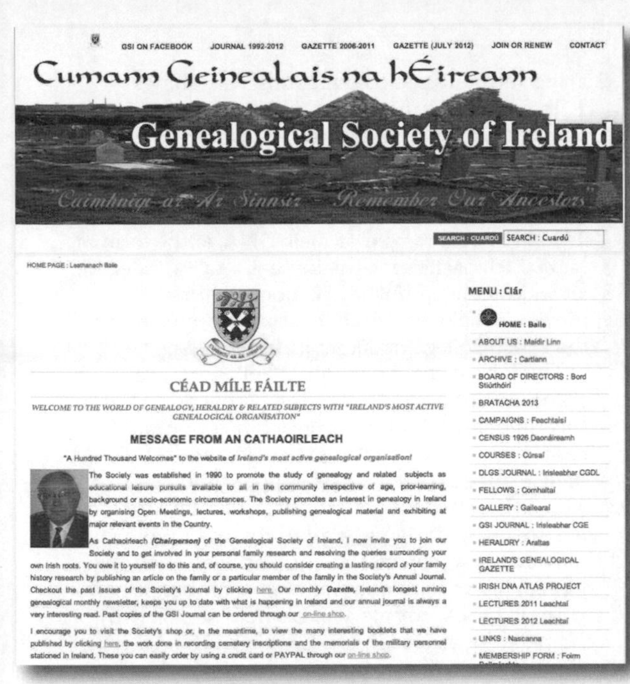

Norman ancestry? Genetics could unravel this mystery by looking at the DNA of persons with the surname Walsh from different parts of the country.

There has been a growing interest over the past decade or so in One-Name Studies particularly in England, however, attempts to replicate such studies in Ireland are fraught with difficulties, not least, because of the history and structure of Irish surnames which has been further complicated by the shift from the Irish language to the widespread use of English over the eighteenth and nineteenth centuries. Patronymics which had evolved over millennia and yet, kept a traditional association with the ancestral sept name, became almost frozen in time with the arrival of the English language and, of course, with officialdom in the form of land records. Similarly this process of Anglicisation produced some very strange and often fanciful mistranslations of some Gaelic surnames which completely masked their true origins and, in many cases, these became indistinguishable from surnames of English or continental European origin that arrived from the seventeenth century onwards. Sometimes differences in the religious denominations of the persons gave a hint to the ethnic origin of the surname, but this is fraught with difficulty and requires much local knowledge to ascertain correctly. This is where genetic genealogy can help.

Aims of the Irish DNA Atlas Project

This joint academic research project is compiling an ***'Irish DNA Atlas'*** through the collection of genealogical information and DNA samples to investigate the diversity of the Irish genome. The specific objectives of the *'Irish DNA Atlas'* are:

(1) To create a DNA collection that allows genetic analysis of population structure within Ireland and distinct groups of Irish. Analysis of such a collection will reveal ancient demographic movements and inform on the ancestry of specific regions and groups within Ireland.

(2) To create a DNA collection to help inform population based studies of health in Ireland.

The collection and scientific analysis of this type of data assists in the identification of genetic risk factors for disease (e.g. diabetes, heart disease etc). With this information, we can contribute to improvements in the nature of future treatments, including drug design or indeed lifestyle decisions on how to prevent the development of disease in the first place. As the Royal College of Surgeons is one of Ireland's foremost health research institutions, this project will have both a national and an international dimension involving researchers in a number of different fields.

An additional activity of the ***Irish DNA Atlas*** team is to promote an awareness, appreciation and knowledge of genetics as a tool for genealogy and history. We are aware that when any complex scientific concept is communicated to a non-expert audience it is exceptionally difficult to convey a full sense of the 'context' of the new knowledge. We will work to communicate the potential of new technology but outlining clearly what the technology can and cannot do.

Who are the IDAP team?

The project is a collaboration between the Genealogical Society of Ireland, based in Dún Laoghaire, Co. Dublin, and Dr. Gianpiero Cavalleri a population geneticist at the Royal College of Surgeons in Ireland (RCSI) in Dublin's St. Stephen's Green. Since its foundation in 1784, RCSI has played a major role in medical education and training in Ireland. Today the College provides extensive education and training in the healthcare professions and has an enviable international reputation in the performance of high levels of research activity. Dr. Cavalleri is of Italian parentage but was born and raised in the west of Ireland. He trained with Prof. Dan Bradley (a pioneer of genetic genealogy in Ireland) at Trinity College, Dublin before completing his PhD at University College London under Prof. David Goldstein. He is currently researching the genetics and pharmacogenetics of epilepsy at RCSI. Dr. Cavalleri collaborated on a number

ISSN 2009-4345

IRISH DNA ATLAS

PROJECT NEWSLETTER

Scientia Pro Bono Humani Generis

Vol. I No. I — www.familyhistory.ie — October 2011

RCSI

A collaboration between the Genealogical Society of Ireland and the Royal College of Surgeons in Ireland

GENETIC GENEALOGY

NEW ALL-IRELAND PROJECT

The Genealogical Society of Ireland and the Royal College of Surgeons in Ireland have launched an important All-Ireland project to create a collection of DNA samples from individuals of Irish origin, which will be used to explore human genetic variation in the Irish population.

Over the past decade or so genealogists from around the world have become increasingly intrigued by the possibilities afforded through the advances in genetic genealogy to augment or confirm our traditional record based research.

This new project is aimed at promoting an awareness, appreciation and knowledge of genetic genealogy. Operation-

College of Surgeons in Ireland (RCSI) will direct all the scientific aspects of this new and exciting project.

For over 200 years the RCSI has played a major role in medical education and training in Ireland. Founded in 1784 to train surgeons, today the College provides extensive education and training in the healthcare professions at undergraduate and postgraduate level.

The RCSI is committed to performing high levels of research activity, and helping to drive the Irish economy through the commercialising of intellectual property arising from its research, and the development of collaborative links with industry, educational and research institutions both nationally and

lation on the edge of Europe, Ireland has a rich cultural heritage that is the product of ancient migrations from the neighbouring island and from mainland Europe.

Understanding and preserving this history enriches our culture. Although historical records and archaeological studies have uncovered many wonderful aspects of Irish history, there are many questions left unanswered.

This new group project will provide valuable information on the migration and settlement patterns across the island of Ireland. This research will assist historians and archaeologists in their analysis of existing records or studies.

of recent TV programmes on genetic genealogy including *'The Blood of the Irish'* and the more recent series *'The Blood of the Travellers.'* Dr. Gianpiero Cavalleri will direct all the scientific aspects of this new and exciting project.

The genealogical aspects of the project will be directed by the Genealogical Society of Ireland through its Archives & Research Centre – *An Daonchartlann* – based at the Carlisle Pier, Dún Laoghaire Harbour, Co. Dublin. The Society appointed its Director of Archival Services, **Séamus O'Reilly, FGSI**, to coordinate the collection of the genealogical data.

How to participate:

We are seeking to recruit participants, male and female, from all parts of the island of Ireland who can trace their eight great grandparents to an area within a 15kms to 20kms radius of the main ancestral homestead. The reason the project is not based on the Irish county boundaries is simply that communities near to or indeed, straddling the county boundaries create a *'Natural Area of Social Cohesion'* or *'NASC.'* For example, the local communities in south County Wicklow often had more in common with their counterparts in north County Wexford than with the communities in north or west County Wicklow. This cross-county-boundary *'NASC'* situation exists throughout the country and, in some cases, can involve communities in many different counties which, over the centuries, became linked socially, commercially and, of course, through marriage. Whilst, much of the genealogical information required by the participant is readily available in civil registration, census or church records, the Genealogical Society of Ireland will advise participants on the location and accessibility of such records. There are a number of very useful on-line resources listed on the Society's website www.familyhistory.ie

Participants satisfying this criteria will be sent a recruitment pack, requesting two things –

1. To complete a *'Birth Brief'* (Pedigree Chart) provided by the Genealogical Society of Ireland. This document is designed to capture ancestry (name, date of birth, place of birth) back to the eight great grandparents.

2. To provide a sample of their DNA, in the form of saliva. Each participant will be sent a saliva collection kit which contains full instructions on how to provide sample etc which is forwarded directly to the Royal College of Surgeons for analysis.

Thinking of participating? Well, here are some essential guidelines for all participating in this unique and hugely important scientific research project. Participation in the *Irish DNA Atlas* Project is strictly on a pro bono basis for all participants. All genetic data will be studied in a specially designed coded format by which individual participants cannot be identified by name. This special code linking each participant to their DNA sample will be held securely by the main investigator Dr. Cavalleri. This information will not be used for any other purpose other than for this particular project. The results of the study, including data generated, may be shared with other scientists and published at a later date, but the names of the participants will not appear in such publications.

Participants are free to choose whether to partake in both the 'historical' and 'health' components of the work or indeed, just the 'historical' component if they so wish. The Project has been approved by the Ethics Committee of RCSI.

Analyzing the Genealogical Data

The Genealogical Society of Ireland is currently analyzing the data extracted from the pedigree charts completed by each participant to ascertain the possible origins and classifications of the surnames of the participant and their ancestors back to their great-grandparents.

The classification will be based on two sets of criteria, one for the surname of the participant, and the other for the each of the eight great-grandparents.

The general classification of the surnames of the great-grandparents will be

1. Gaelic (Irish, Scottish, Manx)
2. Welsh (including Cornish)
3. English (including Anglo-Norman and Anglo-Scottish)
4. Other (including all surnames outside the above irrespective of the area of origin)

As for the participant's own surname, a further analysis will determine whether it is (1) Gaelic Irish; (2) Old English (including Anglo-Norman etc – 12th to 15th centuries); (3) New English (Tudor and Stuart protestant plantations – 16th and 17th centuries) (4) Ulster Plantation (including Gaelic Scottish, Anglo-Scottish, English and Welsh in Ulster – 17th century); (5) Cromwellian Plantation (English and Welsh – 17th century); (6) Williamite Plantation (including English, Scottish, Welsh, Dutch etc – late17th century); (7) European Protestant (Huguenots – 16th to 18th centuries; Palatines – 18th century); and (8) Other (including Jewish and other ethnic or religious groups).

These classifications allow for the correlation of the data within a historical timeline which will be of considerable assistance to historians and may challenge some of our accepted narratives on the settlement of Ireland. This information will be analyzed and compared to the genetic data to create the ***'Irish DNA Atlas'***.

Research drives innovation

Although participating in this study will not be of direct benefit to each participant, it is important scientifically. Information arising from this study has the potential to improve our understanding of common diseases such as cancer and cardiovascular disease and, of course, provide valuable new information of the origin and movement of populations on the island of Ireland. Information from a participant's sample could be used for research involving the commercial sector including pharmaceutical companies. Through the collection and scientific analysis of this type of data it may be possible to predict diseases and help improve the nature of future treatments, including drug design or lifestyle decisions. It should be fully understood that any involvement of the commercial sector will be through collaboration or partnership with the RCSI involving formal assurances that equivalent data protection measures will be upheld by the commercial partner.

Participants are strongly advised to download and keep a copy the Irish DNA Atlas Project Newsletter for future reference. The newsletter is available on the website of the Genealogical Society of Ireland www.familyhistory.ie. It is the responsibility of each participant to ensure that he/she understands all the information presented by the Project team before agreeing to participate in this study. The Project team will endeavour to answer any queries that intending participants may have on the Project.

For further information or to participate contact the Director of Archival Services at the Genealogical Society of Ireland, Séamus O'Reilly, FGSI, by e-mail on Irish.DNA@familyhistory.ie

The Genealogical Society of Ireland is a registered charity in Ireland (CHY 10672) promoting the study of genealogy, heraldry and related subjects as open access educational leisure pursuits available to all. The Society is a membership based organisation that hosts to Open Meetings each month, publishes an Annual Journal and a monthly newsletter *'Ireland's Genealogical Gazette'* and operates an Archive and Research Centre – An Daonchartlann – at the Carlisle Pier, Dún Laoghaire Co. Dublin, Ireland. For further information see: www.familyhistory.ie or www.facebook.com/familyhistory.ie or follow us on Twitter @GenSocIreland

About the authors:

Dr. Gianpiero Cavalleri is a population geneticist at the Royal College of Surgeons in Ireland (RCSI), St. Stephen's Green, Dublin 2, Ireland.

Michael Merrigan, MA, FGSI, General Secretary of the Genealogical Society of Ireland based at An Daonchartlann, Carlisle Pier, Dún Laoghaire, Co. Dublin, Ireland.

The Sad Side

Joseph O'Neill

Ellis Island, New York

'After you, Madam,' said the Austrian. He stepped back from the gangplank with a gallant bow. Even in the cold January air, she felt a blush warm her pale skin. A smile danced in her dark eyes and she stepped forward into history, the first of twelve million.

It was 1st January 1892 and Annie Moore, a fifteen-year-old Irish girl, was the first to pass through America's new immigrant station, Ellis Island. Before it closed, in 1954, another 520,903 of her race would follow.

Today, the north of the Island houses a spectacular Emigration Museum, opened in 1990 at a cost of $200 million. An enormous three storey redbrick building with limestone piping forms its centre piece. But the structures on the south of Ellis Island lie derelict, a mouldering network of buildings, abandoned to the mice and birds.

This area is known as the *'sad side'* of the island. All the immigrants were not like Annie, young and healthy, full of hope and energy.

In its heyday, the island was a modern Babel, humming with a hundred languages, a throng of crushing bodies. Built to process several thousand immigrants in a day, nearly twelve thousand bodies passed through in one twenty-four-hour period.

For most it was a fleeting visit. After a cursory medical check and a meal, they bought a white lunch box and a railroad ticket for Boston, San Francisco, Pittsburgh, Cleveland, Cincinnati, Chicago, St. Louis or wherever there was work and friends.

But for some the Island was the end of the road. They were the ones who ended up on the sad side.

Arriving at Ellis Island

Ellis Island 1905, New York

Every immigrant was tagged with the number of his ship. But the other men who mingled with the throngs, a piece of white chalk at the ready, were not immigration officers. They were doctors, watching for those who looked sick. They marked their backs with an 'X'.

The immigrants formed lines to be examined. A common belief in America was that poor immigrants were the carriers of contagious diseases. Many, it was said, were so decrepit that they immediately became a charge on the public purse. The marked ones were closely scrutinised.

The commonest ailments were measles - a potential killer in the 1900s - tuberculosis, for which there was no cure and trachoma, a contagious eye disease, often led to blindness. Immigrants' health was so bad that one in five was consigned to the hospital complex.

Even for most of these, this was only a temporary inconvenience, like the fourteen hundred women who gave birth on the island. But for others, the Island that was their first site of America, became the graveyard of all their hopes.

On the sad side it was easy to feel the desolation of the place. Before an eighteen-century New York merchant, Samuel Ellis, gave his name to the Island, it was known for the execution of a soldier in 1765 and called Gibbet Island. In winter it is a desolate spot, lashed by the cruel Atlantic rain. In summer, stifling humidity envelops the place, spawning swarms of midges and sucking energy from sweating limbs. It's no place for the sickly.

Many of the sick were wasted by the Atlantic's buffeting; others were near the end. In total, over three thousand five hundred died, including fourteen hundred children.

Many spent restless days in the large, airy wards or the high rooms of the psychiatric wing with its meshed windows. When fit to travel, they were sent back to their place of origin.

In many ways, these were the most pitiable of all. Some had travelled to be with their family who would support them in their illness. Now they were condemned to poverty and sickness, often returning to die in the poorhouse. Most had travelled with relations who now faced an agonising decision: abandon a sick mother or a dying father or else forsake their hopes of a better life.

Arrivals Hall, Ellis Island

But for the courtesy of an Austrian gentleman, Annie Moore would be just another nameless immigrant, one of the anonymous millions. Sean Keane's song will ensure that she won't be forgotten. It's as it should be, for she stands for all those whose hope and courage carried them to a new life in America.

As for the unfortunate ones, those whose experience of America began and ended here, they still haunt the buildings of the sad side.

Upon Your Honour Sir!

Duelling in Ireland 1750-1820

Stephen Wade

The notion of a face to face confrontation over a point of honour goes back a very long way. Where there has been a military elite or an aristocratic high culture, there have been fights concerning reputation. European life in the higher circles of power and status always had an element of preserving one's name and the honour attached. As Roderigo says to Iago in Othello, *'I have lost my reputation! I have lost the immortal part of myself and what remains is bestial . . .'* The duel came into use in the forms we think of today, however, late in the sixteenth century; at that time there was a growing body of writing concerned with manners and courtly behaviour, notably the universally read *Il Libro del Cortegiano* (*The Courtier*) by Castiglioni.

There were codes of behaviour, governing the correct protocols for dealing with insults, and the mindset behind this stretches back to the time of trial by combat in the early medieval years. Duelling was banned under Cromwell, and also under Charles I and it was not until 1819 that the intricate and binding rules of duelling were taken from the statute books. The practice was universal, but certain places seemed to take to the custom with alacrity, and one of these locations was Ireland. Such was the esteem given to one who had taken part in a duel that in some quarters, such activity was thought to be essential to a proper education into the higher echelons of society. A question sometimes asked of a young man of quality was *'Did he blaze away?'* The phrase was often used at the opening of the fight, one man shouting *'Blaze away!'* to incite a response.

In 1777 the practice of duelling was so rife that Ireland had to sort out some kind of regulations. The men involved came up with an Irish Code and this was always referred to as the *'Twenty-six Commandments.'* The interesting point about that event is that the men who decided on the commandments were at Clonmel assizes at the time. This happened at the summer assizes, and the rules were agreed on by men from five counties. The guidelines were so important that a copy of them, referred to as the *'commandments'* was ordered to be kept by a man, usually in his pistol case, so that if required, they could be consulted on points of proper behaviour and ritual. Maybe the men at Clonmel had done the legal business and had time to spare, so they put together some rules for what had always been a chaotic affair, with insults being given and responded to in all areas of the land where the gentry and their profligate sons were active.

The rules were very specific regarding the order of statements and events, so that, for instance, the first rule is complex and undoubtedly long-winded:

'The first offence requires the apology, although the retort may have been more offence than the insult. Example: A tells B he is impertinent; B

The shooting of D'Esterre
***Irish Magazine* Vol. 8 1815**

O'Connell
The Liberator's statue on the street named after him

though political factors such as election encounters, were also common triggers to action; there were many deaths – one estimate suggests that the death rate was 1 in 4 at that time, although of course, there were very many confrontations which ended with no casualties.

The problem with the duel has always been that there was no scale of insults which was generally agreed on. As the historian V G Kiernan has explained: *'For some offences an exchange of two or more shots was held to be the minimum purgation. Cheating at cards was one of the crimes equivalent to a blow. An enlightened provision was that challenges should not be delivered at night, 'for it is desirable to avoid all hot-headed proceedings' Irish heads were usually too well heated at night with claret.'*

From the beginnings of recorded history in Ireland, there had been duels, even extending back to folklore and myth. But when the Restoration brought with it a conquest of the land by the Anglo-Irish class, duelling became a part of the ideology of their power and indeed their culture. A duel became a very common matter; the Victorian historian Froude referred to these people as *'Irish chiefs of the sixteenth century in modern costume.'* Being engaged in duelling was a crucially important part of the code of being a *'gentleman'* of course and it was often said that a man was not able to take his place in the hierarchy of that power of the landed gentry until he had *'smelt powder.'*

retorts that he lies; yet A must make the first apology because he made the first offence and then (after one fire) B may explain away the retort by subsequent apology.'

The rules give us an insight into the wider culture of course, and to the various degrees of insults, such as number 10: *'Any insult to a lady under a gentleman's care and protection is to be considered as by one degree a greater offence than if given to the gentleman personally, and be regarded accordingly.'* Built into the code was the very practical direction that *'challenges must not be given at night'* thus avoiding, one assumes, the potential frequency of drunken challenges which would be regretted in the sobriety of the morning after.

In the last decades of the eighteenth century in Ireland, most duels were fought over insults,

In the eighteenth and early nineteenth centuries, there are numerous duels, some involved famous characters and some with very obscure people in the drama. Even Wolfe Tone acted as a second in a duel while at Trinity College, and one of his friends died in that encounter. So common was the habit that even the provost of the college was a duellist at one point. One particular area around the city was known for its duels - a place known as Clontarf Wood. The reputation of that place was that it was 'where men of heart go to bleed one another in duels.'

One of the very last duels in Dublin took place in 1838, when a Galway man called O'Hara made a joke at the expense of Mr

Robert Napoleon Finn. He refused to apologise and the duel had to go ahead so seconds were appointed and the assignation was settled, to take place at North Bull, around three miles from Dublin. They arrived at the scene and put their coats on the sand; a man called Ireland was a witness and he later gave an account of what happened to William Le Fanu.

An experienced second said he would give the signal to fire and the two men stood at each side of him, ready to walk their twelve paces. What happened next was farcical. The second said that there would just be the one signal, the words, *'Ready, fire.'* But the nervous Finn, when he heard the man say the word fire, turned and pointed the pistol at him. The second told him to settle down, saying, *'Do you want to shoot me?'* What followed was more like something from a melodrama:

'At the word "fire" Finn again lost his head, pulled the trigger of his pistol, which was pointed downwards, and lodged the bullet in the calf of his own leg. O'Hara, thinking that Finn had shot at him, immediately took aim at him, crying out, "For God's sake, don't fire. It was all a mistake!" But O'Hara did fire, and his bullet struck the ground close to Finn.'

Mr Ireland, watching from close by, was sprayed with sand, and then before any more developments could take place, four constables arrived and arrested everyone who was present. They were all put into carriages and taken back to Dublin. Ireland points out that Finn's injured leg was dangling out of a carriage to keep it cool. A Dublin joker said that Finn had gone to the Bull, got cow'd and shot the calf.

The famous Daniel O'Connell was also involved in a Dublin duel. After he criticised the Dublin corporation, he made enemies, and a character called D'Esterre challenged him to fight. O'Connell was a married man, having wed Mary, his cousin, in 1802. There was no doubt that D'Esterre had provoked the argument, but it went to the actual confrontation and he was shot. It took him a few days to die, but before he did so he exonerated O'Connell from any blame, and his second, Sir Edward Stanley, made it clear to O'Connell that there would be no prosecution. O'Connell was later to be on the wrong side of the law (while he was Mayor of Dublin) and was in jail for three months for conspiracy.

Aubrey de Vere, in his memoirs, says that *'In those days (1830s) a duel was the most mirthful of pastimes'* and he described a meeting of two lawyers in Dublin who met at sunrise in Phoenix Park; *'one was the biggest and one the smallest'* in Dublin society. But the big man had problems with his eyesight and said he could not see his opponent. The other instructed his second to draw a white chalk line of his own shape on the large *'carcass'* of his opponent. Such jocularity in chatty memoirs does not even hint at the terrible tragedies that occurred in duels, such as the fight in 1786 between Robert Keon of Leitrim and George Nugent Reynolds. Keon and Reynolds arrived at the place for the duel before their seconds and went on without them; Keon shot Reynolds dead, then he was tried, found guilty and hanged, in March 1788.

Joseph Le Fanu
wrote about the experience of a duel
in his memoirs - *Seventy Years of Irish Life* 1893

In the late eighteenth century there had been some really prominent duels and some, such as a fight between Blaquerre and Bagenal in 1773 had such an effect that there was a public condemnation of the whole nasty business. But for a long time it was impossible to outlaw the practice; all that happened over the course of these years was that the fights were regulated, but not banned. There was always the added problem that when it was linked to army life and manners, there was a code of honour which ran contrary to the law.

Some duels were so high profile that they affected public opinion, and one notable confrontation between Flood and Agar led to duelling being given more general respect and support. This was because Flood, being accused of bribing magistrates, had such support and

Honours Preſervati[(]
WITHOUT
BLOOD
OR,
A Sober Advice
TO
DUELLISTS
Being a Compendious Tract of the *moſt* Exq[u]
Nature to *Appeaſe* the Sudden Fits of *Fury*, w[.]
ENGLISH-SPIRITS
have of *Late* been too much Subject to.
With many *Cautions* how without the *Loſs* of R[...]
tation, or the leaſt Imprint of *Cowardiſe*, as well the
Nobility as Gentr[y]
of this Nation may Refuſe to Hazard their *Lives* and *Fortunes* on
mean Pretences of Vindicating a
Miſcalled Honour, or *Unmanly Gallantry*:
Shewing likewiſe, into what Dangerous Inconveniencies M[...]
thruſt themſelves forward in ſuch Caſes.
With an Account how ſuch *DUELS* prove [...]
Murther, and are contrary to the *Laws* of *God* and *Man*.

Written by a Well-wiſher to both Peace *and* Honour.

London, Printed for *Phillip Brookſby*, 1680.

Title page of a typical anti-duelling tract of the late 16th century

sympathy from the new middle classes that they took an interest in the case and in the words of one historian, the duel was *'the talk of the salons as well as the coffee houses.'* The result was that duelling and its code of honour, were understood and perhaps tolerated more by the public.

It has often been said and written that the notion of a duel, which is of course linked inextricably to notions of honour, reputation and class status, is deeply set in the Irish folklore and literature of earlier times. So much was this embedded in the later stereotypes of Irish character that *the 'stage Irishman'* of the eighteenth century English drama included the satirical depiction of the duelling temperament. The character of Sir Lucius O'Trigger in Sheridan's play *The Rivals* is typical of this. His name suggests his aggressive and volatile nature. That tradition of taking stock characters from Irish life and culture led to distortions and misunderstandings, but nevertheless, the historical record shows that Dublin people in these years had a penchant for settling disputes and matters of 'good name' by arranging a duel. The procedure and etiquette involved appealed so much to the general love of display and theatre that in terms of the media and the general civic gossip, at times a duel took its place as just another variety of slightly questionable but respected manly behaviour.

If we are to look for the kind of duel that would be more ordinary and typical, it would be the meeting between Standish O'Grady and Captain Smith in 1830. O'Grady, son of Edward O'Grady, chairman of the county of Waterford, was riding in Dawson Street when he smashed into a cabriolet driven by Captain Smith of the 32nd Regiment. O'Grady hit the officer's horse in order to free himself from the entanglement and Smith rounded on O'Grady and cracked him repeatedly with his own stick. O'Grady was merely a commissioner of bankrupts: Smith was a soldier, so the confrontation would be dangerous for the civilian generally, but he chased the cab and asked who had insulted him. Smith shouted out his name.

A message was sent by Lieutenant McNamara and they met at six in the morning, when O'Grady was shot, mortally wounded in the groin. Medical attention was given after he had been rushed to Richmond barracks, but he soon died.

The last death in a duel fought in Ireland is arguably that between Joseph Daunt of Kilcascan Castle, who was killed by his cousin from Manch House in 1826. This was, according to some, a duel fought over a suspected affair with the wife of the cousin. In England, as a contrast, the last duel on record happened in 1852 when a certain M. Barthelemey killed fellow Frenchman, M.Cournet at Egham in Surrey.

What does the story of duelling in Ireland in the Augustan and Regency years tell us? Mainly, such ritualistic affairs reflect the intricacy of the web of relationships in that social world of fast climbing and even more rapid falling from power or esteem. Reputations were a part of that fabric, but so were the demands made on people to maintain their status and name by established protocol in every walk of life. In an age of performance and display, of public showing-off of wealth and surface worth and vitality (as captured in the caricature art of Gillray and Rowlandson for instance), a duel was surely the extreme sensation, even more worthy of scandal and society chit-chat than an elopement or a suicide through disastrous gambling debts.

Further reading:

Gentlemen's Blood: A History of Dueling from Swords at Dawn to Pistols at Dusk Barbara Holland ISBN 978 1582344409 Bloomsbury, 2003

Pistols at Dawn: A History of Duelling Richard Hopton ISBN 978 0749951023 Portrait, 2007

That Damned Thing Called Honour: Duelling in Irish History, 1570-1860 James Kelly ISBN 978 1859180396 Cork University Press, 1995

The Duel in European History: Honour and the Reign of Aristocracy V G Kiernan ISBN 978 0192851284 Oxford Paperbacks 1989

The General Valuation of Rateable Property in Ireland

Mary P McConnon MA

Generally known as *'Griffith's Valuation'* it is one of the most important surviving nineteenth century Irish records available for genealogical purposes. It was a nationwide valuation of land, buildings and other tenements in order to assess the amount of local taxes, known as rates, payable. It was also used, at one time, to determine who was eligible to vote. However with its accompanying maps and manuscript material etc. it is not as simple a record to use as is sometimes suggested. This article is an introduction to these records.

In genealogy the term is normally used to describe the manuscript and printed documentation produced under the Rateable Property (Ireland) Act, 1846 (9 & 10 Vict. c.110) and the final publication in 1865 of the original printed sources prepared under the Valuation (Ir.) Act, 1852 (15 & 16 Vict. c.63). In practice, though, it only refers to the valuations prepared under the Act of 1852 and published between 1852 and 1865. This latter collection is also the most frequently used in genealogy. This will be explained later when looking at its history.

Although sometimes described as a census substitute it is not a census that shows family relationships or indeed those living in a particular household. It concerns the particular premises or land etc. that was valued, the amount of valuation on which the local taxes were assessed and the person liable to pay such as the main occupier and 'immediate' lessor from whom the occupier leased, rented or otherwise held the property.

GENERAL VALUATION OF IRELAND.

Acts 15 and 16 Vic., Cap. 63, and 17 Vic., Cap. 8.

NOTICE IS HERBY GIVEN, that the Tenement Valuation of the COUNTY OF CAVAN, has been commenced under the above Acts, and it is requested that the several Landholders, Agents, and others, will be good enough to afford every facility to the Surveyors who are now engaged defining and marking on the Ordnance Maps, the boundaries of the different Farms and Holdings.

RICHARD GRIFFITH,
Commissioner of Valuation.

General Valuation Office, Dublin, 12th June, 1854.

History

To gain an understanding of this important record, undertaken during and after the Great Famine, one has to go back to the 1820s when decisions were made to map every townland in Ireland on a scale of 6 inches to 1 mile. Prior to that time there was no standard countrywide survey. There were various maps produced such as estate maps by individual landlords and by local Grand Juries (forerunners of the County Councils) showing roads, natural features etc..

The Ordnance Survey - Maps and Boundary Survey

In 1824 the Ordnance Survey, as it became known, had commenced at first under Colonel Coleby and later under Sir Thomas Larcom. It resulted in the publication between 1833 and 1846 of six-inch maps of Ireland in about two thousand sheets. Since that time these maps have been revised. For further information on the actual publication dates for each county see *Andrews J.H., A Paper Landscape The Ordnance Survey in Nineteenth-Century Ireland, Dublin, 2002 (2nd edition), Appendix F, pp.327-32, & Appendix G, pp.333-7.*

The surveyors plotted the different features of the country, streams, rivers, roads, and principal houses as well as the boundaries, but it did not include the fences. However, difficulty was experienced in determining the boundaries of counties, baronies, civil parishes and townlands (approx. 69,000) upon the ground and so a separate Boundary Survey was introduced.

Under the Manors (Ireland) Act 1825 (6 Geo. 4 c.99) the Grand Juries were required to draw up tables of the names of parishes, townlands, ploughlands etc. in each barony and the high constable for each barony was to provide a return of same. In order to 'mark out' the boundaries of the divisions for the Ordnance surveyors the Lord Lieutenant was authorised to appoint persons to ascertain the boundaries. *(The Manors (Ireland) Act 1825 (6 Geo. 4 c.99) amending the The Boundaries (Ireland) Act, 1824 (5 Geo. 4 c.112 , The Statutes of The United Kingdom of Great Britain and Ireland, 6 Geo. IV. 1825, London 1825, pp.536-544.)*

The person appointed to conduct this

Boundary survey, as it was known, was Richard Griffith. On the work undertaken he told a House of Commons Select Committee on 6 May 1869:

'We had district boundary surveyors; corresponding with those of the Ordnance survey; we preceded them. The boundaries were determined by a meersman appointed by the proprietors. They were all marked with numbers; a sketch map of each parish was made by the boundary surveyors appointed by me, in which they introduced the same marks. When the Ordnance surveyors afterwards commenced the survey they had the sketch map in their hands, and a meersman, and they never made a mistake.' *(Report from the Select Committee of the House of Commons on General Valuation, etc. (Ireland): together with proceedings of the committee, minutes of evidence, and appendix, vol.IX, 1868-9, (362), 6 May 1869, parg.1357 in answer to question by The O'Conor Don).*

The initial high constables' lists of the townlands were obtained, the boundaries and names were checked and disputes settled. Townlands that bore the same name were distinguished by adding the term 'lower', 'upper', 'north', 'south' etc.. Further amending legislation was required to give the Boundary surveyors the necessary power to make the alterations.

In addition to the sketch maps descriptions of the boundaries were written into registers. Like some previous estate maps that included a written commentary such as names of tenants etc. this was also proposed for the Ordnance Survey but soon ceased. According to Andrews:-

'... it was felt in some quarters that the historical and social sections of the memoir might have an exacerbated effect on Irish patriotic feeling and so accentuate the divisions between planter and native, protestant and catholic, government and governed ... Larcom's ideas were also involved in another kind of political conflict ... the conflict of state action versus private enterprise. Why not leave memoir writing to local initiative, as in the case of the Statistical account of Scotland?' (Andrews, op. cit., pp.173-4).

Richard John Griffith
Born on 20th September 1784
Died 22th September 1878 aged 94 years

Richard Griffith.

Richard John Griffith was born on 20th September 1784 at 8 Hume Street, Dublin, and baptised in St Peter's Church of Ireland Parish, the son of Richard and Charity Griffith. His father made a fortune while working for the East India Company and had an estate at Millicent, County Kildare. His mother was stated to be Charity Bramston of Oundle in Northamhtonshire *(Davies, Gordon L. Herries & R. Charles Mollan, editors, Richard Griffith 1784 - 1878, Dublin, 1980, artlcle by Davies, pp.1-31, p.1)* but died when Richard was about 5 years old. His father Richard then married Mary the daughter of Hussey de Burgh in 1793.

He attended schools at Portarlington, Rathangan and Dublin. For a short time in 1800 to 1801 he joined the Royal Regiment of Artillery. He afterwards went to London and studied chemistry, geology and mineralogy. His interest in geology brought him to Edinburgh and here he became acquainted with preparing geological maps and also land valuing. On his return to Ireland he was involved in a number of public works including investigations into geology and bogs. The Dublin Society appointed him mining engineer and professor of geology from 1812 to 1822. From 1836 to 1844 he was also engineer for roads in the southern district in counties Cork, Limerick, Kerry and Tipperary. In 1825 he was placed in charge of the Boundary survey and later in charge of the Valuation survey. On 30 October 1868 he resigned as Commissioner of Valuation. He was made a baronet in 1858. Sir Richard John Griffith died 22 September 1878 age 94 years, at 2 Fitzwilliam Place, Dublin.

Valuation - Townland Valuation

Besides the tithes payable to the Established Church there were two other local taxes in existence by 1840. The County cess or Grand Jury rate was used to build and maintain roads, bridges, gaols etc. while the poor rate under the Poor Relief (Ireland) Act 1838 (1 & 2 Vict. c.56) was to provide for the relief of destitution. Each had its own form of assessment. The resulting documentation produced by the Ordnance and Boundary surveys began to be used to standardize the local cess in the various counties and also later the poor rate.

The Lord Lieutenant was empowered by the Valuation of Land (Ireland) Act, 1826 (7 Geo. 4 c.62) to appoint valuators. Houses for the first time ... were to be assessed at letting value, and land on the prices of wheat, oats, barley, potatoes, butter, beef, mutton and pork. The townland was adopted as the unit of valuation. (Street, Howard A. 'The Law Relating to Local Government, Dublin 1955, Appendix C, p.1313). In the beginning only houses over a certain valuation were included.

The 1826 Act did not come into operation until 1830 because the Ordnance maps were not completed until that time of the northern counties, namely Londonderry and Antrim.*(Griffith to Select Committee, op. cit., 6 May 1869, parg.1313, in answer to question by Col. French)*. On its commencement Richard Griffith states:-

'The old townland valuation was commenced in the county of Londonderry in 1830 . . . it was a universal practice there (fortunately for me) to let lands by valuation, and not by tender or proposal, as in other parts of Ireland; I . . . obtained the names of a number of professional surveyors and valuators who had been engaged in those counties, and in the adjoining county of Tyrone; and after a great deal of trouble I fixed upon nine of them, . . .we began at Coleraine. I read the Act of Parliament to them, and told them that the principle of valuation that I wished to follow was, "Live and let live," the principle, in fact, on which the landlords in the north of Ireland let their lands; that of a low moderate scale. I explained to them that they were bound to value the land according to the scale of prices contained In the Act; that they were to ascertain the quality of the land by digging up the active soil and the subsoil . . .' (ibid, 6 May 1869, parg.1335)

He further stated that information gained on some townlands from above valuation was used as standards for valuing:

' . . . I took the whole district of the northern parts of the counties of Londonderry and Antrim, which represented a greater variety of soils than any other part of Ireland; I took that as a scale; I was in the habit for many years of sending people to value the different townlands for the purpose of testing them, to see whether they adhered to the same scale or not. (ibid, 13 May 1869, parg.1483, in answer to question by The O'Conor Don)

The Valuation of Land (Ireland) Act 1836 (6 & 7 Will. 4 c.84) repealed the Act of 1826 and in effect re-enacted it. As will be seen later the 1836 Act was replaced by The Rateable Property (Ireland) Act, 1846 (9 & 10 Vict. c.110) and the Valuation (Ireland) Act, 1852 (15 & 16 Vict. c.63). On the published versions from 1852 to 1865 of Griffith's Valuation, at the beginning of the Barony listings, these Acts under which the particular barony survey was carried out are listed. In understanding the House Books (see later) knowledge of the dates of the legislation as well as how the valuing progressed is helpful.

Valuation - Tenement Valuation

In 1844 a Committee was appointed to inquire into the townland valuation of Ireland. Local rates varied greatly between grand jury areas and it was believed a general valuation, using certain standard criteria, would be more equitable. Two years later and, in consequence of the introduction of the poor laws, The Rateable Property (Ireland) Act 1846 (9 & 10 Vict. c.110) providing for a Tenement Valuation was passed. The word 'tenement' included land and buildings.

In comparison to the previous valuation this tenement valuation was, according to Griffith, undertaken *'on the same principle, but not according to the actual practice, because in the first Act we had three valuators together; and in the second we had only one. Then I adopted the principle of check valuations ... I had only a few men, who were constantly employed in checking the others . . .' (ibid, 13 May 1869, parg.1490).*

However, it appears to have been limited to the counties of Dublin, Cork, Limerick, Kerry, and Waterford.' *(ibid, 13 May 1869, parg.1489)* before the Act was revised in 1852

On being queried that not a single county was completed between 1844 and 1853 Griffith stated:

There were other counties finishing. The counties

List of COUNTIES and CITIES, showing the Dates at which the Valuation of each was completed

COUNTIES	Date of issue of Valuation	COUNTIES	Date of issue of Valuation
Carlow	28 June 1853	Clare	3 July 1856
Cork	20 July 1853	Galway Town	14 July 1856
Cork City	9 July 1853		
Dublin	5 May 1853	Cavan	25 June 1857
Kerry	19 July 1853	Galway	29 June 1857
Kilkenny	8 July 1853	Leitrim	6 July 1857
Kilkenny City	8 July 1853	Mayo	13 July 1857
Limerick	29 June 1853		
Limerick City	29 June 1853	Donegal	6 July 1858
Queen's	28 June 1853	Roscommon	1 July 1858
Tipperary	29 June 1853	Sligo	7 July 1858
Waterford	5 July 1853		
Waterford Borough	5 July 1853	Londonderry	16 July 1859
Dublin City	31 October 1854	Tyrone	13 July 1860
Kildare	18 July 1854		
Wexford	7 July 1854	Monaghan	1 July 1861
Wicklow	4 July 1854		
		Antrim	10 July 1862
King's [Offaly]	2 July 1855	Carrickfergus	10 July 1862
Longford	6 July 1855		
Louth	5 July 1855	Fermanagh	4 July 1863
Borough of Drogheda	6 July 1855		
Meath	10 July 1855	Down	12 July 1864
Westmeath	5 July 1855		
		Armagh	1 June 1865

FIGURE 2: Source: Report from the Select Committee on General Valuation, op. cit., Appendix No.8, p.241. In Appendix 1 (pp.213-19) is also given for each Poor Law Union the dates it or parts of it were printed.

that were previously valued . . . were to be calculated and issued . . . Then the tenement valuation was commenced, which was a very costly valuation. In Tipperary . . . the changes were very great. Part of the barony of Owney and Arra was valued three times, and all of it twice, because the changes of tenement were so numerous that we had to go over them again. It was not only that new tenants came in, but the boundaries were altered, and new fences were made. We were weary going over it.' (ibid, 13 May 1869, parg.1497).

The valuations prepared under the 1846 were deemed too high so in the 1852 Act the tenement valuation was continued but a new scale of agricultural prices was included. The method used in valuing buildings was described to the Select Committee by Griffith thus:

We value a house everywhere at what it will fairly let for. There is a guiding scale of prices in the valuation instructions, given according to the cubical measurement; this scale includes every variety of building. This scale was made in the north, but in the south the price would be too high and we reduced it. In valuing towns, we work by the same scale, increasing the price per cube according to locality. In the best streets in a town the country scale will be multiplied by four, or even more, and in the inferior by two, as the case may be. (ibid, 13 May 1869, parg. 1603, in answer to question by Sir Frederick Heygate).

In the case of the cabins of the poor he stated that there *'are no cabins so bad in the north as there are in the south. They are rarely so dilapidated . . . They are valued according to an arbitrary scale of cubic measurement, according to quality, local circumstances being taken into consideration; they are based on measurement.' (ibid, 13 May 1869, parg. 1604-5).* The value of mountain lands in the south of Ireland was determined, in the spring or early summer *'according to the quantity of cattle they feed in the summer; the soil is divided according as it is adapted to young or full-grown cattle.' (ibid, 13 May 1869, parg. 1703, in answer to Mr Herbert).*

It appears from the Minutes of the Select Committee that counties valued under the 1846 Valuation Act were subsequently reduced to the same scale as the counties valued under the 1852 Act. Griffith stated that the valuations under the 1846 were not published until they were reduced and that the reduction was *'a percentage' (ibid, 13 May 1869, parg* 1734, in answer to question by The O'Conor Don) and it was calculated in the office. It appears also that some smaller areas had to be redone because of the amount of errors while Dublin was valued in anticipation of an amendment to the 1852 Act being passed.

So far as records are concerned it appears that some of the listings of these valuations, and corrections, are included in the House Books (see later).

According to H.A. Street:

'Griffith's valuation *made under the Valuation (Ir) act, 1852 . . . was to apply to "all public and local assessments" and (s. 11) "to every valuation hereafter to be made". The "tenement" is the unit of valuation, as in the Act of 1846. The valuation was completed in 1865 . . . but no development of importance in the legal history of this branch of law took place until 1898, when the grand jury and poor rates were unified.' (Street, op. cit., pp. 1313-4).*

Who or what type of properties were actually rated depended, until 1946, on the legislation relating to the particular type of local authority such as towns, boroughs etc.. Normally it was the occupier but in e.g. boroughs it also included the lessor and tenant.

Griffith's valuation provided the basis on which local decisions relating to the rates were made. In brief the valuations were sent to the local authorities for publication, appeal etc., returned for amendment and afterwards sent back to the local authority to make the necessary changes in the local rate books and assess the rates. What has survived of these rate books are held in the local county library or archives of each county. A small number are also in the National Library of Ireland and the National Archives of Ireland.

Figure 3. Source: The Statutes of The United Kingdom of Great Britain and Ireland, 15 & 16 Victoria, London, 1852, 15 & 16 Vict. c. 63, p.242.

FORM.

VALUATION OF TENEMENTS.—(No. 1.)

County of / City of / *or* Town of / *or* Borough of — Union / Barony / Parish

Reference to Map.	Names.		Description of Tenement.	Area.	Rateable Annual Valuation.		Total Annual Valuation of Rateable Property.
	Townlands and Occupiers.	Immediate Lessors.			Land.	Buildings.	
				A. R. P.	£ s. d.	£ s. d.	£ s. d.

(Signature)
A——— *B*——— Commissioner of Valuation.

The Dates of completion of Griffith's Valuation.

After each barony or Poor Law union was completed it was published. These dates are listed at the end of each such section. In the case of some online versions it is given under 'details'. A rough guide as to the length of time the valuation survey in each county took can be determined from the date of publication of the notice to enter properties and the final date of publication of Griffith's Valuation. For example the survey had begun by 12 June 1854 in County Cavan (see Figure 1) and was completed by 25 June 1857 (see Figure 2).

Records included in the collection.

The Published Griffith's Valuation.

As stated the most frequently used part of the collection, in genealogy and local history, is the result of the survey made or revised under the 1852 Act and published before 1865. It is widely available either in hard copy or microfiche in local county libraries (on county only) and national repositories. It is also available online, on subscription websites, such as www.origins.net, www.findmypast.ie and www.ancestry.com and for free to view on www.askaboutireland.ie. These latter online versions include a name and place name indexes. There is also available in hardcopy and microfiche *The Index to Surnames in Griffith's Valuation and the Tithe Applotment Books* also known as *The Householders' Index*.

What information does it contain?

The template to be used was included in the 1852 Act (see Figure 3).

Most tenements are houses, offices, yards, gardens and land but other properties liable to rates such as forges, coach factories, stables, flax mills, corn mills, flour mills, kilns, distilleries, malt houses, dairy yards, markets, tan yards, timber yards, iron works, coal yards, quays etc. are listed as well as properties exempt from rates such as churches, graveyards, schools, cavalry and infantry barracks, police barracks, courthouses, gaols, dispensaries, poor-houses, workhouses, railway lines, etc.. Besides agricultural land (in statute measure) also included are plantations, mountainous land, bogs, orchards, gardens, lakes, rivers etc.. In short an invaluable local history record.

In Figure 4 is an example, from the printed version of Griffith's Valuation, for house at 8 Hume St, Dublin City, where Richard Griffith was born in 1784. It was valued at £52 while small two roomed thatched houses in rural areas were valued at about 5s to £1.

The boundaries of each plot were marked on the available Ordnance Survey maps. There plots were numbered and the corresponding number is the 'no. of reference on map' listed in Griffith's Valuation. However with the various changes that took place sometimes new numbers were inserted on the same maps. In above example in a city the plot number is 8 on Hume St. In smaller built up areas sometimes the area is listed with a number for the townland and a sub-number for each plot. In rural townlands the plots are marked 1,2, 3 etc. with A & B listed as divisions of the holding while the small letters a, b, c, usually refer to a house. So locating a name of an occupier on this survey and with the plot number listed it should be possible to locate the actual situation of the property where the person lived. Here, however, care has to be taken. Is the OS map the one that corresponds with the actual valuation or with a revision? For example in Marshes Upper Townland, south of Dundalk, County Louth, 44 properties are marked on the OS map, sheet 7, but only 43 plots are listed in the printed Griffith's Valuation for the townland.

Some townlands were left out e. g. in County Louth the plots in Rockmarshal Townland are

12 PRIMARY VALUATION OF TENEMENTS.

MANSION HOUSE WARD.

No. of reference to Map.	Local Numbers	Names.		Description of Tenement.	Area.	Rateable Annual Valuation.		Total Annual Valuation of Rateable Property.
		Streets, &c., and Occupiers.	Immediate Lessors.			Land.	Buildings.	
		HUME-STREET. (*Ord. S.* 27 & 28.) PARISH OF ST. PETER.			A. R. P.	£ s. d.	£ s. d.	£ s.
1	1	Robert Harrison, .	Immediate Lessor, .	House,offices,and & yd,	—	—	90 0 0	90 0
2	2	Miss Doran, . .	Court of Chancery (*Christr. Lodge, Receiver*)	House and small yard,	—	—	44 0 0	44 0
3	3	Susan Bacon, . .	Captain Butler, . .	House and small yard,	—	—	42 0 0	42 0
4	4	Thomas Berry, . .	Reps. —— Maunsell,	House, office, and yard,	—	—	65 0 0	65 0
5	5	Matthew R. Sausse, .	Jane Moore, . .	House, office, and yard,	—	—	56 0 0	56 0
6	6	Rev. R. H. Wall, .	John Ensor, . .	House, office, and yard,	—	—	68 0 0	68 0
7	7	Mrs. Ruxton, . .	Edward Walsh, . .	House, office, and yard,	—	—	56 0 0	56 0
8	8	Trustees of Orange Hall *Here Ely-place intersects*	Rt. Hon. T. B. C. Smith,	House and yard, .	—	—	52 0 0	52 0

Figure 4. With permission of Commissioner of Valuation.

Figure 5.

County	House Books		Rent Books	Miscellaneous Books
	Parish	Town		
	Page	Page	Page	Page

Figure 6.

Houses in Townland of ______								
No	Name and Description	Quality Letter	Length	Breadth	Height	Number of Measures	Rate per Measure	Amount £. s. d.

listed as 1 to 13 in Annaloughan Townland, Civil Parish of Ballymascanlan.

Some occupiers can be listed twice. This may arise from the occupier moving to another area that was valued later e.g. the County Louth valuations were published by 1855 but that of neighbouring County Monaghan were published by 1861. It is possible this can occur also within counties as civil parishes were surveyed at different times. One person in County Louth, who would have been known to Richard Griffith, was Sir John McNeill, the well-known engineer and freemason, yet he is listed as occupier at plot 1a in Milltown Townland, Civil Parish of Dromiskin, for house, offices, 137 acres 1 rood and 17 perches of land, tilery and a brickfield and also for plot 2abcde in Aghaboys Townland, Civil Parish of Ballymascanlan, for house, offices, 115 acres 2 roods and 13 perches of land, flax-mill and offices, Villa and offices, office and Lime-kiln. He is best known in the county for building the Boyne Viaduct which is not listed in Griffith's Valuation as it was not completed until 1855.

Other Records available.

These are listed under the three main repositories where valuation records are held.

NATIONAL ARCHIVES OF IRELAND, Bishop St., Dublin 8 [NAI].

On open shelf in the NAI, in addition to the indexes for the Ordnance Survey Collection, there are three Indexes relating to the Valuation Office Collection. A short note on each of these indexes is given below. These records are only available to view on microfilm if available. Some have also been microfilmed by the Church of Latter Day Saints, Utah.

Valuation Office: House Books. Of the unpublished records prior to the published Griffith's Valuation these are probably the most important. Normally the houses listed are the main residences in the townland, i.e. valued

1	Slated house or office built with stone or brick and lime mortar
2	Thatched house or office built with brick and lime mortar
3	Thatched house or office with dry stone walls pointed.
4	Basement of 1
5	Thatched offices with dry stone walls
Classification with reference to Age and Repair New [or nearly new]	
A+	Built or ornamented with cut stones and of superior solidity and finish
A	Very substantial building, and finished without cut stone ornament
A-	Ordinary building and finish or ether of the above when built 20 years.
Medium	
B+	Not new, but in sound order and good repair
B	Slightly decayed but in good repair
B-	Deteriorated by age and not in perfect repair.
Old	
C+	Old but in repair
C	Old, out of repair
C-	Old, dilapidated, scarcely habitable

Figure 7. *Source: Index 'Valuation Office: House Books', NAI*

over about £5, but also included are some valuations made later especially for counties in the south-west of the country. Therefore for some districts it is possible to locate, in these records, people who emigrated at the end of the Great Famine or immediately afterwards.

Index on open shelf: It lists what is available for each county as in *Figure 5*

On the county page in the index are the reference numbers for the particular books available. These references range from OL 5.0001 to OL 5.4254 so about 4254 books. The microfilm numbers range from MFGS 46/1 to MFGS 46/157 or 157 microfilms.

The actual House Books. See Figure 6 for headings in the House Books. This format differs slightly in some books.

The number corresponded with the number on the Ordnance Survey Map used by the surveyor. Under 'Name and Description' was listed the name of the occupier and underneath the type of property occupied such as houses including outside sheds like 'cow house', 'piggery', 'stable' etc. Buildings like chapels were divided into 'long isle', 'right isle, 'left isle' and 'sacristy'.

The 'Quality Letter' refers to the type of building and was classified as in Figure 7

For each division of property listed e.g. the dwelling house, the cow house, the isle of the chapel etc. was listed in feet and inches the 'length', 'breadth' and 'height'

The calculations obtained, along with the 'measure' obtained from the Act, were used to determine the remaining columns (see History above).

The date it was prepared can be written in margins at the end of the civil parish or townland or, if copied, checked or recalculated the date can be noted in the margin.

8 Hume Street, Dublin where Richard John Griffith was born on 20th September 1784

Valuation Office: Boundary Survey 1826-1841. These records seem proper to the Ordnance Survey Collection but because the way the Valuation survey developed they are included in the Valuation Office Collection. The material includes sketch maps of parishes drawn by the Boundary surveyors at a scale of 1 inch to 40 Irish or plantation perches (1:10,080). There is considerable variation between sketches in the information and detail shown and in their physical condition. Other records include the Boundary Remark Books or field notebooks and the Boundary Registers which are office or fair copies of same. The records transferred to the NAI in 1946 were listed as part of the Valuation Office Archives while those transferred in 1996 were listed as part of the Ordnance Survey Archives. *(Source: Valuation Office: Boundary Survey 1826-1841, Index on open shelf, NAI).*

Index on open shelf: Under each barony name is listed in Irish and English, under the headings in Figure 8, the reference numbers for the records available.

These range from OL 3.0001 to OL 3.5571 so about 5571 books.

Valuation Office: Field, Tenure, Mill, Quarto and Miscellaneous Books.

(i) The Field Books.

Index on open shelf: Under the County page is listed the reference numbers under the following headings in Figure 9.

The reference numbers range from OL4.0001 to OL4.4607 or 4607 records.

The microfilm numbers range from MFGS 54/1 to MFGS 54/170 (i.e. 170 microfilms)

The actual Field Books describe the different

qualities of soils. Explanatory words used were, for example,
'strong' where the soil contained a considerable portion of clay;
'deep' where the soils exceeds ten inches in depth;
'cold' where the soil rests on a tenacious clay subsoil, and has a tendency when in pasture to produce rushes and other aquatic plants;

[Barony Name is given]					
Paroiste	Uimhir an Chláir	Log-uimhir	Uim. na Léarscailte	Data	Log-uimhir
Parish	Register Number	Destination of Register	Map No.	Date of map	Destination of Map

Figure 8

[County]			
Ref. No	Barony	Parish	Shelf No

Figure 9

'hungry' where the soil contains a considerable proportion of gravel or course sand etc.

(ii)The Tenure Books 1841-1851.

Index on open shelf: Under the County page is listed the reference numbers under the headings in Figure 10.

Books are only available for Counties Carlow, Cork, Dublin, Kerry, Kildare, Kilkenny, King's County [Offaly], Limerick, Mayo, Tipperary and Waterford.

The reference numbers listed range from LO6.0001 to OL6.0467 or 467 books.

The microfilm numbers range from MFGS 47/1 to MFGS 47/22 (i.e. 22 microfilms).

[COUNTY]			
Ref. No	Barony	Parish	Shelf No

Figure 10.

(iii) Preliminary List – The Mill Books.

The Books are numbered 1 to 23, the year and County included in each.

That is Mill Books:-

1 (Armagh), 2 (Cavan), 3 (Clare), 4 (Cork), 5 (Down), 6 (Galway), 7 (Kerry), 8 (Kilkenny), 9 (King's County [Offaly]), 10 (Leitrim) – all for year 1839;11 (Limerick), 12 (Limerick City), 13 (Longford), 14 (Louth), 15 (Mayo), 16 (Queen's [Laois]), 17 (Sligo), 18 (Tipperary) & 19 (Waterford) – all for year 1851 and 20 (Waterford - the Barony of Upperthird), 21 (Westmeath), 22 (Wexford) and 23 (Wicklow) – all for year 1848.

(iv) The Quarto Books.

Index on open shelf: Under each county is listed the town or city and reference number for relevant book ranging from OL 7.001-7.0090 or microfilms MFGS 48/1 to MFGS 48/6. Books are only available for towns or cities in Counties Antrim, Cavan, Donegal, Dublin, Kilkenny, Louth, Mayo, Meath, Offaly, Tipperary, Waterford and Wexford.

(v) Miscellaneous Books.

Index on open shelf: Under each county are listed the references numbers for records available. The heading for the counties varies depending on the type of manuscript record. The reference numbers range from OLX.001 to OLX.169 or 169 records.

The microfilms range from MFGS 61/1 to MFGS 61/8

(b) Valuation Office, Irish Life Centre, Abbey Street Lower, Dublin 1 [VO].

The VO has the printed versions of Griffith's Valuation, the original maps and scanned images of the maps, the books showing the revisions after Griffith's Valuation known as The Revision or

Cancelled Books and some pre Griffith's Valuation material similar to the House Books but including some information from the Field and Tenure Books and based on the barony.

The Revision or Cancelled Books. These volumes show changes made to Griffith's Valuation each year to the name of occupier, the immediate lessor, the property or to the valuation. The information is rewritten about every ten years sometimes in the same volume or in a new one depending on the size of the administrative area it applies to. The changes are usually made in different colours of ink and year of alterations are usually given. For all properties these records survive up until the late 1970s when the rates on domestic property were abolished.

The core business of the VO is still valuing property but limited research facilities are available. A member of staff will provide assistance. However it is advisable to know the townland or street name before searching in the VO.

(c) Public Record of Northern Ireland, 2 Botanic Boulevard, Titanic Quarter, Belfast BT3 9HQ [PRONI].

Similar material for the counties of Antrim, Armagh, Derry/Londonderry, Down, Fermanagh, Tyrone is available in PRONI. They are organised under The Townland Valuation (*VAL/1B*); Griffith's Valuation (*VAL/2B*) and accompanying maps (*VAL/2A*); Annual Revision Lists (*VAL/12/B*) and associated maps (*VAL/12D*) and town plans (*VAL/12E*); valuers' note books from 1894 (*VAL/12A*) and revaluation of Belfast 1900-6 (*VAL/7B*). Unlike the Republic of Ireland a general revaluation of all six counties took place in 1935 (*VAL/3*), 1956-7 (*VAL/4*), 1975 (*VAL/14*) and 1993. Leaflets in *Your Family Tree Series* 4 and 20 give further information.

Before searching any manuscript material it is advisable to locate the area first in the printed Griffith's Valuation.

John (Count) McCormack
(The Peerless Irish Tenor)
Brian Parnaby

John Francis McCormack was born of Scottish parents on the 14th June 1884, at The Bawn, in Athlone, Province of Leinster, Ireland (then a part of the United Kingdom), the fourth child of working-class Roman Catholic parents. There was little to suggest that John McCormack would grow up to be recognised as one of the premier tenors of his generation – with a voice by which all future Irish tenors would be judged!

John followed the usual route so many of his contemporaries did: emphasis on Church and School. He was fortunate to receive a sound education from the Marist Brothers (Boys only) in Athlone followed by attendance at Summerhill College in Sligo. In 1903, at the age of only nineteen, with a natural, yet untrained voice, John was entered into the prestigious Dublin Feis Ceoil and won the Irish singing prize for Solo tenor, being awarded the Association's Gold Medal. This success persuaded John where his future lay. An annual music festival in Athlone now commemorates McCormack's life and work as a world-renowned tenor.

It may seem rather peculiar that, around that time, John McCormack should form an association with a man who, subsequently was to become one of the most famous of Irish Authors – James Joyce, author of *'Ulysses'* amongst other works. However, this encounter, if not a meeting of minds, was a meeting of voices. Joyce himself had had singing lessons and the pair practised together on several occasions. Indeed McCormack persuaded Joyce to enter the Feis Ceoil that year and he won the Bronze medal (3rd place.) There is no truth in the rumour that McCormack had actually beaten Joyce the previous year when he himself had won the Gold medal. (Feis Ceoil is Irish for 'Festival of Music': an Irish Musical Society founded in 1897 for the purpose of stimulating musical studies in Ireland and encouraging native performers and composers.)

It is said that, when Mc Cormack was singing Handel, in English, he sang it *'as no American or Englishman will ever sing English; that is, English as it was spoken before all other countries in the world forgot how to speak it.'* This passage appeared in a book *'Serenade'* written in 1937 by the American Crime writer James McCain, as part of a dialogue on Mc Cormack.

John McCormack - New York 1910
The voice by which all Irish Tenors are judged.

John married Lily Foley, a local girl, in 1906; subsequently, there were two children of this union, Cyril and Gwen.

Following his success in Dublin, word of John's prowess as a tenor soon spread throughout the country and fund-raising enabled him to travel to Italy (the home of Tenors) in 1905, for training by Italy's foremost voice-coach Vincenzo Sabatini (Father of the novelist Rafael.) Sabatini quickly discovered that McCormack's voice was 'naturally tuned;' he therefore concentrated on the singer's voice control to the extent that this factor would become an integral part of the tenor's renown; this breath control training eventually resulted in McCormack's amazing ability to sing sixty-four notes on one breath as he later, and repeatedly, demonstrated; particularly in Mozart's *Il mio tesoro* from the Opera *Don Giovanni;* and also in various works by Handel.

In 1906 McCormack made his opera début at the Teatro Chiabrera in Savona, followed by a season at Covent Garden in 1906. There, in *Cavalleria Rusticana*, he became that theatre's youngest principal tenor at the age of just 22 - a remarkable accomplishment and a tribute to his prowess. Within three years McCormack had travelled to the United States of America, to commence what would become almost a life-long association with that country. John sang operatic arias in what was then known as the *'Italian'* style and also in French.

Spreading his operatic wings even further, in 1911, still only 27 years of age, he travelled to Australia, having been engaged by the world-famous Dame Nellie Melba, for the Melba (Melbourne) Grand Opera Season as its star tenor. McCormack had now become a fixture on the operatic world stage. The following year, increasing his repertoire into the world outside formal Opera venues, he embarked on a series of concert performances, though he did not relinquish his operatic career for a number of years, until 1923 when, by that time, his control over the top notes had begun to diminish. The number of concert performances McCormack had now embarked on cemented him into the affection of the general public. His general deportment and charisma, allied to a wonderful voice made him the most celebrated lyric tenor of his time and the public flocked to his performances. Some of the songs he sang - and recorded the on the new-fangled phonograph cylinder in 1904 – included the most popular songs of the day.

Following the outbreak of the Great War (1914-1918) McCormack was the first artist to record one of the most enduring songs of that War (and since) – *'It's a Long Way to Tipperary,'* in 1914; later (in 1917) he was to record Ivor Novello's touching tear-jerker *'Keep the Home Fires Burning'* which one still hears sung in movies about the Great War. With Irish nationalism on the march during the Great War and McCormack himself probably being a nationalist at heart, he also recorded patriotic Irish songs. One such was *'The Wearing of the Green'* - possibly a veiled incentive to fellow-Irishmen to press for Home Rule for the Irish as this song had its origin in the failed Irish rebellion of 1798. However, this was balanced by other popular Irish songs of the time which survive to the present day, examples being; *'The Minstrel Boy', 'The Last Rose of Summer', 'Believe me if all those endearing young charms'* – all perennial favourites. *'Kathleen Mavourneen'*(1927) and *'Mother Machree'* (also 1927), *'The Rose of Tralee'* (1930) and *'Macushla'* were particular

"For sheer pleasure, simple beauty, true emotion and all the things that make life worth living, there is nothing to beat a McCormack concert."—Ernest J. Hopkins, San Francisco Bulletin.

John McCormack

World-Renowned Irish Tenor

(Edwin Schneider, Accompanist)

American Concert Tour 1915-16

Management: Charles L. Wagner
(D. F. McSweeney, Associate Manager)
1451 Broadway, New York
Steinway Piano Used

CARNEGIE HALL

SUNDAY NIGHT, AT 8.15 APRIL 9th

TICKETS: $2.00, $1.50, $1.00, and 75c — Now at Box Office

By special request Mr. McCormack will sing: "The Snowy Breasted Pearl," "The Bitterness of Love" and the "Agnus Dei," the latter with piano, violin and organ accompaniment.

John McCormack Carnegie Hall 1916

Irish favourites. For a while McCormack fell out of favour with the British public because of his support for Irish nationalism, but this disappeared once his fund-raising concerts began to raise money in support of the War effort.

In 1917 John McCormack became a naturalised United States citizen and made a substantial donation to the United States' war effort when it eventually entered the war.

In the same year McCormack bought a home in County Kildare where he spent time as a country gentleman, also becoming a keen racehorse owner, with an unrealised ambition to win the Epsom Derby with his horse *Golden Lullaby*. He also had apartments in London and New York. Later, in 1930, he purchased an estate in Hollywood, having viewed it whilst filming a musical '*Song of my Heart*' He named his new American home *San Patrizio*, after Saint Patrick, the patron saint of Ireland. Whilst he was on tour the estate was often rented out to friends and acquaintances, many of whom were the film stars of the day.

In 1937, now 53 years' old, having completed a farewell tour of the country, he left America and returned home to Ireland, intending to return at some time. This never happened as the Second World War intervened in his plans. His final public performance was at the Royal Albert Hall, London in 1938 but, on the outbreak of the Second World War, he returned to the stage in performances in aid of the Red Cross and the general war effort; he toured. broadcast and recorded, many of his most popular songs being requested repeatedly as would be expected from such a well-loved artist.

Finally, and unhappily, in 1943 he was forced, through ill-health, to retire. Afflicted with emphysema, he retired to the Irish coast, purchasing a house by the sea.

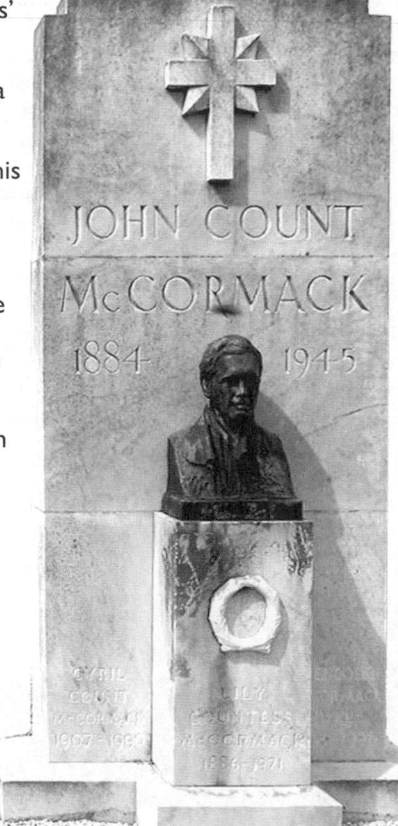

John McCormack's Grave
in Deansgrange Cemetery
Dún Laoghaire–Rathdown

Complications including pneumonia and influenza finally ended his life on the 16th September 1945, at only 61 years of age.

John McCormack will be remembered by all lovers of music as a man with an incomparable voice noted for its elegant phrasing, vocal quality and diction, and marvellous breath control. Allied to these qualities was his determination to sing only those songs which would project his utter conviction to his audience. Were he not convinced that he could do justice to a particular song then he would reject it; it must have conviction for the listeners or not be acceptable to him.

As a postscript to this article, attention must be drawn towards the honours he received from the Catholic Church during his lifetime.

From Pope Pius XI in 1928 he received the title of Papal Count (which became incorporated into his name: John Francis Count McCormack); all in recognition of his work for the Catholic Church. He had already received three Papal Knighthoods and was also created a Knight of Malta and a Privy Chamberlain of the Sword and Cape, now known as a Gentleman of His Holiness. Though these honours specifically apply to the Roman Catholic Church and are in the gift of the Pope, throughout the Christian world they are universally recognised as of great importance.

By 1920, his permanent accompanist had become Edwin Schneider and the two travelled and worked together for twenty-five years, forming an almost inseparable bond.

A peculiarity of his career was that he was never invited to sing at *La Scala*, Milan. The reason for this omission has never been divulged. Counted amongst one of the greatest acts of McCormack's career was his singing of *Panis Angelicus* in Phoenix Park, Dublin, at the 1932 Eucharistic Congress. McCormack actually confessed that a *'lack of acting abilities'* had persuaded him to give up Operatic work and concentrate on concert work; to the great benefit and pleasure of the general public.

A life-sized bronze statue of John Francis Count McCormack stands in the Iveagh Gardens, near the National Concert Hall, Dublin.

The Irish in Wales

Beryl Evans M.A.

Migration of the Irish to Wales has been taking place for centuries, but, it was during the urbanisation and industrialisation of South Wales during the first half of the nineteenth century that saw a growth in Irish settlements in and around Swansea, Cardiff, Newport and Merthyr Tydfil areas. Some also migrated to the developing industrial areas around Wrexham in North Wales. The copper works in the Swansea area depended greatly on the importation of copper ore from the counties Wicklow, Waterford, Cork and Kerry during this period; this was easily transported from Ireland to the South Wales ports, therefore creating a link between both countries. Potential markets in both countries were also realised for iron and coal during the this period, Welsh and Irish businessmen alike saw opportunities in both countries which saw the development of both industries and transportation in South Wales.

The main influx of Irish migrants came to Wales during the great potato famine of the 1840s. The failure of the potato crop, due to blight in successive years, meant that there was a lack of food for the peasants as this was a staple food that sustained the poor in Ireland. As a result, the Irish had few options available to them – starvation, death or mass emigration. About a million died and another million Irish fled the country, with many thousands arriving in ports along the South Wales coast after travelling in the holds of cargo ships from Ireland. The journey itself was horrifying taking sometimes weeks in bad weather conditions, some dying on route others arriving in an appalling state starving and diseased. The migrants were often met with hostility on their landing in the Welsh ports. Port officials did their best to discourage ship captains from bringing the migrants to Wales, so far so that in June 1848 Cardiff Board of Guardian officials issued a poster advertising a £10 reward leading to a conviction of such captains.

"The above Reward will be paid to any person or Persons who shall give such information to the undersigned, as will lead to the conviction of any Commander of a Vessel, who shall illegally Land any Irish passengers on the coast between Aberthaw and the River Rhumney".

Many saw South Wales as a better option due to its proximity to Southern Ireland and that it was a growing industrial area at the time with opportunities and a better life than was offered in Ireland.

The Irish were not always warmly welcomed by the Welsh with tensions running high in many areas of Wales where incomers were accused of working for lower wages than the Welsh, much research has been published on this topic, but there is no hard evidence to suggest that this was actually true. During the nineteenth century as many as twenty anti-Irish riots took place all over Wales from Holyhead to Cardiff, between 1826 and 1882.

Swansea at the turn of the nineteenth century was more populated than Cardiff and was a very important town in Glamorgan at the time, with a population of 6099 in 1801 compared to 1870 in Cardiff. The Greenhill area of Swansea was densely populated by the Irish even before the mass migration of the 1840s and is often referred to as *'Little Ireland'*. This was the result of the growing development of copper works to the North of the town. For more

The Colliery Treharris and General View Trelewis.

information relating to the Irish in this area see R T Price's book *Little Ireland: Aspect of the Irish and Greenhill, Swansea*.

Anti-Irish disturbances tended to be as a direct result of tensions in the workplace caused by grievances relating to loss of jobs for local people and undercutting wages. Other disturbances occurred due to pub brawls or circumstances surrounding a murder. However, both affected the relationship between the Welsh and Irish in and out of the home and workplace. The Irish tended to be given the heavy manual work, work not often wanted by the Welsh, whereas they would undertake the skilled and semi-skilled jobs. The Irish were not considered to be unskilled but more often than not were overlooked in favour of native locals.

The first unrest associated with such tensions occurred at Rhymni in 1826 after the Marquis of Bute brought Irish workers to the area specifically to build three blast furnaces. On the 1st of March that year hundreds of Welshmen tried to oust the Irishmen from their homes. Unrest occurred when William Forman an ironmaster struck a miner with a stick and as a result of the ensuing siege had to seek refuge in a nearby house with the miner until calm had returned to the streets. William Forman's opinion was that the Welsh miners were *'dissatisfied that any people but their own countrymen should be employed.'*

Some of the unrest experienced during the nineteenth century came about after incidents such as the murder of John Bowling, an Irishman by six Welshmen in August 1842 in Swansea. A detailed account of the horrific

Colliery Explosion 1879
Dinas Colliery
Rhondda Valley
Wales

attack with a knife and hatchet is described in the report of the Coroner's Inquest in the *Cambrian* newspaper 20th August 1842. The gang firstly attacked Timothy Leary in the street before entering his home; John Bowling was attacked after coming to the aid of Leary and was subsequently bludgeoned to death with the hatchet and stabbed with the knife. The prisoners were committed to Swansea House of Correction to await their trial at the Glamorganshire Spring Assizes in 1843; a report appears in the *Swansea Journal Supplement*, 1st March 1843. The verdict given by the Judge *'Taking all the circumstances of the case into consideration I cannot pass a less sentence upon you than the utmost which the law allows, therefore the sentence of the Court is, that each of you be transported beyond the seas for the terms of your natural lives.'*

In 1848 again a series of events caused tensions which saw the murder of two Welshmen in May 1848 in Swansea by a group of Irishmen which sparked more aggression within the area and another stabbing of a Welshman by an Irish man in November 1848 resulted in the first riot in Cardiff.

It must be remembered that not all the Irish migrants to Wales were poor and had arrived as the result of the famine. Many had decided to come to Wales because of better prospects in the developing industrial areas of South Wales. Many were skilled workers and people of prominence in the community and in public life such as Edward Dowling, the editor of the Newport newspaper *Monmouthshire Merlin* in the 1830s and 1840s. Other Irishmen became mayors – James Murphy in Newport in 1868

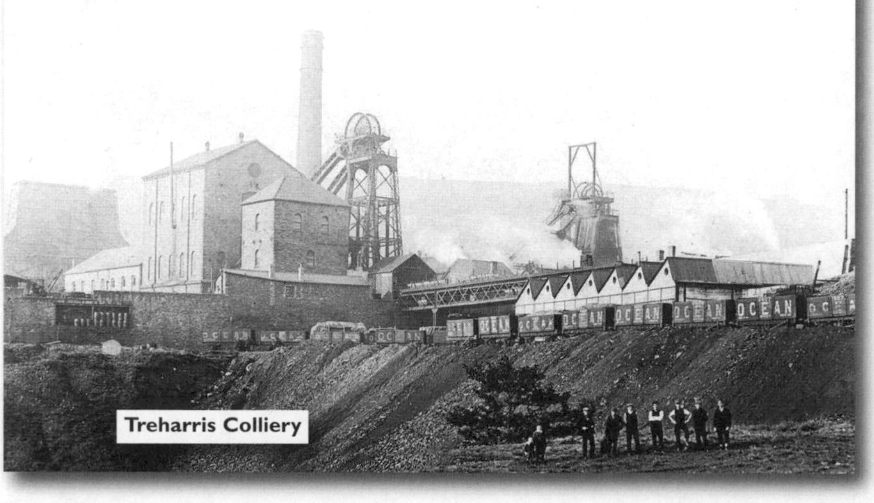

Treharris Colliery

and John Beirne in Wrexham 1877 are but two. Many Irishmen were also prominent in the trade unions in the ports of South Wales. Others became prosperous business people building commercial companies in South Wales and employing many local and Irish people.

For a more in-depth understanding of how the Irish integrated, lived and contributed to the history of Wales I recommend that some of the titles below are read, it is a fascinating topic that should be researched much further. There are numerous topics that I have not touched upon, such as the Catholic religion, Benefit Societies, Irish communities in various areas of Wales. For possible records relating to the Irish the Archives Wales website should be visited at www.archiveswales.org.uk/ also county record offices and also The National Library of Wales www.llgc.org.uk

One resource that will prove to be invaluable to those researching the Irish in Wales will be Historical Newspapers and Journals Project at The National Library of Wales. The project aims to digitise 2 million pages of out-of-copyright newspapers and periodicals – generally those published in Wales up to 1911. Many researchers who have written about the Irish in Wales have used newspapers as one of their main sources for information. Therefore, with the digitisation, these newspapers will be available worldwide with free access to discover countless nuggets of facts, forgotten incidents and interesting miscellany that would otherwise remain hidden within the covers of heavy and dusty volumes in Aberystwyth. It is envisaged that the release date at present will be January 2013.

Further Reading

Immigration and integration: the Irish in Wales, 1798-1922 by Paul O'Leary (University of Wales Press, Cardiff, 2000)
Irish Migrants in Modern Wales edited by Paul O'Leary (University Press, Liverpool, 2004)
My Struggle for Life by Joseph Keating (University College Dublin Press, 2005)
Little Ireland: Aspect of the Irish and Greenhill, Swansea by R T Price (Swansea City Council, 1992)

Beryl Evans is the Research Services Manager, The National Library of Wales, Aberystwyth

The National Archives of Ireland

Aideen M. Ireland

Head of Reader Services Division

The National Archives of Ireland was established by legislation on 1 June 1986 and was created out of the original State Paper Office (founded in 1702) and the Public Record Office of Ireland (founded in 1867). It is situated on the site of the original Jacob's Biscuit Factory in Bishop Street, Dublin 8.

The primary function of the National Archives is to collect, evaluate, preserve and make available the records for which it has responsibility.

The primary role of the National Archives is the preservation of departmental records and records transferred from other government agencies and making them available for public research under the terms of the National Archives Act, 1986 when they are thirty years old.

Apart from departmental records the National Archives holds testamentary and other court collections which are over twenty years old and business, charitable, estate, family, personal and trade union collections. The National Archives also holds some Church of Ireland parochial registers or abstracts or transcripts thereof.

Records of all Government departments which have existed since the foundation of the State (subject to legal restrictions) are now in the National Archives.

Reader's Tickets & Rules for Readers

The Reading Room may be used by any member of the public who holds a current Reader's Ticket. Members of the public may apply for a Reader's Ticket on the day of their first visit to the National Archives provided they have photographic identification. They must obey the Rules for Readers, which they must sign before a Reader's Ticket will be issued to them. Failure to observe the Rules for Readers may result in the cancellation of the individual's Reader's Ticket. An application for a Reader's Ticket may be downloaded in advance of visit - www.nationalarchives.ie/contactus/tickets.html - although the Reader's Ticket is only given on personal application.

Readers must have their Reader's Ticket with them at all times - both for entry to and exit from the building as well as for ordering documents or microforms. If a reader fails to bring along a Reader's Ticket, no records or microfilms will be issued for consultation.

Reading Room

The National Archives is open to the public for research. The Niall McCarthy Reading Room and Microfilm Room are fully equipped with finding aids to the various categories and forms of records held and staff at the public counters are available to give advice and assistance.

The Reading Room is open to the public from 10.00 a.m. to 5.00 p.m. Monday to Friday, excluding public holidays, the December media preview and a period over Christmas and the New Year. For further information on opening / closure dates please consult the National Archives website - www.nationalarchives.ie/contactus/closures.html

For information on ordering records and on record ordering times - www.nationalarchives.ie/contactus/opening.html

Readers should be aware that not all records are held on the Bishop Street

College Green, Dublin

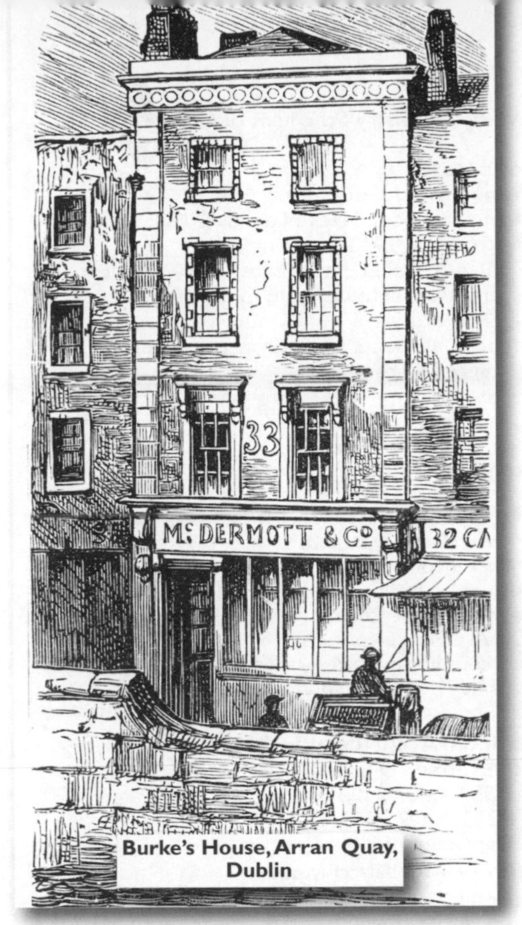

Burke's House, Arran Quay, Dublin

site. For those holding a valid Reader's Ticket records may be ordered in advance of a visit - www.nationalarchives.ie/contactus/records.html

Genealogy Service

A Genealogical Service, staffed by professional genealogists, is also available on the same floor as the Reading Room. It operates the same hours as the Reading Room. The Genealogy Service is intended primarily for first - time researchers and visitors but more experienced researchers are also welcome to use it. No appointment is needed.

Responsibility for Records

The National Archives Act is primarily concerned with Departmental records (the records of Government Departments, the Courts, and the other state bodies listed in the Schedule to the Act). The National Archives Act enables the National Archives to give advice to state sponsored bodies, local authorities and other public service organisations on records under their control, and to acquire records from them

The National Archives also has overall statutory responsibility for Church of Ireland parish registers of marriages which pre - date 1 April 1845 and baptisms and burials which pre - date 1 January 1871 since they were declared to be public records by Acts of 1875 and 1876. Until recently almost all the surviving registers were still held by the parish clergy, although most of them have now been transferred to the Representative Church Body Library, Churchtown, Dublin 14 - http://ireland.anglican.org/index.php?do=about&id=42

The National Archives Act also permits the National Archives to acquire records from private sources.

Major Collections

Almost all of the records accessioned by the Public Record Office of Ireland before 1922 were destroyed by fire and explosion during the Civil War in June 1922. Included were some collections transferred from the State Paper Office, although most of these survived intact. All collections which are open to public research are held in the National Archives in Bishop Street or are available, on request, from off - site storage.

Records of Government and State Agencies:

Board of Health / Cholera, 1832 - 4
Board of Trade, 1840s - 1930s
Commissioners of National Education, 1831 - 1963
Commissioners of Intermediate Education, 1879 - 1918
Commissioners of Charitable Donations & Bequests, 1801 - 1961
Crime Branch Special, 1887 - 1920
Famine Relief Commission, 1845 - 7
Fenian Papers, 1857 - 83
Irish Crime Records, 1848 - 93
Irish Record Commission, 1810 - 30
National Archives (formerly P.R.O.I. & S.P.O.) 1867 -
Office of Public Works, 1831 - , and its precursors, Directors General of
Inland Navigation, (1730 -), 1800 - 31
Civil Buildings Commissioners, 1802 - 31
Ordnance Survey (part of), 1824 -
Penal Transportation, 1788 - 1868
Poor Law Commission
& Local Government Board, 1822 - 1922
Prison administration records, including the
- Government Prisons Office, 1836 - 80
- General Prisons Board, 1877 - 1928
- Prison registers, 19th - 20th centuries

Proclamations, 17th - 19th centuries
Quit Rent Office, 17th century - 1942
Registrar General of Shipping and Seamen and Mercantile Marine Office, 1863 -
Royal Hospital Kilmainham, 1684 - 1933
Shipping agreements and crew lists, 1863 - 1979
Tithe Applotment Books, 1828 - 37
Valuation Office, and Boundary Survey, 1827 - 1925

Chief Secretary's Office, 1790 - 1924; and its constituent departments / records including :
- Chief Crown Solicitor's Department, (1815 -), 1859 - 90
- Convict Department, 1778 - 1922
- Official Papers, 1790 - 1880
- Privy Council Office, 1800 - 1922
- Rebellion Papers, 1790 - 1807
- State of the Country Papers, 1790 - 1831

Official and non Official Sources

Census of Ireland, 1821 - 1911:

Enumerator's Returns / Heads of Household returns, 1901, 1911 are complete, survive for the whole country and are available on - line - www.census.nationalarchives.ie/

Partial survivals, 1821 - 51, which are incomplete or in transcript or abstract form, survive for:

Antrim 1851: Cavan 1821, 1841: Cork 1841: Fermanagh 1821, 1841, 1851: Galway 1821: King's County (Offaly) 1821: Londonderry (Derry) 1831 (supplemented 1834): Meath 1821: Waterford 1841

There are no census returns for the period 1861 - 91.

Church of Ireland Registers of baptisms, marriages and burials including:

- Original registers of some parishes; microfilms of surviving registers of some diocese, as well as abstracts and transcripts from other parishes.
- There are also thirteen volumes searches in parish registers against baptisms undertaken in the early part of the twentieth century as evidence of age.
- Some genealogical researchers, in the early decades of the twentieth century, have made specific surname searches in parochial registers.
- Parochial registers (including those for the Church of Ireland) are becoming available on-line at www.irishgenealogy.ie/.

Court Records

- Probate Office of the High Court (formerly the Principal Probate Registry) and the District Probate Registries, mostly 20th century.
- Incumbered / Encumbered Estates Court, Landed Estates Court, and Chancery and Land Judges, mostly 1850 - 20th century, Many of the Landed Estates Court Rentals now available at www.findmypast.ie/content/landed-estate-court-records

Diocesan Court Records / indexes

Records of the former Prerogative and Diocesan Registries, 16th century - 1858 :
Administration Bonds, 1612 - 1858
Administration grants, 1595 - 1804
Marriage licence bonds, 1623 - 1867
Wills, 1536 - 1858

Genealogical Abstracts

Abstracts compiled by Betham, 16th - 19th centuries
Genealogies etc. compiled mostly by Crosslé, Tennison Groves, Groves - White, Jennings, Thrift, 17th - 19th centuries
Parish registers, 17th - 19th centuries
Baptism, marriage, burial abstracts, 17th - 19th century
Wills and grants of probate, 16th - 19th century

Testamentary Records / calendars

Grants of administration, 1858 -
Grants of probate, 1858 -
Principal Registry Schedules of Assets, (1873 - 90, with gaps) 1924 -
Wills, 1858 -

Transcripts / Calendars

Abstracts and indexes of archives which were destroyed in 1922, including:

- Calendars of court records, 13th - 19th centuries
- Fergusson, extracts from Exchequer records, 13th - 18th centuries
- Lodge, abstracts from Chancery patent rolls, mainly 17th century

Also:

Commissioners of Charitable Donations and Bequests, 1800 - 1961
Irish will registers and indexes, 1828 - 79
Irish administration registers and indexes, 1828 - 79
Marriage licences, 1629 - 1818
Marriage settlements, 18th -
Miscellaneous copies, transcripts and abstracts
Also older finding aids, 16th - 20th centuries
Searches in Census returns, 1841 & 1851 - largely for Old Age Pension purposes
Searches in parochial registers, 19th century - largely for Old Age Pension purposes

National Archives of Ireland
Bishop Street, Dublin 8
T: + 353 1 407 2300
F: + 353 1 407 2333
E: mail@nationalarchives.ie
W: www.nationalarchives.ie
All enquiries should be addressed to The Director

Opening Hours:
Monday to Friday 10.00 - 5.00

Facilities
Photocopying, photography:
Instant photocopying (small orders):
Self service microfilms: Genealogy Service

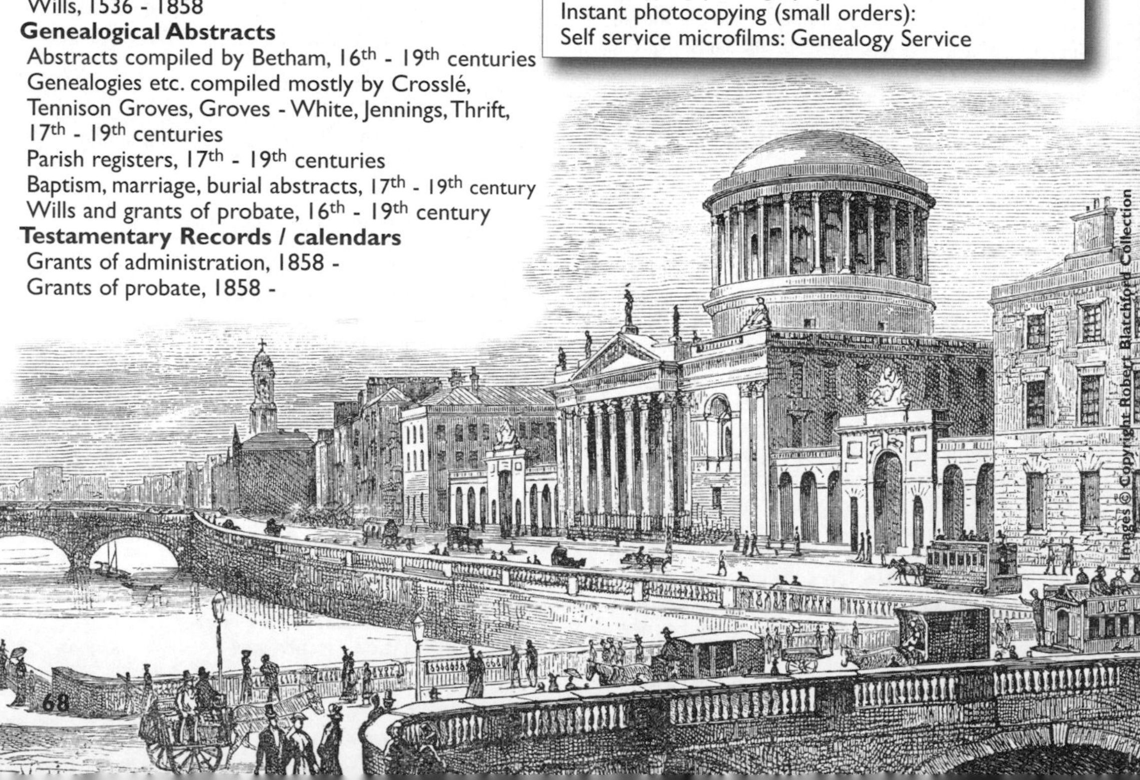

The National Museum of Ireland
www.museum.ie

The Museum of Science and Art, Dublin was founded on 14th August 1877 after requests by the Royal Dublin Society for government funding for its expanding museum activities. The Science and Art Museums Act of 1877 transferred the buildings and collections of the Royal Dublin Society into state ownership. Other notable collections from the Royal Irish Academy and Trinity College Dublin were also incorporated. The Museum became the responsibility of the Department of Science and Art who were responsible for the South Kensington museums in London.

A purpose built new building on Kildare Street was opened to the public in 1890. The museum brought together significant Irish antiquities from the Royal Irish Academy including the Tara brooch and Ardagh chalice. Ethnographical collections and material from Captain Cooke's voyages were transferred from Trinity College Dublin together with material from the Geological Survey of Ireland. The old Royal Dublin Society museum on the Merrion Street side of Leinster House, which had opened in 1856, was devoted to natural history, zoology and had an geology annexe.

The building on Kildare Street was designed by Thomas Newenham Deane and was used to show contemporary Irish, British and Continental craftsmanship in its construction. Considerable benefit came from steady funding and a liaison with the state museums in London and Edinburgh. The collections grew over the years through purchase, donations and bequests. In 1900 control passed to the Department of Agriculture and Technical Instruction and in 1908 becoming the *'National Museum of Science and Art.'* However in 1921 the museum's name was changed to the *'National Museum of Ireland.'*

After the foundation of the Free State in 1922, the old Royal Dublin Society buildings of Leinster House were chosen to house the new parliament (Dáil). The Natural History building was given a new entrance directly onto Merrion Street and the architecture was altered to allow the present opening at the east end and the development of new staircases. Responsibility for the Museum went to the Department of Education in 1924 then to the Taoiseach's Department in 1984. In 1993 responsibility passed to several governement departments before becoming an autonomous state agency with its own Board in 2005.

Throughout the latter half of the 20th Century there was a great deal of pressure on available exhibition, storage and staff space for the Museum. In 1988 the Government decided to close Collins Barracks, Dublin. Established in 1702 *'The Barracks,'* changed its name in the early 19th Century to the *'Royal Barracks,'* and when the Free State was established in 1922 was re-named *Collins Barracks*. The original buildings were designed by Colonel Thomas Burgh and the complex, which includes 18th and 19th Century buildings, housed troops for three centuries. It was assigned to Museum use in 1994 and opened in 1997 with the first exhibitions, and development continues on the site. In September 2001 the Museum's Country Life branch was opened at Turlough Park, County Mayo. Turlough Park House (a Venetian Gothic building designed

Bank of Ireland, Dublin

by Thomas Newenham Deane) and its gardens house the Museum's National Folklife collections; these are devoted to traditional crafts and everyday life in rural Ireland in the century or so since the Great Famine.

The Collections

The Royal Dublin Society, founded in 1731, collected plaster casts, geological minerals, fine art and ethnographical material, in order to train artists and encourage industry. *The Royal Irish Academy*, founded in 1785, sought to advance the study of Irish antiquities, science and literature. *The Museum of Irish Industry*, established in 1847, sourced its material largely in the Great Exhibition of 1851 and the Dublin Exhibition of 1853.

The Science and Art Museum, established in 1877, brought all three collections together and expanded them through loans, purchases and donations, with the aim of developing the institution into *'a source of recreation and instruction.'* In 1900 it became the *National Museum of Science and Art*, placing much emphasis on the development of rural craft and contemporary design. The aim was that the Museum and its collections should be *'of commercial value to the country as well as of historical and scientific interest.'*

With the foundation of the Irish Free State, the institution was transferred to the Department of Education and became the National Museum of Ireland. Its concentration was now on collecting and exhibiting material of Irish interest and its stated aim was *'to increase and diffuse the knowledge of Irish civilisation, the natural history of Ireland and the relations of Ireland in these respects with other countries.'* The collections on view here reflect the various stages of the Museum's development, the political changes that altered its status, and the shaping of its collecting policy over the years.

The National Museum of Ireland has three locations in Dublin and one in County Mayo. Admission is free to all four museums.

Archaeology, Kildare Street, Dublin 2
The National Museum of Ireland - Archaeology is centrally located on Kildare Street, Dublin 2, next door to Leinster House (Government Buildings).

Decorative Arts & History, Collins Barracks, Dublin 7

Natural History, Merrion Street, Dublin 2
The National Museum of Ireland - Natural History is centrally located on Merrion Street, Dublin 2, next door to the National Gallery.

Country Life, Turlough Park, Castlebar, Co. Mayo
The National Museum of Ireland – Country Life has modern exhibition galleries in the spectacular grounds of Turlough Park House with its magnificent gardens and lake.

Opening Times: (All four museums)
Tuesday to Saturday 10.00.a.m – 5.00.p.m.; Sunday 2.00.p.m. – 5.00.p.m. Closed Mondays (including Bank Holidays), Christmas Day and Good Friday

Dublin City Archives

The City of Dublin has been governed by its own elected representatives since the 12th century. *The Dublin City Assembly* which flourished during the Middle Ages and survived until 1840, met at the great feasts of Christmas, Easter, Midsummer and Michaelmas for the transaction of business, but extra meetings could be held if necessary. The Mayor presided at meetings of the Assembly, whose members consisted of two sheriffs, 24 aldermen, 48 sheriffs' peers and 96 representatives of the Dublin trade guilds. The municipal franchise was not democratic in the modern sense, as it was largely confined to members of the trade guilds and to their descendants.

Dublin City Archives hold the historic records of the municipal government of Dublin from the 12th century to the present. The City Archives contain a significant number of medieval documents, including two important bound manuscripts written on vellum: the *White Book of Dublin*, also known as the *'Liber Albus,'* and the *Chain Book of Dublin*. This book contains transcripts of documents in abbreviated Latin, French and old English relating to the administration of Dublin illustrating civic

transactions with lands, buildings, mills and water-supplies. It contains one hundred and eleven leaves written on vellum. The Archives also hold a series of Assembly Rolls, written on parchment, which record the minutes of the Dublin City Assembly (a forerunner of today's City Council) from 1447 to 1841. *The Assembly Rolls*, together with the *White Book* and *Chain Book*, were transcribed and translated by Sir John T and Lady Gilbert and published as Calendar of Ancient Records of Dublin (19 volumes, Dublin, 1889-1944).

Dublin City Charters 1171 - 1727

The magnificent series of 102 Charters granted to the city by successive English monarchs. The earliest charter was issued by Henry II in 1171-1172, giving the men of Bristol the right to live in the City of Dublin. Later charters contain grants to the city of rights, privileges and property, and taken together they form the basis of municipal law in Ireland.

In addition to these published materials, the Dublin City Archives contain a wealth of records which have not been published and are available for research. These records include City Council and committee minutes, account books, correspondence, reports, court records, charity petitions, title deeds, maps and plans, photographs and drawings, all of which document the development of Dublin over eight centuries. The Archives hold the magnificent series of 102 charters granted to the city by successive English monarchs. The earliest was issued by King Henry II in 1171 giving the men of Bristol the right to live in the city of Dublin. Later charters contain grants to Dublin of rights, privileges and property, and taken together they form the basis of municipal law in Ireland.

Guild Records 1192 - 1841

Guilds were mutual benefit associations which flourished in western Europe from the 11th century. The Guild system in Dublin was licensed under a charter by Prince John in 1192 and dominated the commercial and political life of the city. There were four types of Guilds: Guild Merchant or Merchant Guild, Craft Guilds or Trade Guilds, Religious Guilds and Military Guilds. Guild membership could be acquired by three means:

Service – by completion of an apprenticeship with a guild member

Birth – obtained by sons of guild members

Freedom – honorary membership to be conferred on dignitaries

Freedom Records 1225 - 1922

The ancient Freedom of Dublin was instituted at the time of the Norman Invasion. The inhabitants of Dublin in the middle ages were either free or non-free. Holders of the freedom of the city were known as *'Free Citizens'* and were entitled to special trading privileges and the right to vote in parliamentary and municipal elections. In order to qualify for the freedom it was usually necessary to have been born within the city boundaries or *'franchises'* and to be a member of one of the trade guilds of Dublin. Members of 'the Irish nation' were excluded, but in practice many people with Irish surnames succeeded in obtaining the freedom. Under the Penal Laws, Roman Catholics were excluded from the Freedom of Dublin from 1691 until 1793. Under the Representation of the Peoples Act, 1918, the ancient Freedom of Dublin was abolished to make way for a more democratic franchise. Nowadays all inhabitants of the city of Dublin who have reached the age of 18 are entitled to vote in municipal elections. It is possible to trace several generations of old Dublin families through these lists which form a useful source of genealogical research.

There were six main categories of admission:

1. Admission by Service was granted to those who completed an apprenticeship in one of the Trade Guilds of Dublin.
2. Admission by Birth was granted to sons, and sometimes daughters, of Free Citizens. Several generations of one family could hold the Freedom of Dublin.
3. Admission by Marriage was granted to sons-in-law of Free Citizens.
4. Admission by Fine was confined to prosperous professional men who were required to pay a substantial sum of money into the city treasury. Sometimes the Fine consisted of the presentation of a pair of gloves to the Lady Mayoress.
5. Admission by Grace Especial also known as

Entrance to St Stephen's Green, Dublin

Special Grace was the equivalent of the modern Honorary Freedom, and was reserved for dignitaries and for craftsmen who were not in a trade guild.

6. Admission by an Act of Parliament to '*Encourage Protestant Strangers to Settle in Ireland*' was granted to French Huguenots and Quakers from England.

Lists of those admitted to the ancient Freedom of Dublin survive for the period 1225-1250, 1468-1512 and 1575-1918. These lists may be consulted at Dublin Corporation Archives, City Hall, Dublin 2. A computerised index to the lists is being prepared by the Dublin Heritage Group. The lists are of interest to students of social and economic history and are also important for genealogical research.

Honorary Freedom of the City of Dublin

The Honorary Freedom of Dublin was instituted under the Municipal Privileges Act, 1876 and is presently conferred under the provisions of the Local Government Act 1991. The founder of the Home Rule Party, Isaac Butt, was the first person to receive the Honorary Freedom of Dublin. Other illustrious recipients include Charles Stewart Parnell, George Bernard Shaw, John Count McCormack and John Fitzgerald Kennedy, President of the United States of America. In recent years, it has been conferred on Pope John Paul II; Mother Teresa of Calcutta; the world champion cyclist Stephen Roche; and the former President of Ireland, Dr. Patrick Hillery. Nelson Mandela received the Freedom in 1988, whilst still a political prisoner. It has also been conferred on Jack Charlton, manager of the Republic of Ireland football team; & Bill Clinton, President U.S.A.

Dublin City Surveyors – Book of Maps 1695 - 1827

Dublin City Assembly acted as one of a number of landlords with estates in the city following a policy of leasing its lands to improving tenants. The City Estate was leased to Dublin's merchant class who built houses, stables, warehouses and outbuildings on their holdings.

The post of the City Surveyor was established in the late 17th century when there was no overall planning authority for the city. The role of the City Surveyor was to record rather than to plan such development. His involvement in planning was confined to dividing ground in lots for setting. The collection is an example of urban cartography and documents the development of the ancient Dublin City Estate within the original walled city.

Wide Streets Commission

The Wide Streets Commission was established in 1757 to develop wide and convenient streets through the city of Dublin. Among its other achievements, the Commission built Parliament Street, Westmoreland Street and D'Olier St. as well as Carlisle Bridge (now O'Connell Bridge). The minute books, maps, title deeds and architectural drawings produced for the Commission before it was abolished in 1849 are all held in the Dublin City Archives. These important records tell the story of the layout and development of much of Georgian Dublin.

Dublin Mansion House Relief Fund 1880

Ireland was beset by harvest failure during the 1870's and in 1880 famine threatened the country. To prevent this, the Mansion House Fund was set up to collect money from Irish emigrants all over the world. The records of the Fund are held in the Dublin City Archives and are important for local history because they contain reports from 800 local committees who distributed relief in every county in Ireland. Records of other relief committees are also available for inspection.

Edmund Dwyer Gray, Lord Mayor of Dublin, set up the Dublin Mansion House Relief Fund on 2nd January 1880. Administered by a voluntary central committee moneys were raised in Europe, North America, India and Australia. It was an all-Ireland relief fund with over 800 local committees set up in the thirty-two counties, of which membership of clergy of all denominations and poor-law medical officers was a pre-requisite. The central committee provided funds to voluntary committees who distributed in kind, supplying Indian Meal, turf and clothes to the most needy. The '*Little Famine*' lasted a comparatively short time, autumn 1880 yielded a good harvest and the Mansion House Fund was no longer required for the relief of distress. It was wound up in December of that year.

Records of Urban District Councils

The areas of Rathmines and Rathgar and of Pembroke each had their own local government until 1930, and their records are preserved in the Dublin City Archives, describing the development of these suburbs from the mid 19th century. The records of the Howth Urban District Council are also available, from 1318 to 1940.

The Reading Room is open to all readers holding a current Research Card available on application to Dublin City Public Libraries. The City Archives are for reference and research and may not be borrowed; access to the storage area is not permitted. An advance appointment is essential. Some records, because of their antiquity or fragile condition, may be withdrawn for conservation treatment and may not always be available. The Archivist will be pleased to answer any queries relating to the records. Photocopying, photography and microfilm services are provided as appropriate. The Archivist can advise on costs and conditions of copyright.

Reading Room First Floor, 138 - 144 Pearse Street, Dublin 2 Tel: +353 1 674 4999 Fax: +353 1 674 4881E: dublinstudies@dublincity.ie E: cityarchives@dublincity.ie

Opening Hours:

The Reading Room is open from 10am to 8pm Monday to Thursday and from 10am to 5pm on Friday and Saturday. We do not close for lunch.

Dublin City Library and Archive is closed on the Saturdays and Mondays of Bank Holiday Weekends.

The Genealogy Advisory Service

at National Archives of Ireland & National Library of Ireland

Eneclann Ltd - Ancestor Network Ltd Consortium

From June 2012 the National Library of Ireland (NLI) and National Archives of Ireland (NAI) has offered a new *free* genealogy advisory service to visitors. However those people who cannot visit Dublin queries by email sent to the National Library of Ireland, and marked 'genealogy' will also be answered by the service.

A consortium of genealogists from Eneclann Ltd and Ancestor Network Ltd are providing this new genealogy service. These professional genealogists, including some of Ireland's best known family history experts, are now 'on call' weekdays in the Library and Archives, and on Saturday mornings in the Library. Whether just beginning family history research, or are an experienced researcher, the genealogists from the consortium are there to answer questions on family history and to act as research guides.

The Eneclann-Ancestor Network consortium has more than doubled the number of genealogy experts delivering the genealogy advice service, from what was previously available. In increasing the numbers of genealogists, the consortium also looked to extend the range of specialist knowledge available to anyone tracing their family history.

'The real strength of the consortium is it's a platform for some of the best Irish genealogists to collaborate, so that each person can work to their skills. We can draw on specialist language and palaeography skills if required, but more importantly we can draw on the depth of knowledge and experience of our team members,' says Fiona Fitzsimons of Eneclann. *'The genealogy advisory service in the Library is also supported by the Assistant Librarians Mr. Fran O'Carroll and Ms. Christina O'Donnell. They're great people to work alongside, and everyone has a real sense of purpose – to deliver the best service we possibly can.'*

The Director of the National Library, Fiona Ross, has also welcomed the consortiums' new collaborative approach, particularly in these straitened times: *'We are delighted that Eneclann and Ancestor Network have been awarded the contract for providing the genealogy advisory service,' 'They offer an enhanced family history service at a significantly reduced cost to the tax payer.'*

The reception of Irish and overseas visitors to the genealogy advisory service in the Library and Archives, has been very positive. Visitors have been impressed with the calibre of professional advice they are receiving from the genealogists working on the panel.

One other exciting aspect about the new genealogy service is that the consortium partners, Eneclann and Ancestor Network, have also provided a programme of free lunchtime genealogy talks in the National Library of Ireland. The range of speakers included genealogists, librarians, archivists, writers, broadcasters,

Advice for visitors from Tom Coughlan

academics and a geneticist! The range of topics will range from introductory talks on beginning Irish family history research to online research, Irish surnames and heraldry, Gaelic genealogies, connecting to the Irish Diaspora, genetic genealogy, and a focus on major collections of documents, as well as many other intriguing topics.

'The variety of speakers lined up proves what a 'broad church' genealogy is, but also that people from these diverse groups and organisations are capable of coming together to support the NLI.' said Aiden Feerick of Ancestor Network.

Reviews of the Genealogy Advisory Service include:

'Greeting with a smile, helpful people; excellent service'
'Thanks very much for your help – was invaluable.'
'Excellent direction and advice; thank you.'
'Thank you very much for all your help. You are doing a great job!'
'Your advisor was fantastic! So knowledgeable and very helpful. Looking forward to coming back to Ireland!'

John Hamrock of Ancestor Network says *'We take great pleasure in assisting Irish people and overseas visitors alike in tracing their roots. We're promoting Irish genealogy from within the national cultural institutions, and the response has been overwhelmingly positive.'*

Genealogy Advisory Service National Archives of Ireland

www.nationalarchives.ie: Monday to Friday, 10.a.m to 1.30.p.m The National Archives is located in Bishop Street, Dublin 8, close to the city centre and within ten minutes' walk of the St Stephen's Green Luas line.

Genealogy Advisory Service
National Library of Ireland (www.nli.ie):
Monday to Friday, 9.30am to 1pm, 2-5pm, Saturday 9.15am to 12.45pm The National Library of Ireland is located on Kildare Street in the centre of Dublin.

Eneclann Limited
Eneclann Ltd. is a Trinity College Campus company, incorporated in 1998. Since then it has become the largest historical and genealogical research and consultancy service in Ireland, with tens of thousands of clients worldwide.

The company is probably best known internationally for its research for the hit T.V. series *WDYTYA*, as well as the successful T.V. series *Faces of America* (2010), and *Finding Your Roots* (2012) presented by Prof. Henry Louis Gates. Eneclann has traced the Irish roots of President Barack Obama, Meryl Streep, Jeremy Irons, Harry Connick Jr., Steve Colbert, and Graham Norton.

Since 1998 Eneclann has also developed significant skills in archival management, and expertise in digital technology. The company was instrumental in the founding of the online service www.irishorigins.com in 2003, and more recently launched the web service www.findmypast.ie with their Scottish partner Brightsolid. To date the company has brought over 12 million new genealogical records online, and has acted as a trusted partner of several archives, libraries and other public institutions in making their historic records available to a wide audience.

Eneclann's clients include the National Museum of Ireland, the National Library of Ireland, the National Archives of Ireland, Trinity College Library, the Military Archives, the OPW, the National College of Art & Design, the GAA archives, Dublin City Library & Archives, Cork City & County Archives, Clare County Archives, and the RDS.

About Ancestor Network Ltd
Ancestor Network Limited was established in May 2009 to help promote knowledge and learning of genealogy (family history) and heraldry in Ireland. Ancestor Network is a professional genealogy organisation that helps people search for their Irish ancestry and discover their family history and surname origin. The company is focused on Irish Family History or Genealogical Services including; professional research and advice, teaching, tours, DNA testing, and book sales. Ancestor Network also advises on DNA tests for genealogy, heraldry, and adoption searches. The company websites are www.ancestor.ie and www.24-7genealogist.com.

For further information about Genealogy Advisory Service please contact:
Fiona Fitzsimons, Research Director, Eneclann Ltd. T: +353 (01) 671 0338 E: info@eneclann.ie
or
John Hamrock, Managing Director, Ancestor Network Ltd. T: +353 (0) 87 0505296 E: info@ancestor.ie

Mary Beglan helps a visitor

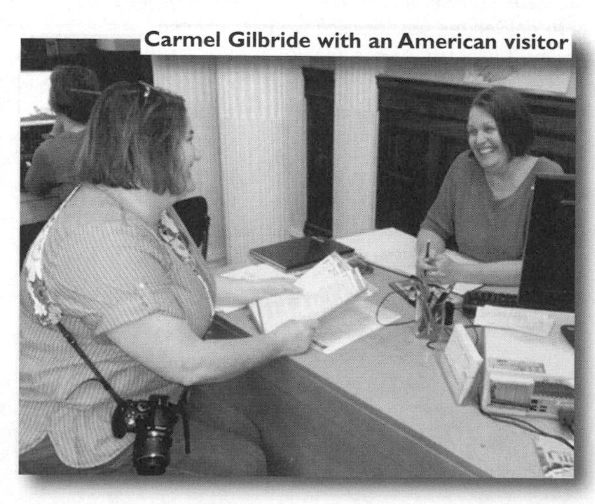
Carmel Gilbride with an American visitor

The Irish in London

Emma Jolly

From the Middle Ages, there has been an Irish presence in London. Like many early immigrants, Irish people of all social classes came to London for work. Agricultural labourers made regular seasonal visits and aristocrats retained houses. Whilst there is evidence of Irish merchants, bankers and lawyers in the English capital, the largest influx of immigration from Ireland took place in the 1840s, in the wake of the notorious famine. However, it was from the 18th century that a notable Irish community emerged. Descendants of those who settled in the city became known as *'London Irish,'* a term still used today.

Before 1800, the Irish can be traced using general London genealogy search aids, such as parish registers, land records, and documents from the parish chest. Other useful sources for this period include contemporary newspapers, published histories or genealogies, and online material. An excellent website for tracing ancestors in late Stuart/ early Georgian London, London Lives 1690-1800 www.londonlives.org/ enables a search of 240,000 manuscripts from eight archives and fifteen datasets. The Irish are found here amongst City parish records, criminal sessions (including the Old Bailey), and the records of coroners and St Thomas's Hospital. Other Irish in the city before 1800 may be discovered in the Society of Genealogists' Inhabitants of London index, compiled by Percival Boyd www.sog.org.uk

London's parish material is spread amongst a number of archives. The city's main repository, and the largest local authority archive in Britain, is London Metropolitan Archives (LMA). LMA holds microfilmed copies of most of London's parish registers. Where LMA retains the original register, the baptism, marriage and burial entries have been digitised on www.ancestry.co.uk A full list of what has been digitised can be found via the LMA website: http://c.mfcreative.com/offer/UK/Search/MoreHelp/LMA-AtoZ-of-London-Parishes.pdf

Irish residents of Westminster, from the aristocrats of Belgravia to the slum-dwellers of Great Peter Street, are found in records held at Westminster City Archives www.westminster.gov.uk/services/libraries/archives/ The parish registers have been uploaded to www.findmypast.co.uk (FindMyPast) and further records are to be added shortly. The most useful of these for researching Irish ancestors are cemetery registers, rate books, settlement examination books, removal registers, poor relief lists, workhouse books, and militia records.

London's historical court records, and those of institutions, like schools, hospitals, and asylums, are also held at LMA. A number of these records, but certainly not all, can also be found on Ancestry. Individual names, indexed from a small percentage of the archives, may be found via LMA's online catalogue: http://search.lma.gov.uk/opac_lma/index.htm The catalogue can also be used to order documents in advance of a visit.

From the creation of the United Kingdom of Great Britain and Ireland in 1801 to 1921, when Ireland was granted independence, the Irish were officially British citizens. This did not prevent them being treated as a distinct group in the increasingly cosmopolitan world of Georgian London. London was expanding quickly in this period, and offered many opportunities for those wishing to flee the pressures of greedy landlords in Ireland. Some Irish men became known for their boxing prowess, but there were also negative portrayals in the press of the Irish as brawlers and drinkers. Many Irish poor settled in the parish of St Giles in the Fields, often working as hawkers or beggars. The Rookery or 'Little Ireland', a notorious slum area of the parish, has been immortalized in the satirical imagery of William Hogarth (1697-1764). Records of St Giles can be found at LMA or Camden Local Studies & Archives, and a small number have been digitised on Ancestry. Original parish records are retained by the church www.stgilesonline.org/heritage-resources/genealogy.php

Ancestors who were unable to find work in this period may have spent time in the local workhouses. Detailed information on workhouses, such as that of St Giles in the Fields and St George Bloomsbury, can be found at www.workhouses.org.uk/ Many workhouse registers are held at LMA, and some have been digitised on Ancestry.

For those researching back from 1850, the Irish Genealogical Research Society www.igrsoc.org/index.htm is particularly useful. Based in London at the Church of St. Magnus the Martyr, Lower Thames Street EC3 6DN, the Society holds the largest private library of Irish genealogical material in London, and is particularly useful. Amongst records held are the Hussey-Walsh Manuscripts, genealogical annotations to the covert rolls, the Nugent

Collection, and the Betham Index of pedigrees. The Society offers a Members only service for those who cannot access the library.

Civil registration began in England in 1837. Addresses on birth certificates of children born from this date can be used to trace families, particularly those who moved regularly to evade the rent collector. Used in conjunction with ratebooks (held at local borough archives), later electoral registers and contemporary maps, civil certificates can assist in plotting where a family lived – a sometimes give a clue as to how. Early marriage certificates are useful in providing father's names and occupations for family back in Ireland. When used with birthplaces given on censuses, these may provide the essential link back home.

Birth, marriage and death certificates can be used in conjunction with censuses to narrow down the date of immigration. London parish registers can also help with this, and many have been digitised on Ancestry. Not all Irish will appear in Anglican parish registers, however. Although Catholics were legally required to marry in a church of England church between 1754 and 1837, many married illegally. A large proportion of the Irish in London were Roman Catholic and the Church was keen to retain their loyalty in the face of discrimination in the 19th century and secularism in the 20th. During this time, the Irish comprised the majority of London's Catholic population. Local priests still retain many of the registers, but some may be found in the transcriptions and indexes of the Catholic Record Society. Some of these can be found at the library of the Society of Genealogists. From 1850, London's Catholic churches came under the jurisdiction of the Archdiocese of Westminster. Church magazines can be a useful resource, along with records of local Catholic schools. In 1858, the Royal Commission on Popular Education found in Middlesex 117 Roman Catholic schools or departments educating 15,574 children, as well as 8 Roman Catholic Sunday Schools with 1,324 pupils, and one Jewish Sabbath school with 35 pupils. The Catholic Family History Society has useful resources and publishes indexes on London churches: www.catholic-history.org.uk/cfhs/

Sadly for researchers, too often Irish birthplaces in censuses were given only as *'Ireland.'* Even if a county is named, locating an

London 1888

exact parish is difficult. This is where some of the London parish records outside of the registers can prove essential.

During the years of famine in Ireland from summer 1845 to 1850, 1.1 million people died of starvation. Many in Ireland blamed the English, particularly the aristocratic landowners, for taking their corn (for bread) and driving them off their land. Although many Irish would have preferred to flee to the USA, with little money and less choice thousands sailed to England and Scotland for a new life. By 1851 there were 108,500 Irish-born people in London – almost 5% of the city's population.

The Irish who fled the famine were usually too poor to travel far from the port where they landed. This can often provide a useful clue as to their place of origin. Those who settled in London during the years of the famine tended to have sailed from Cork. They originated either from a parish in County Cork, or from southern Irish counties like Munster and South Leinster.

Poverty and crime are often closely associated and there are many examples of Irish names in London's court and prison registers. Some of these cases were covered in contemporary newspapers. Child criminals may have been sent to be rehabilitated at special schools, such as the Catholic Girls' Reformatory at Brook Green, Hammersmith. Reformatories were used increasingly for Catholics from 1868. Names, ages and residences of Irish paupers or low-earning labourer may be found in the *'Police Intelligence'* or other columns of newspapers, which gave details of families receiving aid from local poverty relieving officers. These newspapers can be searched at local record offices or online via the British Newspaper Archive www.britishnewspaperarchive.co.uk/ or British Newspapers 1600-1900, which can be accessed at the British Library and other local libraries.

Although many of the Irish in London suffered poverty, many were unwilling to risk being removed back to their parish of origin in Ireland. Thus many avoided asking for relief. Those who did apply can be found in poor law records, which are usually held at LMA or the relevant borough archives. Others may have received charitable help from organisations such as the Catholic Poor School Committee, (established 1847) or the Benevolent Society of St Patrick (LMA: A/FWA/C/J/06), which was founded in 1783. Notably, the Benevolent Society gave relief to Irish of all religious backgrounds.

As the decades wore on, more Irish migrated to London. In 1861, there were 600,000 Irish-born people in Britain, and 5% of the London population was Irish. Compared with 25% of the population in Liverpool and in 18% in Glasgow, the London Irish were a relatively small group. Nevertheless, by 1871 there were more Irish in London than in Dublin. Working class Irish labourers made a vital contribution to the London economy and infrastructure. Many found work in the docks of the Port of London. The docks were central to London's – and Britain's – economy. Many dock labourers were employed on a casual basis - as a result of the unpredictable nature of shipping - and the

London Borough Archives

Besides the records at LMA, thousands of documents on the lives of Londoners is held at local borough archives. Those boroughs which have, or have had, large Irish communities include:

Brent - www.brent.gov.uk/archives
Camden - www.camden.gov.uk/ccm/navigation/leisure/local-history/
Hammersmith and Fulham - www.lbhf.gov.uk/Directory/Leisure_and_Culture/Libraries/Archives/17430_Archives_and_Local_History.asp
Islington - www.islington.gov.uk/islington/history-heritage/heritage_lhc/Pages/default.aspx
Lambeth - www.lambeth.gov.uk/Services/LeisureCulture/LocalHistory/Archives.htm
Lewisham - www.lewisham.gov.uk/inmyarea/history/archives/Pages/default.aspx
Southwark - www.southwark.gov.uk/info/200161/local_history_library
Tower Hamlets - www.towerhamlets.gov.uk/lgsl/1001-1050/1034_local_history_archives.aspx

Some parish records for all of the above can be found on Ancestry and some of Tower Hamlets records, which includes many docklands areas, have been uploaded via www.ideastore.co.uk/en/articles/information_local_studies_and_archives_archives_online

A full list of London boroughs can be found at the Genuki London webpage: http://homepages.gold.ac.uk/genuki/LND/parishes.html

Useful Contacts and Resources in London

Irish social clubs have provided important support for those in London. Records of these may be held at surviving clubs or in the local borough archives. The present London Irish Centre in Camden www.londonirishcentre.org/ offers a service to trace missing persons for close relatives currently living in Ireland.

London Metropolitan University has an archive dedicated to Irish in Britain, including records of those who settled in London www.londonmet.ac.uk/research-units/iset/projects/archive-of-the-irish-in-britain.cfm

East of London Family History Society - www.eolfhs.org.uk/
London, Westminster & North Middlesex Family History Society -www.lwmfhs.org.uk/
Museum of London - www.museumoflondon.org.uk/

work could be dangerous. When there was no work, the labourers were paid nothing. Baptisms of some parishes in the London Docklands area have been digitised on FindMyPast.

Other Irish labourers helped to build the railways, canals, bridges and roads that were essential to London's position as a great international city and capital of an expanding empire. Irish working class women took in piece work or laundry, whilst others worked in factories. Names of those from the Bryant And May factory in Bow who took part in the matchworkers' strike of 1888 can be found on FindMyPast.

Instead of being valued for their essential contribution, the Irish often suffered discrimination. As Robert Winder explains life could be very difficult for the recent Irish immigrants:

The Irish were viewed as violent, angry, lazy, noisy, uneducated, scary and drunk . . . They were harshly discriminated against in employment, housing and all areas of social welfare; and badgered both by squads of racist citizens and by a police force dedicated to the defence of non-Irish property . . . there was much logic in the usual caricature of the Irish refugee as a diseased and undernourished alcoholic. The Irish did society's heavy lifting. And they were strong enough to do it, week after week, year after year. Disease and malnutrition cannot have been the norm.

Bloody Foreigners, Robert Winder (Abacus, 2004)

Charles Booth's Online Poverty Map of 1898/9 can be used to find streets where Londoners lived at this time and to discover the social class of those who lived there. Booth labelled his classes A-H, where A was *'The lowest class of occasional labourers, loafers and semi-criminals'* and H was the *'Upper middle class – Wealthy.'* The website at http://booth.lse.ac.uk/ also includes further details from Booth's survey into life and labour in London, dating from 1886 to 1903.

For the London Irish who Booth would have categorized as G or H, those of the middle and upper classes, probate records can be useful in locating family members in London, Ireland and elsewhere. Between 1384 and 12 January 1858, richer Londoners' wills were proved at the Prerogative Court of Canterbury (PCC). These are indexed on TNA's website: www.nationalarchives.gov.uk/documentsonline/default.asp Records of smaller London courts can be found in the Bank of England wills 1717-1845 and London Probate Index 1750-1858 that have been digitised on FindMyPast. The Corporation of London's London Signatures index, including 10,000 Archdeaconry Court of Middlesex Wills 1609-1810 can be found on Ancestry. The probate records of the London Consistory and Commissary Courts, and the Peculiar Court of the Dean & Chapter of St Pauls are held at LMA. The online PDF http://bit.ly/KVvh2U gives full details on these and their available indexes.

From 1858, probate records of those who died in London can be found at the Principal Probate Registry in Holborn. Copies of the wills and administrations can be obtained in person or via the Court Service www.courtservice.gov.uk The official index of these records (or National Probate Calendar) from 1858 to 1966 can be found online at Ancestry.

Many middle and upper class Irish visited London to attend school or university. Published and online alumni records are easily accessible in large libraries and online. Ancestry has lists of names from Westminster School up to 1927, a selection of schools and universities. www.thegenealogist.co.uk has a larger selection.

London Docks

The Petty Session Order Books

Ross Weldon

Introduction

The Petty Sessions Order Books are one of the greatest untapped resources for Irish genealogical research. Containing almost 15 million cases they are also one of the most extensive sets of records about the general population of Ireland in the nineteenth century. Most surviving records for the Republic of Ireland are held by the National Archives of Ireland (MFGS 58/1–3393), although others are held privately or by local libraries. The records for Northern Ireland are either held by the Public Record Office of Northern Ireland or still reside in the court houses.

There are very few registers which pre-date 1851, and none for Dublin City, Dun Laoghaire (Kingstown), and some other districts either which were excluded in the 1851 act which established them or simply because the records do not survive.

The Petty Sessions Order Books records held at the National Archives of Ireland have now been scanned by Family Search and transcribed and made fully searchable by findmypast.ie.

The Petty Sessions Order Books available on findmypast.ie

In February 2012 findmypast.ie released the first tranche of its 15 million records. This first batch comprised 1.5 million cases and is particularly useful for areas of the country for which family history records are notoriously sparse, such as Connaught and Donegal. A second batch of 4 million records was released in May and another 10 million will follow throughout the year.

The records cover all types of cases, from allowing trespass of cattle to being drunk in charge of an ass and cart. The reasons for cases being brought before the Petty Sessions Court are incredibly varied, but unsurprisingly the most common offence was drunkenness, which accounted for over a third of all cases.

The top five offences tried before the courts were: - Drunkenness - 33%; Revenue/Tax offences - 21%; Assault - 16%; Local acts of nuisance - 5%; Destruction of property - 4%

The nature of these cases was significantly different from those in England. Figures show that the rate of conviction for drunkenness was three times greater, four times greater for tax offences, 65% higher for assault, and we were twice as likely to be charged with *'malicious and wilful destruction of property'* than our nearest neighbours. (British Parliamentary Papers 1864)

Brian Donovan, Director of findmypast.ie, commented at the time of their release:

'These court records open up a unique window into Irish society in the 19th century. Most families interacted with the law in one way or another, being perpetrators or victims of petty crime, resolving civil disputes, to applying for a dog licence. The records are full of the trauma and tragedy of local life, as family members squabbled, shop keepers recovered debt, and the police imposed order. These records help fulfil our mission to provide more than just names and dates, to get to the stories of our ancestors' lives.'

What were the Petty Sessions?

These were the lowest courts in the country, which dealt with the vast bulk of lesser legal cases, civil and criminal. The Court was presided over by two or more unpaid *Justices of the Peace* (JPs), or by a single paid Magistrate. There was no jury so judgements were made summarily by the JPs or Magistrate. Each Court met daily, weekly or monthly, depending on the volume of cases to be heard. Some localities established a small courthouse for the purpose of holding sessions but many held court wherever they deemed appropriate. In addition, every Court had a Clerk who kept the registers that are published on findmypast.ie, and collected fees from those involved in cases.

The earliest surviving Petty Sessions records held in the National Archives of Ireland date from 1822 for the district of Castlemartyr in county Cork. This has previously been taken as evidence that the Courts of Petty Sessions were first introduced into Ireland in the southern province of Munster, and then gradually into other parts of the country.

This system is still in place in Northern Ireland and Britain and usually referred to as the Magistrates Court. In the Republic this type of court was replaced by the District Court in 1924.

Who were the Judges?

As JPs were unpaid, they were invariably local landowners who were untrained and often more interested in their own private gain. It was for this reason that over the course of the 19th century the government slowly replaced the use of JPs with paid and trained Magistrates. Where did the Magistrates come from? Who paid them? Why did they take the jobs?

Origins and development of the Petty Sessions Court

From the medieval period the government appointed JPs in each county to act as judges and arbiters of legal cases that were not of the most serious nature (i.e. murder, treason, rape, insurrection, etc.). In practice the JPs set up Quarter Sessions (courts held 4 times a year) to

deal with cases that had to be tried by jury or summarily (without a jury). JPs were given the right to try and convict people summarily at different dates and for different reasons from the 1500s onwards. Due to the vast number of cases it became apparent that it would be more efficient to deal with the lesser matters at local courts called *petit* sessions more commonly called *Petty Sessions.*

The system governing how Petty Sessions worked was only set out by statute (despite centuries of operation) in 1827 with the *Act for the better Administration of Justice at the holding of Petty Sessions by Justices of the Peace in Ireland, 2 July 1827* (7 & 8 George IV c.67). This specified that the Grand Jury in each county (the forerunners of modern county councils) should set out Petty Sessions districts in a formal manner. It also required proper registers to be kept, trained clerks, and regular courts. The system was overhauled again in 1851 with the *Petty Sessions (Ireland) Act* which sought tighter regulation of the keeping of records and meeting of courts.

Why is it an important resource?

Family historians will find this an essential resource. There were few families that did not need to interact with the courts at some level, from licensing a dog, to resolving a civil dispute to being the perpetrator or victim of a petty offence or infraction of the law. This extent of coverage can help pinpoint a person in a place at a specific date. In light of the relatively late start date for civil records, and the destruction of the 19th Century Census, these records are an effective census substitute, and can allow you to pick out your ancestor from their doppelganger, i.e. someone of the same name, who flourished in the same timeframe.

However the real value of the Petty Sessions records is that they open a window into the past, so that you can see clearly the events that shaped your ancestors' lives. Knowledge of a family dispute, a disagreement over a field boundary, a petty criminal action or even being arrested for drunkenness at the time of a birth or death in the family provides context and enables you to construct stories around your family narrative.

Used in conjunction with other sources the Petty Sessions Court records can be even more powerful. For example, many of the more serious disputes and cases are likely to have spawned a local newspaper report close to the date of the hearing. Newspaper accounts can often add additional detail to the summary of the case in the registers. Used alongside other local sources, like church records and estate papers, researchers can build community profiles to put their ancestors' and their neighbours' actions in context. For example, prosecutions for poaching game say much about social class, poverty and survival, while frequent cases for *'playing [sports] on the roads,'* or *'making an ice-slide'* on a public right of way, tell us something of the indomitable high spirits of children and young people at any time in the past.

As with previous record sets released on findmypast.ie, their value reflects family historians growing interest in finding out more than just the names of their ancestor and when they were born and died. These records, along with the Landed Estate Court Rentals and the Irish Prison Registers, help the family historian to build up a picture of not just when their ancestors lived but how they lived, and in this case what kind of trouble they were involved in, the victims of, or bore witness too.

The Petty Sessions Order Books are available exclusively on findmypast.ie.

Level of Detail in the Petty Sessions Records

The level of detail found in the Petty Sessions records sets them apart from records which simply provide us with names and dates. The structures of the Petty Sessions were set out by statute and include comprehensive details of the case including:

Column	Description
Date	
Name of Justice(s)	
Complainant(s)	*The person or persons who bring the charge (often police)*
Defendant(s)	*The person or persons charged with an offence*
Names of witnesses	
Cause of Complaint	*Summary of charge*
Particulars of order or dismissal	*The judgement*
Act under which order made	*The statute governing sentence*
When and how amount ordered to be paid	*The fine payment details*
Imprisonment	*Details of custodial sentence*
Name etc. of person receiving compensation	*If ordered by the magistrate/justice*
Name of defendant against whom order made	*Name of defendant sentenced*
Amount to be paid	
Stamps and Signature	*Stamps for court fees and Judges signature.*

Case Studies

The Petty Sessions are full of incidents of minor squabbles, none more so than some of the cases below which not only give an indication of how busy these courts must have been but also give a wonderful insight into Irish life in the late 19th and early twentieth century. These case studies show both the wealth of information available in the records as well as the often minor cases which were brought before the courts.

Michael Downey

This entry for Michael Downey of Athlone, Co. Westmeath shows he was charged with being *'drunk while in charge of an ass and cart.'*

Date of Order *January 23rd 1911*
Name of Justices by whom order made *J. Byrne, Col. Brereton, M.J. Hughes, R. English, M. Geoghegan*
Complainant(s) *Thomas Craddock (Royal Irish Constabulary)* ,**Defendant(s)** *Michael Downey from Clonohill*
Names of witnesses *S. Donohue*
Cause of Complaint
Drunk in charge of an ass and cart - *That on the 11th January 1911 at Athlone, defendant was found drunk while in charge of an ass and cart on the public street.*
Particulars of order or dismissal *Defendant convicted and ordered to pay for fine the sum of s7.16 and for costs the sum of 1/6 and in default of payment to be imprisoned in His Majesty's prison at Tullamore for 7 days with hard labour*

County of Westmeath ORDER BOOK, as approved of by the Lord Lieutenant (with the advice and consent of

1 No.	2 Date of Order.	3 Name or Names of Justice or Justices by whom Order made; and if made out of Petty Sessions, or if entry in this Book made from a Certificate, same to be here stated.	4 PARTIES—COMPLAINANT AND DEFENDANT. (The Christian and Surname, Rank, Occupation, or other addition, and Residence, stating Parish and Townland, to be given, and the parties to be distinguished by prefixing their appellation—Complainant or Defendant.) Complainant.	Defendant.	5 Names of Witnesses examined, and whether for Complainant or Defendant.	6 CAUSE OF COMPLAINT as set forth in Summons.	7 PARTICULARS OF ORDER OR DISMISSAL. If Dismiss, whether with or without prejudice, and whether with or without Costs, &c. In Ejectment, when to be evicted, and from what and whose Premises, &c. If to be Whipped, whether in or out of Prison, &c., &c. (Where Money ordered to be paid by or to any Person, the amount to be written in Words at full length in this Column, as well as to be entered in Figures in the Money Columns.)
75	1911 Jany 23rd	J Byrne RM Col Brereton MJ Hughes R Bairle R English J Green M Geoghegan	Michael Hughes Athlone	Thomas Meehan Templeboy Co Sligo	C R. Alaco. P. Hughes.	That on the 24th Decr 1910 at Dublin Gate Street Athlone in said district and County you being quarrelsome & disorderly on the licensed premises of the Compt did unlawfully refuse to leave such licensed premises on being requested to leave by the Compt or his duly authorized Manager	Defendant convicted and ordered to pay for Fine the sum of 20/= and for costs the sum of 3/ 8/= and in default of payment to be imprisoned in His Majesty's Prison at Tullamore for 14 days with Hard labour unless he shall sooner pay the before named sums
76	"	do	Michael Hughes Athlone	James Kemp otherwise Carroll of no fixed residence	C R. Al P. Hughes	Malicious injury — adjd Case That on the 24th Decr 1910 at Dublin Gate Street Athlone you did unlawfully wilfully and maliciously commit certain damage injury and spoil to and upon a door of Compts licensed house whereby he sustained loss and injury to the amount of 8/.	Defendant convicted and ordered to pay for Fine the sum of 8/= and for costs the sum of 8/= and in default of payment to be imprisoned in His Majesty's Prison at Tullamore 7 days with Hard labour unless he shall sooner pay the before named sums — and to pay for Compensation 8/=.
77	"	do	Michael Hughes Athlone	James Kemp otherwise Carroll of no fixed residence	C R. Al P. Hughes	adjourned Case Quarrelsome disorderly on lic premises That on the 24th Decr 1910 at Athlone you being quarrelsome and disorderly on the licensed premises of the Compt at Dublin Gate Street Athlone aforesaid did unlawfully refuse to leave such premises on being requested to do so by the Complainant or his duly authorised Manager	Defendant convicted and ordered to pay for Fine the sum of 20/= and for costs the sum of 8/= and in default of payment to be imprisoned in His Majesty's Prison at Tullamore for 14 days with Hard labour unless he shall sooner pay the before named sums Warrant to follow that in No 7

A Day of Violence in Cloonakilla, Co. Roscommon

Image © Robert Blatchford Collection

Here is a page from a sitting of the Athlone Petty Sessions court in Co. Westmeath on the 1st of September 1908. The entry names four individuals involved in what seems to be a full day of tit-for-tat petty offences against each other in Cloonakilla, Co. Roscommon.

The four defendants are named as Edward Gallagher, James Fitzgerald, Patrick Curley and Patrick Goodman and from the evidence contained in this record the events seemed to play out like this:

1. In the first entry Edward Gallagher and James Fitzgerald are accused of having *'assault and beat one Patrick Goodman.'*
2. On the same day they were alleged to have assaulted Patrick Curley.
3. They were also accused of *having 'maliciously committed certain damage injury and spoil to and upon a bicycle, the property of the complainant, whereby he sustained a loss of £1.5.0d'*
4. However it appears that Patrick Curley and Patrick Goodman decided

to team up and get their own back. Iin the fourth case they were alleged to *'unlawfully assault and beat'* Edward Gallagher.

5. Finally in the fifth entry we can see the balance of events coming full circle with the original victims again ganging up and allegedly assaulting and beating James Fitzgerald, one of the original assailants.

County of Westmeath ORDER BOOK, as approved of by the Lord Lieutenant (with the advice and consent of

2 Date of Order.	3 Name or Names of Justice or Justices by whom Order made; and if made out of Petty Sessions, or if entry in this Book made from a Certificate, same to be here stated.	4 PARTIES—COMPLAINANT AND DEFENDANT. (The Christian and Surname, Rank, Occupation, or other addition, and Residence, stating Parish and Townland, to be given, and the parties to be distinguished by prefixing their appellation—Complainant or Defendant.) Complainant.	Defendant.	5 Names of Witnesses examined, and whether for Complainant or Defendant.	6 CAUSE OF COMPLAINT as set forth in Summons.	7 PARTICULARS OF ORDER OR DISMISSAL. If Dismiss, whether with or without prejudice, and whether with or without Costs, &c. In Ejectment, when to be evicted, and from what and whose Premises, &c. If to be Whipped, whether in or out of Prison, &c., &c. (Where Money ordered to be paid by or to any Person, the amount to be written in Words at full length in this Column, as well as to be entered in Figures in the Money Columns.)
1908 Septr 1st	J Vaughan, J Glover, R English, M J Lennon	F. W. Jones Sergt R.I.C.	Edward Gallagher of Cartron and James Fitzgerald of Cloongowna	Sergt Jones Plaintiff, Pat Goodman for Pat Curley (Wt)	Adjourned Case See No 96. Assault. That Defts on the 8th day of August 1908 at Cloonakilla in said district and County of Roscommon did unlawfully assault and beat one Patrick Goodman and that said Patrick Goodman declined to prosecute	Dismissed OM
"	do	Patrick Curley Dernasee	Edward Gallagher and James Fitzgerald	Pat Curley Plt, Pat Goodman for Plaintiff, Sergt. Jones	Adjourned Case — 97 — Assault. That Defts on the 8th August 1908 at Cloonakilla did unlawfully assault and beat the Compt	Dismissed OM
"	do	Patrick Curley	Edward Gallagher and James Fitzgerald	Pat Curley, Pat Goodman, Jas. Fitzgerald	Malicious injury to bicycle. Adjourned Case — 98 — ~~[struck out]~~ That Defts on the 8th August 1908 at Cloonakilla did unlawfully wilfully and maliciously commit certain damage injury and spoil to and upon a bicycle the property of the Compt whereby he sustained a loss of £1:5:0	Dismissed OM
"	do	Edward Gallagher Cartron	Patrick Curley and Patrick Goodman of Dernasee		Adjourned Case — 99 — Assault. That Defts on the 8th August 1908 at Cloonakilla did unlawfully assault and beat the Compt	Dismissed OM
"	do	James Fitzgerald Cloongowna	Patrick Curley and Patrick Goodman both of Dernasee		Adjourned Case — 100 — Assault. That Defts on the 8th August 1908 at Cloonakilla did unlawfully assault and beat the Complainant	Dismissed OM

Note.—No erasure to be, on any account, made, and every interlineation or other change to be initialed by the Justice who affixes his Signature ... Order. The greatest care to be taken that the cases be kept distinct from each other

Five men and women convicted of 'tippling in a sheebeen'"

In another case five men and women were convicted of *'tippling in a sheebeen'* (drinking in an unlicensed premise) on Queen Street, Athlone and given fines of between £1.0s.0d. and £5.0s.0d. The transcribed details from this record are:

Date of Order *October 17th 1911*

Name of Justice(s) *John Byrne R.M., Col. Brereton, R. English, M.J. Hughes*

Complainant(s) *Detective Inspector C. Berne (Royal Irish Constabulary)*

Defendant(s) *Kate Barnes, William Logan, James Geoghegan, Michael Kelly, Annie Louring*

Names of witnesses *A.J. Campbell, P. Slua, R. Taylor*

Cause of Complaint

Drinking or Tippling in a Sheebeen

That on the 7th October 1911 at Queen Street, Athlone you were unlawfully drinking or tippling on the premises of one Kate Barnes – the said premises not being duly licensed for the sale of wine, spirits, beer, cider or perry.

Particulars of order or dismissal

Convicted and fined £5.0s.0d

County of Westmeath ORDER BOOK, as approved of by the Lord Lieutenant (with the advice and consent of

1 No.	2 Date of Order.	3 Name or Names of Justice or Justices by whom Order made; and if made out of Petty Sessions, or if entry in this Book made from a Certificate, same to be here stated.	4 PARTIES—COMPLAINANT AND DEFENDANT. (The Christian and Surname, Rank, Occupation, or other addition, and Residence, stating Parish and Townland, to be given, and the parties to be distinguished by prefixing their appellation—Complainant or Defendant.) Complainant.	Defendant.	5 Names of Witnesses examined, and whether for Complainant or Defendant.	6 CAUSE OF COMPLAINT as set forth in Summons.	7 PARTICULARS OF ORDER OR DISMISSAL. If Dismiss, whether with or without prejudice, and whether with or without Costs, &c. In Ejectment, when to be evicted, and from what and whose Premises, &c. If to be Whipped, whether in or out of Prison, &c., &c. (Where Money ordered to be paid by or to any Person, the amount to be written in Words at full length in this Column, as well as to be entered in Figures in the Money Columns.)
20	1911 Octr 17th	John Byrne R.M. Col Bredeton R. English, E Baile, M J Hughes	The King at the prosecution of Berne D. I. R. I. C.	Kate Barnes Queen Street Athlone	C R. Taylor RC, A. Shea RC, A. Campbell RC	Keeping Beer or Porter for Sale on unlicensed premises. That on the 7th October 1911 at Queen Street Athlone in said district & County you the said deft not being duly licensed to sell wine spirits beer ale cider or perry did unlawfully keep for sale on your premises a quantity of beer or porter	Convicted and fined £2 and 1/- costs, in default imprisonment in Tullamore Gaol for one calendar month unless said sums be sooner paid
21	"	do	Same	William Fogan Athlone	C A Campbell RC, A. Shea	Drinking or tippling in Shebeen. That on the 7th October 1911 at Queen St Athlone you were unlawfully drinking or tippling on the premises of one Kate Barnes - the said premises not being duly licensed for the sale of wine spirits beer ale cider or perry	Convicted and fined £5/- and 1/- costs - in default imprisonment in Tullamore Gaol - for 7 days unless said sums be sooner paid
22	-	do	Same	James Geoghegan Queen Street	C A. Shea RC, A Campbell	do. That on the 7th Octr 1911 at Queen St Athlone you were unlawfully drinking or tippling on the premises of one Kate Barnes - the said premises not being duly licensed for the sale of wine spirits beer ale, cider or perry.	Like rule as last No 21
23	-	do	Same	Michael Kelly Queen Street	C P Shea RC, A Campbell RC	do. That on the 7th Octr 1911 at Queen St Athlone you were unlawfully drinking or tippling on the premises of one Kate Barnes - the said premises not being duly licensed for the sale of wine spirits beer ale cider or perry	Like rule as last No 22
24	-	do	Same	Annie Fourig Queen Street	C A Campbell RC, P. Shea	do. That on the 7th Octr 1911 at Queen St Athlone you were unlawfully drinking or tippling on the premises of one Kate Barnes - the said premises not being duly licensed for the sale of wine spirits beer ale cider or perry.	Like rule as last No 23

NOTE.—No erasure to be, on any account, made, and every interlineation or other change to be initialed by the Justice who affixes his Signature to the Order. The greatest care to be taken that

British Parliamentary Papers Relating to Ireland

William Roulston
Ulster Historical Foundation

The papers generated by the Westminster Houses of Parliament form a vast and relatively untapped source of information of immense value to local historians and genealogists interested in Ireland. This essay seeks to present a selection of those papers from the implementation of the Act of Union in 1801 to 1845, the eve of the Great Famine, and to draw attention to the sort of information they contain. A fully comprehensive definition of parliamentary papers would include everything to do with the machinery of government, even the somewhat tedious procedures of day to day business. However, to the researcher three groups of material are of primary importance.

First, there are the journals which record the things done in parliament. Second, there are the debates which record the things said in parliament. These are better known as Hansard which began as a private venture supported by a public subsidy and only later became an official publication. Third, there are the papers arising in or presented to parliament which deal with the formulation, development and execution of policy. This collection of papers has come to be known as the 'Blue Books' because of the blue paper with which most of the volumes were covered. It is with this last category that the term, 'parliamentary papers' has come to be most closely associated. To the local and family historian the papers of greatest interest and value are those providing information to Parliament in the form of select committee reports, Royal Commissions and returns.

In the 45 years after the Act of Union 114 commissions and 61 special committees reported on Irish matters. Often these reports include minutes of evidence and appendices, sometimes running to several hundred, or even, in a few cases, over one thousand pages. These are generally of much more interest than the reports themselves. Returns are documents printed under the direction of Parliament which provide specific information about a certain subject. When they provide names and addresses of individuals they can be of immense value to the genealogist.

House of Commons at time of King Charles II

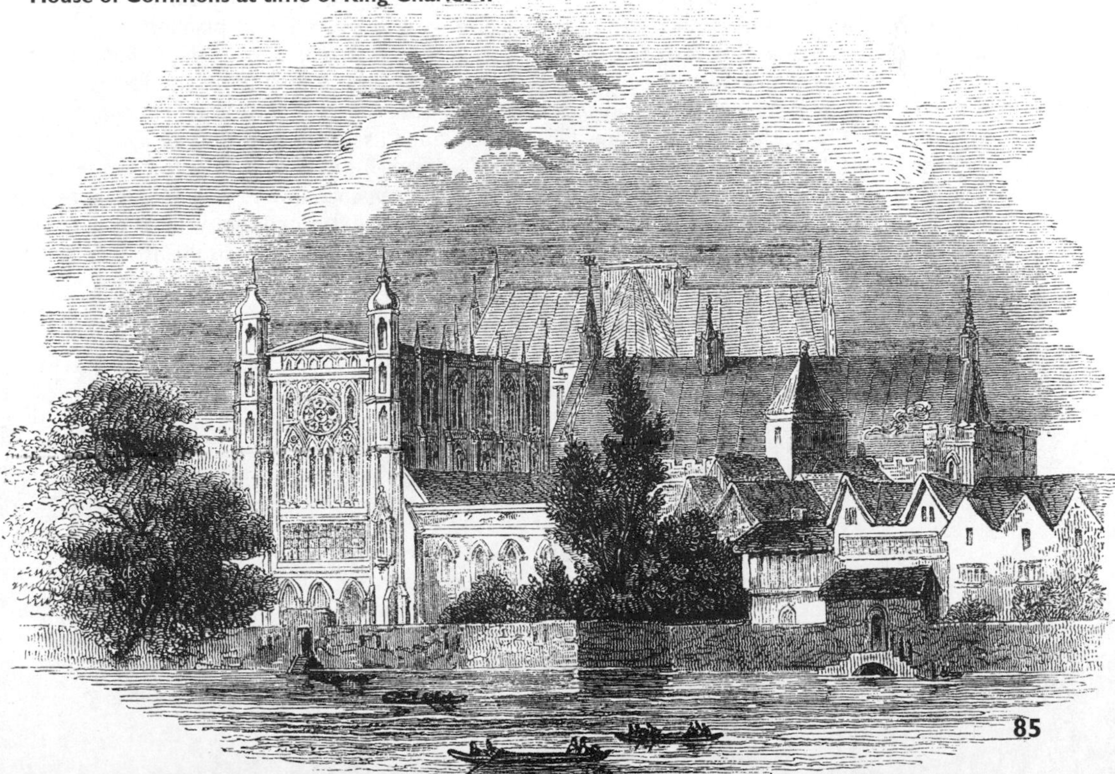

Freeholders, freemen and elections

Numerous parliamentary papers deal with issues arising from elections. These provide much of value to the genealogist. For Carrickfergus in Co. Antrim, among several interesting papers from the 1830s, there is a report on the forgeries election petition, which lists the names of over 50 witnesses.[1] Following on from this there is a return giving the names of freeholders, leaseholders, and £10 householders in Carrickfergus[2] and another listing the names, occupations and residences of freemen in the town.[3] A further return gives the names, occupations and residences of the mayor, sheriffs, aldermen and burgesses of the corporation of Carrickfergus.[4] For Belfast there is a report on the 'election compromise' which lists the names and occupations of nearly fifty witnesses.[5] There are also a number of useful papers relating to Coleraine listing the names of freemen and aldermen of the town.[6]

The *First report from the select committee on fictitious votes, Ireland* of 1837 is a veritable treasure trove for genealogists. This committee was ordered to be appointed on 6 February 1837 to 'inquire how far the intentions of the Reform Bill are defeated by creating and registering fictitious and improper votes in Ireland'. The report is interesting enough in itself, but the appendices to it are of incredible value, listing as they do thousands upon thousands of names of people and quite often where these individuals lived, down to the very street. The lists include the names of freeholders and leaseholders in Co. Fermanagh (unfortunately without addresses); the names of marksmen (illiterate voters) in the boroughs of Armagh, Belfast, Carrickfergus, Coleraine, Downpatrick, Enniskillen, Londonderry and Newry etc.; the names of freemen admitted to the corporations of Carrickfergus, Coleraine and Londonderry etc.; houses and householders in towns which returned MPs, including Armagh, Coleraine, Dungannon, Lisburn, Londonderry and Newry.

Law and order

The administration and enforcement of the law form a major part of parliamentary papers relating to Ireland. Returns dealing with crime are usually presented statistically. Occasionally, however, the names of perpetrators of criminal acts are given, together with the nature of their offence. A return of 1843 lists the names, residences and crime of individuals prosecuted for offences against the excise laws.[7] The offences varied: William Madill was convicted of *'having raw grain in his brewery'*, while James Dunlavie of Morass in Co. Donegal was guilty of 'keeping a still without licence and harbouring illicit spirits'. From 1837–8 there is a *Return of all rewards offered by proclamation of the lord lieutenant or lords justices of Ireland for the discovery of the perpetrators of murders and other outrages from 1st January 1836 to 12th December 1837*.[8] This lists the date, the county, the nature of the outrage, the name of the victim, the reward offered and whether or not it was claimed.

If not executed or transported those who broke the law were likely to end up behind bars. The appendix to the *Ninth report of the Inspectors General on the general state of the prisons of Ireland, 1831* includes brief accounts of each gaol in Ireland.[9] In the town of Antrim the prison consisted of only two cells. It was, however, 'kept clean and the pauper prisoners are fed and provided with blankets etc.' In Lurgan, Co. Armagh, a new prison was nearly finished, but in the meantime the former prison, described as a *'wretched old dungeon', continued in use. With regard to the Tyrone County Gaol in Omagh the inspectors noted: 'Criminals will find that a sentence to imprisonment is more than a privation to liberty, and that while a gaol is, on the one hand, a place of punishment, it opens on the other, a door to reformation through the*

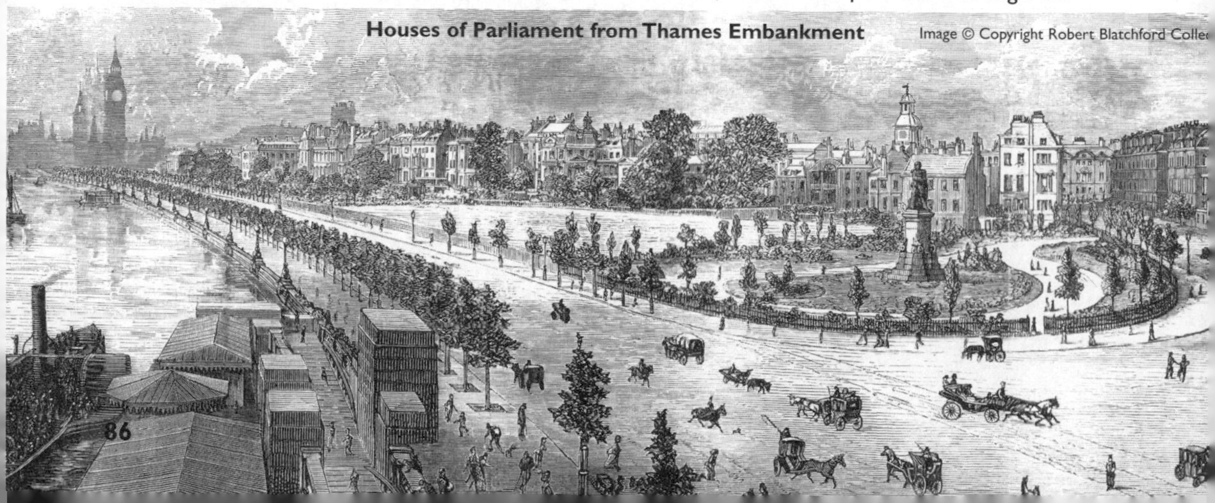
Houses of Parliament from Thames Embankment

medium of industry, instruction and moral government'. The gaol included a *'treadmill for those sentenced to hard labour'*.

Those enforcing the law are the subject of a fairly large number of papers. These include a return listing the names of all stipendiary magistrates in Ireland[10] as well as a return of the magistrates included in a commission of the peace in Ireland.[11] Several returns list the names of retired police officers who were receiving pensions.[12] These returns include the rank of the policeman, the date of his commencement of service and the date of his retirement. Unfortunately residences are not given. A return of 1842 lists the names of barristers appointed to 'supernumerary prosecuting counsel' in each circuit in Ireland, as well as those who declined the offer.[13]

The inquiries into the Orange Order in 1835 reveal much about the organisation and about secret societies and law and order in the 1830s.[14] The minutes of evidence make fascinating reading and give a real insight into the perception of the Order and its activities at this time. The appendix to the first report records the names, where known, of all the principal office bearers, such as the committee members, county grand officers and district and lodge masters. The appendix to the third report includes further lists of office bearers as well as some additional lists of names such as those seen marching at various Orange parades in Ulster, including Kilrea in Co. Londonderry, as well as a list of members of the Lurgan yeomanry.

The *Report from the select committee on manor courts, Ireland; together with the minutes of evidence, appendix and index of 1837* reveals much about the workings of local justice in rural Ireland in the early nineteenth century.[15] Most of the manor courts in Ulster had been established in the seventeenth century as part of the Ulster plantation scheme, but by the beginning of the nineteenth century probably the majority had fallen into abeyance. One of the most interesting cross examinations involved T. Davison, seneschal of the manors of Glenarm and Oldstone in Co. Antrim. When asked about the sort of person he chose to serve on the juries of the manor courts he replied, 'My object has been to summon the most respectable class of persons, shopkeepers and farmers.' Davison revealed that his predecessor as seneschal of Glenarm had been an elderly man 'of very good intentions, but I think he was an indolent man, and did not give himself much trouble in selecting the jurors'. From 1842 there is a return of the seneschals or stewards of manors in Ireland, giving the date of appointment, and the names of the sureties as well as, in some cases, the name of the manor.[16]

Occupations and professions

Parliamentary papers dealing with particular occupations and professions in Ireland appear with regularity. Most of these are concerned with individuals employed by the government, but a significant number relate to the private sector. The 1822 *Report from the select committee on laws which regulate the linen trade of Ireland together with minutes of evidence and appendices* includes the names of the officials and employees of the Linen Board of Ireland, ranging from inspectors to watchmen, for both 1797 to 1822.[17] Their salaries and emoluments are also given. The report also includes a petition signed at Londonderry on 16 June 1822 by over sixty dealers in linen, yarn and flax.

A *Return of the names of the several officers employed under the butter acts of Ireland* of 1829 gives the name of each officer, by whom and when appointed, account of fees received by such officers in each of the last seven years.[18] It is arranged by county and provides much miscellaneous material provided. A return of all apprentice apothecaries in Ireland between 1791 and 1829 lists names and addresses arranged by year and county.[19] This is followed by other returns listing the names of assistant apothecaries,[20] practising apothecaries,[21] and those apothecaries who had been prosecuted for various offences, such as practising without a licence or selling arsenic.[22]

Returns of the name of every person who has been appointed in Ireland to any situation producing an annual income of £100 and upwards since 1 September 1841 to 1843 list various officials including the Lord Chancellor (salary of £8000), stipendiary magistrates, customs and excise officers and coast guards.[23] It also includes those discontinued or dismissed. *A return of the names of the officers of each and every yeomanry corps in Ireland* comprises nine pages of names covering the whole of Ireland in the 1840s.[24]

A report on pawnbroking includes returns of pawnbrokers in each county in Ireland made to the Marshall of Dublin and Register of Pawnbrokers in Ireland, 1832–7, with towns, sums lent, date of registry and observations such as 'since dead'.[25] It also gave the names and residences of all pawnbrokers who had lodged bonds in the offices of Treasurers of

State Opening of Parliament by Queen Victoria at the Peer's Entrance

Counties, and with town clerks. A return of registered blacksmiths is disappointingly poor for Ulster with only one name for Co. Down, six for Co. Donegal, eleven for Co. Monaghan and twenty- two for Co. Cavan, none for any of the other counties in Ulster.[26] It is, however, good for some of the other counties of Ireland. A return from 1845 lists the names of all those who had renewed or taken out a spirit grocer's licence between 5 July 1838 and 5 July 1844.[27] Over 200 names and residences are listed for the excise districts of Armagh, Coleraine, Lisburn and Londonderry.

Fisheries

The appendices to the *First report of the commissioners of inquiry into the state of the Irish fisheries* contain an incredible amount of material on the fishing industry and indeed the entire coastal economy in Ireland at that time.[28] There are reports from each of the coastal counties in Ireland, together with additional reports dealing with fishing grounds, harbours for fishermen and markets for fish. The importance of the fishing industry to Co. Donegal in terms of employment is highlighted by the fact that the number of men employed in fishing here was 6,613: in Co. Down it was 2,305 and in Co. Antrim 816. Many of the fishing boats in Co. Donegal were in poor condition. The commissioners wrote that the *'county boats are small, in bad repair, bad oars, and never carry sails; and from never being coated regularly with tar or paint, they are water-soaked'.*

On the subject of harbours we read that: 'There was a harbour at Ballycastle [Co. Antrim], with a handsome pier, but the former is filled with sand; the latter is broken down by the sea, and suffered to go to ruin; and there is now not any shelter except for boats of about two tons burden'. The contractor for erecting the pier at Greencastle in Co. Donegal, *'by ingenious manoeuvring, got a great part of the work raised by the peasantry on credit, for which he never paid the poor men one farthing'.* To give an example of the markets for fish the commissioners found that at Enniskillen the supply of haddock was usually good, while herrings, lobsters and oysters were abundant. All other sea fish were, however, very scarce. There was a good and regular supply of salmon and eels, while cured herrings from Scotland could also be purchased. The second fisheries report follows on immediately after the first report and includes lists of coast guard stations and officers in Ireland.

The *Report from the committee on the petition relating to Ardglass harbour* of 1809 can probably be included here.[29] It includes a petition from the merchants, traders and shipowners of Downpatrick, 37 names in total, and also a detailed map of the harbour and town of Ardglass.[30] It was reckoned that the cost of a new pier at Ardglass would come to £14,662. If it were extended 70 yards further seaward this would add an additional £16,886 to the overall expenditure.

The Poorer Classes

In the 1830s a massive parliamentary inquiry dealt with the condition of the poorer classes in Ireland.[31] Interviews were carried out with individuals from every district in Ireland and the answers given to specific questions were included in the supplements to the appendices of the official report. Those interviewed included landowners, clergy and the more prosperous farmers. The questions ranged from the diet and clothing of the poorer classes to the type of houses they lived in and what their wages were. The different answers given to the same question, even from interviewees from the same parish, reveal much about the varying perceptions of the problem of poverty in Ireland at this time.

Three men were interviewed for the parish of Leckpatrick in County Tyrone and their answers to a selection of the questions will be analysed here. James Gamble was the minister of the Secession Church in Strabane, while Robert Hume was the Church of Ireland minister in Leckpatrick. The third interviewee was James Sinclair of Holy Hill, a local landowner. The answer each man gave on the question of the condition of the poorer classes and whether or not it had improved since 1815 was different. Gamble believed that it was much worse. However, Sinclair believed that, on the whole, the poorer classes were 'better off in all respects'. He pointed out that the handloom weavers were busily employed and if this continued, *'we shall have little reason to envy any district in Europe.'*

Hume's opinion on the subject was that the conditions of beggars had improved. However, he was concerned that the parish was 'diminishing in its best features' with the emigration of so many of its active and industrious young people. He estimated that about one hundred people left the parish every year, mainly to the United States, but some to Canada. Hume was also disgruntled at the fact that during the minority of the second marquis of Abercorn the parish had become *'studded with pauper tenements'* and he was the only person to whom the *'wretched peasantry'* could apply for aid. All three interviewees gave nearly the same answer to the question on the diet of the labouring classes – generally potatoes, milk and herrings. On the subject of their clothing James Sinclair stated that it was *'generally, pretty good',* while the Rev. Robert Hume said that *'their week-day clothes are very bad, but on Sundays they turn out very comfortably clad'.*

Workhouses, asylums & medical charities

In 1838 the Poor Law system was introduced to Ireland largely as a response to the increasing problem of vagrancy and destitution as revealed in the abovementioned parliamentary inquiry. The island was divided into 130 poor law unions, each of which would have its own workhouse and board of guardians. Of major interest for those studying the provision of accommodation for the destitute in Ireland is a series of returns from 1842 detailing correspondence and documents concerning the construction of a number of

Prime Minister Benjamin Disraeli addresses Parliament

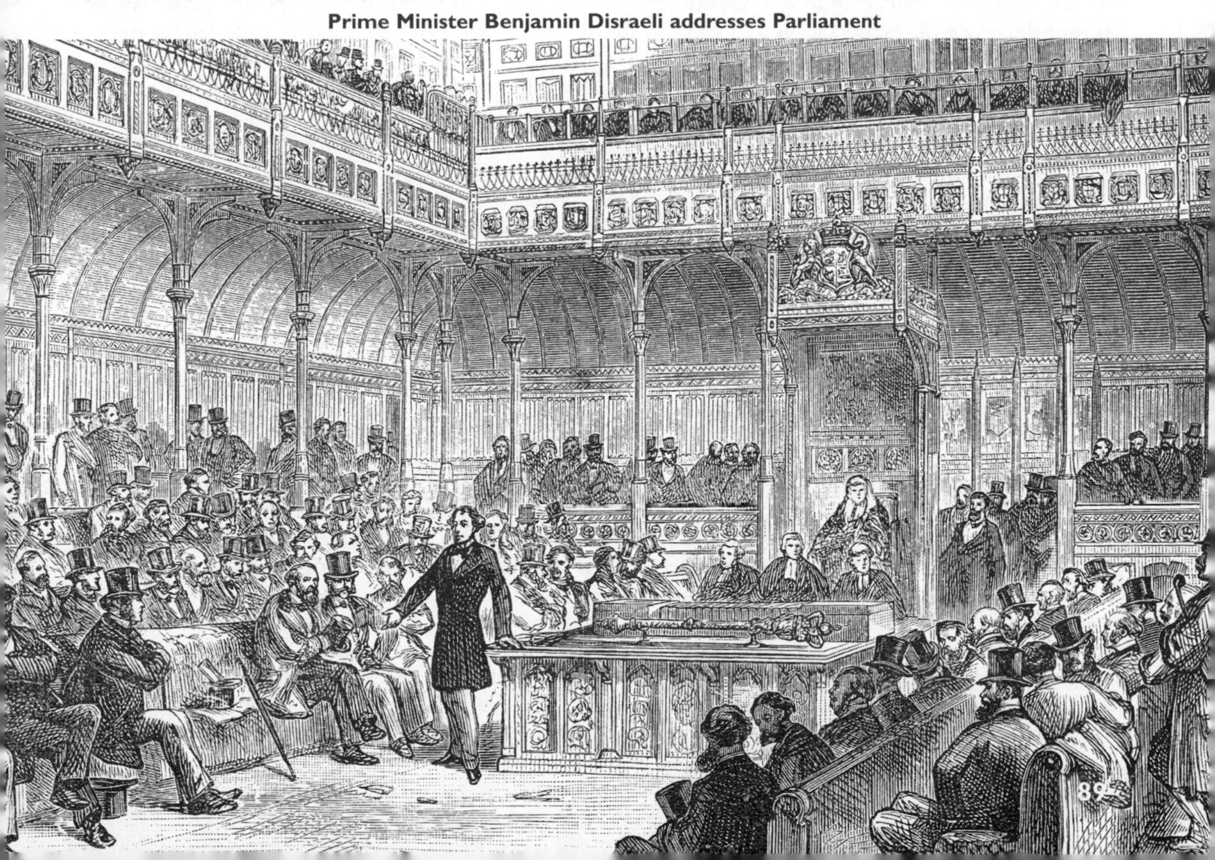

The Clock Tower Houses of Parliament 1870

workhouses in Ireland, including Castlederg, Londonderry and Lowtherstown (Irvinestown).[32] The documents provided include architects' estimates, building contracts and specifications. In the case of Castlederg there are 86 items of correspondence and documents, all of which are presented *verbatim*. In the return for Lowtherstown there is a map showing the extent of the poor law unions of Enniskillen, Lisnaskea and Lowtherstown, mainly in Co. Fermanagh, but also in adjoining parts of counties Cavan and Tyrone.

Following on from this is the *Report from the commissioners for inquiring into the execution of the contracts for certain union workhouses in Ireland* of 1844.[33] The report was commissioned in response to a number of serious complaints by the local Boards of Guardians about the new workhouses. The commissioners investigated these complaints and prepared their own reports on the condition of those workhouses which had been criticised. They also drew up a series of requisites for a workhouse, ranging from where it should be built to the way in which it should be constructed. A suitable site for a workhouse was one near the principal town in the poor law union and which had a good spring water supply and good drainage. A very useful map accompanying the report shows the location of all 130 workhouses in Ireland.

The reports on the individual workhouses varied considerably. At Belfast it was found that *'the stone walls have been badly executed; in parts the stones were badly laid, with very wide and irregular joints, and the walls would certainly have admitted more wet than they do, but that they were, at the request of the Guardians, lined with brick'*. There were other problems as well: *'the stone steps and pavement of the stairs are of a soft material, which is wearing away fast'*. Worst of all was the workhouse in Castlederg, Co. Tyrone, which was, according to the commissioner sent to inspect it, *'the worst built workhouse I have seen – that it is in my opinion, a disgrace to the builder'*. On the other hand the workhouse in Londonderry was 'generally very good' with well built walls keeping out damp. The timber was of red pine and *'well done'*. The workhouse in Armagh was 'a well built house'. For Strabane extracts from the minutes of the Board of Guardians are included to show how the site of the workhouse was finally settled upon.

The workhouse returns of 1842 and the

report of 1844 ought not only be of interest to those studying the type of accommodation being offered to the destitute in the early 1840s, but also to those interested in the building industry in the early nineteenth century. Many aspects of this industry are discussed, such as the different types of contract and various constructional details.

Also dealing with public buildings is the *Report of the Inspectors General on the district, local and private lunatic asylums in Ireland 1843: with appendices* of 1844.[34] This includes reports from the asylums in Belfast, Armagh and Londonderry which provide details on the diet and treatment of the patients. The names of a number of employees are given. A ground plan of the Belfast district asylum is also provided. In a similar vein is the *Report of the Poor Law Commissioners on Medical Charities, Ireland* of 1841.[35] This provides reports from the poor law unions on local medical provision in Ireland. For example, in the poor law union of Omagh in Co. Tyrone there were five dispensaries, a fever hospital and an infirmary. In the dispensary in the town of Omagh it was noted that 'the medicines are supplied in a manner that renders the parties liable to suspicion, as to the prices charged, even though there are, I am sure, no just grounds for it'. In the Omagh infirmary the kitchen, washhouse and some of the wards were *'so constantly filled with smoke as to render them completely useless'.*

The Devon Commission

In 1843 the government commissioned a major inquiry into the state of agriculture in Ireland.[36] Known as the Devon Commission after its chairman, Lord Devon, this commission heard evidence from more than 1,100 witnesses and visited nearly one hundred places during the course of its investigations. There are two lists of those interviewed, one alphabetical, the other arranged by county. Three men from the north-western part of Co. Tyrone were interviewed in 1844 in the course of the inquiry and their evidence is analysed here. The men were Robert McCrea of Grangefoyle, a tenant farmer, Francis O'Neill of Mount Pleasant, a linen bleacher, and James Sinclair of Holy Hill, a landlord.

McCrea told the Devon Commission that he believed that the state of agriculture in the country was improving and this was largely due to the establishment of agricultural seminaries. He considered the seminaries at Templemoyle near Eglinton and Loughash near Dunnamanagh to be 'both excellent of their kind'. He himself had had his eldest son educated at Templemoyle. Ploughing and draining had much improved and liming had become much more common. Other fertilisers and manures which were used in the district included farmyard manure, sea shells, bone dust and guano. Draining was an expensive improvement and McCrea estimated that it cost from £5 - £8 to drain one Cunningham acre. He himself had drained a field of seven acres and it had cost him £50 besides his own time. However, he believed that it would repay him in 6 - 8 years.

Francis O'Neill was a prominent figure in the district in the mid nineteenth century. He was the lessee of the bleach green at Burndennet, and had been so from at least the early 1830s, while he himself lived at Mount Pleasant in the neighbouring townland of Gloudstown where he possessed a farm of 60 Cunningham acres. Before the Devon Commission O'Neill revealed that he had laid out about £700 - £800 on his farm in Gloudstown and had made all the improvements before he had received a lease. The lease that he was eventually granted was for 31 years or three lives, but O'Neill felt that this was not long enough. The house he had built on the farm was for his own accommodation; he admitted that it was not necessary for him to have built such a house for the farm alone. On the subject of improvements O'Neill believed that the want of tenure militated against the tenants making them. He pointed out that any improvements that were made were carried out by the tenant and not the landlord. Robert McCrea's opinion on this subject was that the landlord ought to do all the permanent improvements to the farm and charge the tenant an increased rent.

While Francis O'Neill was dissatisfied with his lease of 31 years or three lives, James Sinclair told the commission that he believed that a tenant never considered 'whether he has a lease or not or asks for it'. He revealed that he had no leases on his Holy Hill estate. Sinclair was of the opinion that the tenants were improving their farms with the confidence that they would not lose anything. When asked about the subdivision of farms he responded by saying that it had been checked by the landlords without much difficulty. O'Neill confirmed this in his interview with the commissioners.

All three men painted a rather bleak picture of the state of the labouring classes. Robert McCrea believed that the labouring classes were in a 'wretched state' with regard to their clothing, homes and food supply. When asked whether he believed the condition of the labourers and cottiers was improving, James Sinclair replied, *'No, I am sorry to say it is not'*. At the same time he made the following statement to the commission: *'I have a property in this county in which no man can recollect a pauper'*. Francis O'Neill blamed the poverty of the labouring classes on the 'want of employment and attention to their wants by the farmers'. In some instances the condition of the small tenantry was as bad as that of the labourers. On the other hand, McCrea believed that the large farmers had *'an appearance more comfort'* and *'a taste for a better style of living and appearing in public'*, though he was of the opinion that *'their circumstances are not better by any means'*.

The report includes drawings of farmhouses and cottages as well as maps showing how landholdings in a particular townland could be reorganised to the advantage of the occupiers. The appendix includes a list of the names of the subscribers to Templemoyle Agricultural Seminary near Eglinton in Co. Londonderry, 72 in total. There are also lists of tenants recently evicted from several townlands in Co. Monaghan.

Towns

It would be impossible to study towns fully in the first half of the nineteenth century without examining the many parliamentary papers that relate to them. The most important is the *First report of the commissioners appointed to inquire into the municipal corporations in Ireland* of 1835.[37] The report includes sections on the existing state of municipal corporations, defects in their constitution, the privileges of freemen and other members, their jurisdiction and powers in the administration of justice, and the nature of their tolls and customs. The appendix to the report contains a vast amount of information on Irish towns in the early nineteenth century. It is arranged by circuit: southern, midland, western, south-eastern, north-eastern and north-western. The reports from the towns provide information on such things as the charters of each town, the fairs and markets held there, the property owned by the corporation and its regulations. Occasionally there is a final section commenting on the present condition of the town.

Much is revealed about the historical origins of these towns, many of which were founded in the early seventeenth century as part of the scheme for the plantation in Ulster. St Johnstown in Co. Donegal was created a borough by a patent granted in 1618 to the Duke of Lennox, a kinsman of the king and one of the principal plantation grantees. Under the terms of the patent Lennox was to bring thirteen English or Scottish settlers, *'chiefly artificiers and mechanics'*, to St Johnstown along with their families. Each of the families should be assigned a plot of ground measuring 20 feet broad by 96 feet long for a house and garden. All of the houses were to be arranged *'in the form of a street'*, with six houses on one side and seven on the other. The thirteen settlers were to become the burgesses of the town. St Johnstown was intended to be a place of refuge and defence for the settlers living in its vicinity, but in the view of the commissioners writing in the mid-1830s, it *'appears never to have reached a state of strength or population in which it could have been qualified to effectuate that purpose'*. At that time it was no more than a *'collection of a few houses'*.

The returns from other towns include detailed accounts of expenditure by the corporation on such things as paving streets, repairing the market house etc. The return for Londonderry includes lists of individuals who received charitable donations from the corporation going back to 1811. For Londonderry there are also extracts from the town's bye-laws for the seventeenth century.

Most of these accounts of expenditure are from the 1820s or early 1830s, though the return for Enniskillen includes a detailed account for the middle of the eighteenth century. Some of the reports provide an indication of the nature of the relationship between the town's proprietor and its inhabitants. The corporation of Enniskillen, for instance, was dominated by the Earl of Enniskillen and it was here, more so than anywhere else, that the commissioners found among many of the town's inhabitants there was *'a strong sense of apprehension of offending the patron by coming forward to give evidence in open court, singularly coupled with a disposition to acknowledge his private virtues'*.

Several other papers relate to towns and are worth looking at. Among the Accounts and Papers for 1831 - 2 is a return entitled *Parliamentary representation: boundary reports (Ireland)*.[38] The Ulster towns covered include Armagh, Belfast, Carrickfergus, Coleraine, Downpatrick, Dungannon, Enniskillen, Lisburn, Londonderry and Newry. The return for each town covers such things as a general description of the town, its manufactures and trade and a list of its MPs since 1801.

Of additional interest for those studying municipal government is *A return of the names of those towns in Ireland in which the act of 9 Geo. 4, c.82 has been brought into operation*, 1843.[39] The act in question concerned the provision of *'lighting, cleansing and watching'* of towns in Ireland. This provides the names and occupations of town commissioners appointed in each town affected by the above act; towns in Ulster include Armagh, Ballymena, Ballyshannon, Banbridge, Belturbet, Cavan, Coleraine, Downpatrick, Dromore, Dungannon, Lisburn, Lurgan, Monaghan, Newry, Newtownards, Portadown and Strabane. The returns provide an indication of the status and occupations of the town commissioners. For example, the commissioners for the town of Armagh included five esquires, eight merchants, four innkeepers, two woollen drapers and a land surveyor and a tanner. Elsewhere doctors, surgeons and priests served as town commissioners.

The Established Church

For anyone seeking information on the Church of Ireland, the Established Church in Ireland until 1869, the most valuable paper is the *Third report of His Majesty's commissioners on ecclesiastical revenue and patronage in Ireland* of 1836.[40] The digest of the inquiry lists all of the parishes in Ireland and includes much information on ecclesiastical matters of the Church of Ireland in each parish. In addition to the acreage and population of the parish, the name of the minister and his income, together with information of the glebe house (minister's residence) and church are given. The information on the glebe houses and churches should be of interest to architectural historians.

According to this report, the glebe house in the parish of Leckpatrick, Co. Tyrone, was built in 1792, though at what cost was not known. It was described as 'very commodious'. The church was built in 1817 and enlarged in 1824, and was capable of accommodating 600 people. The report also revealed that in the past year the parish had spent more than £13 on the care of abandoned children and on providing coffins for the poor. In the parish of Maghera in

House of Commons Debate

Co. Londonderry the glebe house was built in 1825 at a cost of more than £3,000. Nearly £1,800 of this had been provided by the rector from his own private funds. On the other hand, in the parish of Learmount, also in Co. Londonderry, there was no glebe house and instead the minister rented a house at a cost of £30 per annum.

A major part of the Church of Ireland's income was derived from tithes and this subject can be examined in some detail in the *Report from the select committee on tithes in Ireland* of 1831 - 2.[41] The minutes of evidence include interviews with various individuals on the setting and collection of tithes and the problems and difficulties associated with this. The appendix contains letters from across Ireland on the collection of tithes from different parishes.

Education

Numerous reports in the parliamentary papers deal with the issue of education. In the mid to late 1820s nine reports were produced by the Commissioners on the Irish Education Inquiry. Of particular interest is the *Second report of the commissioners of Irish education inquiry* of 1826 - 7.[42] The results of this make interesting reading and provide a fascinating insight into local education provision in Ireland at this time. The appendix to the report lists all the schools then operating and is arranged by parish. Information is provided on the name of the schoolmaster, the type of building in which classes were held, the number of pupils and the way in which the school was supported financially.

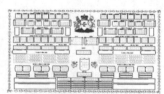

The return for the parish of Leckpatrick in Co. Tyrone can be examined in more detail. In 1826 there were seven schools in this parish: Leckpatrick, Strabane, Ballee, Ballylaw, Balnegran and two in Cloghcor. All of the schools were mixed, though there was only one Catholic pupil in Ballylaw. The buildings in which classes were held varied greatly. The parish school in Leckpatrick townland was stated to have been a *'good slated house'* which was believed to have cost £40.0s.0d. Margaret Gibson's girls' school in Strabane was a good house costing £200. The rest were held in either thatched houses or small cabins which were worth as little as £3.0s.0d. All of the schools were pay schools and the total income of the master or mistress could vary from the £37 10s 0d. received by Margaret Gibson in Strabane to £6 5s 0d. received by Andrew Stephenson in Ballylaw.

The school with the largest attendance was Ballee where there were over one hundred pupils, while there were fewer than thirty pupils at Ballylaw and Balnegran. The funding of each of the schools also varied. The rector of Leckpatrick contributed £5 towards the parish school. The Kildare Place Society contributed towards the running costs of the schools in Strabane, Ballee and James McDavit's school in Cloghcor. The school in Ballee was particularly fortunate, because not only did it have funding from the Kildare Place Society, the master, Thomas Edmonson, received annually £5.0s.0d from the Rev. F. Brownlow and another £5.0s.0d from the marquis of Abercorn. The patron of James Kelly's school in Cloghcor was a Mr McCrea who each year paid £7 4s..0d towards Kelly's salary. The rest of the schools were not connected to any outside society and depended solely on pupils' fees for their maintenance.

Accessing the papers

Having discussed the value and importance of parliamentary papers to the local and family historian, it is important to provide some information on how they can be accessed, particularly in view of the fact that many people are put off using them because of the perceived difficulty in accessing near complete sets in near perfect condition. There are a number of useful guides to the papers. Of these the weightiest is Peter Cockton's recently published five-volume index with an additional volume serving as a guide to the papers on microfiche. Also of tremendous value and very handy to use is A. and J. Maltby, *Ireland in the Nineteenth Century: a breviate of official publications* (Oxford, 1979).

The work of Professor and Mrs Ford should also be acknowledged. In 1968 they reprinted with an introduction the *Catalogue of parliamentary reports and a breviate of their contents, arranged under heads according to the subjects, 1696–1834*, first published in 1834. They were also responsible for the *Select list of British parliamentary papers, 1833–99* (Shannon, 1969). Joseph Canning's article, 'British Parliamentary Papers as a source for local history', in *Ulster Local Studies*, vol.11, no.1 (Summer, 1989) provides a useful introduction to the subject and was very helpful in the writing of this essay.

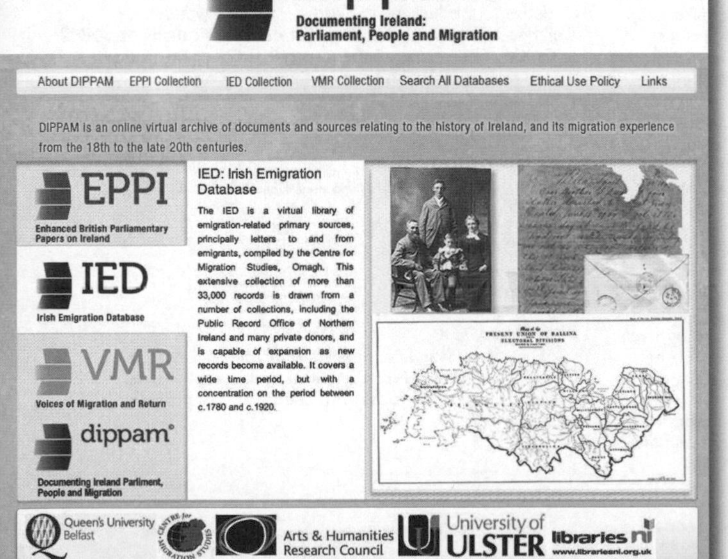

Prior to the advent of internet, one of the biggest difficulties for researchers was in accessing reasonably complete sets of the papers. Most university and major public libraries across the British Isles will have good collections, though with varying degrees of comprehensiveness. One of the more complete collections is housed in the library of Queen's University Belfast, and this was extensively drawn upon in the preparation of this essay. In addition to the original papers, there is also the Irish University Press set of over 1,000 volumes into which were grouped all the basic source material on a wide range of significant subject areas – the largest single printing project undertaken by a publishing house (www.britishparliamentarypapers.com).

There are now several ways of accessing parliamentary papers online. Researchers will find helpful the Enhanced British Parliamentary Papers on Ireland (EPPI) database which is now available via the DIPPAM (Documenting Ireland: Parliament, People and Migration) website (www.dippam.ac.uk). The completed EPPI archive contains over 14,000 documents, comprising bill, reports, commissions of enquiry and statistics from 1801 to 1922. The House of Commons Parliamentary Papers website (http://parlipapers.chadwyck.co.uk) also allows access to British parliamentary papers via subscribing institutions. Some of the volumes of parliamentary papers are available through Google Books (http://books.google.com).

Conclusion

The importance of parliamentary papers lies not just in their value to social and economic historians looking at Ireland as a whole, but also in their usefulness to the local historian wanting to find out more about his area and the genealogist seeking information on his or her family history. Much of the value of the reports lies in the fact that the oral evidence is printed *verbatim*. It is thus possible to find out exactly what people were saying and what they thought about specific issues. The island-wide coverage of some of the reports, such as the Devon Commission, means that it is possible to make comparisons between different parts of Ireland and place one's own area in a wider context. The papers highlighted here can be used in conjunction with other sources such as the Ordnance Survey Memoirs and landed estate records to build up a picture of what life was like for everyday people in Ireland in the nineteenth century.

Notes

There are several different ways of referencing parliamentary papers. I have chosen the rather simple method of giving the title of the paper, the year in which it was published and the volume it appears in for that year. I have resisted the temptation to include page numbers so as to avoid confusion between the page number of the paper and the page number of the volume. If the title of the paper appears in the main text it does not reappear in the endnotes.

1 *Report from select committee on Carrickfergus forgeries election petition*. 1830–1: III. Their expenses are given in 1830 - 1: X.
2 *A return of the names, occupations and residences of the registered freeholders, leaseholders and £10 householders, Carrickfergus*, 1834: XLIII
3 *A return of the names, occupations and residences of the freemen of Carrickfergus*, 1834: XLIII
4 *A return of the names, occupations and residences of mayor, sheriffs, aldermen and burgesses of the corporation of Carrickfergus*, 1834: XLIII.
5 *Report from the select committee on the Belfast election compromise, together with the minutes of evidence*, 1842: V.
6 *A return of the persons admitted, elected, or sworn freemen of the corporation of Coleraine, in Ireland, or to whom the freedom was granted from 1st January 1831 to 1st January 1834*, 1834: XLIII; *A return of the several aldermen and other common councilmen, now existing, of the corporation of Coleraine*, 1834: XLIII; *Return of persons admitted or elected in corporation of Coleraine*. 1831 - 2: XXXVI.
7 *A return of the number of informations filed in Her Majesty's Court of Exchequer in Ireland for the recovery of penalties of offences against the excise laws in ... 1841, 1842, 1843 ...* 1843: L.
8 1837–8: XLVI.
9 1830–31: IV.
10 *A return of the names of all stipendary magistrates in Ireland*. 1831–2: XXXIII.
11 *A return of the names of magistrates included in the commission of the peace in Ireland up to the latest period*. 1831–2: XXV.
12 *A return of the names of all persons receiving pensions or gratuities from the superannuation fund or reward funds of the Force*, 1843: L; *A return of the names of all persons receiving pensions or gratuities from the superannuation fund . . . for the year ending 31 December 1843*, 1844: XLIII; *A return of the names of all persons receiving pensions or gratuities from the superannuation fund*'. 1845: XLV.
13 *Returns of the numbers and names of the barristers appointed in the present year to be supernumerary prosecuting counsel in each circuit in Ireland*. 1842: XXXVIII.
14 *Report from the select committee appointed to inquire into the nature, character, extent and tendency of Orange lodges, associations or societies in Ireland; with the minutes of evidence and appendix*. 1835: XV; *Third report from the select committee appointed to inquire into the nature, character, extent and tendency of Orange lodges, associations or societies in Ireland, with minutes of evidence and appendix*. 1835: XVI.
15 1837: XV. *There is a further report with the same title in* 1837–8: XVII.
16 *A return of the name of each seneschal or steward of a manor in Ireland with the date of his appointment and the person by whom he was appointed*. 1842: XXXVIII.
17 1822: VII.
18 1829: XXII.
19 *A return of the names of each person in each year since the 24th of June 1791, who has been examined by the governor and directors of the Apothecaries' Hall in Dublin and who has received a certificate of his proper qualification to become an apprentice to learn the business of an apothecary*. 1829: XXII.
20 *A return of the name of each person in each year since the 24th June 1791, who has been examined by the governor and directors of the Apothecaries' Hall in Dublin, and who has received a certificate of his proper qualification to become an assistant or journeyman to the business of an apothecary*. 1829: XXII.
21 *A return of the name of each person in each year since the 24th June 1791, who has been examined by, and received a certificate from the governor and director of the Apothecaries' Hall in Dublin, of his qualification to open a shop and practise as an apothecary in Ireland*. 1829: XXII.
22 *A return of the number of prosecutions, the name of the person prosecuted, the date of each prosecution, together with the offence committed against the Act 31 Geo. III from the 24th June 1791, until the 25th March 1829; also the number of penalties, with the name of the person from whom recovered, and the date of recovery of said penalty*. 1829: XXII.
23 1843: L.
24 1843: L.
25 *Report from the select committee on pawnbroking in Ireland; together with the minutes of evidence, appendix and index*. 1837 - 8: XVII.
26 *A return ... of the names and places of abode of every blacksmith whose forge has been registered ... during the last ten years*. 1843: L.
27 *A return of the names and particulars as set forth in the excise entries of each separate and distinct grocer or co-partnership in each excise district in Ireland who took out or renewed the spirit grocer's licence ... from 5 July 1838 to 5 July 1844 ...* 1845: XLV.
28 1837: XXII.
29 1809: III.
30 This map has proved to be extremely useful to archaeologists from Queen's University Belfast who were carrying out an excavation at one of the medieval castles in the town.
31 *First report of commissioners for inquiring into the condition of the poorer classes in Ireland*. 1835: XXXII. The appendices and supplements to the appendices are spread over several volumes: 1835: XXXII; 1836: XXX, XXXI, XXXII, XXXIII & XXXIV. In 1845: XLIII & XLIV there are indexes to the reports of the Irish poor law commissioners for 1835 - 39.
32 *Returns of copies of correspondence and documents relative to the building of Castlederg Union workhouse; architects' estimates, building contract, specifications, etc*. 1842: XXXVI. The returns for the other union workhouses have similar titles and are in the same volume.
33 1844: XXX.
34 1844: XXX.
35 1841, 1st session: XI.
36 *Report of Her Majesty's Commissioners of Inquiry into the state of the law and practice in respect of the occupation of land in Ireland*. 1845: XIX, XX, XXI & XXII.
37 1835: XXVII, XXVIII; 1836: XXIV.
38 1831 - 2: XLIII.
39 1843: L.
40 1836: XXV.
41 1831 - 2: XXI.
42 1826 - 7: XII.

This essay was first published in *Familia: Ulster Genealogical Review* No. 18 (2002) and is reproduced here in slightly amended form with the permission of the publisher.

The Spanish Civil War 1936 - 1939

Joseph ONeill

The year 2012 marked the 76th anniversary of the Spanish Civil War. The war divided the nation as Irishmen fought and died on both sides. The National Archives in London released MI5 documents which throw new light on an old controversy.

The Spanish Civil War – in which half a million people lost their lives – sparked profound controversy in Ireland. When Spain's Republican government – a coalition of socialists, communist and anarchists, backed by Stalin's USSR – was threatened by Franco's Nationalists – a mixture of conservatives and fascists, backed by Hitler and Mussolini – the Irish government espoused a policy of neutrality and non-intervention and advised its citizens against involvement.

Yet most Irish people saw the outbreak in July 1936 as something of monumental significance, the outcome of which would determine the fate of Europe. Many saw it as a struggle between the two great ideologies of the 20th century, communism and Fascism. For others, it was a struggle between godless Bolshevism and Christian civilization.

Eoin O'Duffy 1922

When war broke out in Spain Europe was already in the grip of an international crisis. Both Mussolini and Hitler, the leaders of the two great fascist powers, Italy and Germany, seemed determined to undermine the precarious peace that had prevailed in Europe since the end of the Great War. However, a victory for the Republic, backed by Stalin's murderous tyranny, would extend communist influence to the Mediterranean and provide a base from which Bolshevism might conquer Europe. But it was Republican atrocities against the church which most impressed Irish opinion. Early in the war the Republicans massacred four thousand clerics and in total as many as 72,000 civilians – many of them for practising their faith. In addition, churches and convents were burnt in imitation of Stalin's savage suppression of the faith in the USSR. It is hardly surprising that most people in Ireland regarded the Spanish Republic as the enemy of Christianity.

The conflict in Spain also mirrored that in Ireland. Eoin O'Duffy, a general in the Free State army during the Irish Civil War, founded the Blueshirts who had much in common with European fascism and they frequently engaged in violent confrontations with communists on the streets of Ireland's cities.

It was Count Ramirez de Arellano who encouraged Irishmen to come to the defence of Christianity in Spain. His call was taken up by O'Duffy, who by 1936 was the leader of Ireland's National Corporate Party, which looked to European fascism for its inspiration. O'Duffy called for volunteers for his 'anti-Red Crusade' and 7,000 men came forward. Of these 700 were selected for the Irish Brigade – *La Bandera Irelandesa*. Of these two hundred travelled overland to Spain while five hundred more followed in December 1936 on the German ship *Urundi*, out of Galway.

They landed in El Ferrol, from where they travelled to their training camp at Cáceras. (In the church of Santa Domingo, where these men worshipped, there is an impressive plaque commemorating their contribution to the war.) Clad in green uniforms emblazoned with a silver harp, they formed four companies in the Fifteenth Battalion of the Spanish Foreign Legion.

In February 1937 they fought in the crucial battle of Jarama, where immediately they suffered four losses. They again suffered losses in the attack on Titulcia before being withdrawn to defensive positions at La Maranosa.

By January 1937 another six hundred volunteers were ready and waiting at Galway, but were never collected. The political situation in Spain had changed and the Nationalists no longer wanted foreign troops with the result that the Brigade was withdrawn in the summer of 1937. Their homecoming reception was less enthusiastic than they expected and the entire escapade damaged O'Duffy's standing.

'You are legend. We shall not Forget You.'
Dolores Ibarruri
Farewell address to International Brigade, Barcelona 28th October 1938

In September 1936 the Executive Committee of the Communist International – the mechanism by which Stalin sought to control national communist parties – announced that it would raise an International Brigade to fight for the Spanish Republic. Individual Communist parties were assigned the task of recruiting men in their own country, so it was the Communist Party of Ireland which recruited the men who joined what became known as the Connolly Column. Approximately one in three lost their lives.

As the Spanish Civil War broke out Peader O'Donnell – a leading figure in left-wing politics — was already in Spain, participating in the People's Olympics – the alternative to the Olympics being staged in Hitler's Berlin. After fighting with the anarchists he returned to Ireland and spear-headed the drive for Republican recruits. In this he worked with IRA men Bill Gannon of the Irish Communist Party and Robert Hilliard – ex cleric, athlete and Marxist atheist.

In December 1936 Frank Ryan led a group of eighty men to Spain to fight for the Republic. Having reached their training camp at Albacete their extreme Irish republican sentiments brought them into conflict with some of their British counterparts who had served as Black and Tans in the Irish War of Independence. Consequently most joined the largely American Fifteenth Brigade and became known as the Connolly Column, though other Irishmen fought in different units.

Their first action for Republican cause was on the Cordoba front in December 1936 in the attack on Lopera. The Connolly Column also saw action at Jarama in February 1937 as part of the attack on Gandesa. In July 1938 they fought in the Battle of Ebro before being repatriated in September, when the International Brigades were disbanded.

What do we know of the men who fought?

Only 29 of the 104 who fought for the Republic were from Northern Ireland and most were communists or fellow travellers. Many were members of the Republican Congress and trade unionists and had some military experience. Fr. Michael O'Flanagan was unique among Catholic clergy in being the only priest to speak out on behalf of the Spanish Republic.

Many of these who fought for Franco had fought in the War of Independence and the Irish Civil War and were ex-Irish Army soldiers. Many were motivated by religious fervour.

For those trying to trace ancestors who might have fought in Spain the newly released material is invaluable as the Irish government destroyed its own records in 1940.

These Files, labelled KV5/112 at *www.nationalarchives.gov.uk/documentsonline/spanish-civil-war.asp* contains basic information collected by the British Security Service on men and women it believed to be travelling to Spain to fight with the International Brigades, including the date and place of departure, the brigade to which they were attached, and the date of their return to Britain. Other files in the KV5 series provide further details of their activities in support of the International Brigades.

Further Research
The Marx Memorial Library
http://marx-memorial library.org/index.php?option=com_content&view=article&id=28&Itemid=13
houses the records of those who fought in the International Brigades.
Websites devoted to Ireland's role in the Spanish Civil War.
Among the best is ***Ireland and the Spanish Civil War http://irelandscw.com/*** which is a constantly expanding body of articles and research on Irish involvement in the Spanish Civil War.
It includes a Roll of Honour of soldiers from Ireland who died fighting for the Spanish Republic.
You will find a list of survivors of the International Brigades at *http://irishcitizenarmy.tripod.com/spain-surv.html* and a list of notable figures who found for the Republic *at http://cn.wikipedia.org/wiki/Irish_socialist_volunteers_in_the_Spanish_Civil_War.*
The best general introduction to Ireland's role in the war is *Irish Politics and the Spanish Civil War* by Fearghal McGarry Cork University Press ISBN 1 85918 240 2

From Gibraltar to Belfast

Chris Paton

Occasionally in our family history research we may come across a record that radically transforms the story of an ancestor, sending us off in a whole new direction on a relentless pursuit for more information. In the case of my great great grandmother Florence Graham, née Halliday, such a discovery raised as many questions as it provided answers. Little did I know when I first started my research that far from having been born and raised in 19th century Belfast, *'wee Flo'* had in fact originated considerably further away!

Florence was the first of three wives to Edwin Graham, a riveter from Belfast, and the mother of my great grandfather Ernest, who was born in the city in 1893. As many will know, researching Irish ancestry until recent times has not been the easiest of tasks. Often the loss of records in the 1922 civil war in Ireland is cited as the main reason, though in truth it has been as much about the historical lack of effort by Irish authorities to make their surviving records accessible online. Thankfully this is finally changing in a somewhat dramatic fashion, but when I first explored Ernest's story about eight years ago there was little source material readily available online to work with from my home in Scotland. I had a fortunate break in that I discovered that Edwin had been working in Barrow-in-Furness in England in 1881, where he was recorded in the census with his father Thomas, but by 1891 he had left Britain. With the common Ulster surname of Graham I soon found myself on a virtual hiding to nothing, and so parked my research into his story, and that of his family, for a better day.

It was not until the National Archives of Ireland made the 1911 Irish census freely available online at **www.census.nationalarchives.ie** in 2010 that I decided to have another look into the Grahams. I easily located Edwin and Florence in Belfast's Duncairn Gardens, but as well as Ernest, I not only discovered a further seven sons in the house, but also the fact that an additional nine children to the couple had all died prior to 1911. Six of the surviving boys recorded on the form were noted as coming from Ireland, one from England and another from Scotland. The biggest surprise however was to learn that Belfast lass Florence was not in fact Belfast born lass Florence at all. Despite residing at various points in both Britain and Ireland, the place of birth on the census form pointed to something much more remarkable – Florence had been born on the island of Gibraltar! What on Earth was her family doing there?

The fact that Florence's eldest son, also called Edwin, was born in Scotland, provided the starting point for some answers. Using the ScotlandsPeople website - **www.scotlandspeople.gov.uk** - I consulted his birth record and established that Florence's full name was in fact Florence Teresa Halliday. We are extremely fortunate here in Scotland in that from the advent of civil registration in 1855 the

country has provided considerably more information in its BMD records than its British and Irish counterparts, with most birth records noting the place of marriage for the parents. As such, I was immediately able to learn that Florence and Edwin senior had in fact married in Barrow-in-Furness on June 27th 1881. To follow this up I then obtained a copy of their marriage certificate from the English based General Register Office - **www.gro.gov.uk/gro/content/** - and from this I learned that Florence's father was apparently called William Alexander Halliday. The record helpfully noted that William was a deceased bandmaster at this stage, implying a military connection.

The next task was to source Florence's birth certificate in Gibraltar. The indexes to most overseas BMD records concerning British subjects, including military registered events, are freely available to browse on the Family Relatives website - **www.familyrelatives.com** and in a fully searchable format on FindmyPast - **www.findmypast.co.uk**

Through these I located an index entry in the *GRO Regimental Birth Indices* collection for a Florence T. Halliday, and again ordered up the certificate from the English GRO. When it arrived the document duly confirmed her full name and her date of birth as September 7th 1863, but stated that her father was called Corporal Alexander Halliday of the 2nd battalion of the 2nd Regiment of Foot, with her mother's name given as Teresa.

Now knowing the names of Florence's parents I next decided to see if I could find their own marriage record. There was again no entry identified in the domestic British or Irish indexes, and so I tried the overseas records once more. Within the *GRO Ionian Islands Civil Register of Marriages* I soon found a record of an Alexander William Halliday marrying in Corfu in 1862. When the certificate arrived from the GRO a week later, it revealed that Alexander William Halliday, again noted as a corporal, was the son of William Alexander and Martha Ann Halliday, whilst his spouse was noted as Teresa Mooney, daughter of Thomas and Mary Ann Mooney.

On browsing through the indexes I had been keeping an eye out for further mentions of any Hallidays registered with the 2nd Regiment, and discovered the birth of a William Halliday in 1866 in Bermuda. Just how much of the world had my ancestors seen?! On a whim I ordered the record up, and sure enough, I duly found that the couple had had a son there also on August 16th 1866. This William was referred in most records after as *'Alexander'* or *'Alexander William'* the order of his forenames changed as often as his father's! One thing was for certain, however, and that was that all of this was a very long way from Belfast.

It now seemed likely that this branch of my family may not have been from Ulster at all, though with Florence's mum having the surname Mooney, an Irish connection still seemed possible. The next step was to find out more about the 2nd Regiment of Foot, also known as the Queen's Royal Surrey Regiment. I purchased a book from eBay entitled *'The Queen's Royal Regiment (West Surrey)'* by Jock Haswell, which more than anything began to flesh out why the Hallidays had spent the 1860s travelling half way around the world.

The regiment's second battalion was formed in Colchester in 1857, and in 1859 was first posted to Malta, before setting off for Corfu. Whilst the first battalion waged war in China, the second spent a peaceful year in 1860 on garrison duty in Cephalonia and Zante, followed with duty between 1862 and 1865 at Gibraltar. Clearly after marrying Alexander senior in Corfu Teresa must have accompanied him first to Gibraltar, and then onto Bermuda. In 1865 the regiment set sail for Bermuda with over 700 men, and to its first real battle, though tragically it was to be against an enemy that could not be seen.

The regiment arrived on July 15th 1865, with a third of the strength posted to St. George's, an area which from June had been described as a *'tainted district'* with yellow fever, according to the Freeman's Journal

Gibraltar

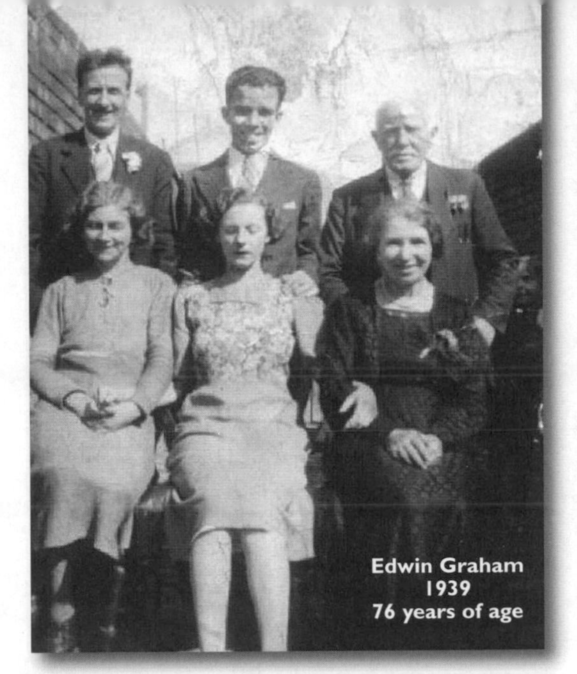
Edwin Graham
1939
76 years of age

newspaper of October 31st 1866. A local doctor urged the military commander not to base his soldiers there, but the advice was ignored, and within a few weeks, almost 250 soldiers were ill with the fever. When it had run its course, well over a hundred men, including fourteen officers, were killed by the plague. The conditions had been appalling, with a Doctor Barrow, one of many brought hurriedly from Canada to treat the victims, providing a grim description of life at the general hospital during the epidemic. 'The sick were not only lying around the wards, but may be said to have covered the entire floor. There lay these unhappy men on the floor of the pesthouse, ejecting black vomit over one another.' All of the doctors were struck down, with four of them also dying. In the aftermath of such a horrific ordeal, Teresa gave birth to her son.

Haswell records that *'The Queen's survived their many ordeals in the Carribean with . . . the highest credit and an enhanced reputation.'* The question now raised, however, was whether Florence's father had made it out alive. In order to establish what had become of him, I made a trip to the National Archives in London where I was able to consult the muster rolls for his regiment. These confirmed that Alexander had in fact been a well travelled man long before he had met Teresa! He had originally enlisted with another unit, the 14th Regiment of Foot, from at least 1844 (most likely as a boy soldier), and as well as serving in Canada, Britain and Ireland, he had also fought in the Crimean War, for which he had received a medal. In 1859, after a period of illness in England, he had transferred from the 14th into the Queen's at Corfu. Had Teresa perhaps met him in England and travelled with him?

One thing the records could confirm was that the family had most definitely been based in Bermuda throughout the epidemic of 1865. The strain of the proceedings had clearly affected Alexander, as he was not only hospitalised in the first quarter of 1865, but also again later in the year in both September and October. Seriously ill by this stage, on January 31st 1866 he passed away. The final entry for Alexander in the regimental muster rolls revealed yet another surprise in that his place of birth was described as the East Indies. I later discovered from records held at the British Library in London that he had in fact been born in Bangalore, India, in 1829, and it is possible that his mother, Martha Taylor, may well have been Anglo-Indian.

With Teresa now stranded in Bermuda in 1866 with two children, Florence and Alexander junior, she was given just eight shillings and sixpence by the military from her husband's pay, after his debts had been deducted. Her movements in the next decade are somewhat vague, but it appears that she somehow managed to make her way towards Ireland, and to settle with her family in Dublin. On August 1st 1878, aged just eleven years and eleven months Alexander junior was admitted to the Royal Hibernian Military School in the city, originally a school set up for military orphans, as confirmed by enrolment records at the National Archives at Kew (TNA: WO 143/22).

Two years later young Alexander joined the 48th Brigade in Dublin, with the record noting his parents' names and two sisters, Florence and Sarah. This is the only reference found for a sister called Sarah to date, and I have as yet to establish when and where she was born, or what became of her. By the 1881 census, just two months before sister Florence married Edwin Graham, Alexander was also noted in England, based in Aldershot as a 14 year old private in the 1st Battalion of the 2nd Regiment of Foot, the Queen's Royals, his father's former regiment.

I later established that Alexander served in the army until 1902, with his Chelsea Pension discharge papers, available on FindmyPast - **www.findmypast.co.uk** - showing that he had served with distinction in India in the 1890s. The records also noted that his intended place of residence was 52 Benburb Street, Dublin. Once again I found myself returning to the resource where my ancestral research trip with the Hallidays had first commenced – the 1911 Irish census.

Using the census I was delighted to learn that Alexander was still in Dublin at this point, he being recorded as residing at 3 Synnott Row and with an occupation of *'motorman,'* as well as a description of being a military pensioner. His birthplace was noted as Bermuda, West Indies, and living with him in the house was his 39 year old wife of two years, Margaret (Hughes). To my

great joy there was also one other resident noted – his 75 year old mother, now listed as Teresa Burns, implying that she had remarried. Even better was the revelation that Teresa was indeed Irish, the record noting that she was a native of the City of Dublin.

One of the more fascinating revelations that I later established was the fact that Teresa, who had married in an Anglican ceremony to her soldier husband in Corfu, was in fact born a Roman Catholic in Dublin in October 1834, as noted on her baptismal record on the wonderful Irish Genealogy website at **www.irishgenealogy.ie**

In 1911 she was described as still being a follower of the Anglican faith – but her son Alexander, who had previously been baptised by the Church of England, was now conversely noted as a Roman Catholic! I later established that Teresa ended her days in Dublin in 1919, and was buried in the city's Glasnevin Cemetery, whilst Alexander also continued to live in the city until his own death in 1947, and was later buried in Mount Jerome Cemetery.

As for my direct ancestor Florence, based further north in Belfast, she tragically passed away just a few months after the 1911 census was recorded, on September 18th 1911, aged 48, with her cause of death noted as chronic nephritis. A simple fallen headstone at a forgotten grave in Belfast's City Cemetery is all that is left in the landscape to bear witness to her extraordinary travels, but her true legacy lies of course with the many descendants who have since succeeded her.

The Public Record Office of Northern Ireland

Dr Ann McVeigh

The Public Record Office of Northern Ireland (PRONI) is now open to the public in its new, state-of-the-art premises. Opening in March 2011, it was two months ahead of schedule, much to the delight of researchers both regular and new.

The new accommodation, which is fully compliant with DDA, comprises an expansive Public Search Room, with seating for 76; an integral microfilm area, accommodating 20 researchers and with two microfilm printers; internet and WiFi access and laptop-enabled tables. There are 35 computers giving access to the e-Catalogue and ordering system, while another 13 PCs will allow easy browsing of our databases, guides and website. The Reading Room, with seating for 80, provides greatly enhanced capacity and facilities for researchers, including access to the e-Catalogue and ordering system. A totally new feature is our self-service digital camera, where researchers can scan a document directly onto a USB pen (a small charge applies).

The storage repositories have been greatly expanded and improved with bespoke 'rolling rack' shelving systems, fully compliant with the British Standard for the preservation of archival documents. The spacious ground floor area houses reception; an exhibition area, which will feature '*A century of conflict, change and transformation*', our opening interactive exhibition; a lecture and a conference room; three information/orientation points; a meeting area; public utilities, and a café with internet access. All public areas are Wi-Fi enabled.

We are happy to welcome both individuals and groups to our new premises (although groups of six or more should book in advance), and we look forward to being a vibrant part of the Titanic Quarter community.

PRONI Website

For those starting their research for the first time, the PRONI website (www.proni.gov.uk) is a great place to begin as it contains information on the most useful archives to consult at PRONI, an updated set of PRONI's family and local history leaflets, and information on other sites that may be useful to your area of study. The '*Frequently Asked Questions*' page covers a host of topics. One of the most useful and popular parts of the PRONI website is our extensive introductions to over 140 major private collections. These give users an excellent overview of each archive as well as detailed historical background information. Increasingly, however, we are putting more databases and guides online.

Records Available On-line

Several major databases are available on-line:

The Freeholders' Records relating to the six counties of Northern Ireland from the mid 18th to early 19th centuries, record the name and place of residence of those who were entitled to vote (or who actually voted) at elections. This online resource of over 5,000 high quality images of the registers is fully searchable and provides direct access to a unique resource for family and local history for a period that has a scarcity of documentary evidence.

The Ulster Covenant contains the names and addresses of those who opposed Home Rule in the early part of the twentieth century. Almost half a million people signed either the Covenant (men), or

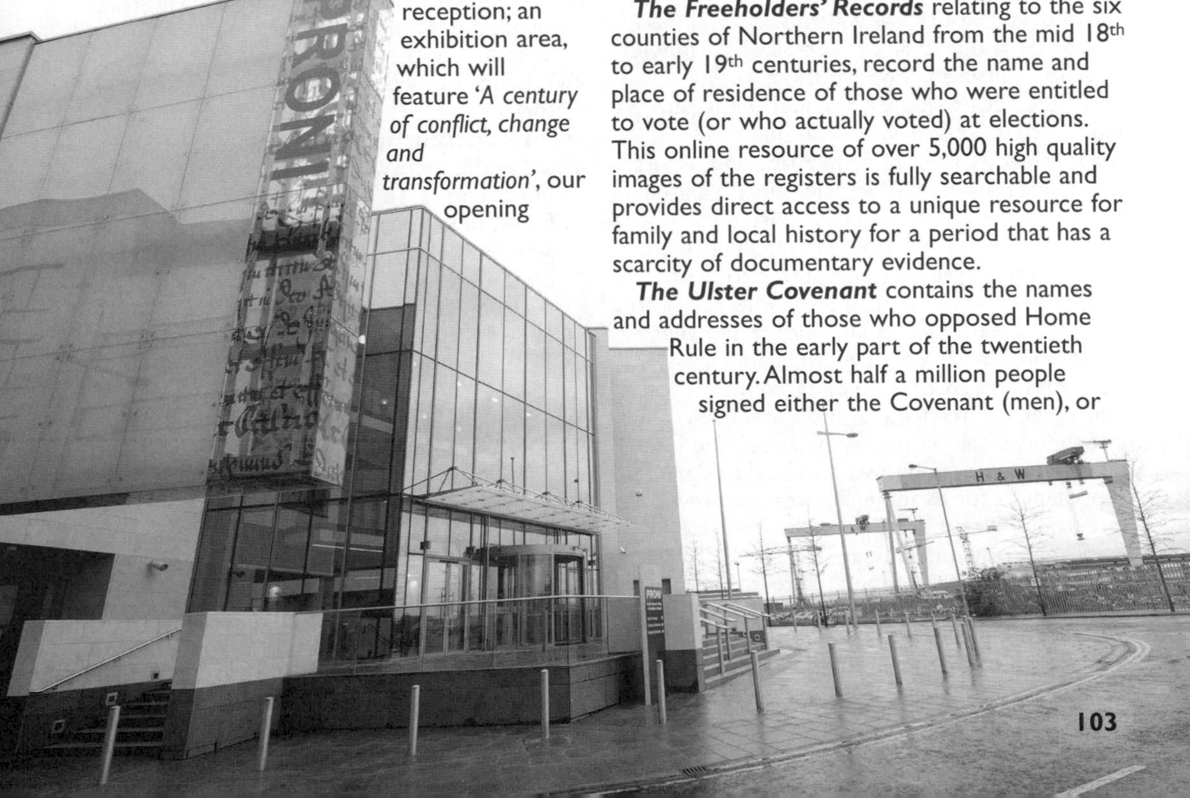

the Declaration (women) in September, 1912. The database is searchable by surname and each surname is linked to an image of the actual document showing the handwritten signature.

The Wills Index is now searchable online. This application provides a fully searchable index to the will calendar entries for the three District Probate Registries of Armagh, Belfast and Londonderry. The database covers the period 1858 - 1919 and 1922 - 1943. Part of 1921 has been added, with remaining entries for 1920 - 1921 to follow in the near future. Digitised images of entries from the copy will books covering the period 1858-1900 are now available online, allowing users to view the full content of a will. 93,388 will images are now available to view.

Although the original wills up to 1900 were destroyed and it is simply copies of these wills that have survived, they are the earliest complete set proved by the Supreme Court of Judicature in Ireland, who assumed responsibility for granting probate and letters of administration in 1858. The index is based on the entries in the will calendars that summarise every will proved and all letters of administration granted, amounting to over 148,000 entries. Although many wills relate to the professional classes and the landed gentry, most walks of life are covered, from farmers, labourers and grocers, to blacksmiths, innkeepers, watchmakers, and even a few people who died in the workhouse! The last testaments of well-known personalities are also represented, for example, Thomas Andrews, the director of Harland & Wolff who was aboard the Titanic when it sank in 1912, and Charles Lanyon, civil engineer and architect, who designed many of the finest buildings in Belfast, including Queen's University, the Custom House, and the Crumlin Road Court House.

Street Directories, previously on open access in the Search Room, were very heavily used and damage was becoming critical. Further handling would have endangered their long term preservation so it was decided to scan the directories to provide an on-line search. The online directories cover the years 1819 to 1900 but with some gaps in the series. PRONI does not hold copies of all street directories and even when the main run of the *Belfast and Ulster Street Directory* begins in 1852 there are gaps in the series up to 1900.

The directories were published for trade and business purposes largely as a result of the growth in trade at home and with the wider world, hence the emphasis on the listing of manufacturers, traders and merchants. Some, for example, Matier's 1835-6 *Directory* and the 1831-2 *Directory* feature only Belfast, but will also generally include a list of the gentry in the neighbourhood. These *'village directories'* include a list of the principal inhabitants living on the outskirts of Belfast, for example in Dunmurry, Jordanstown and Newtownbreda, as well as an alphabetical listing referred to as *'Country Residents.'* Occasionally the directory is only for some provincial towns, for example the 1840 *New Commercial Directory of Armagh, Newry, Londonderry*, etc. While there are problems with their accuracy, they are nevertheless, an invaluable resource for family and local historians.

Name Search, launched in 2009, currently includes the following sets of indexes:

- index to pre-1858 wills (which are to be found in various collections in PRONI) and a selection of diocesan will and administration bond indexes
- surviving fragments of the 1740 and the 1766 religious census returns
- 1775 dissenters petitions
- pre-1920 coroners' inquest papers

The Public Record Office of Northern Ireland (PRONI) is committed to making its archives more widely available. While PRONI's eCatalogue has made access to PRONI's archives easier and speedier, in most instances it does not provide information on the actual content of the archives. PRONI has therefore embarked on a project to improve access tocontent by producing or reproducing indexes to some of the most popular records.

Continued on page 106 . . .

Public Record Office of Northern Ireland

PRONI

Explore your family and local history
Enjoy talks and lectures
Embark on research
Engage with exhibitions

Exhibitions
A century of change, conflict and transformation.
A semi-permanent exhibition exploring economy, society, leisure and governance, featuring a display on the Blitz experience. Also, temporary and travelling exhibitions, including some never before seen in Northern Ireland, such as the ***Ground Zero 360°*** photographic exhibition.

Talks and events
Join our ***Distribution List***.
Simply send your name and email address to proni@dcalni.gov.uk and we will keep you informed by email of all upcoming PRONI events, including lectures, book launches and displays.

Research
PRONI is the official archive for Northern Ireland, holding over three million public and privately deposited records. Many of these can be used to uncover family or local history and are freely available. No appointment necessary.

PRONI promotes and makes available the unique archival heritage of Northern Ireland for present and future generations.

Public Record Office of Northern Ireland (PRONI) 2 Titanic Boulevard, BELFAST, BT3 9HQ
E: proni@dcalni.gov.uk W. www.proni.gov.uk T: (+44) 028 90 534800 F. (+44) 028 90 534900

About the pre-1858 wills index: Although most originals were destroyed in the fire in the Public Record Office of Ireland (Dublin) in 1922, copies of testamentary records or extracts from them survive in a wide variety of PRONI sources. The pre-1858 wills index is an attempt to bring together pre-1858 wills and administrations found within the archives in PRONI. There are over 15,500 entries in this index. If a copy does survive, this will be noted.

About the 1740 and 1766 religious census: These returns are not only of value to the family and local historian but to those interested in Irish surnames and how they have been anglicised. The returns lists the names of heads of households arranged largely by county, barony and parish and in at least half of the returns there is a breakdown by townland. No further information is given about the individuals. The returns show religion as either Roman Catholic (referred to as 'Papists') or Protestant. Protestants were sometimes distinguished as either Church of Ireland, or Dissenters, with Dissenters being mainly Presbyterians. The returns also give an account of any Roman Catholic priests operating in the parish and their names. There is often more than one person of the same name listed in a townland/parish but we have no way of knowing whether this was in fact the case or if names were duplicated in transcription.

About the Dissenters' Petition: The petitions are lists of names of Dissenters arranged either by parish, by congregation, by town and neighbourhood or in one instance by barony. Occasionally, members of the Established Church also signed the petitions. The lists usually indicate whether the signatories were Dissenters or Established Church members, although there are occasions when no such information is recorded.

About the pre-1910 coroners' inquest papers: Coroners in Northern Ireland are either barristers or solicitors and are appointed by the Lord Chancellor. They inquire into deaths that are unexpected or unexplained, a result of violence, negligence or accident, or any other unusual circumstances. Coroners' records held by PRONI date from 1872 to 1997 and are now referenced on the Name Search database. They contain details of the surname, forename, address, date of death and date of inquest.

A relatively small volume of inquests have survived for the former part of this period (1872 - c.1960) in comparison to a much larger volume which has been retained in recent years (including the Troubles period). Name Search has indexed most inquest papers for the period 1872-1920 and the original documents are open to the public for this period. More recent inquest papers are closed to the public but requests for information can be made in writing to PRONI (see below for information on access).

PRONI does not take every inquest record created by the coroners, and indeed many older inquests have not survived. Consequently, if a record does not exist that does not necessarily mean that an inquest did not take place.

PRONI Photographs on Flickr; images from the archives are now available on the photo-sharing website *'Flickr.'* A selection of images from the Allison photographic collection can now be viewed on PRONI's Flickr Photostream. You can view the images without a Flickr account but if you want to leave comments about the photographs, you will have to create a Flickr account. A basic Flickr account is free.

The first collection of PRONI images to be made available on Flickr are wedding and family group portraits taken by the Allison Photographic Studios, Armagh, between circa 1900 and 1955. The photos are arranged in sets alphabetically by family name, or you can use the search box to search for a particular name - just make sure you are searching the PRONI Photostream and not the entire Flickr site! Take a look to see if any of your ancestors appear in the shots and feel free to add a comment. Initially, 200 images were uploaded to Flickr, but now the entire collection of 1,530 wedding and family group portraits are available.

GUIDES

On-line Guide to Church Records: Church records are an invaluable source for the family historian, especially those that pre-date Civil Registration of births, deaths and marriages, introduced in Ireland in 1864. PRONI's *Guide to Church Records* is an easy way to identify what churches are in a parish, what records exist for each church, the covering dates for each series of records (for example, baptisms, marriages, vestry minutes etc.) and their PRONI reference number. Denominations included are: Church of Ireland, Roman Catholic, Presbyterian, Non-Subscribing Presbyterian, Reformed Presbyterian, Methodist, Moravian, Congregational, Baptist and Religious Society of Friends ('Quakers'). Normally, there will be more than one denomination of church in each parish. The denomination of a church can be identified in the Guide by the preceding code (for example, C.I. = Church of Ireland; P. = Presbyterian Church and R.C. = Roman Catholic Church). The majority of parishes covered in the Guide are located within the six counties of Northern Ireland; however, PRONI holds some records from parishes in the Republic of Ireland, particularly the border counties of Donegal, Cavan, Monaghan, Leitrim and Louth. You will still have to visit PRONI to see the actual records but at least by checking this guide, you can be confident that your journey will not be wasted.

Electronic Catalogue: Perhaps the jewel in our website's crown, the Electronic Catalogue (E-Catalogue) enables researchers to browse the lists of practically all our collections from the comfort of their own computers. Providing web access to over one and a quarter million catalogue entries, the E-Catalogue contains approximately 70% of PRONI's total catalogue of which almost 92% is relevant to family history. The database can be searched by keyword, such as a name, townland or subject matter; by date; or by PRONI reference number. Some private documents have been transcribed, thus removing the need to see the original in a number of cases. This resource has made it so much easier to carry out research 24/7.

Public Records

Many people are under the impression that, due to the fire in the Public Record Office of Ireland in the Four Courts in Dublin, there are no surviving public records before in 1922. In fact, there are many series of records that go back to the early 19th and even into the 18th century. For example, the Grand Jury Presentment Books that give the names of those who received money for the construction and repair of roads, bridges, gaols, and other public works, date back to the 1760s.

Other early sources include:

- Valuation records, dating from the 1830s to the present day
- Tithe Applotment books, 1823-37,
- Copy wills, 1838-c.1900,
- Original wills 1900 to 2004
- Registers and inspectors' observation books of approximately 1,600 national/public elementary/primary schools, 1870s – c.1950s
- Grant-aid applications of the Commissioners of National Education, 1832 to 1889;
- Ordnance Survey maps (various scales) 1831 - present;
- Minutes, indoor and outdoor relief registers, and other papers of the Boards of Guardians who administered the workhouse system from 1838 to 1948;
- Records, including admission registers, of lunatic asylums, some dating back to the mid-19th century (but these are subject to extended closure for 100 years);
- Title deeds, leases and wills in the Irish Land

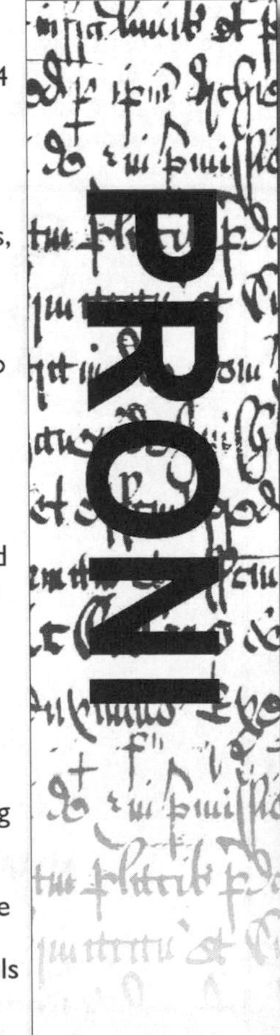

Commission and the Land Purchase Commission archive, some of which date back into the 18th century.

Guides to using the more popular collections, such as the tithe applotment books, the large scale Ordnance Survey town plans, education records and probate records, are available in the PRONI search room.

Private Archives

Privately deposited records are also available at PRONI and can often be very adequate substitutes for those public records destroyed in the Four Courts Fire. The most important of those are:

- records of solicitors' firms, which include copies of wills, leases and title deeds;
- great landed estates (many of which go back into the 17th and 18th centuries);
- railway companies, who bought up a considerable amount of land;
- churches, where generations were baptised and married.

Equally useful are family and personal papers, and the working notes of antiquarians and genealogists who worked in the Public Record Office of Ireland prior to the fire of 1922. These scholars took copious notes from the early records and their notebooks contain information on documents dating back to the mid 17th centuries.

Almost all the major estate archives for Northern Ireland are held in PRONI and you can find descriptions of many of them on the PRONI website. Among the more notable estate archives are: Downshire (Cos Down and Antrim); Antrim (Co. Antrim); Abercorn (Co. Tyrone); Belmore (Co. Fermanagh); Gosford, Brownlow and Caledon (Co. Armagh); and Drapers' Company (Co. Londonderry). Other estate papers are also available.

Opening Times

PRONI is open to the public Mon - Wed and Fri 9.00 am – 4.45 pm; Thurs - 10.00 am – 8.45 pm. Latest time for ordering documents is 4.15 pm (Thursdays, 8.00 pm). There is no need to make an appointment unless you intend to bring a group. Group visits are very welcome but **must** be booked in advance.

Research is free for those pursuing personal and educational research, however, all visitors will need to obtain a Visitor Registration card at Reception which requires photographic proof of identity. PRONI staff look forward to welcoming visitors to our new office.

From the Mixer to the Modem - the Irish Navvy in Britain

Joseph O'Neill

His clothes were as distinctive as a judge's wig or a policeman's helmet. He wore a big donkey jacket, with two wide outside pockets and inside a large poacher's pocket. Moleskin or heavy corduroy trousers, a double-canvass shirt, a velvet or corduroy waistcoat, a billycock hat, a wide, big-buckled belt, to protect the back when lifting, and a large scarf of coloured cotton, tied with a special *'pincher's knot,'* made up the rest of his attire.

The first navvies were the men who built the *'inland navigation system,'* the canal system, between 1745 and 1830. People called them *'navigators'* – later shortened to *'navvies'* – a term that remained in popular and official use for two centuries.

Many of these men were migrant agricultural labourers from the poorer parts of Ireland, working in Scotland or England to earn the rent for their smallholdings. Most were subsistence farmers from the north west, west and south west of Ireland, in England to work on the harvest. When George Stephenson, John Rennie, James Brindley and other pioneering engineers recruited labour for their roads and canals, Irishmen signed up.

Many – the young and unattached – stayed when their comrades returned home in December. They mastered the *'graft,'* a drain-digging spade, the symbol of their trade.

In the years before the Famine these migrant workers came in ever-greater numbers. The Great Hunger, of course, led to a massive exodus of people who would never return home.

The Famine also ended the old inheritance system. Now one child came into his father's land and the rest took to the road in search of work. As the 19th century came to an end the demand for seasonal agricultural labour was replaced by the need for men in construction and civil engineering in Britain's new industrial cities.

The 3,400 miles of canal built in Britain during the 18th and 19th centuries are a phenomenal achievement. Building a canal is more than just digging a big ditch. It involves quarrying, brick-making, joinery and iron working, laying rails and pipes and building locks, bridges, gates, arches and tunnels.

Navvies not only excavated the channel, moving millions of tons of soil with picks, shovels and wheelbarrows. They also lined the bottom and sides with impermeable clay, working it into position with the soles of their boots. This *'heeling-in'* or *'puddling'* process was used for two hundred years. As recently as 1964 the Chew Valley Reservoir in the South West of England was lined by the same method used on the Newry Canal in 1742.

From the outset, the navvy had a proud reputation. No ordinary labourer could match his feats of strength and endurance. Nor would he take the risks. Blasting through rock and undercutting banks were perilous shortcuts which made navvying more dangerous than soldiering.

In return for this the navvy commanded high wages. In 1845 he earned 3s.9d a day – twice the wage of a farm labourer.

To make this money he had to be mobile – to go where the work was. During the years of the great railway boom of the mid-19th century, professional navvies were the norm. In some areas local labourers supplemented their numbers, but on the major lines in urban areas or in remote, thinly populated regions, the seasoned navvy was the bedrock on which the railways were built. From the beginning the navvy was a nomad, following the contractor, always in search of the big money.

Their fame and aura spread with the roads, canals and railways. They were the elite of the labouring class, the renowned *'long-distance men.'* They lived for the moment, taking risks and spending their wages riotously. Free of domestic ties, they lived rough and didn't care what people thought of them. Yet they were good-hearted, generous and loyal to their own.

The middle and upper classes were suspicious of them and there were *'navvy riots'* in Scotland and the north of England in the in the 1840s. Yet local newspapers had nothing but praise for the men building the Manchester Ship Canal, commending them for their generosity and gentlemanly demeanour, and one third of these men were Irish.

Building this famous Canal was so dangerous and the company surgeon, Robert Jones, became so adept at making artificial limbs for disabled navvies that he is acknowledged as the father of orthopaedic surgery. In total, 2,000 men were disabled and 1,100 lost their lives.

The Ship Canal is among the most famous of the great public utilities, which the navvies made their speciality. Between 1845 and 1853 alone they built seven major reservoirs in the Edinburgh area.

Travelling the length and breadth of the country in search of work, they built up a support network, usually based on public houses. Many of these hostelries, like the *Mason's Arms* and the *Bricklayer's Arms*, still bear the mark of their origins. This is one of the reasons why navvies became associated with pubs and drink.

Despite this image as men without responsibilities, most navvies retained a link with home, often through the remittance. This remained the case until the 1970s when the Central Statistical Office estimated that £4.5 billion had been sent to Ireland from Britain in the previous thirty years. Those who sent this money often did so at great personal cost.

It was this innate generosity and decency as much as their skills that so impressed Robert McAlpine when he observed Irishmen building the Mallaig Extension to the West Highland Railway in the 1880s. From then on he showed a distinct preference for Irish navvies, even recruiting them directly in Ireland. With McAlpine they went on to build Wembley Stadium, the Dorchester Hotel and the Mersey Tunnel.

And it was in tunnelling, the most hazardous of all engineering enterprises that the Irish navvy established his supremacy. The Lochaber Power Scheme, 1921-31, was one of the biggest engineering feats ever. A camp housed the 3,000 workers, two-thirds from Donegal. From this time on Donegal men were renowned as the elite of hard rock tunnelling.

The worldwide depression of the 1930s ended the demand for Irish labour. It was only the war that changed this. Between 1940 and 1944 160,000 Irish workers took up employment in Britain. Many played a key role in vital construction work such as the underground aircraft factory at Corsham,

Wiltshire, the vast *'deep shelters'* built under London and the 450 new airfields completed during the war.

Nor was the British government slow to acknowledge the importance of Irish labour to the war effort. The official history of the Ministry of Labour notes that *'Irish labour was valuable out of all proportion to its numbers ... in meeting urgent and difficult needs.'*

The demands of post-war destruction led to a new call for Irish labour. Now Irishmen and women flocked across the Irish Sea in greater numbers than any time since the Famine. The programme of hydro-electrification in Scotland, the housing boom, the growth of the motorway system in the late 1950s and the bonanza of North Sea oil made the years from 1945 to 1970 the golden age of the Irish navvy.

These were the days of the big money. Tunnellers working on the Clyde project in 1964 earned on average £70.0s.0d. a week at a time when a craftsman's wage was £11.0s.0d.

Then everything changed. Developments in the construction industry drastically cut the need for labourers. The great construction projects came to an end. And Ireland too was changing.

With the onset of further education for all in 1968 and Ireland's development as a key player in the Economic Community, expectations were raised. For the first time in generations, there was an alternative to emigration. The Irish working population was on its way to becoming the most highly educated in Europe.

Today many want to erase the memory of our navvy ancestors. Yet their qualities – their endurance, their courage, their generosity – deserve our admiration.

Even if we should forget them, their monuments remain. They span the length of Britain, from the hydro-electric dams in the Scottish Highlands to the London underground. And a network of railway lines and motorways links them.

A Lawless Outrage:

Abductions in Eighteenth Century Ireland

Stephen Wade

'Abductions' is a less frightening word than *'kidnapping'* but in fact that terrible notion of forcible taking away, against the will of the person, has run through European history, since the rape of the Sabine women in ancient Rome. The subject is an aspect of criminal history which has rarely been given any prominence. However, in recent years, it has caught the attention of popular writers and of academic historians.

If we survey patterns of crime in eighteenth century Britain, we find that, in an age with no professional effective police force, violent crime was rife and the value placed on human life was small indeed. We glamorize that Augustan age as a time of romantic highwaymen, dandies and rakes: a period of risk, adventure and dangerous streets. Partly, the reality was rather the same, but there was certainly no glamour in what lawyers would call *'crimes against the person'* in that age of Swift, Johnson and Pope, when people were writing books about style, manners and proper behaviour. While the men of letters were chatting about Shakespeare in their spacious rooms, in the wilder areas of the kingdom there was barbarity- and that could be in the streets of London or the wilds of the mountains.

Lately publish'd, in the same Size with the History of Executions, and very Proper to be bound up with this Year's SET,

THE Case of Mr. *Dan. Kimberley*, Attorney at Law, Executed at *Dublin, May* 27, 1730. for assisting *Bradock Mead* to marry *Bridget Reading*, an Heiress. Contained in his Declaration and Dying Words, deliver'd to the Revd. Mr. *Derry*, at the Place of Execution, and recommended to Dean *Percival, John Hacket*, Esq; and two other Gentlemen, to see it publish'd. Pr. 3d.

II. A Collection of Remarkable Cases for the Instruction of both Sexes, in the Business of Love and Gallantry. Being a modest and clear View of the three following Tryals, *viz.* 1. Of *Richard Lyddel*, Esq; for a criminal Conversation with the Lady *Abergavenny*. 2. Of *Knox Ward*, Esq; for a Promise of Marriage to Miss *Sarah Holt*. 3. Of Col. *Francis Ch-rt-is*, for a Rape committed on the Body of *Anne Bond*, his Servant. Containing the Substance of three Sixpenny Pamphlets (call'd Tryals) on these Subjects. Price 6 *d.*

III. A Second Collection of Remarkable Cases, *viz.* in Love and Law, in Physic, Scandal, and Religion. Containing, 1. The Tryal of Mr. *J. Whaley*, for Breach of a Marriage-Promise to Mrs. *Eliz. Davis*, late of *Haverford-West*; with the Substance of several Love-Letters that pass'd betwixt them. 2. The Tryal of *Eliz. Chamberlain*, on an Action brought against her by *Samuel Stockwell*, alias, *Sam the Potter*, an Independant Parson, for saying he was a Rogue, a Drunkard, a Libertine, and a Singer of bawdy Songs; with the merry Defence of his sanctified Reputation. 3. The Qualifications necessary to set up a raw Independent Parson. 4. The Description and Character of a Novice. 5. A pleasant New Song on a King and a Young Lady. 6. A surprizing Account of the (supposed) Murder of a Gentleman by Pills, Potions, and Chirurgical Operations, in a Letter from a Rev. Divine to his Widow, who was going to marry the suspected Murtherer. Price 6 *d.*

IV. *Scotch* Gallantry Display'd: Or, The Life and Adventures of the unparallel'd Col. *Fr-nc-s Ch-rt-s*, impartially related. With some Remarks on other Writers on this Subject. Pr. 6 *d.*

One crime from that era was notably rife in Ireland and Scotland, although it could happen anywhere. surely one of the most terrifying offences committed anywhere and at any time- abduction or kidnapping. Even today, the concepts of abduction and false imprisonment carry heavy penalties and attract the censure and disgust they deserve from law-abiding people. Back in the Georgian age, Ireland was one hot-spot of the crime, and the reasons are complicated. There also appears to be no pattern in these abductions, and explanations are hard to find.

In the time when the Old Bailey was the centre of attraction for everyone on both sides of the law, there were tradesmen about who were only too happy to cash in on the sensational and sad lives of villains – especially those whose lives had ended dangling on a rope at Tyburn. One such retailer was Richard Wam of the Bible and Sun at Warwick Lane, Amen Corner, London. Among his sick and bizarre items for sale there was a series of chapbooks with narratives on them, and one of these published in 1730 was this, as advertised:

'The case of Mr. Dan. Kimberley, attorney at law, executed at Dublin, May 27, 1730, for assisting Bradock Mead to marry Bridget Rending, an heiress. Contained in his declaration and dying words, delivered to the Rev. Mr. Derry, at the place of execution, and recommended to Dean Percival, John Hacket, Esq', and two other gentlemen, to see it published. Price: three pence.'

Behind that smart piece of advertising there lies not only the complex tale of a learned and educated man who fell into deep trouble, but also a story typical of its age and place – one more abduction in hundreds, a trade (and a crime) totally heartless and unscrupulous – and of course, a capital offence. Kimberley's last dying speech tract was headed, *'Daniel Kimberly, Gentleman'* Those words were unusual for a gallows tale, and his date with death was as meticulously recorded as the events of his own story: *'Executed at St Stephen's Green on*

Wednesday, May 27th, 1730 at 38 minutes past three o'clock in the afternoon.'

The famous historian of eighteenth century Ireland, W E H Lecky, in his account of the spate of abductions of heiresses in that time, explains how many people ascribed them to sectarian enmity, yet he finds little evidence of that. But there were certainly many different abductions, and whatever their nature, they were brutal and cruel and could be like this one described by Lecky:

'On a Sunday in the June of 1756, the Rev. John Armstrong was celebrating divine service in the Protestant church in the town of Tipperary, Susannah Grove being among the congregation. In the midst of the service Henry Grady, accompanied by a body of men armed with blunderbuses, pistols, and other weapons, called out to the congregation that anyone who stirred would be shot, he struck the clergyman on the arm with a hanger and ... hastening to the pew where Susannah was sitting, dragged her out ...'

But we are not dealing with this type of abduction in Kimberly's story, and, as Lecky points out, the Kimberly case is unusual because he was a Protestant, pointing out that

'Among the few persons who were executed for abduction in Ireland was an attorney named Kimberly, at a time when no-one but a professing Protestant could be enrolled in that profession.'

Here then, we have a case of a lawyer and a Protestant being hanged for an offence for which few were hanged. What was so heinous about this particular abduction? Or did Kimberly have powerful enemies?

His own account of the events of the abduction of Bridget Reading (not *Rending*, as the London printer had it) is expectedly, full of bad luck stories and of his being an innocent dupe. Making sense of Kimberly's own garbled and complicated account of what happened, there emerges a bare outline of a plausible story: he was a lawyer and so would have appeared to be hardly a *'heavy'* when it came to applying some pressure on the intended abduction and forced marriage of Bridget Reading, for that is what lies at the heart of this story. Kimberly was contacted by an unscrupulous adventurer called Braddock Mead, with an assignment of visiting the nurse who had the guardianship of Bridget. Now, Kimberly argued that the old couple who had Bridget in care were also after her inheritance, and he said that he was told *'there was a considerable sum of money due to her ... she never having received a penny from her father, who was an ill man.'*

The lawyer then found out that Mead, back in London, had more knowledge of Bridget's situation than he had at first said because he took out articles with a man called Dodamy with a plan to sell Bridget's estate for the then huge sum of £3,600. The pressure was then on Kimberly to get a desired result in his negotiations to prise Bridget from her guardian

Hogarth's Portrayal of Tyburn

and to speed her to the altar with Mead. Again and again, Kimberly insisted that there had been no forced marriage:

'soon after, and by my consent, and inducement, Mead applied to said Bridget by way of courtship and on 11th April, 1728, said Mead married her in Dublin, when and where no force, threats, or compulsion was made use of by any person towards said Bridget to come into said marriage.'

Understanding this case is all a matter of believing Kimberly was *'sold out'* to the law or not. His argument was that Mead was largely responsible for duping him and setting him up, as he was seen as the actual agent of the affair, and so would be assumed to have used force on the girl. When Mead was arrested and imprisoned and the network was about to be destroyed (and heads to roll) Mead was threatened by Mr Reading to apply a charge of rape against him unless he had the marriage annulled, Kimberly was apparently *'stooged.'* He did understand that the right moves had been attempted, though. Applications were made to the Doctor's Commons, and though the intentions may have been good, to dissolve the contract, perhaps the Doctors' Commons was not the right place to go. Later, Dickens was to call that institution of Doctors of Law *'a cosy, dozy, old-fashioned and time-forgotten, sleepy-headed little family party.'*

As with all such convoluted narratives of crime, it all depends who is believed at the time, and by the people who matter. Daniel Kimberly was clearly not believed; we have his side of the story, but we also have the weight of history and statistics to show how hard the authorities were coming down on abductions of heiresses. It may be that, in the end, Kimberly was being harshly punished as a precedent to other professional gentleman not be involved in that nefarious and amoral trade.

He faced his death on the scaffold with courage, offering to dramatic entertainment to the crowd. He even ended his speech with the surprising attitude of forgiveness: *'As for my prosecutors, or such as have persecuted me. Or fought any perjurious or indirect ways to take away my life, I freely forgive them.'* Reading between the lines, there is still rancour there, and *a 'spin'* towards showing himself in a better light than his enemies. But, as with many others in his final minutes, his main concern was for his reputation:

'In order to prevent the publishing of any false or spurious accounts of me . . . I do therefore humbly entreat my very worthy friends, the rev. Dean Percival, Mr Derry, John Hacket, Edmund Fenner . . . to order the printing and publishing of this declaration.'

He did have some friends (Dean Percival has gone down in history as one of the men who lampooned Jonathan Swift in a satirical poem) but clearly their exertions were not strenuous enough to save him from the gallows.

As to trends in abductions generally, Lecky did his own investigation back in 1890 and his conclusion was, after dealing with the theory that most were sectarian, and that Catholic abductions were condoned by priests, he concluded that *'The truth is that the crime was merely the natural product of a state of great lawlessness and barbarism, and it continued in some parts of Ireland later than in other countries, because, owing to circumstances of described in the present chapter [the lack of authority impinging on the state of affairs] the formation of habits of order and respect for law was unnaturally retarded.'*

Lecky looked into archives at Dublin Castle, and there he found that in the presentments of Grand Juries for the years 1700 - 1760, 28 cases were of abduction, and in only four of these is there any evidence that a Protestant victim was taken away by a Catholic band of abductors. He noted that these presentments were created by Protestants of course, and the depositions therein would be sworn by Protestant families, so as he says, *'We may be sure that no element of sectarian aggravation that could plausibly be alleged is omitted.'* He weighs the evidence of the material carefully and sees no certainty that the old tales of Catholic dominated abductions had truth in them.

Although there were undoubtedly many abductions related to profits from marriage at the time, as in Kimberly's case, a factor that must be recalled was that an Act of 1745 made marriages celebrated by priests between Protestants and Catholics null and void.'

But the stories and myths went on, into the regency years. Arthur Young, the agrarian traveller and farmer, in his tour of Britain at the turn of the eighteenth century, noted that abductions were fairly common, but again, he has no explanation which relates to sectarian violence. What is of interest with regard to how the tales graduated to perhaps fictional proportions is that the English Victorian historian, J A Froude, wrote of them in his popular work, *The English in Ireland in the Eighteenth Century*. Froude wanted the historiography to be one of religious interplay and depredation. Lecky took the opposite view. But in the end, as Kimberly's case shows, the reasons for the crime being fairly common

SACKVILLE-STREET, DUBLIN.

across the centuries is a very different one.

We owe this largely to research done by James Kelly in his work, *'The Abduction of Women of Fortune in Eighteenth Century Ireland'* in which he explains the economic basis of this nefarious crime. Kelly notes that going back to an Act of 1634 which stated that those who *'take away . . . and deflower . . . maidens that be inheritors'* were subject to imprisonment for between two and five years and also, their next of kin would be disinherited. In other words, the economic factor is uppermost. Partly for this reason, there were such things as arranged abductions, involving no rape, for instance. Kelly explains that a writer of 1682 telling tales of abduction often uses what were in fact *'ritualistic'* ones – not forcible abduction. This means that, although a girl had rebuffed a suitor, the father and family had actually pressurised her into relenting, and agreed that an apparent abduction should take place. This seems not dissimilar to a situation akin to Shakespeare's *The Taming of the Shrew* in that a girl was designed to be off-loaded to a suitor, even though he might be a rough type, likely to step over moral or legal lines, to get his woman.

An account from the later fifteenth century explains what this was:

'When a man is in love with a woman but is repulsed . . . he often has recourse to the following stratagem. He causes a report to be spread in the neighbourhood that he intends to carry her off. This seldom fails of gaining the point. He is now permitted to pay his addresses without interruption, and is generally looked on by the family as a true and sincere love . . .'

The debate on Irish abductions brings out several interesting elements of the social and legal history, not the least of these being that historians of the past have wanted to find sectarian aspects of the events – common of course in all areas of Irish writing – but this also highlights the now (with hindsight) obvious and rather clumsy bias of Victorian writers on this very emotional theme. This partly falls in line with the disgusting representations of Irish people as in Victorian periodicals and the literary stereotypes, but we also have here an example of how some of the most heinous crimes of the past were sometimes interpreted without any real feeling for the human situation beneath the legal situation. That is, perhaps, left to the novelists and documentary writers. Yet the case of abductions presents the reader of Irish history with something open to a number of interpretations, while it must be said that in the end, much of the answer lies in the parental machinations in a period of paternal governance, when the family unit was part of a clan, for self-preservation and survival.

In the novels of Jane Austen, the reader may be asked to be appalled at the event of two young lovers engaging in a dangerous elopement, following romantic attachment rather than economic and social sense, and yet the supposed opposite situation of a forced kidnapping for a beneficial marriage was arguably too much for popular fiction. Though it may at times have had a willing, artificial aspect, on the whole it was a *'barbarous'* practice as Lecky expressed it, and historians are now engaged in digging for further truths about the practice.

Further Reading

The English in Ireland in the Eighteenth Century J A Froude - Longmans Green 1886 [ISBN: 978 0559835377 BiblioBazaar 8 Dec 2008]

'The Abduction of Women in Eighteenth Century Ireland' James Kelly - *Eighteenth Century Ireland* (Eighteenth Century Ireland Society, 1994)

A History of Ireland in the Eighteenth Century W E H Lecky - Longmans Green 1892 - A History of Ireland in the Eighteenth Century was published in this five-volume version in 1892, and aimed at providing a less sectarian history than was currently available. It remains an important source, particularly on the 1790s, as Lecky made use of records which have since been destroyed. - Cambridge University Press 2011 Five volumes ISBN 978 1108024440; 978 1108024457; 978 1108024464; 978 1108024471; 978 1108024488

Attempt at Abduction at Tipperary

Illustrated London News 8th July 1854

Fred Feather

At attempt at abduction , which fortunately failed in its object, was made at half past two o clock last Sunday, by Mr John Carden, a large land proprietor in Clonmel, assisted by six or seven ruffians, supposed to be some of his tenancy. It appears that the Hon.Mrs Gough, accompanied by her sister Mrs Arbuthnot, Miss E. Arbuthnot, and another lady, who is on a visit at Mrs Gough's, proceeded to Divine Service, at Rathronan Church, a short distance from their residence, Rathronan House, and upon their return at half past two o'clock, they were met by Mr Carden and his associates, armed with knives, bludgeons, &c., who stopped the car, cut the reins and traces , and desired the driver not to stir or they would kill him,for refusing to comply with this order, he was severely beaten as were two of Mr Gough's men, who came to the rescue.

In the meantime Mr Carden succeeded in dragging Miss E. Arbuthnot out of the car, but was prevented by her sister and another lady from doing her any injury. The alarm having reached the house, and the servants being seen approaching, the discomforted Lothario and his suite fled, as one of his men had a carriage and pair, and four or five saddle horses, close by, leaving his hat cane and a portion of his coat in the hands of the victors. Shortly after the occurrence, the steward to Captain Gough, hearing of the circumstance, set chase after Mr Carden, and, after a desperate race of twenty miles, at the end of which on of Mr Carden's horses dropped dead, they laid hold of him at Farley Bridge, and lodged him in Cashel Bridewell, along with four of his associates. The lady whom he attempted to carry off is an heiress, with a fortune of £50,000.

Mr Gough's Steward set chase after Mr Carden

Seeking Irish Ancestors in South Africa

Rosemary Dixon-Smith

On 20th November 1857 the barque *Lady Kennaway* brought a cargo of 153 single Irish women to the port which would later be named East London, situated at the Buffalo River mouth in the Cape Frontier district known as British Kaffraria.

It's hard to imagine these women's first impressions when they saw the wild country which would be their future home. They had willingly agreed to undertake a risky sea voyage of nearly three months - in a forty-year old ship which had seen service as a convict transport. The passengers had been given scant detail about their destination. However, they had the promise of a fresh start, and husbands, and these factors must have been strong incentives for young women from Northern Ireland who had been living in poor conditions, many of them in workhouses.

The expedient of bringing in unmarried women to the colonies to correct the imbalance of the population (too many men and not enough women) was nothing new. It had been tried in North America in 1850 where, if the advertising of the time is to be believed, thousands of men *'having made their fortunes at the mines, are now anxious to throw themselves at the feet of the first passable specimens of womanhood whom fate and a happy wind may cast upon their shores.'* In the Cape Colony there were two attempts, in 1849 and 1851, to introduce small numbers of Irishwomen sent out under the auspices of British philanthropic societies.

So Cape High Commissioner Sir George Grey's suggestion that a group of Irish women should be shipped to British Kaffraria in the *Lady Kennaway* was not unprecedented. His intention was that the women should become wives for German military men, ex-legionaires who had been settled in the Eastern Cape as part of the frontier defence policy. It might have been anticipated – except, apparently, by Grey – that such a scheme was unlikely to succeed.

British Kaffraria was far from the civilized delights of Cape Town: the ship had not stopped there in case disappointing comparisons were made when the passengers reached the port on the Buffalo River. Here there was as yet no developed harbour and the *Lady Kennaway* had to anchor off shore with passengers being landed by boats in a protracted four-day disembarkation. Though accorded a warm welcome, particularly by the male segment of the population, it seems the attractions of the soldiery were not highly-rated and though a few women were married soon after arrival (not necessarily to Germans), many preferred to seek domestic or other employment in centres such as King William's Town and Grahamstown.

To add to the general air of disillusionment, the *Lady Kennaway* ran aground within the mouth of the Buffalo River in a gale on 25th November 1857, becoming a total wreck.

Thanks to Colonial Office record keeping, the names of the *Lady Kennaway* women, their ages and their counties of origin, have been preserved. A list can be viewed at www.eastlondon-labyrinth.com/cybertrails/kennaway-09.jsp#girls

Despite the fact that the venture wasn't a resounding success the *Lady Kennaway* story remains romantic, in the best sense: 153 Irish women chose to do something astounding and courageous, making history and changing their lives in the process.

Lady Kennaway

Destination

South Africa is not a country that springs readily to the minds of family historians seeking Irish ancestors. Certainly, the flow of Irish immigrants to South Africa at no time resembled the huge tide which turned towards the shores of North America. An authority on Cape 19th century aided immigration, Esme Bull, says that government-assisted schemes brought approximately 14,000 Irish settlers to the Cape between 1823 and 1900. By comparison with American statistics,

Cape Town Harbour

immigrants who formed part of this 1820 initiative. Ireland, like England, was in the throes of economic difficulties including large-scale unemployment.

Several men of Irish origin formed their own settler parties, notably John Ingram who recruited would-be colonists, many of them Roman Catholics, from his own county, Cork. Ingram took them on as his employees, undertaking to pay them a wage and at the end of the three year period of service to give each man 10 acres of land, or ten pounds.

This group disembarked at Saldanha Bay in May 1820. Their names, including Ingram's, are listed at www.genealogyworld.net/nash/ingram.html

Ingram later continued his emigrant enterprise, recruiting more settlers from Cork. Under his auspices, 352 people came to the Cape in the ship Barossa, arriving on 12th December 1823. A list of the relevant surnames can be seen at www.genealogyworld.net/immigration/immigration.html

Another Cork merchant, William Parker, brought 75 men and their families to the Cape aboard the East Indian in February 1820. Their names are listed at www.genealogyworld.net/nash/parker.html

Captain Walter Synnot of County Armagh, arranged for a party of 10 labourers and their families of that county to sail from Cork on 12 February 1820. See www.genealogyworld.net/nash/synnot.html

Captain Thomas Butler of the Dublin Militia recruited labourers in Wicklow, his home county. Butler undertook to support them until they harvested their first crops, while the men promised Butler 200 days work each year for 4 years. This group sailed on the same vessel as Synnot's party, on 12th February 1820. See www.genealogyworld.net/nash/butler.html

The source for information on these immigrant groups is M D Nash's *The Settler Handbook*. For more by Nash on this vast topic,

this is a drop in the ocean.

Nevertheless, for family historians this figure (which refers only to government-aided immigration schemes during the time-frame mentioned above) is sufficient to suggest South Africa as a possible destination for that elusive Irish forebear.

Cape Immigration Schemes

In the early 19th century there had been minor private schemes involving Irish immigrants. Henry Nourse, for example, a London merchant who had settled at the Cape, brought out a small group of Irish people as his employees in 1818, and advised that a government-sponsored immigration scheme would be beneficial to the Colony.

The authorities had already come to that conclusion. By 1819 the troubled eastern frontier of the Cape had become a permanent headache for the colonial government, while in Britain unemployment and discontent were rife. Sponsored emigration would reduce pressure at home, offering new prospects to many. At the same time, installing a buffer strip of farming colonists would be a way of defending the frontier. This thinking led to the arrival of what are today generally referred to as the 1820 Settlers. They were not one large unit, as this title seems to imply, but comprised a number of different parties each in the charge of a leader, making the journey out to the Cape in various ships.

Overshadowed by the mass of information available on the 1820 Settlers are the Irish

Handbook. For more by Nash on this vast topic, including recent corrections and additions to the original volume see www.genealogyworld.net/nash/index.html

Regrettably the policy-makers had decided that Irish immigrants would be separated from the main body of 1820 settlers, placing the Irish in the Clanwilliam district on the Cape west coast – a remote and arid region. When the Irish became aware of conditions at Clanwilliam most of them successfully made representations to be moved to Albany, where the majority of the 1820 Settler groups were situated. Their problems did not end there, for the wheat crop failed due to disease in the first few years followed by floods in 1823. A few of the Clanwilliam settlers clung tenaciously to their allotments in that area.

Later Irish Settlers

Between 1846 and 1851 there were further arrivals based on a government-aided scheme. Of the 4 200 immigrants brought to the Cape about a third were Irish. Not all the passenger lists have survived. One of the ships, *The Eclipse*, brought 20 women from Irish workhouses.

Towards the end of the 1850s there was a shortage of labour at the Cape and the government hoped immigration might solve the dilemma. Esme Bull estimates that more than 11,000 British settlers were brought to the Cape between 1858 and 1862 in 32 ships. Of these immigrants nearly 5000 were Irish.

In Natal, the largest and most well known immigration scheme of the 19th century was the brain-child of a Dubliner, Joseph Byrne. Of the approximately 2200 British settlers who came out in 20 ships between 1849 and 1851, some were of Irish origin. Historian Shelagh Spencer suggests that most of the latter arrived on *The Unicorn* which sailed for Natal from Liverpool in June 1850. Names include Deane, Connelley, MacMinn, White, Scott and Williamson. All Byrne settlers and the ships on which they arrived are listed in John Clark's Natal Settler-Agent (see Further Reading).

There was a tendency, usually actively encouraged by government, for people already in residence in the South African colonies to send for other family members to join them.

Independent Arrivals

Not all Irish immigrants came to South Africa as part of a private or government-sponsored scheme. During the course of the 19th century families or solo travelers made the voyage in merchant ships at their own expense. Of these, my Waterford-born great grandfather is a typical example. In 1863 he paid his own passage out and chose to settle at Port Natal (Durban), where his descendants still live today.

It wasn't easy trying to find evidence of his arrival at Natal, though handwritten passenger registers have been preserved. Independent arrivals are more difficult to trace, especially if, as in my great grandfather's case, the surname is so curiously misspelled as to be almost unrecognizable. Checking the passengers' names against a list published in the press satisfactorily confirmed that it was the correct person. In this type of search the Natal European Immigration Index and Registers, held at Pietermaritzburg Archives Repository, are invaluable. (Pietermaritzburg Archives Repository Post address: Private Bag X9012, PIETERMARITZBURG 3200 Street address: 231 Pietermaritz Street, PIETERMARITZBURG T: (033) 342 4712 Fax: (033) 394 4353 E: pmbarchives@kzndac.gov.za) For family historians at a distance, it is possible to delegate to a local researcher to check this source. Further details on the EI Index and Registers can be seen at www.genealogyworld.net/rose/euimmigr.html

Cape passenger records reflecting independent arrivals at Table Bay and other ports such as Algoa Bay (Port Elizabeth) exist for 1822-1917. These are limited to names of first class or 'cabin' passengers, ignoring those in second class or steerage - the latter being the people we generally want to know more about.

There are also Cape sources such as the so-called Permissions to Remain in - or to Leave - the Colony, Applications for and Letters of Naturalization, Correspondence received from settlers etc. These are useful alternatives to records of passenger arrivals.

One of the factors adding to the difficulty of identifying individual 19th century travelers is that people of British origin (including the Irish) were free

to come and go at will throughout the Empire. There were no restrictions such as passport control.

Early Arrivals

From the earliest days of British government at the Cape, the Irish were among the civil servants and other officials involved in the day-to-day running of the Colony. They did not regard themselves as settlers. Most had no intention of remaining at the Cape and would eventually return home to Ireland.

Some were exotic personalities like Benjamin Green from Wexford who arrived in Table Bay on the *Lovely Maria* in December 1819. Not your average civil servant, he is said to have killed a leopard with his bare hands. After a brief but action-packed decade in South Africa, during which he became a pioneer trader in Natal and Zululand, Green succumbed to fever near Delagoa Bay in 1829.

There were Irish mariners at the Cape, too, mostly just passing through – or so they hoped. James Hooper, born in Ireland circa 1782, was accidentally left ashore at Cape Town in May 1808 when the East Indiaman on which he was employed as a Captain's servant sailed away without him. Perhaps being *'marooned'* in this way had an adverse psychological effect on Hooper, for he and Dubliner Michael Kelly later conspired together in the instigation of a slave revolt. There was no worse crime in the Colony. Both men were arrested and tried, Kelly being deported and Hooper hanged.

These individuals are among numerous Irishmen included in a fascinating list of 4 500 British residents occurring in a variety of Cape records between 1795 and 1819. (*British Residents at the Cape* by Peter Philip.)

Military

Family historians might not immediately perceive the military as a possible avenue for research into Irish ancestors in South Africa. Yet, wherever the British army served it included soldiers of Irish origin. These cannot be thought of as immigrants in the accepted sense of the term, but there's no doubt that many Irishmen having taken their discharge from the army while serving in South Africa, decided to stay in the country.

The Irish as members of the military were present from the time of the first British occupation of the Cape (1795 to 1803) and again from 1806 when British rule was re-established after a short hiatus. From then on there was no campaign in South Africa in which Irishmen did not serve, including the Cape Frontier Wars. Some had careers cut tragically short, such as Richard *Armstrong 'of Ireland,'* a Lieutenant in the 8th Light Dragoons (King's Royal Irish Hussars) who died in June 1798 aged 18; his regiment was in South Africa from 1796. The more fortunate completed their period of service, married local girls of Dutch or other nationality and settled down after leaving the army.

Names of men, including some of Irish origin, who retired to pension between 1818 and 1826 and chose to remain at the Cape, were at www.genealogyworld.net/immigration

These names were transcribed from WO 23/147 at TNA, Kew; the list includes birthplace and regiment.

In the South African colonies fear of tribal incursions was endemic. British regiments garrisoned forts and towns throughout the 19th century. An example of an unusually long-serving garrison, the 45th Regiment was stationed in Natal for 16 years, from the early 1840s, and of the men finally discharged from the regiment a high proportion were Irish. Many elected to put down roots in Natal.

Later Conflicts

Irish troops saw service in various regiments during the Anglo-Zulu War and Irishmen were among the defenders of Rorke's Drift on 22nd January 1879. The popular belief that the 24th Foot, present at Rorke's Drift, was a Welsh regiment, is not accurate. The 24th Foot was originally the 2nd battalion of the Warwickshire Regiment. At the time of the famous Defence the 24th was an English Regiment, with over 20 Irishmen in its ranks. Their names include Horrigan, Turner, Lyons, Meehan, Gallagher, Hayes, Bushe, Caine, Connors, Minehan, Galgey, Connolly and others.

Irish Brigade - Anglo-Boer War 1899 -1902

Not a member of the 24th Regiment but one of the

defenders awarded the Victoria Cross for his valiant part in the action was Surgeon James Reynolds, born in Dublin. Gunner John Cantwell of the Royal Artillery was another Dubliner present at the Drift: he lived in Natal for many years and lies buried in Durban.

During the Anglo-Boer War 1899-1902, about 30,000 Irish troops fought for the British cause. Irish regiments included the famous Connaught Rangers, the Inniskillings, the Royal Dublin Fusiliers, the 5th (Royal Irish) Lancers, the Royal Irish Rifles and others. Many saw action in the Natal theatre of the war, particularly during the Siege of Ladysmith.

It's well-known that a relatively small number of Irishmen fought on the Boer side, in two *'Irish Brigades.'* The first and most effective of these was formed by John MacBride, born in County Mayo. The unit – about 700 strong - fought at Colenso, Spioenkop, Dundee, Tugela Heights and the Siege of Ladysmith. This meant that they found themselves fighting against their own countrymen, recognizing in the enemy ranks a cousin or a neighbour from *'back home.'* A list of Irishmen who fought for the Boers, compiled by D P and C S McCracken, is given in *Southern African Irish Studies, vol. 2.*

After the Anglo-Boer War, some Irishmen who had fought in British regiments remained in South Africa, or returned with their families to settle in the country.

NAAIRS - South African National Archives and Record Service

It's always worth checking NAAIRS, the online index of the South African National Archives and Record Service, to see if there is any reference to the ancestor you are trying to find. Access the index at www.national.archives.gov.za/ Enter the relevant surname and forenames. Include a date parameter if possible.

If you have no clue as to which area of South Africa is appropriate, search on the database RSA which covers all provinces. There are some useful guidelines on the site for those new to navigating the index.

To cover the wide spectrum of people of Irish origin who left their imprint on South Africa is beyond the scope of this article: they included missionaries, clergymen, merchants, entrepreneurs, journalists, members of police forces, diamond diggers, gold miners and railway workers. Your ancestor could have been among them.

Sources and Further Reading

Bull, E: Aided Immigration from Britain to South Africa, 1857-67 (HSRC Pretoria 1991)

Dickason, G B: **Irish settlers to the Cape: History of the Clanwilliam 1820 Settlers from Cork Harbour**. (Balkema Cape Town 1973)

Philip, P: **British Residents at the Cape 1795-1819.** (David Philip 1981)

McCracken, D P (ed.): **The Irish in Southern Africa 1795-1910.** (Southern African Irish Studies vol. 2 1992)

Nash, M D: **The Settler Handbook,** A new list of the 1820 settlers. (Cape Town 1987)

Clark, Dr J: **Natal Settler-Agent; the Career of John Moreland, Agent for the Byrne emigration scheme of 1849-51**. (Balkema Cape Town 1972)

Spencer, S O'Byrne: **British Settlers in Natal 1824-1857**. 7 vols. (UNP, Pietermaritzburg)

Rorke's Drift Memorial

Harry Furniss : Illustrator

Fred Feather

Harry Furniss aged 20

Harry Furniss was born on 26th March 1854 was an artist and illustrator, born in Wexford, Ireland. His father was an English engineer and his mother who was Scottish was the miniaturist painter Isabella Mackenzie. He was educated at the Wesleyan College School, Dublin. Whilst there he started and edited *The Schoolboy's Punch.*

After leaving school he worked firstly as a clerk to a wood-engraver, who also taught him the trade. He worked as an artist in Ireland but in 1876 he moved to England and found work as an illustrator was for the *Illustrated Sporting and Dramatic News* transferring to *The Illustrated London News* when it was purchased by the owner. Over the next eight years he developed a reputation as an outstanding illustrator and contributed to *The Pall Mall Gazette*, and *The Graphic*. He moved to *The Graphic*, initially writing and illustrating a series of supplements

William Gladstone
Harry Furniss always drew William Gladstone with a large collar

Harry Furniss in 1893

titled *'Life in Parliament,'* and he commented that *'from this time forward it would be difficult to name any illustrated paper with which I have not at sometime or other been connected.'*

In October 1880, Francis Burnand, the editor of *Punch Magazine*, invited Furniss to contribute to the magazine. Several of his cartoons were published and in 1884 he became a member of the staff at the magazine. For the next ten years he illustrated the *'Essence of Parliament.'* He also supplied articles, jokes, illustrations and dramatic criticisms for other sections of the magazine. It is estimated that over the years he contributed more than 2600 drawings to the magazine. Harry Furniss always drew William Gladstone with a large collar, and although he never wore collars like this, the public become convinced that he did.

He left *Punch* in 1894 when its owners discovered that he had sold one of his *Punch* drawings to Pears Soap for use in an advertising campaign.

On leaving *Punch* Furniss brought out his own humorous magazine *Lika Joko*, but when this failed he moved to America where he worked as a writer and actor in the fledgling film industry and where, in 1914, he pioneered the first animated cartoon film for Thomas Edison.

His two-volume autobiography, titled *The Confessions of a Caricaturist* was published in 1902, and a further volume of personal recollections and anecdotes, *Harry Furniss At Home*, was published in 1904.

Furniss wrote and illustrated twenty-nine books of his own, including *Some Victorian Men and Some Victorian Women* and illustrated thirty-four works by other authors, including the complete works of Charles Dickens and William Makepeace Thackeray.

In his autobiography he said that his illustrations should not always be thought of as being produced by a witness to the events depicted.

One boat race, for example, is very much like another. Some years ago I executed a panoramic series of sketches of the University Race from start to finish, and as they were urgently wanted, the drawings had to be sent in the same day. Early in the morning, before the break of fast, I found myself at Putney, rowing up to Mortlake, taking notes of the different points on the way — local colour through a fog. Getting home before the Londoners started for the scene, I was at work, and the drawings — minus the boats — were sent in shortly after the news of the race.

In 1877 he married Marian Rogers in the Strand, London. He died on 14th January 1925.

Irishman 1893
Harry Furniss

The Origin of the Species

Fiona Fitzsimons

Research Director of Eneclann

How Bram Stoker drew on his own family history as inspiration for the Dracula story

'I myself am of an old family' **- Count Dracula to Jonathan Harker**

Count Dracula is one of the most terrifying figures in popular culture. He first appeared in print in 1897, as the title character in Bram Stoker's book. Since then the name *'Dracula'* has become shorthand for all vampires.

In the century since its publication, critics and biographers have dined out on the blood-sucking aristocrat from Transylvania. They have pored over Bram Stoker's early life and formative experiences, to try and explain how this former civil servant could have imagined the gothic horror of Dracula. Now new research has uncovered aspects of Stoker's family history, previously unknown, which reclaims the story as essentially Irish. Our research has proven links between the writer's family, the oldest surviving Irish manuscript in existence, and one of the greatest treasures held in the National Museum of Ireland.

We began research using records from the Landed Estates Court Rentals on the Findmypast.ie website. An 1855 document lists *'Abraham Stoker and Charlotte Stoker, his wife'* co-owners of lands in Garracloon, County Mayo. Charlotte Stoker inherited a share in Garracloon, through her mother Matilda Blake, a younger daughter of Richard Blake (d. 1801) and Eliza O'Donnell. The Blake family in Ireland are very well documented from ca. 1300 onwards.[1]

Stoker's biographers have made much of his Blake ancestors, notably his great-uncle *'General'* George Blake who led the Irish rebels in Connacht during the 1798 Rebellion, and was afterwards hung for treason. All his biographers have passed over Stoker's O'Donnell connexion, typically noting only that Eliza's father was Colonel Manus O'Donnell, *'a landed gentleman'* of Newport County Mayo.[2] What they failed to see was the potential significance of the name 'Manus O'Donnell'.

Bram Stoker

Traditionally aristocratic and gentry families in Ireland, be they of English feudal stock or of Gaelic origin, used names as *'cultural signifiers'* to identify themselves as a distinct family group.[3] We developed a working hypothesis that the O'Donnell family of Newport used the Christian name *'Manus'* as an explicit statement of their family's origins. It required many hours and days further research to take this hunch, document it and prove it as fact.

As the O'Donnell family of Newport were a landed family we found their pedigree in the Genealogical Office manuscripts – G.O. Ms. 169. It quickly became

Family crests of the main branches of the O'Donnell family including 'O'Donnell of Newport', the branch of the family from which Bram Stoker was descended on his mother's side.
Reproduced by kind permission of the National Library of Ireland, G.O. MS 169

evident that the O'Donnell family of Newport traced their direct descent from the main O'Donnell family, formerly lords and Earls of Tir Conaill. The immediate consequence of this was that we could trace Bram Stoker's direct descent in twelve generations from Manus O'Donnell, (*'Manus the Magnificent'* d. 1563), a warrior lord who led the Geraldine League in revolt against Henry VIII. Furthermore, as the O'Donnells of Newport traced their descent from the main O'Donnell line, its possible to document Stoker's direct lineage even earlier, back to the 11th Century.

Even as we consulted G.O. Ms. 169, we noticed a very unusual drawing of a box or shrine decorated in high medieval relief, with the following explanatory note: *'the book or relicks of St. Columbanus descended, and . . . left . . . by will to O'Donnell of Newport.'* We set to work to research what were these relics. Our research showed that the book of St. Columbanus, also known as the *'Psalter of Saint Columbcille'* or *'the Cathach'*, is a 6th Century manuscript which survives to the present day, and is held by the Royal Irish Academy. The book-shrine which held the manuscript also survives, and is in the National Museum of Ireland in Kildare Street.

Between A.D.561 and A.D.1843, the O'Donnells were the hereditary keepers of these relics, which were passed by descent to every succeeding generation. Even allowing that descent was not always by primogeniture, it was always within the ruling dynasty. The fact that the Psalter and the shrine passed by descent into the hands of the O'Donnells of Newport provides de facto evidence to trace Bram Stoker's direct lineage back to the 6th Century. Clearly, historical truth has proven stranger and more fantastical than any of Stoker's own fictions.

The history of the Psalter and shrine is this. Apparently in A.D.561 after the battle of Cul Dremhne the O'Donnells took the *Psalter* which was subsequently passed by descent within the family. Ca. A.D.1062 the O'Donnell commissioned a manuscript shrine to hold the book, decorated with crystals, pearls and silver trace work, with an inscription in Irish around the base. Throughout the medieval period, the book and its shrine remained in O'Donnell's possession:

> *the manuscript was named 'Cathach' or 'Battler' from the practice of carrying it thrice right-hand-wise . . . as a talisman [before battle]. It was taken to France in 1691 and brought back to Sir Neal O'Donel, Newport, Co. Mayo, in 1802. [From the Royal Irish Academy website] www.ria.ie/library/special-collections/manuscripts/cathach.aspx*

The manuscript was re-discovered in 1813 when Sir William Betham, the Ulster King of Arms was invited by the O'Donnells of Newport to open the trunk sent from France.

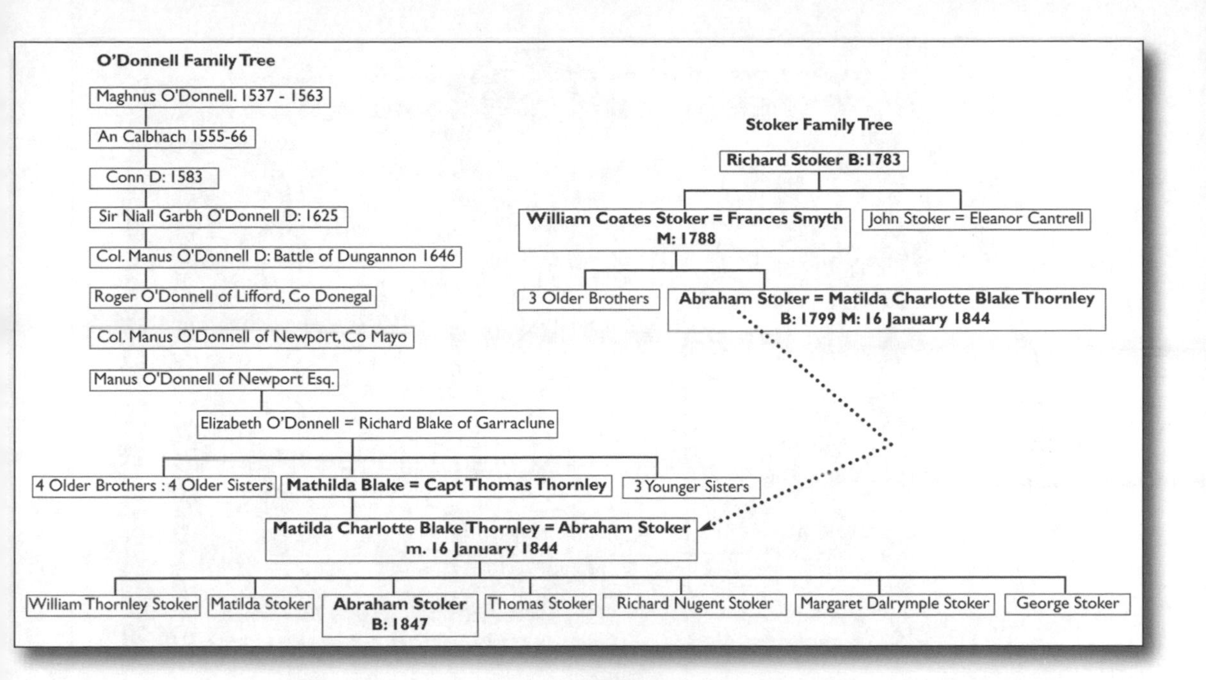

The silver shrine (Cumdach) made to contain the Psalter, and now on display in the National Museum of Ireland, Kildare St. Image courtesy National Museum of Ireland

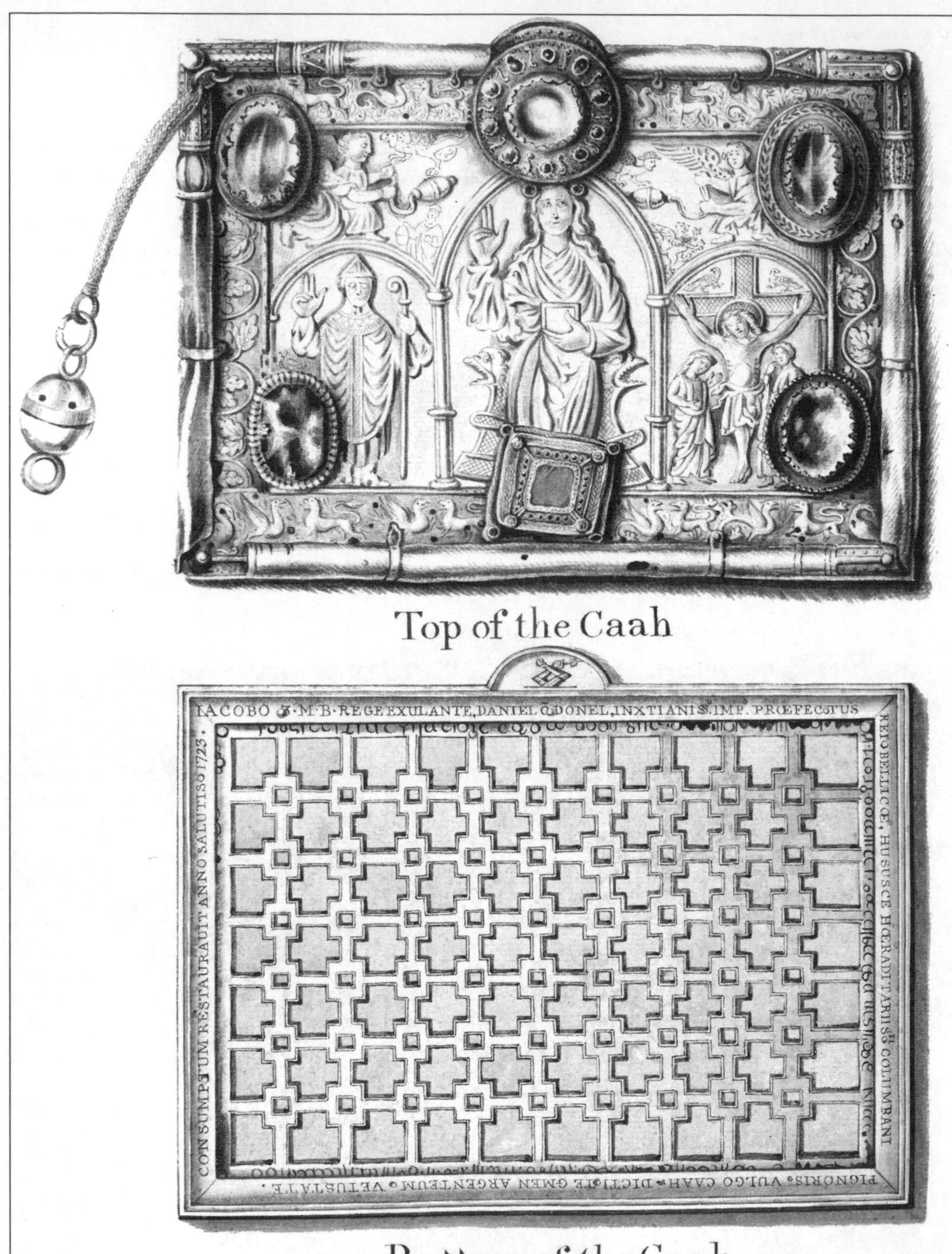

Illustration of the Cathach, also known as the Psalter of St. Columbcille, the earliest surviving Irish manuscript.
Reproduced by kind permission of the National Library of Ireland, G.O. MS 169

Inside he discovered the battered but elaborately decorated shrine, and inside this the Psalter. The rediscovery of these artefacts had a dynastic importance recognised by Betham who wrote '*it was a tacit acknowledgement of the O'Donnells of Newport being now the chief of this illustrious family.*'[4]

In 1843 inspired by the Celtic Revival, the O'Donnells deposited the Psalter with the Royal Irish Academy. The donation was covered

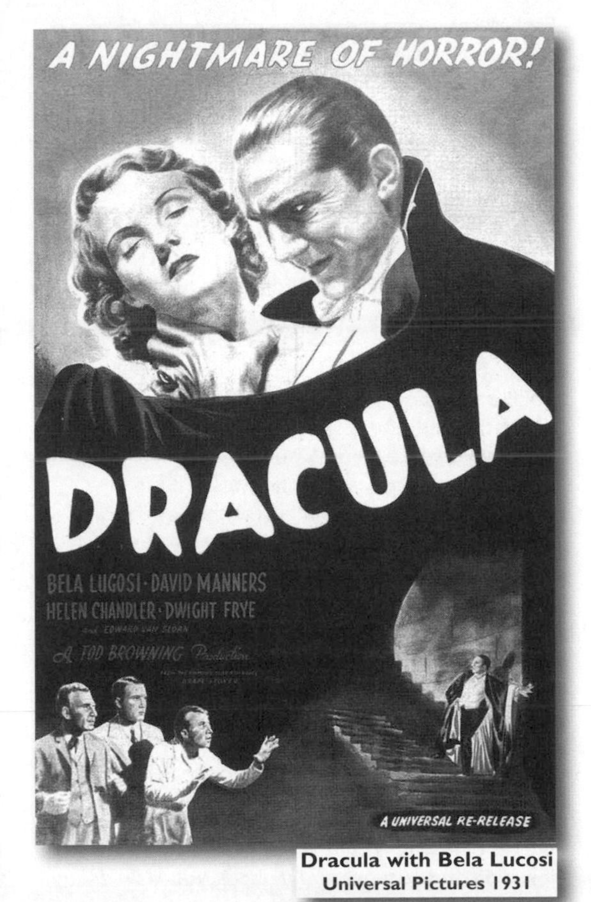

Dracula with Bela Lucosi
Universal Pictures 1931

enthusiastically by the Irish press, and the story of how St. Columbcille's relics passed for 1,300 years by descent in the O'Donnell family until they were given to the Academy, was welcomed as a cause célèbre among the Dublin intelligentsia, which included Abraham Stoker Sr. and his wife Charlotte.

Charlotte Stoker (Bram's mother) knew that her own grandmother was Eliza O'Donnell of the Newport family, and that Sir Neal O'Donnell who deposited the relics in 1843 was a close cousin. She remained in contact with her family in Mayo, and cannot have failed to understand the dynastic significance of the find.

In 1847 Charlotte gave birth to her third child Abraham Stoker junior, just four years after the manuscript book and shrine were given to the Academy. Young Bram Stoker was a sickly child, bed-ridden until the age of seven. We know from his own account, that his mother entertained him with tales, including stories from her own childhood and family history as well as tales of Irish folklore. It is inconceivable that Charlotte would not have told Bram that her grandmother's own family were the last hereditary keepers of St. Columbcille's relics, or of his own O'Donnell lineage. Bram himself later wrote of this period, *'I was naturally thoughtful, and the leisure of long illness gave opportunity for many thoughts which were fruitful according to their kind in later years.'* The true significance of his mother's stories has not been appreciated, until now. The discovery of his deep family history is a timely one, and we hope will allow readers to *'rescue'* Stoker's Dracula from its critics.

Between the 16th and 20th April 2012, critics writing in the *Irish Times* alone claimed that Stoker drew his inspiration for Dracula from a wide range of his own neuroses, ranging from sexual repression caused by his wife's supposed frigidity, to his own homosexual feelings for Henry Irving and Oscar Wilde. Other influences trotted out have included fear of syphilis or other diseases of the blood, and vices ranging from misogyny

Dracula with Christopher Lee
Hammer Films 1958

and xenophobia to anti-Semitism.

We argue against trying to *'shoe-horn'* Dracula into a metaphor for all these things and more. Instead, we maintain that in light of Stoker's own family history, that Dracula is more Irish than Transylvanian. In addition that the driving force of the story is taken from Irish history recast in the fire of the writer's own creation. Dracula is the story of a decayed aristocracy with a glorious warrior past, bypassed by history and that survives only in the shadows. Certainly Stoker hinted heavily at this when he put the following words into Dracula's mouth:

'the Szekelys, and the Dracula as their hearts blood, their brains, and their swords, can boast a record that mushroom growths like the Hapsburgs and the Romanoffs can never reach. The warlike days are over. Blood is too precious a thing in these days of dishonourable peace, and the glories of the great races are as a tale that is told.'

It is this interpretation alone that allows the text to be read as Stoker originally intended it.

The Cumdach (book shrine) is on display at the National Museum of Ireland – Archaeology, Kildare Street Dublin, while the Cathach (commonly known as the Psalter of St. Columba) is held in the library of the Royal Irish Academy and can be viewed by appointment.

Notes:

1. The Blake Papers are held by the National Library of Ireland, and in the early 20th Century Martin J. Blake published some of these genealogies and transcripts of documents.

2. Paul Murray, *From the shadow of Dracula: A life of Bram Stoker*, (Jonathan Cape), p. 8.

3. I have previously demonstrated how genealogists can identify and use *'founder's names'* to advance their research, see F. Fitzsimons, President Obama's Irish ancestry, published in *Irish Roots*, vol. 78, Summer edition 2011.

4. NLI, G.O. Ms. 169, O'Donnell pedigree.

All research for this article was undertaken by Fiona Fitzsimons, Helen Moss and Jennifer Doyle of Eneclann.

About Eneclann

Dublin based Eneclann is the leading provider of Irish history and heritage services. Established as a Trinity College Campus Company in 1998, the award-winning company's offerings include historical and genealogical research, digitisation and digital publishing services, and archives and records management. Eneclann's customer base ranges from individuals to public institutions and private companies. Clients are located within Ireland and across the Irish Diaspora of 80 million people. Eneclann traced President Barack Obama's Irish ancestry to the late 1600s and the company's research has featured in television programmes such as Faces of America, *Who Do You Think You Are? and Finding Your Roots*.

In May 2011 Eneclann formed findmypast.ie, a joint venture with brightsolid, the online publishing and technology group. If you would like Eneclann to research your Irish family history for you, please contact us at genealogy@eneclann.ie, or visit our website – www.eneclann.ie - for further information about our services.

Bram Stoker's House Kildare Street, Dublin

Roman Catholic Parish Registers
Mary McConnon

For the period preceding the introduction of civil registration in 1864 Roman Catholic parish registers are the main sources, and in some instances the only source, of information on Irish Catholic families. Because of their importance to family history research some brief historical note on their keeping is required.

Unlike Church of Ireland parishes where a law was passed in 1634 to keep registers no such law was made for Roman Catholic registers. This was because up until 1 January 1871 the Church of Ireland was in effect the State Church.

Within the Church itself various orders were made from the Synod of Drogheda in 1614 and later in 1670 to keep registers of baptisms and marriages. However the seventeenth century was a period of upheaval In Ireland with the Flight of the Earls in 1607 bringing to an end the power of the Gaelic Chiefs, the Ulster Plantation in 1609, the Rebellion of 1641, the Cromwellian Wars and Settlement and later the Williamite Wars followed by another plantation where lands were confiscated and given to the victors.

The defeat at the Battle of the Boyne in 1690, of the Catholic King James II by the Protestant William of Orange for the English throne, resulted in the enactment of various laws, known as the Penal Laws, against Roman Catholic in order to prevent the growth of Popery. A law passed in 1697 required all regular clergy and all clergy exercising jurisdiction to leave Ireland by the 1 May 1698. However as this was difficult to enforce further legislation was passed in 1704. This required the diocesan clergy to register with the civil authorities, to indicate the parish or parishes where they ministered, and enter into a bond with two sureties of £50 to be of good behaviour on pain of transportation. In all 1,089 registered as parish priests. According to Patrick J. Corish the law proposed *'the gradual extinction of the Catholic priesthood in*

Going to Mass

Ireland, because it made no provision for successors to those who registered' (The Catholic Experience - a Historical Survey, Dublin, 1984, p.125). A further Act in 1709 provided for an oath of abjuration renouncing the Stuart claim to the throne. About forty priests took this oath and the remainder lost their status under the 1704 Act. As a result

'Lay Catholics might be summoned on oath to testify where they had last heard Mass and who had been the celebrant. There emerged a new type of 'popish discoverer', who was rewarded for turning in priests. It was not a highly regarded occupation. There was some sympathy even among Protestants for priests who had refused to take the oath.' (Ibid)

Such conditions did not allow for the general keeping of records. However by 1730 the persecution began to decline. By that time almost every diocese had a bishop and the parish structure was being formed. But some parishes were too large, some were poorly equipped, and the appointment of assistant priests was forbidden. In 1760 with the founding of the Catholic Committee efforts began to secure the repeal of the Penal Laws. By the turn of the nineteenth century their enforcement and effect had declined further although this differed from parish to parish. It was not until the Catholic Emancipation Act of 1829 that most of the remaining Penal Laws were abolished. The position in the capital city of Dublin, the centre of government and commerce, from 1745 to 1865 is summed up in a Catholic Directory:

'So late as 1745 ... Catholics were first permitted to attend public worship in the few miserable churches of the city, and scores of persons now living heard mass in a thatched chapel in the very heart of the metropolis. After the comparatively brief space of 120 years, we now find the city studded with magnificent churches, there being upwards of 40 places of Catholic worship in Dublin and the suburbs, and nearly half as many priests in the Diocese as there were in all Ireland in 1704.' (Keogh, Very Rev. Canon, Catholic Directory, Almanac and Registry of Ireland, England, and Scotland, Dublin, 1865, p.186)

While for the period 1800 to 1865 in the

Kilsaran Church, County Louth
Foundation stone laid July 1814
Kilsaran Church, Kilsaran, County Lou

Diocese	Total Parishes	Counties covered
Armagh	54	Almost the whole of Louth & Armagh, a greater part of Tyrone and a part of Derry
Meath	68	Meath, Westmeath, the greater part of King's County [Offaly], and a small portion of Longford and Cavan
Derry	37	Nearly the whole of Londonderry, a large portion of Tyrone and a small part of Donegal,
Clogher	38	Monaghan and Fermanagh with parts of Tyrone and Louth
Raphoe	28	Nearly the whole of Donegal
Down and Connor	45	Antrim, the greater part of Down, and the Liberties of Coleraine, in Londonderry.
Kilmore	43	Nearly all Cavan, and parts of Leitrim and Fermanagh
Ardagh	41	Nearly all Longford, and parts of King's County [Offaly], Westmeath, Roscommon, Cavan, Leitrim, Sligo
Dromore	18	Parts of the Counties of Down, Armagh and Antrim
Armagh Province	**372**	
Dublin	52	Dublin, nearly all of Wicklow, and portions of Kildare, Queen's county [Laois], Carlow and Wexford
Kildare and Leighlin	48	The entire of Carlow, and Parts of Kildare, Queen's County [Laois], King's County [Offaly], Kilkenny and Wexford
Ossory	40	Kilkenny, and portions of King's County [Offaly] and Queen's County [Laois]
Ferns	40	The entire of Wexford and part of Wicklow
Dublin Province	**180**	
Cashel & Emly	46	Most of Tipperary and part of Limerick
Cork	34	Cork, and part of Kerry
Killaloe	55	Most of Clare and parts of Tipperary, King's County [Offaly], Galway, Limerick, Queen's County [Laois]
Kerry	48	Kerry and part of Cork
Limerick	48	Most of Limerick and a small portion of Clare
Waterford & Lismore	38	Waterford and parts of Tipperary and Cork
Cloyne	45	A large portion of Cork
Ross	11	Part of Cork
Cashel Province	**325**	
Tuam	53	Portions of Galway and Mayo
Clonfert	24	Parts of Galway, Roscommon, and King's County [Offaly}
Achonry	22	Portions of Mayo and Sligo, and a small part of Roscommon
Elphin	41	Most of Roscommon, and a large portion of Sligo
Kilmacduagh & Kilfenora	18	Clare and part of Galway?
Galway	13	Part of Galway
Killala	22	Portions of Mayo and Sligo
Tuam Province	**193**	
IRELAND	**1070**	

Roman Catholic Dioceses in Ireland with the number of Parishes and Counties in each

Diocese of Ferns in the south east of the country it states:

'The opening of this century found it with few decent chapels, many of the humble fabrics that bore the name having been burned during the rebellion, in 1798. It has now some of the most tasteful and elegant churches in the kingdom, and not alone in the leading towns, but also scattered over the rural parishes.' (ibid, p.197).

The Celebration.

These were the conditions for the saying of Mass but the celebration of baptisms, marriages and burials was also affected and were normally performed at home. It was not until well into the nineteenth century that the church was required to be used for baptisms and marriages services.

Again Patrick J. Corish states:

'The 'rites of passage', traditionally celebrated in the home, made there way to the church. In 1850 the Synod of Thurles laid down that baptisms should normally take place there, and I Maynooth (1875) allowed only very few exceptions to this rule. The practice of marriage in church, with Mass and the nuptial blessing, spread more unevenly, but it too became the rule. The traditional funeral Mass in the house also drifted slowly towards the church. In 1917 the new Code of Canon Law laid down that all funeral rites must take place in the church ...' (Corish, The Catholic Experience, p.234).

Administrative Divisions.

For administrative purposes Ireland was divided into provinces or archdioceses and these were sub-divided into dioceses and further into parishes. The size of the latter varies and, unlike Church of Ireland parishes, are not exactly co-terminus with the boundaries of the civil or former medieval parish and some cross county boundaries.

Diagram 1 lists the names of the dioceses in 1865 per the Catholic Directory with the number of parishes in each and the counties covered.

So what records are available, where are they and what do they contain?

Records Available

The Roman Catholic records that exist are baptisms and marriages but unlike Church of

Dromiskin Graveyard, County Louth

Ireland parish registers very few church burial registers were kept.

Dates

The growth in parish registers, from what is known to be extant, appears from the early nineteenth century. From the beginning of the 1820s *'it became the norm for each Catholic parish to have its own register of baptisms and marriages. Particularly in the towns and cities, a number of registers do go back well into the eighteenth century, but most begin about the year 1829 except in Ulster and the more deprived areas elsewhere.' (Ibid, p.157).*

By 1865 there were 1070 parishes (see *Diagram 1*) but only about 31 of those parishes are known to have an extant register or registers dating pre 1750 and about half of them are in Dublin County, Dublin City and Waterford City.

However even though a register can begin at a certain date there can be parts missing or difficult to read. Also while some registers may date from the middle or late eighteenth century this may arise from a parish being formed out of an earlier parish. So if a particular baptism or marriage is not found it is always advisable to search registers of neighbouring parishes.

Where are they?

The original registers are normally held in the local parishes. However in the 1950s and early 1960s the National Library of Ireland, 2 – 3 Kildare Street, Dublin, [NLI] microfilmed most of the registers to 1880. These are available to view in the self service room in the NLI. Photocopying facilities also exist. In more recent times some registers have been filmed to 1900. Copies of the microfilms for parishes in the six counties of Northern Ireland and for a number of those in the adjoining counties of Donegal, Cavan, Louth, Leitrim and Monaghan, are available in the self-service microfilm room of the Public Record Office of Northern Ireland, 2 Titanic Boulevard, Belfast [PRONI]. The Church of Jesus Christ of the Latter-Day Saints Family History Libraries [LDS] also hold a number of the microfilms.

From more recent years efforts have and are being made to computerize these registers and many are now available online from the date

Dromiskin Church, County louth
Foundation stone laid September 1923

Dromiskin Church, Dromiskin, County Louth

commenced to 1900. It is advisable to view on the website concerned the actual sources for each county as not all of a particular parish is indexed. The indexes are gradually being added to and proposals are to include a link to the scanned page of the original register.

The largest digital index is to be found on the website of the Irish Family History Foundation [IFHF] at www.rootsireland.ie. Part of this database relating to registers for parishes in counties Antrim and Down is also available on the website of the Ulster Historical Foundation at www.ancestryireland.com .The county indexes too are available in the IFHF heritage centres of the particular county and in some diocesan centers such as in Armagh for parishes in the dioceses concerned but access is only by a member of staff.

In the case of some parishes in the Diocese of Cork and Ross and in the Dublin Diocese the online index is to be found at www.irishgenealogy.ie For some parishes, on this website, the actual digital image of the page of the register is linked to the index entry.

Various transcriptions made by individuals on a voluntary basis for a particular surname or parish are available online and some can be found in published form in local parish histories or journals. These may related to period of years or just for particular surnames. One of the main printed ones is: *O'Casey, Albert, O'Kief Coshe Mang, Slieve Lougher and Upper Blackwater in Ireland: Historical and Genealogical Items relating to North Cork and East Kerry (Knockagree Historical Fund, Birmingham, Alabama, 1952-68).*

What information do they contain?

While the information may be minimal it is more than one normally finds on Church of Ireland parish registers for the same time period. Some registers can be written in Latin but most are in English although the handwriting ranges from a scribble to copperplate. There are also gaps in some and with the passage of time parts in others have become indecipherable. However today with the zoom feature on computers and microfilm machines it is possible to enlarge an image and so it may be easier to view an entry on computer or microfilm than on the actual manuscript register.

While the registers relate mainly to baptisms and marriages and to a lesser extent burials there can also be included some local information such as confirmations, local censuses, famine relief and other details not usually found in records.

Baptisms

The basic information given is date of baptism, name of child baptised (usually only one forename is given) and names of parents and sponsors to the baptism. In the case of the mother her maiden name is usually but not always provided. Some registers included address such as the townland or well known local district within the townland and in the case of urban parishes a street address, the name of the priest and sometimes the contribution made. In a small number of registers fuller information is provided such as addresses of sponsors.

Marriages

In the case of marriages the normal information is date, names of parties marrying and of witnesses to the marriage. The witness can be close relatives but sometimes neighbours. Fuller information found on some registers is an address and in a lesser number the addresses of the parents and the witnesses. In the case of the parents sometimes it is stated the name of both the father and mother and whether each are deceased although this latter information relating to both parents cannot always be relied on.

Burials

Not many parishes maintained burial or death registers pre 1900. They may only contain basic information such as a name but usually an address such as in baptism above, sometimes age at death and of most value the cemetery where the deceased was interred. These burial registers relate to the actual religious service. It should be remembered, however, that the local graveyard may not belong to the Roman Catholic parish and so burial information may be found on registers belonging to other religious denominations.

Michael Leader in his article on *'Irish Parish Registers'* states that

'Church of Ireland burial registers are a far better hunting-ground for Catholic entries. The first volume of St. Anne Shandon-beginning in 1778- has some forty thousand burials. Of these, I would estimate, at least three quarters are Catholics. In some parts of the book, it specifies the denomination, and you find '1808, Oct, 24, James Trant, roman, buried in a vault' (The Irish Genealogist, vol.3, no.2, (1957), pp.61-2).

This, however, will differ between parishes. Dromiskin cemetery, in County Louth, has both Protestants and Catholic burials. There was a Church of Ireland Burial register 1802-1902 for the parish which was lodged in the Public Record Office, Four Courts, Dublin but perished in 1922. The Roman Catholic burial register for the Parish of Darver which included Dromiskin for the period 1787 to 1828 is in the O'Fiaich Library in Armagh City but although in good condition is, as the writer found, not easily accessible. It was actually located among family papers of a relative although how it got there is unknown except that the family did purchase property in the townland where the priest of the time once lived. Unfortunately all were dead before the writer became aware of its existence. It is not on microfilm in the NLI.

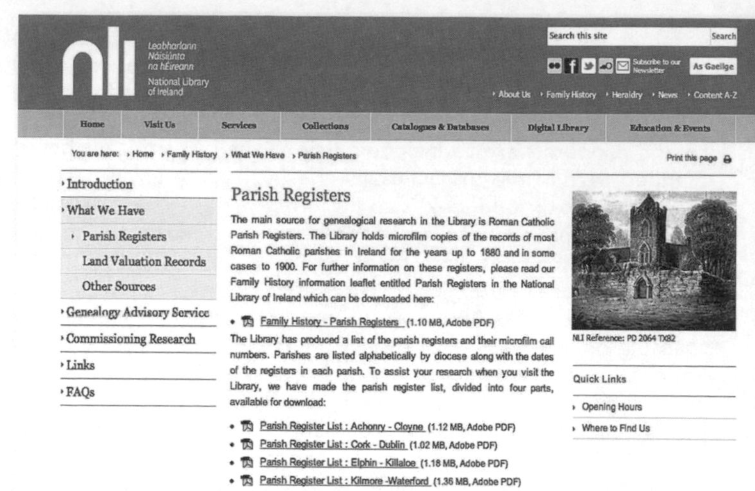

Information on it is to be found in an article by Noel Ross, *'Darver Burial Register, 1787-1828', County Louth Archaeological and Historical Society Journal, vol.XXIV, no.3 (1999), pp.435-6.*

There are other non parish sources which do not come under the term *'parish registers'* and so are not within the scope of this article but a brief mention is needed. Information on deaths are not only to be found in the civil deaths records from 1864 and from inscriptions from actual headstones but also from what are termed *'burial registers'* which relate to the actual plot of ground and who was interred and when internment took place. In the nineteenth century the local Boards of Guardians were given powers to provide burial grounds and these functions passed to the main local authorities. A register was and possibly is still maintained for these cemeteries. Unfortunately not much effort has been made to-date to locate or make the older records available to the public and they remain an untapped source. Families still tend to bury in the same family plot so the older records may be in use.

Also a Trust could have been set up to manage and maintain a particular burial ground as in the case of the large Glasnevin Cemetery in Dublin. The records of the latter are available online at www.glasnevintrust.ie

In short obtaining some knowledge of the local parish area can be of assistance.

How to Research?

While digitization has made searching easier it is always advisable to view the original register. The database on the website www.rootsireland.ie not only includes church baptisms, marriages and burials but also civil birth, marriages and deaths and other records. In all over fourteen million records are in the index.

Searching the index is free once registered but payment is required to view a particular entry. A search by surname returns variants of that surname and the number of entries of baptisms, marriages and burials for it. But before commencing it is important to know as much information as possible about an ancestor. For example a search, in May 2011, for just the surname *'Morgan'* returns 11,756 baptism, 6,435 marriage and 1.685 death entries. By clicking on each 'view' button a breakdown is giving on a county basis but only for the first 10 entries unless a period of years is selected.

However transcriptions bring in human error as well as difficulties encountered with computer searching of Irish surnames and forenames and the website does not provide for a wildcard search. From a study, in early 2011, of the family of John Sarsfield Casey *'The Galtee Boy'* and his siblings the errors found were unacceptably high. The errors ranged from 15% major ones to 25% having minor errors. For example in the case of the 13 baptism entries located:

- *one son Timothy Stanislaus was listed for 1866 instead of 1886.*
- *a sister Ellen had a date of baptism as 22 August 1855 instead of 22 April 1855.*
- *on a baptism entry of a sister 'Honora' the father was listed as 'Jeremiah' instead of 'Jerry' and a sponsor was listed as 'Daniel' instead of 'Dan'.*

In general, however, it is believed the error margin may be and is hopefully much less. With the implementation of future proposals to link the digital image of the page to the indexed entries these errors will lessen.

The next main database is on the website www.irishgenealogy.ie but so far only relates to parishes in County Kerry and for some in Counties Cork and Dublin including the Cities. The total number of entries for all religions can be seen in the left column of the website (*Figure* 2) as well as totals for each diocese and each parish within the diocese so far digitized. The parish with the largest available entries is St. Andrew's, Dublin City, with 223,993 baptism entries online. Provision is made to search by name(s) of person, parish, religion, event, time period including year, or browse the entries in each parish. It is free to search and view the available images.

The combining of these two databases would seem appropriate considering both projects were provided directly or indirectly by public funding in both Northern Ireland and the Republic of Ireland and by other funding sources provided to help with the Peace Process between North and South. The development of research services from these database projects and the proposition that they provide local employment should also take into consideration the position of private local businesses.

Until a digital image is made available online the other main source to view the original entry is the microfilm copy of the register. For any serious researcher viewing the original entry must be stressed. It is a must for anyone involved in searching for legal purposes where civil records of births and marriages are unavailable and in the case of locating baptisms of children to specific parents it involves searching for a period of years, sometimes at least thirty, but depending on the age of the mother, from the date of the marriage.

How to search the registers on microfilm?

For those unfamiliar with microfilms I will provide a brief note. Basically microfilms are like ordinary photo negatives but in a continuous strip on a reel. Special microfilm machines are used to view the images on each microfilm.

In some cases, such as rural parishes, the registers of a couple of parishes are on the same reel but note these may not be neighbouring parishes. In larger parishes such as in cities the parish registers cover two or more reels.

So having as much specific information on an ancestor is important if deciding to search the parish registers.

How to find the correct reel?

To locate the correct reel you must first find the microfilm call number. The NLI has produced *Parish Register Lists* which are available on their website at **www.nli.ie/en/parish-register.aspx**

The parishes in each diocese are listed alphabetically showing which registers are available with the relevant dates together with the microfilm number. In the case of PRONI, as at January 2010, an alphabetical list of parish registers of all denominations entitled *An Irish Genealogical Source A Guide To Church Records* is available online at *www.proni.gov.uk/index/research_and_records_held/catalogues_guides_indexes_and_leaflets/online_guides_and_indexes.htm*

It should be noted that the NLI, PRONI and the LDS have they own system of referencing microfilms. Some published sources on Irish genealogy have also listed the various call numbers. But all of these are available within the relevant Research Room for anyone visiting the NLI & PRONI. Once the reel is located and on the microfilm machine scroll through it until the correct parish is found and then through the parish until the relevant section is found.

Enjoy the search!

Representative Church Body Library

Dr Raymond Refaussé
Librarian & Archivist

Introduction

The Representative Church Body Library in Dublin is, among other things, the reference library and archives of the Church of Ireland – the Anglican/Episcopalian Church in Ireland. From the Reformation until disestablishment by the Irish Church Act of 1869 the Church of Ireland was the established church – the official church of the state – and so its records were not only the chronicles of a religious denomination but also part of the records of state. Its parishes were units of local government, its courts were the centres for matrimonial and testamentary jurisdiction, its prelates and clergy were often important officers of state, and its parish churches were, for periods, the locations of the only acts of worship which were permitted under the law.

The Church of Ireland was always a minority church but membership of the established church was critical not alone to ecclesiastical advancement but also to the attainment of office and the ownership of land. And so to the ranks of the Church of Ireland were attracted not only those who were convinced by its theology but many who out of political, social or economic expediency found it prudent to become, at least nominally, members of the established church. Thus the archives of the Church of Ireland reflect a much wider spectrum of Irish life than might otherwise be supposed. And so the Library is a place of first resort for those engaged in genealogy and family history and for those interested in local history from an ecclesiastical perspective, but is not exclusively a source for those with an Anglican background.

History & Development

The Library was founded in 1931 as a reference and lending library for the Church of Ireland but from its earliest days it was also a place of deposit for homeless church records. The archival side of the Library's work increased significantly from the 1960s with the amalgamation of parishes and dioceses and this responsibility was formalized in the 1980s with the appointment of the Church's first archivist. Today the Library manages archives from 1025 parishes, chapels and chaplaincies, 20 dioceses, 20 cathedrals, and the non-current records of the General Synod (the Church's parliament) and Representative Church Body (the Church's civil service) as well as almost 900 collections of related ecclesiastical manuscript collections.

The Library seeks to acquire a copy of all material published about or by significant members of the Church of Ireland. This of course, can never be any other than an aspiration, but the process has ensured that the Library has, *inter alia*, considerable holdings of parish, diocesan and cathedral histories; biographical studies of laity bishops and clergy; family histories; ecclesiastical directories and a wide range of ephemera about Church of Ireland people and places.

Parish Records

Parish records and, especially parish registers, are the most widely consulted sources in the Library. Although some registers have been printed and others are available on microfilm in other repositories and although, with the advent of genealogical websites, much information from registers is now available online, yet it is still the case that the information in many of the registers in the Library is not available elsewhere. Added to this, of course, is an understandable desire by researches to see the original records of their ancestors and, in some cases, a reluctance to believe that the microfilmed or digitized records have successfully captured all the information in the original. The earliest Church of Ireland parish register, that of St John the Evangelist, Dublin, dates from 1619, but few registers are extant for the years before 1650 and only a modest number begin in the second half of the 17th century.

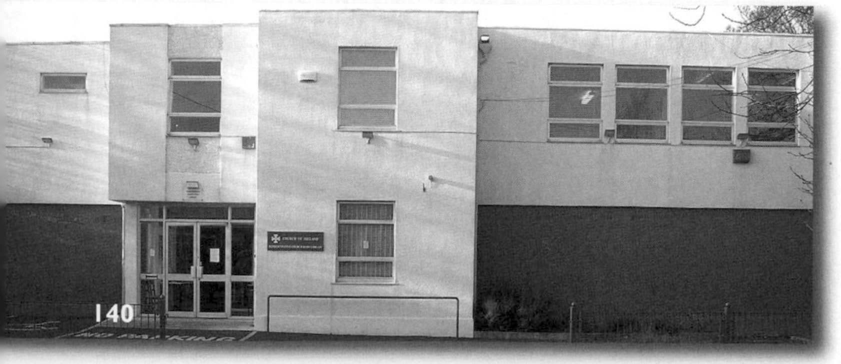

Archbishop John Vesey

The earliest and most substantial parish registers are, for the most part, from the old sea port towns and cities, notably Cork, Derry, Dublin, Galway, Limerick and Waterford and, with the exception of Derry and Limerick all these records have been transferred to the Library. The Library's holdings of parish registers are largely, but not exclusively, from parishes in the Republic of Ireland, and these are augmented by microfilm copies of many of the registers from parishes in Northern Ireland. The National Archives of Ireland holds a small number of original registers as does the Public Record of Northern Ireland, but these custodies apart, registers may only be held by the Library or in parish custody.

Many registers were destroyed in the fire in the Public Record Office of Ireland in 1922 but rather more survives in copy and extract form than was initially supposed. Much of this is among the papers of local genealogists, historians and antiquarians while some exists in the form of transcripts made before the transfer of the original registers to the PROI but not recorded. In general the Library can advise on surviving parish registers, both in original and copy form, and on the location of registers which remain in local custody.

Parish registers, of course, provide only basic information on the Christian rites of passage – baptism, marriage and burial, and it is the records of the vestries, the committees which ran parish affairs, which can often put flesh on the bare bones of the registers. Vestry minutes, churchwardens' accounts and cess books, in particular, can provide a feast of detail on the role of individuals in local life with information on poor relief, fire fighting, policing, property values and much more. Like the parish registers, these records are richest for the cities and in some cases predate the registers, the earliest of them dating from the late 16th century.

Diocesan and Cathedral Records

Diocesan and cathedral records are a much less used source largely because most of them were destroyed in the fire in the Public Record Office of Ireland. However, where they survive they are especially valuable as they are the only significant corpus of pre-Reformation Irish church records.

The Library holds the medieval registers of the diocese of Dublin and Ossory and the cartularies of the cathedrals of Christ Church and St Patrick's, Dublin. Because the archbishops, bishops and cathedral chapters were significant property and landowners until the late 19th century their records often contain much about tenants and employees, as well as clergy, both in their immediate locality and farther afield. For example the maps of the estates of the archbishops of Dublin contain information on landholding in Dublin, Wicklow, Westmeath and Cork from 1654 to 1850 while the records of the diocese of Ossory include records of the inhabitants of the borough of

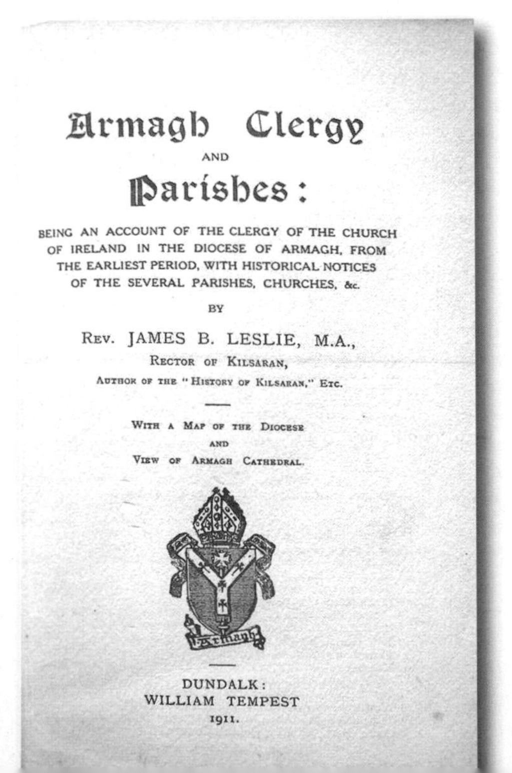
Armagh Clergy

AND

Parishes:

BEING AN ACCOUNT OF THE CLERGY OF THE CHURCH OF IRELAND IN THE DIOCESE OF ARMAGH, FROM THE EARLIEST PERIOD, WITH HISTORICAL NOTICES OF THE SEVERAL PARISHES, CHURCHES, &c.

BY

REV. JAMES B. LESLIE, M.A.,

RECTOR OF KILSARAN,

AUTHOR OF THE "HISTORY OF KILSARAN," ETC.

WITH A MAP OF THE DIOCESE AND VIEW OF ARMAGH CATHEDRAL.

DUNDALK:

WILLIAM TEMPEST

1911.

Irishtown in Kilkenny from the 14th to the 18th century.

The records of the cathedrals especially in Dublin, Kilkenny, Cork and Cloyne, and to a lesser extent in Kildare, Leighlin and Waterford are invaluable sources for their local communities and often further afield.

Clerical Succession Lists

During the first half of the 20th century Canon J.B. Leslie compiled a series of what he called biographical succession lists of Irish clergy. The sources which he used were largely destroyed in the fire in the Public Record Office of Ireland in 1922 and so his work, which he bequeathed to the Library, is the principal resource for information on Church of Ireland bishops and clergy. He produced a volume for most dioceses and to this added a four volume index of all his work. Some of his volumes were published during his lifetime and some more recently. However, some of his work still subsists only in typescript from in the Library. The information in Leslie's lists is variable both in quality and quantity but for most clergy there will be details of family, education and career.

Miscellaneous Ecclesiastical Manuscripts

One of the principal functions of the Library following the loss of so many church records in 1922 was to gather together copies and extracts of destroyed material. Pre-eminent among the copyists of the time was Tension Groves who had worked as a record agent in the years before the fire. From him the Library acquired, among other items, abstracts from the 1766 Religious Census and the 1740 Lists of

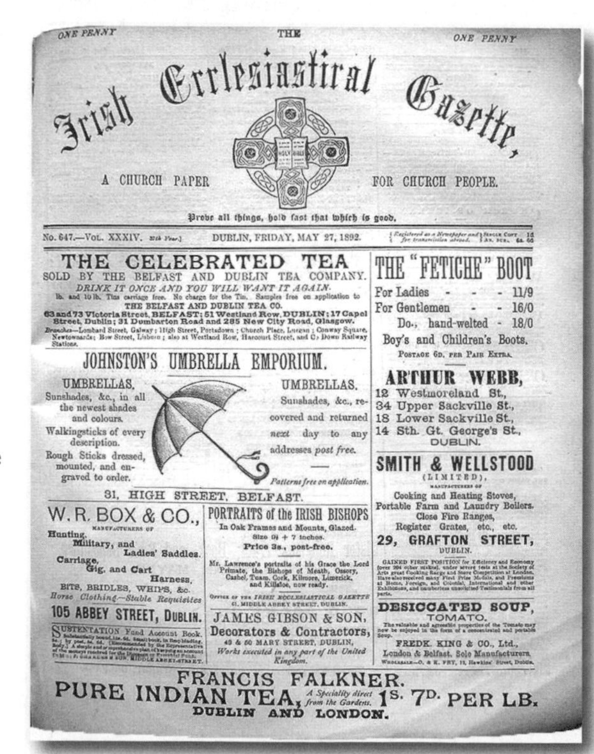

ONE PENNY THE ONE PENNY

Irish Ecclesiastical Gazette,

A CHURCH PAPER FOR CHURCH PEOPLE.

Prove all things, hold fast that which is good.

No. 647.—Vol. XXXIV. DUBLIN, FRIDAY, MAY 27, 1892.

THE CELEBRATED TEA
SOLD BY THE BELFAST AND DUBLIN TEA COMPANY.
DRINK IT ONCE AND YOU WILL WANT IT AGAIN.
lb. and 10 lb. Tins carriage free. No charge for the Tin. Samples free on application to
THE BELFAST AND DUBLIN TEA CO.
63 and 73 Victoria Street, BELFAST; 51 Westland Row, DUBLIN; 17 Capel Street, Dublin; 31 Dumbarton Road and 285 New City Road, Glasgow.
Branches—Lombard Street, Galway; High Street, Portadown; Church Place, Lurgan; Conway Square, Newtownards; Bow Street, Lisburn; also at Westland Row, Harcourt Street, and Co. Down Railway Stations.

JOHNSTON'S UMBRELLA EMPORIUM.
UMBRELLAS. Sunshades, &c., in all the newest shades and colours. Walkingsticks of every description. Rough Sticks dressed, mounted, and engraved to order.
UMBRELLAS. Sunshades, &c., recovered and returned next day to any addresses *post free.*
Patterns free on application.
31, HIGH STREET, BELFAST.

W. R. BOX & CO., MANUFACTURERS OF Hunting, Military, and Ladies' Saddles. Carriage, Gig, and Cart Harness, BITS, BRIDLES, WHIPS, &c. *Horse Clothing—Stable Requisites*
105 ABBEY STREET, DUBLIN.

SUSTENTATION Fund Account Book.

PORTRAITS of the IRISH BISHOPS
In Oak Frames and Mounts, Glazed.
Price 3s., post-free.
Mr. Lawrence's portraits of his Grace the Lord Primate, the Bishops of Meath, Ossory, Cashel, Tuam, Cork, Kilmore, Limerick, and Killaloe, now ready.
OFFICE OF THE IRISH ECCLESIASTICAL GAZETTE 61, MIDDLE ABBEY STREET, DUBLIN.

JAMES GIBSON & SON,
Decorators & Contractors,
49 & 50 MARY STREET, DUBLIN,
Works executed in any part of the United Kingdom.

THE "FETICHE" BOOT
For Ladies - - - 11/9
For Gentlemen - - 16/0
Do., hand-welted - 18/0
Boy's and Children's Boots.
POSTAGE 6D. PER PAIR EXTRA.

ARTHUR WEBB,
12 Westmoreland St.,
34 Upper Sackville St.,
18 Lower Sackville St.,
14 Sth. Gt. George's St.,
DUBLIN.

SMITH & WELLSTOOD (LIMITED), MANUFACTURERS OF
Cooking and Heating Stoves, Portable Farm and Laundry Boilers. Close Fire Ranges, Register Grates, etc., etc.
29, GRAFTON STREET, DUBLIN.

DESICCATED SOUP, TOMATO.
The valuable and agreeable properties of the Tomato may now be enjoyed in the form of a concentrated and portable Soup.
FREDK. KING & CO., Ltd., London & Belfast, Sole Manufacturers.

FRANCIS FALKNER.
PURE INDIAN TEA, *A Speciality direct from the Gardens.* 1s. 7d. PER LB.
DUBLIN AND LONDON.

Protestant Householders, extracts from 17th century hearth money returns, poll tax records and subsidy rolls, and copies of 17th and 18th century episcopal visitations. H.B. Swanzy, the Dean of Down, presented his notebooks of genealogical research from chancery, exchequer and prerogative court records, first fruits returns and diocesan visitations, together with his notebooks of pedigrees of 120 Irish families and his abstracts of some 800 wills mostly relating to Ulster.

Following the death in 1960 of the genealogist, W.H. Welply, the Library acquired, by bequest, a considerable body of his research dealing mostly with Co. Cork from the 17th to the 20th century – abstracts of over 1600 wills, marriage licence bonds, deeds, chancery and exchequer bills and pedigree notebooks.

In addition to copy material the Library has become the place of deposit for records of Church of Ireland organizations and the papers of families and individuals. Records of missionary societies, youth organizations, educational bodies, orphan societies and related charities such as, for example, the Charitable Musical Society of Dublin which hosted the first performance of Handel's *Messiah*, reflect Irish life at every level of society. The correspondence of leading churchmen such as Lord John George Beresford, Archbishop of Armagh, 1822 - 1862, and Euseby Cleaver, Archbishop of Dublin, 1809 - 1819, reflect the preoccupations of those in authority while, for example, the deeds of the Hamilton family of Cos Tyrone and Londonderry and the records of the Youghal Protestant Relief Society reveal something of the lives of the laity in the 18th and 19th century.

Printed Material

As the principal point of reference for information on the Church of Ireland, the Library holds a wide range of printed material which is likely to be of interest to family and local historians. Most important are the two Church of Ireland serials – the *Church of Ireland Gazette* and the *Church of Ireland Directory*. The *Gazette* is a long running church weekly publication having begun life as the *Irish Ecclesiastical Gazette* in 1856 before changing to its present title in 1900. It is bursting with information on people, places, property, publications and services – the advertisements being a particularly rich source for commercial activity. The *Directory* began publication in 1862 as the *Irish Ecclesiastical Directory* and appeared every year until 1965. There was no issue in 1966 but it reappeared in 1967 as the *Church of Ireland Directory* and has been published annually since then. It is a particularly valuable source for tracking the movement of clergy and amalgamations of parishes and dioceses, while the current edition is the main source for names and addresses of clergy who may have custody of church records.

The Library has a large collection of parish, cathedral and diocesan histories, many of which appeared only as local publications with very small print runs and so are rarely to be found in the national reference collections or in the copyright libraries. The Library's catalogue of printed material is in the process of being transferred to an online catalogue and bibliographical information on much of it can already be accessed through the Library's website.

Publications

Since 1994 the Library has been publishing editions of parish registers and, so far, twelve volumes have been produced. More recently the Library, in association with Four Courts Press, has been publishing editions of older vestry records with substantial introductions and notes, and four volumes in this *'Texts and Calendars'* series have appeared. Details of the Library's publications programme is available on the Library website.

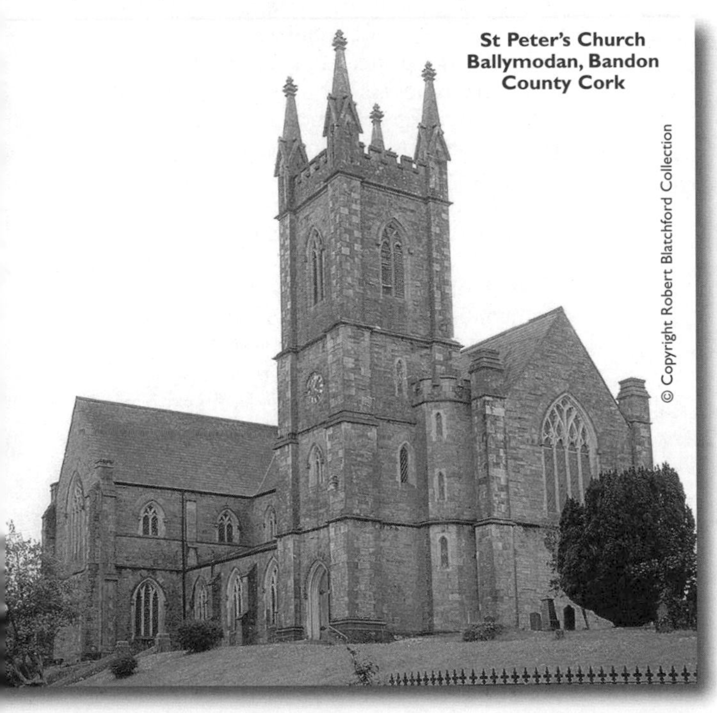

St Peter's Church
Ballymodan, Bandon
County Cork

Image© Copyright Robert Blatchford Collection

St Patrick's Cathedral Dublin

Non-Written Sources

The Library maintains databases of the Church's collections of episcopal portraits and church plate. Some of the portraits are by leading artists such as Reynolds and Orpen and so are substantial works of art. Others are more modest commissions but since many of the portraits pre-date the age of photography they are often the only representation of leading churchmen. To complement the portraits the Library is building up a photographic collection.

This is mostly of church buildings and clergy but the growing number of photographs of *'church events'* provides valuable illustrative material on the laity. The Church's extensive collection of church plate – mostly patens, chalices and flagons - are in part by the leading Dublin and provincial silversmiths and are remarkable for their beauty and rarity. However, from an historical and genealogical perspective their principal value is that they are mostly inscribed and so often have valuable information on individuals and organizations. The databases are not open to public inspection but queries regarding them will, for the most part, be dealt with by the Library staff.

Access to the Collections

The archives and manuscripts collections are, for the most part, subject to a 40 year access rule (the principal exception to this rule is that there is access to all parish registers) and in some cases collections are closed for longer periods. Otherwise collections are available to researchers in the Library's reading rooms. No appointment is necessary and most material can be produced within 15 minutes. However, it is always prudent to make contact in advance of a visit especially if travelling from a distance. General information about the Library and details of the collections are available on the Library website and all researchers should consult the website before making contact with the Library. For those who are unable to visit the Library, the Library staff may, for a fee, undertake specific searches but the Library does not offer a general research service – for the most part researchers are expected to undertake their own wok or to commission an agent to undertake it for them.

Representative Church Body Library
Braemor Park,, Churchtown, Dublin 14
T: +353 1 492 3979 F: +353 1 492 4770
E: library@ireland.anglican.org
W: www.library.ireland.anglican.org

Irish Records at The National Archives, Kew

Audrey Collins

TNA Records Specialist - Family History

Until 1922, all of Ireland was part of the United Kingdom. Since that date the six counties that make up Northern Ireland are still part of the UK. So most of our Irish ancestors would be classed as British, whether they liked it or not.

As a result, many useful records of their lives and activities are to be found in British sources, and the largest collection of these is held by The National Archives (TNA) at Kew, in south-west London.

The National Archives keeps records that were generated by or collected by United Kingdom government departments, and by the English legal system. Some of the records held there relate only to England, or to England and Wales, but many others cover the whole of the UK.

Most of the United Kingdom wide record series held in The National Archives cannot be split into *'English,' Irish,' 'Scottish'* or *'Welsh'* elements, and therefore can only be treated as a single unified collection. From a genealogical point of view the most significant example of this is the records of the armed forces and the merchant navy, where Irish men and women served alongside people from other parts of the United Kingdom and beyond.

Other records are in collections that relate specifically to Ireland, such as an extensive series known as the *Dublin Castle* records, dealing with the British administration of Ireland from the late 18th century until independence. Before that, the collection of *State Papers, Ireland 1509-1784* records the administration of first English and then British rule in Ireland. The service records of the *Royal Irish Constabulary 1816-1922* and other records kept by the Home Office form another important resource. For the 20th century there is a good deal of documentation on the dismantling of the old Dublin Castle administration, and claims for compensation for damage caused by both sides during the Troubles. There is even one early record series that appears to be Irish, but is much less useful for Irish research than it appears to be; the records of the *Irish Tontine* in series NDO 3 1773 - 1871 contain much useful information about individuals, but on inspection it turns out that only a minority of the subscribers were Irish.

The key to the holdings of The National Archives is the online Catalogue, which can be searched at www.nationalarchives.gov.uk /catalogue. There were more than 11 million catalogued items at the last count, and catalogue additions and improvements are constantly being made. However, the level of detail still varies considerably; some parts of the Catalogue can be searched by name, while others have only the briefest of descriptions. One of the best illustrations of this is in the aforementioned Irish Tontine records, where the description of NDO 3/49 reads *'Packet of sundry loose papers - more or less interesting!'*

So a keyword search for a name or a place may produce some results, but these will only reveal a fraction of the potential sources of information on your Irish ancestors. To get the best research results you will need to combine Catalogue searches with guidance from other online and printed sources. The website contains a useful series of brief guides called Research Signposts, and a range of more detailed Research Guides to help you identify the records you need to consult. You will find links to dozens of Research Signposts on the page *'Looking for a person'* www.nationalarchives.gov.uk /records/looking-for-person and most of them lead in turn to some of the In-depth Research Guides. These also have a page of their own where they are listed alphabetically www.nationalarchives.gov.uk /records/research-guide-listing.htm and they include a dedicated guide to Irish genealogy.

Some of the most popular and heavily used records in The National Archives have been digitised, indexed and made available online, so they can be accessed and downloaded anywhere in the world. Some of this work has been done *'in house'* and the results can be found at www.nationalarchives.gov.uk /documentsonline

Only one record series within DocumentsOnline is exclusively Irish – *Early Irish maps from State Papers c1558-c1610* – but most of the record sets in the military and naval categories, and some in wills and probate, include many Irish individuals.

Most of the very large digitisation projects have not been conducted in-house, but in partnership with commercial sites such as Ancestry or Find My Past. Access to these digitised images is always free on-site at The National Archives, Kew, and at some other record offices and libraries, such as Family History Centres run by the Church of Jesus Christ of Latter-Day Saints. The largest digitisation projects to date are the census for England and Wales 1841 to 1911, incoming and outgoing ships' passenger lists, and soldiers' service records from approximately 1760 to the First War. All of these are of great interest to researchers in Irish genealogy.

Census Returns

The England and Wales census may not appear to be an obvious choice, but it can be useful to establish birthplaces in Ireland for ancestors who were in England and Wales at the time of the census. Much of the time it may be of limited use, since Irish birthplaces often appear simply as *'Ireland.'* This is all the information that was required from 1841 to 1901, although sometimes a county, or even a parish, was listed. In 1911, however, the parish and county of birth was required for anyone born anywhere in the United Kingdom, including Ireland. This is great news if you have Irish born ancestors in England and Wales at that time, but if they had died before 1911, it may be worth checking for any of their siblings or other relatives who were still alive then, and who are likely to have the same birthplace.

Even if your Irish ancestor never set foot in England or Wales, it is worth remembering that the census also includes the Channel Islands and the Isle of Man as well as some returns from the Royal Navy and from merchant vessels. Additionally, the 1911 census includes for the first time a full enumeration of the army stationed abroad. Since there were always many Irishmen in the armed forces and the merchant navy, this census could be the one to provide a breakthrough for some Irish researchers.

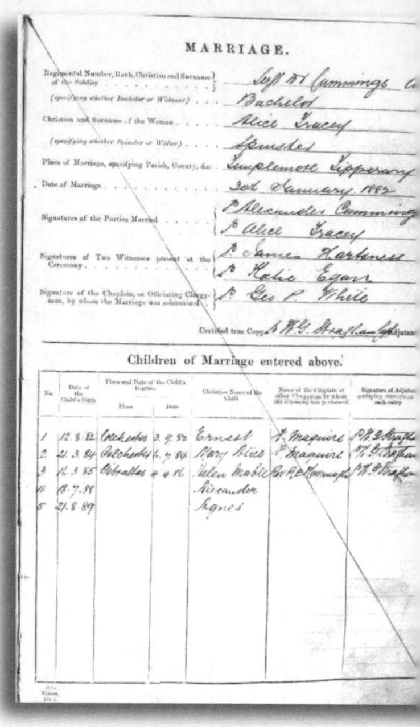
MARRIAGE.

Children of Marriage entered above.

Military Records

Before *The Act of Union 1801*, The British army had a separate Irish establishment with its own organisation and headquarters at Kilmainham, but the British army also drew heavily on Irish recruits. From 1801 Ireland remained a separate command, and Irish regiments kept their own identity, but the army was merged with the British army.

Estimates vary, but in the 18th, 19th and early 20th centuries it is likely that a quarter or even more of the men in British army were born in Ireland. And although many of them served in Irish regiments, they can be found in all regiments and corps throughout the army. Service records survive for many of these men, especially those who those who served long enough to earn a pension before 1913. Records for other ranks, though not for officers, may contain astonishingly detailed physical descriptions; height, chest measurement, eye colour, scars and tattoos. These are some of the most heavily used resources at The National Archives.

Unfortunately about 60% of the service records from the First World War were destroyed by enemy action during the Second World War, but the surviving ones are online and searchable by name at www.ancestry.co.uk

IRISH GRANTS COMMITTEE.

(The Information given on this Form will be treated as Confidential, but inquiries will in all probability be made from the references given.)

1. Name (in full, and in block letters) JOHN SCANLON
2. Age 32 years
3. Address (for correspondence) St.G. Robinson Williams, Solicitors, Sligo County Sligo
4. State here the nature of the loss in respect of which application is made, giving material dates. Detailed particulars need not be furnished at this stage.

A Ford Motor Car, my property was forcibly taken from me by masked men at 4 am. on 7th November 1921

Where there is no service record, medal rolls and unit war diaries may provide some information about an ancestor. Service records of many men who left the army before 1913 are searchable by name at www.findmypast.co.uk

For the soldiers who do not appear in these records, for example those who died in the service, there are many other records, muster rolls, casualty lists, and description books.

Some Irishmen served in the *Royal Navy*, the *Royal Marines* and the *Royal Air Force*, and fortunately there have been no major losses from these records. Many of them can be searched and downloaded from www.nationalarchives.gov.uk /documentsonline which also includes some service records for women in the *Women's Auxiliary Army Corps*, the *Women's Royal Naval Service* and the *Women's Auxiliary Air Force* during the First World War. Those for the *Women's Auxiliary Army Corps* are particularly detailed.

After the First World War, the *Irish Sailors' and Soldiers' Land Trust* was set up to provide cottages in Ireland for ex-servicemen. Over 4000 cottages were built, up to 1932 in the Republic of Ireland, and as late as 1952 in Northern Ireland. The tenancy files are in series AP 7, and are arranged by locality, so you need to have at least an approximate address, since there are no name indexes.

For the records that are not digitised, and which have to be consulted in original format or on microfilm, there is still some good news; the Catalogue information is being improved all the time, so that some records can be searched by individual name and other keywords. Information about these can be found in the *Research Signposts and Research Guides* already mentioned.

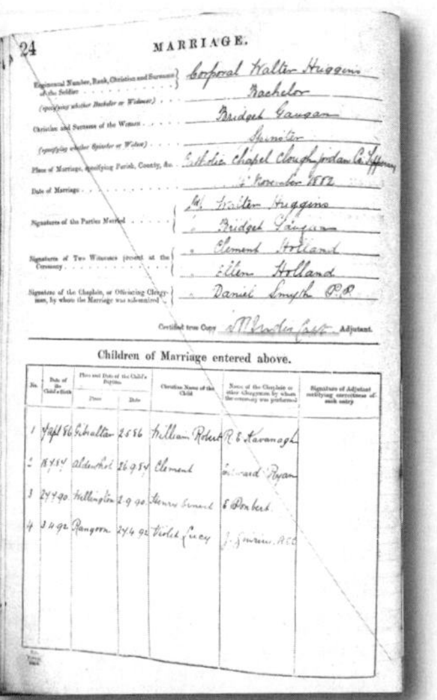
24

MARRIAGE.

Corporal Walter Huggins
Bachelor
Bridget Gaugan
Spinster
Catholic chapel Clough jordan Co Tipperary
November 1882
Walter Huggins
Bridget Gaugan
Clement Holland
Ellen Holland
Daniel Smyth P.P.

Certified true Copy — Adjutant.

Children of Marriage entered above.

No.	Date of the Child's Birth	Place and Date of the Child's Baptism: Place	Date	Christian Name of the Child	Name of the Chaplain or other Clergyman by whom the ceremony was performed	Signature of Adjutant certifying correctness of each entry
1	[illegible] 86	Gibraltar	2.5.86	William Robert	R. E. Kavanagh	
2	18.7.84	Aldershot	26.9.84	Clement	Edward Ryan	
3	24.7.90	Wellington	2.9.90	Henry Ernest	E. [illegible]	
4	3.4.92	Rangoon	24.4.92	Violet Lucy	J. [illegible] RCC	

As well as the armed forces, there are records of other services - *Coastguard, Customs and Excise and the Merchant Navy.* Members of the coastguard and customs and excise services were moved around the country at regular intervals, so your Irish ancestors in those services could be anywhere in the United Kingdom.

Unfortunately, few of these records are available online at the moment, although you can manually search some service records of *Coastguards,* as part of the Digital Microfilm project on www.nationalarchives.gov.uk /documentsonline

Digital Microfilm records are not indexed, but are basically rolls of microfilm converted into large pdf files. This means you can search through a roll of microfilm on your computer, or a terminal in The National Archives, instead of on a microfilm reader. Although this may be no quicker that searching through a film, the good news is that Digital Microfilm records are completely free to download, so you can do your searching at home. Many *Coastguards,* had previously served in the *Royal Navy,* so if you have a coastguard ancestor it is worth checking the *Registers of Seaman's Services* at www.nationalarchives.gov.uk /documentsonline

Merchant Navy

If you are looking for an Irish ancestor in the merchant service you will find that research in this area is less straightforward than for men in the Royal Navy and the other armed forces. You need to bear in mind that the merchant navy was not a unified service, but a large collection of private employers. They had to deposit various records relating to men and vessels with the Board of Trade, some of which are now held in The National Archives. As a result, there is a great deal of variation in the type, extent and survival of the records, and their current location. Other records of merchant navy ships and sailors may be found in a variety of record offices. However, The National Archives and its range of Research Guides is a good place to start. Although The National Archives holds only a small proportion of service records of merchant seamen, the good news is that they include some as recent as the mid-20th century, unlike the armed services, whose more recent personnel records are mostly retained by the Ministry of Defence. Merchant seamen's resisters of service 1918-1949 are being digitised, and will appear on www.findmypast.co.uk

Passenger Lists

Passenger lists collected by the Board of Trade from all ports in the United Kingdom to destinations outside Europe between 1890 and 1960 are online at www.findmypast.co.uk and incoming lists are on www.ancestry.co.uk The incoming series also includes a few earlier lists, back to 1878, but it was only from 1890 that all lists were required to be kept. The outgoing lists comprise a wonderful source for emigrants

Dublin after The Easter Uprising 1916

to Australia, New Zealand and of course to the USA and Canada, many of whom were Irish. It is worth looking at the incoming, as well as the outgoing, lists for them. Not only will you find that some people travelled back and forth, particularly across the Atlantic, but the lists will often include members of the crew, so if your Irish merchant seaman ancestor served on a passenger ship, you might find him here.

Other Sources

Although personal records of Irish people who served in the armed forces and other United Kingdom services form a large proportion of the items of interest for Irish research, they are by no means the only ones. There are also many *Home Office* files rich in information about Ireland and the Irish, and some of these have been catalogued in detail. These include many records on crime and criminals, such as transportation registers; no matter where a crime was committed in the United Kingdom, anyone sentenced to transportation would sail from an English port, so criminals sentenced in Irish courts, under the Irish legal system, might still appear in records in England. The Home Office commissioned reports on the Irish poor, particularly during the famine years; these deal with not only with conditions in Ireland itself, but also with the many thousands of Irish people who fled to England, and how the authorities dealt with them. Sometimes they give the names of individual paupers. Home Office correspondence also covers Catholic emancipation, poor law reform and peerage claims, to name but a few, in series HO 100. These include an interesting set of records known as *'Reports of Outrages' 1836 to 1840,* weekly reports arranged by county and parish, of reported crimes. These range from petty theft, to riot and serious assault, listing the victims, and sometimes the perpetrators or suspects too. Staff records of the Royal Irish Constabulary are also part of the Home Office collection, in series HO 184, and there is a dedicated Research Guide to using this important collection. The service records are due to be digitised and indexed, and should appear online in due course.

The Irish Reproductive Loan fund provided small loans to the industrious poor in the provinces of Munster and Connaught in the mid

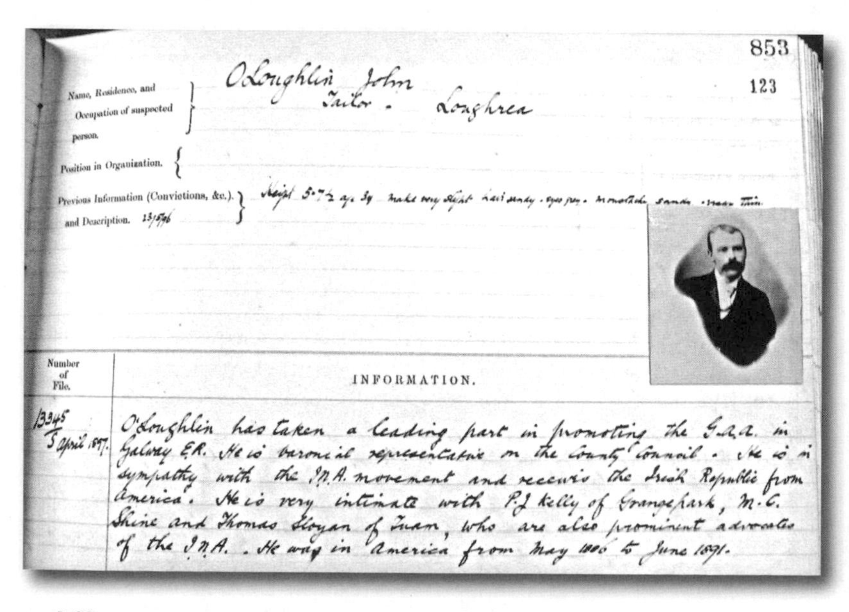
853

123

Name, Residence, and Occupation of suspected person. O'Loughlin John Tailor. Loughrea

Position in Organization.

Previous Information (Convictions, &c.). and Description. 23/5/96 Height 5·7½ age 34 make very slight hair sandy · eyes grey · moustache sandy · nose thin

Number of File.	INFORMATION.
13345 5 April 1897.	O'Loughlin has taken a leading part in promoting the G.A.A. in Galway E.R. He is baronial representative on the County Council. He is in sympathy with the I.N.A. movement and receives the Irish Republic from America. He is very intimate with P.J. Kelly of Grangepark, M.C. Shine and Thomas Sloyan of Tuam, who are also prominent advocates of the I.N.A. He was in America from May 1886 to June 1891.

19th century. Some of these records have been digitised and can be downloaded free of charge at www.movinghere.org.uk . They consist of the returns to the Clerk of the Peace for the counties of Cork, Galway, Limerick, Mayo, Roscommon and Tipperary.

Wills

The very first records to be digitised and published on DocumentsOnline were the Prerogative Court of Canterbury wills, which covers England and Wales. Although Ireland has always had its own completely separate system of probate, some Irish wills can be found in this series. They are mainly those left by members of Anglo-Irish landed families, or of English people who were temporarily resident in Ireland, or vice versa, such as army officers. It is therefore worth checking here for the wills of Irish people who fall into one of these categories.

Irish Nationalism

Most of the material relating to the British administration of Ireland is held in the Dublin Castle records, mainly held in record series CO 904. Many of these records deal with the rise of Irish nationalism and British attempts to deal with it.

There is a whole Research Guide devoted to the considerable amount of material on *The Easter Rising 1916*. This includes extensive records on people who were involved in the rising, especially those who were arrested and tried by court martial afterwards. When most of Ireland finally achieved home rule, a great many records were created concerning the separation of the administrative functions of the two states; these include applications for passports, and questions regarding the status of Irish people resident in mainland Britain. There are also extensive records of claims for compensation for damage caused by both sides in the years leading up to independence, from all parts of Ireland. These are the records of the Irish Distress Committee, later re-named the Irish Grants Committee, comprising more than 3000 files on individual claims which can be searched by name in the Catalogue, in series CO 762.

Maps of Ireland

Finally, The National Archives holds hundreds of maps of Ireland, from the 16th century onwards. They include military maps, railway maps and some relating to property and taxation. They come in many shapes and sizes

This has been just a brief summary of some of the Irish family history resources held in The National Archives in London; further exploration would certainly reveal much more. You can find out more about records in The National Archives that might be useful to your Irish research by consulting some of the in-depth Research Guides, available for download from the website. As well as the three specifically Irish guides on Irish Genealogy, the Royal Irish Constabulary and the Easter Rising of 1916, many of the other guides on the subjects mentioned above will be helpful to you.

You can also find a detailed list of records with Irish content in Alice Prochaska's *Irish History from 1700: A Guide to Sources in the Public Record Office,* published by the British Records Association in 1986, now out of print It is not aimed at the genealogist, and is often charmingly out of date – it refers to records being held at the old Public Record Office building in Chancery Lane, which closed in 1997. There is, understandably, no mention of The National Archives, which only came into being in 2003 as a result of the merger of the Public Record Office with the Royal Commission on Historical Manuscripts. It remains, however, the most comprehensive list of Irish material held in The National Archives, and the introduction gives a good explanation of the historical background and the origins of the records.

For the majority of records that have not been digitised or filmed, you will need to visit The National Archives at Kew in person, or have someone search the records on your behalf. You can find all the information you need about visiting at www.nationalarchives.gov.uk/visit/ including opening hours, travel directions and details of how to obtain a Reader's Ticket, which you will need to view original documents.

The National Archives, Kew, Richmond, Surrey, TW9 4DU. T: +44 (0) 20 8876 3444 W: www.nationalarchives.gov.uk/

Uncovering Family History at a Local Library

Anne Marie O'Dwyer

Would you like to learn more about your family history but are not sure where to begin? You'll usually get off to a good start by noting down what you already know and asking relatives. However for most of us, the family connections we discover from others are unlikely to paint a full picture. It is usually necessary to explore different avenues to find those extra pieces of information. Other issues are then likely to arise such as: *Are there historical records I can easily search? Where can I find these? How much will it cost?*

Public libraries are very well equipped to meet your needs and make family history research a much easier and straightforward pursuit. There are currently 348 public libraries throughout the country and with 16.1 million visits each year, the number of us using the library service is growing rapidly. In addition to local studies' book collections, including histories of the local area, many libraries provide access to church records, indexes to baptisms, marriages and burials, land, emigration, biographical and court records as well as deeds, maps, newspapers, photographs, local journals, plans and drawings related to the local area. Some of the most popular records include local directories, the census online for 1901 and 1911, the Irish civil registration indexes from 1845 to1958 and the *Irish Times Digital Archive* from 1859 to the present. Libraries throughout the country generally have local newspaper collections which can add extra colour to family histories. Many library holdings also include unique collections of manuscripts and early printed books. Each county has a local studies librarian with expertise on local history and on the documents to assist your search. If you haven't already used your public library, you might wonder how much this resource will cost. The good news is that access to local studies material available through the public library service in Ireland is completely free of charge.

Many records and indexes are available in hard copy in the libraries and an increasing number are available via the internet, making searching much easier and quicker. One of the most valuable services used for family research on the nineteenth century is the Griffith's Valuation database which provides

Ask about Ireland

Names: Townlands & Occupiers	Immediate Lessors	Description of Tenement	Area A. R. P.
Poulacurry South - cont.			
13 Lodgers	Henry Maunsell	House	-
14 Lodgers	Same	House	-
15 Denis Crimeen	Same	House & forge	-
16 Lodgers	William Thorley	House (dilapidated)	-
17 Lodgers	Same	House (dilapidated)	-
18 Lodgers	Same	House (dilapidated)	-
19 Lodgers	Same	House (dilapidated)	-
		Waste of lot	1. 0. 3
9 1 Edward Phair	Rev. John K. Woodroffe	House, offices & land	1. 1. 5
2 Unoccupied	Daniel Cantillon	House	-
3 Daniel Cantillon	Joseph Martin	House & sm. garden	-
4 Joseph Martin	Anthony B. St. Leger	Building ground	0. 0. 29
5 Patrick Hurley	John Bullman	House	-
6 William Callaghan	Same	House & yard	-
7 Timothy Sheehan	Same	House, offices	-
8 John Manning		House	-

access to records of tenants and landlords in the mid 1800s for the whole country. This free online service from public libraries includes detailed maps with markings for houses, out-houses and ownership boundaries for every townland in the country. Griffith's Valuation can be accessed on the public libraries' website www.askaboutireland.ie/griffith-valuation either at home or in your local library. The name of an ancestor, the county, parish or townland where they lived can be searched as well as lists of people who lived in each townland at the time of the valuation. The website also provides direct access to maps from the periods 1837 to 1842 and 1888 to 1913, available in an easily searchable format via the new Digital Map Archive from Ordnance Survey Ireland.

Another treasure from the public libraries is the selection of useful historical material and family history guides on the website www.askaboutireland.ie. All content on the site can be freely accessed via the internet. The website's virtual *Reading Room* includes information, pictures, audios and videos on historical, geographical, scientific and environmental topics from all parts of the country. Digitised photographs, maps, documents and illustrations on various aspects of Irish culture and history, past and present, can be located from among hundreds of articles and from all parts of the country. Many historical collections from the public libraries are also available on the site from different periods, for example *The Limerick Leader 1944-50* and *The Waterford News 1915-17*. A collection of historic film clips from the early 1900s onwards is also available to view and include many of Ireland's most important historical events such as Queen Victoria's visit to Ireland in 1900, the Easter Rising, the War of Independence, President Kennedy's visit to Ireland and the bombing of Nelson's Pillar. Video collections on traditional Irish cooking and traditional Irish crafts can also be enjoyed including videos on spinning wool, making butter, a thatcher at work and laying cobblestones. Another excellent collection on the site is the ebooks' section which provides free access to an online library with over five hundred historical books from the 1700s onwards. The collection is organised by both county and topic and a full copy of each book can be viewed. The section also includes full access to the statistical surveys conducted between 1801 and 1832 for most counties.

Each public library offers a unique contribution to your family history research. Many libraries arrange talks from local historians and hold interesting exhibitions related to the history of the local area. If you haven't already, it's definitely time to explore what your library can offer for uncovering your family secrets . . .

www.askaboutireland.ie is managed by The Library Council and The Public Library Authorities.
E: askaboutireland@librarycouncil.ie

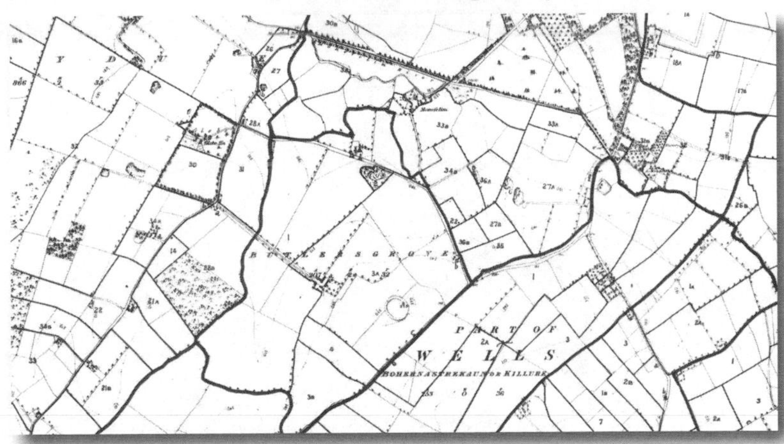

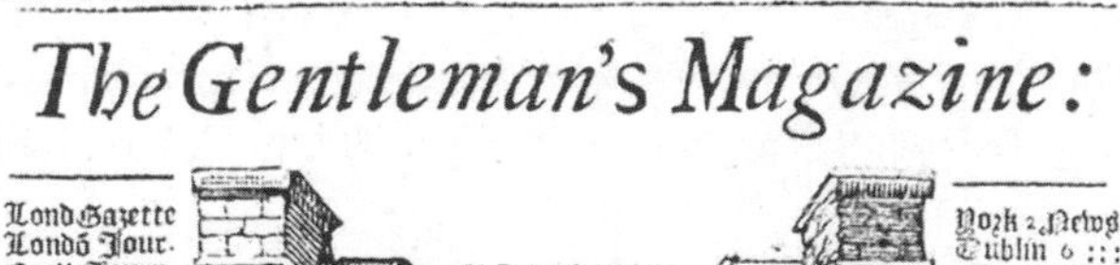

The Gentleman's Magazine - Irish Happenings

Fred Feather

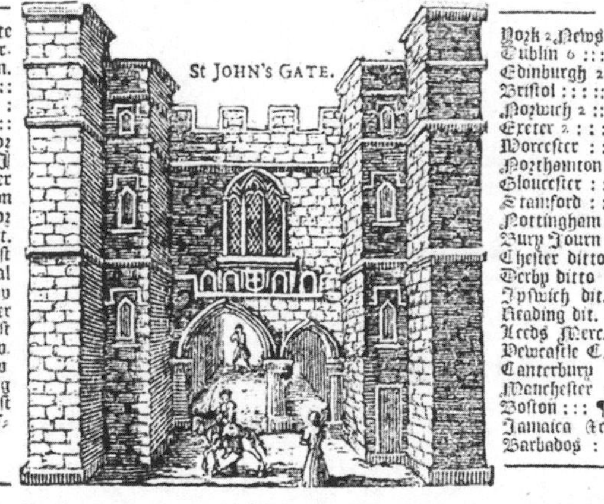

The Gentleman's Magazine:

Lond Gazette
Londô Journ.
Fog's Journ.
Applebee's
Read's
Craftsman
D. Spectator
Grubstreet J
W.ly Register
Free Briton
Hyp Doctor
Daily Court.
Daily Post
Dai. Journal
Da. Post-boy
D. Advertiser
Evening Post
St James's Ev.
Whitehal' Ev
Lòdon Eve'g
Flying Post
Weekly Miscellany
Auditor

St John's Gate.

York 2 News
Dublin 6
Edinburgh 2
Bristol
Norwich 2
Exeter 2
Worcester
Northamton
Gloucester
Stamford
Nottingham
Bury Journ
Chester ditto
Derby ditto
Ipswich dit.
Reading dit.
Leeds Merc.
Newcastle C.
Canterbury
Manchester
Boston
Jamaica &c
Barbados

Or, Monthly Intelligencer.

On 15th April 1731 Mary Meddan was try'd at Ennis in Ireland for the murder of her husband and son, by giving them a blow with a hatchet on the temple, of which they immediately died. The Jury brought her in guilty. Tis believed she murdered her first husband.

In April 1731 Wm. Peters was committed to Goal in Ireland, being found alive on a journey, 3 days after he had been executed for Horsestealing. Again in September 1744 at Roscommon, one Patrick Hurley, condemned to the gallows for robbing, after a considerable time, was perceived to have an iron collar about his neck, on which he was cut down, not being in the least hurt, the collar taken off, and he hung up again until dead.

In October 1737, Andrew Newton, aged 117, lately in Ireland, married to a young woman of 19, who is big with Child by him; he has a Son living above 80, and is as hale and hearty as any man of 50 in the kingdom.

On 28th July 1742 past, a Trial came on before the Court of Kings Bench at Dublin, wherein a Servant Girl was Plaintiff, and a Gentleman Defendant, for a Promissory Note of £50 on her admitting his Embraces; and the Jury not only gave a Verdict for the £50 and for the interest, together with Sixpence Costs.

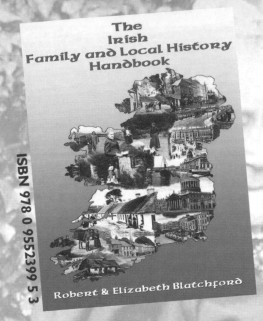

Presbyterians in Ireland:

a guide to denominations and documentary records

William Roulston

Research Director - Ulster Historical Foundation

Over many years, I have met people looking for Irish ancestors who were Presbyterians. For some there is understandable confusion at the bewildering array of manifestations of Presbyterianism in Ireland – *Seceder, Non-Subscribing, Reformed, Free*, and *Evangelical*. The aim of this article is to help those with Irish Presbyterian ancestors find out more about their forebears. It considers the different strands of Presbyterianism in Ireland, distinguishing between each of the historic Presbyterian denominations, and explores the range of records generated by these churches.

The Presbyterian Church in Ireland

Presbyterianism emerged in Scotland in the late sixteenth century. It is characterised by worship services where reading the Bible and preaching have greatest importance and where there is a lack of emphasis on ritual and liturgy. The basic unit in the Presbyterian Church in Ireland is the congregation. In terms of church government it is democratic rather than hierarchical: every minister is considered equal, and to assist him each congregation will appoint a number of *'elders,'* collectively known as the session. Church buildings have historically been known as *'meeting houses'* reflecting the belief that the significance of the edifice lies not in and of itself, but rather in the group of people who have gathered there.

In the early seventeenth century, with the influx of large numbers of Scottish settlers, a number of clergymen with Presbyterian convictions arrived in Ulster from Scotland. To begin with they were accommodated within the Church of Ireland and were allowed a certain amount of freedom to practise their beliefs. However, in the 1630s there were moves to bring the Church of Ireland more closely into line with the Church of England. This resulted in the expulsion of those ministers with Presbyterian beliefs.

In 1642 an army from Scotland landed at Carrickfergus to defend Scottish settlers from attacks from Irish insurgents. Accompanying this army were a number of Presbyterian ministers acting as chaplains, and here the first Irish presbytery was founded. In the 1650s, during the Cromwellian regime, there was considerable freedom of worship and many ministers in Ulster were Scottish Presbyterians. Following the Restoration of 1660, ministers who refused to conform to the teachings and government of the newly reinstated Church of Ireland were dismissed. Despite periods of persecution, Presbyterians began to form congregations and build their own churches from the 1660s. In 1690 an overarching ruling body known as the General Synod or Synod of Ulster was established.

For many members of the establishment, Presbyterians were regarded as more of a threat than Catholics, especially because of their numerical superiority over Anglicans in much of Ulster. Certain restrictions were placed on Presbyterians as a result of the Penal Laws passed in the Irish parliament. For example, in 1704 the *'Test Act'* was extended to Ireland which required persons holding public office to produce a certificate stating that they had received communion in an Anglican church. Twenty-four Presbyterian members of the Londonderry corporation resigned rather than submit to the *'Test Act.'* Even after the passing of the Toleration Act in 1719, under which Presbyterians were granted freedom of worship, there was a strong sense of estrangement from the Anglican and landed

Presbyterian College, Belfast

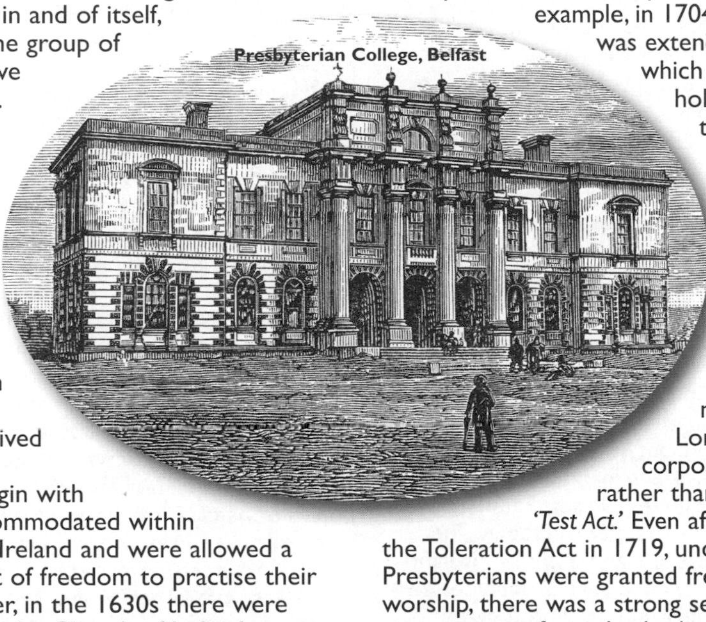

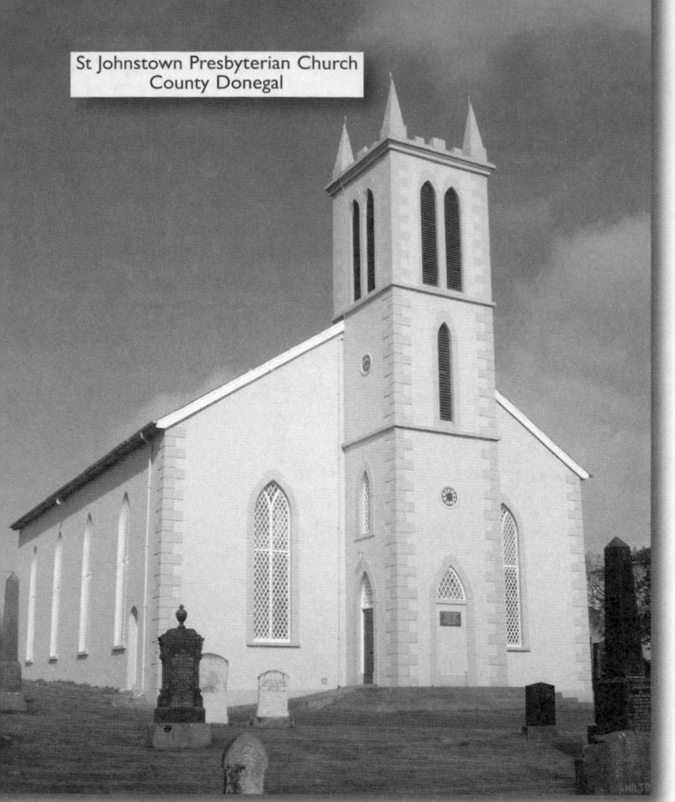
St Johnstown Presbyterian Church County Donegal

establishment, and this was a contributory factor in the large-scale emigration of Presbyterians from Ulster to America in the eighteenth century.

The distinguished historian ATQ Stewart famously observed, *'The Presbyterian is happiest when he is being a radical.'* Political radicalism was never more obvious than in the 1790s when Presbyterians were instrumental in the creation of the United Irishmen and were heavily involved in the revolutionary activities that led to the 1798 Rebellion. In the nineteenth century Presbyterians were active in the movement for land reform that resulted in the dismantling of the landed estate system. With the rise of Irish nationalism and the campaigns for Home Rule in the late nineteenth century, the great majority of Presbyterians became unionist in their political outlook.

Today the Presbyterian Church is the largest Protestant denomination in Northern Ireland with some 560 congregations, overwhelmingly in Northern Ireland, but with a significant number of congregations in other parts of the island, especially counties Donegal and Monaghan as well as the city of Dublin. The website of the Presbyterian Church in Ireland is www.presbyterianireland.org. This includes an extensive, though incomplete directory of congregations.

Published Works relating to the Presbyterian Church in Ireland

Histories

There is no shortage of published works on Irish Presbyterianism. In the nineteenth century several men, usually ministers in the Church, began to write detailed histories of Irish Presbyterians. Foremost among them was James Seaton Reid who wrote the magisterial *History of the Presbyterian Church in Ireland*, ed. W. D. Killen (3 vols, 2nd edition, Belfast, 1867). Others works include Thomas Witherow, *Historical and literary memorials of Presbyterianism in Ireland* (2 vols, Belfast 1879-80) and W. D. Killen, *History of the congregations of the Presbyterian Church in Ireland* (Belfast, 1886). Some of these early volumes can now be read on Google Books or Archive.org.

Most of these books look at the Church from an institutional point of view, focussing on structures of government and prominent ministers. In the twentieth century academics began to research and study Presbyterianism from different viewpoints. An academic study that considers the mental worlds of Presbyterian is *The Shaping of Ulster Presbyterian Belief and Practice, 1770-1840* by Andrew Holmes (Oxford, 2006). A recent handsomely-produced volume that provides a good overview of Irish Presbyterianism is *Presbyterians in Ireland: An Illustrated History* by Laurence Kirkpatrick (Holywood, 2006). This volume includes photographs of virtually every Presbyterian meeting house in Ireland. Presbyterianism in Dublin is expertly covered in *Dictionary of Dublin Dissent – Dublin's Protestant Dissenting Meeting Houses 1660-1920* by Steven C. Smyrl (Dublin, 2009)

Information on Congregations

An indispensable guide to the Presbyterian Church in Ireland is the *History of Congregations* published by the Presbyterian Historical Society in 1982. It provides brief sketches of each of the congregations, mainly focusing on the succession of ministers. It is particularly useful in determining when a particular congregation came into being. A *Supplement of Additions, Emendations and Corrections with an Index* was published in association with the Ulster Historical Foundation in 1996. The text of both publications can now be read online on the website of the Presbyterian Historical Society - www.presbyterianhistoryireland.com

In many of the larger towns and villages in the north of Ireland there are two or more

Presbyterian congregations and the *History of Congregations* is particularly useful in working out their chronology and how they relate to one another. Newtownards, for example, has several Presbyterian congregations. First, Newtownards is the oldest and dates back to the seventeenth century. Second, Newtownards originally had Seceder connections, while Regent Street was established in 1834. The formation of the Greenwell Street congregation can be linked to the 1859 Revival. Strean Presbyterian Church outside the town came into existence following a disagreement in First Newtownards in 1865. It was named after its main instigator, Thomas Strean, who gave over £8,000 to build a meeting house.

Information on Presbyterian Ministers

Biographical information on Presbyterian ministers was published as *Fasti of the Irish Presbyterian Church, 1613–1840* compiled by James McConnell and revised by his son Samuel G. McConnell (Belfast: Presbyterian Historical Society, 1951). After 1840 biographical information was published as *Fasti of the General Assembly of the Presbyterian Church in Ireland, 1840-1910*, compiled by John M. Barkley, and issued in three parts by the Presbyterian Historical Society of Ireland (1986-7). The biographical sketches are fairly succinct, but can include the name of the father and possibly mother of the minister, his own family details, where he was educated and where he served. Publications, if any, may also be noted, and perhaps something exceptional about his career.

Congregational Histories

In his book, *The Shaping of Ulster Presbyterian Belief and Practice*, the historian Dr Andrew Holmes has observed that there is a 'seemingly unique obsession of Ulster Presbyterians with writing and reading congregational histories.' To a large extent this is a reflection of the importance of the congregation within the Presbyterian system, and the way in which its identity is intertwined with its locality and the families who, often for generations, have been associated with it.

A great many congregations have their own published histories. Many of these will include appendices providing very useful information on past members of the congregation and surrounding district. For example, the appendices to John Rutherford's *Donagheady Presbyterian Churches and Parish* (1953) include the following lists of names – ratepayers in the electoral divisions of Dunalong, Ballyneaner, Dunamanagh, and Mountcastle in 1856; Donagheady wills pre-1858, the Donagheady poll book of c.1662, and hearth money rolls for Donagheady from the 1660s, as well as various other extracts from sources.

The best collection of congregational histories is in the Presbyterian Historical Society Library. There are also good collections of these histories at the Linen Hall Library and Central Library in Belfast, and in the library of the Public Record Office of Northern Ireland.

Seceders, Non-Subscribers, and Covenanters

The Secession Presbyterian Church

The Secession Church was a branch of Presbyterianism that emerged following a split in the Church of Scotland in 1712 over the issue of official patronage. Before long it had gained a foothold in Ulster and began to spread rapidly, especially in those areas where the Presbyterian Church had hitherto not been as strong. In the nineteenth century nearly all of the Secession churches were received into the Presbyterian Church in Ireland. Therefore, in the Guide to Church Records congregations that originated as Secession churches will be found listed as Presbyterian churches.

Essential reading for an understanding of the Secession Church in Ulster is David Stewart's *The Seceders in Ireland: With Annals of Their Congregations*

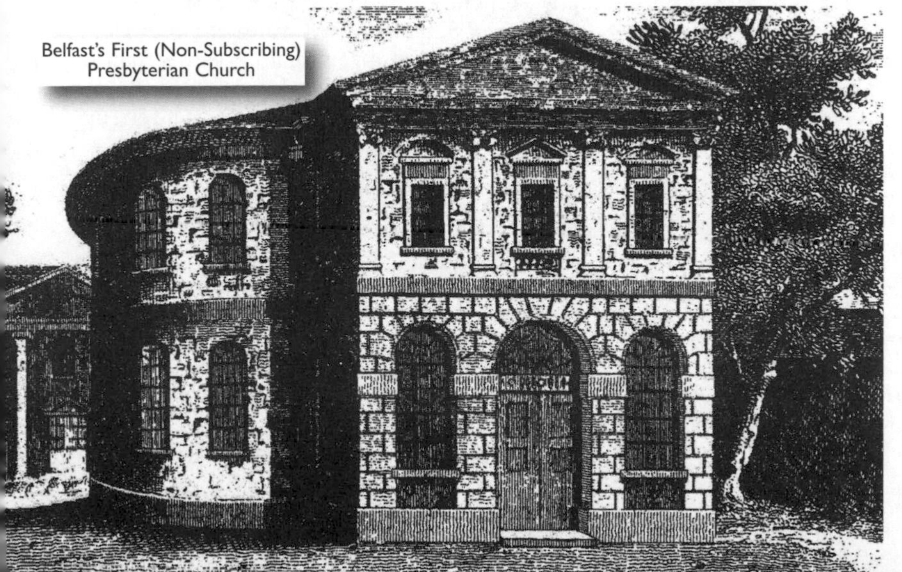

Belfast's First (Non-Subscribing) Presbyterian Church

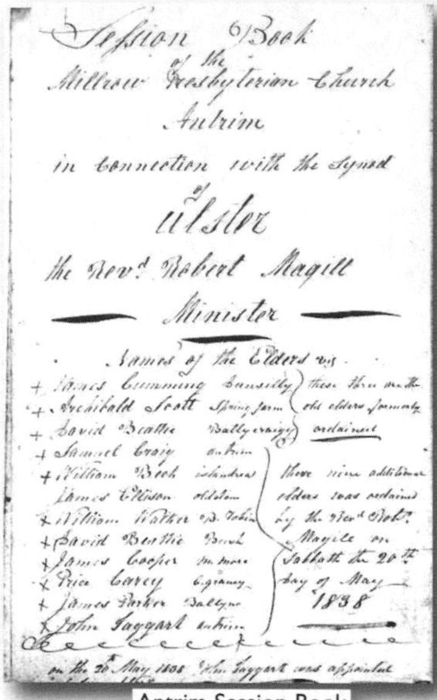

Session Book of the Millrow Presbyterian Church Antrim in connection with the Synod of Ulster the Rev.d Robert Magill Minister

Antrim Session Book

(Belfast, 1950). Brief biographical sketches of Secession clergy appear in *Fasti of Seceder Ministers Ordained or Installed in Ireland 1746-1948*, arranged and edited by W.D. Bailie and L.S. Kirkpatrick, published by the Presbyterian Historical Society in 2005.

The Non-Subscribing Presbyterian Church

The ethos of the Non-Subscribing Presbyterian Church is *'faith guided by reason and conscience.'* The origins of this denomination go back to a dispute within the Presbyterian Church over the issue of subscription to the Westminster Confession of Faith, the statement of doctrine of the Presbyterian Church. Those who denied the necessity of subscribing to this work were known as *'New Light'* Presbyterians or *'Non-Subscribers.'* In 1725, in an attempt to deal with the situation, ministers and congregations of the *'New Light'* persuasion were placed in the Presbytery of Antrim (this did not mean that all the congregations were in County Antrim).

About 100 years later the issue of subscription again became a source of contention within Presbyterianism, and in 1829 a small section of the Presbyterian Church withdrew and the following year formed what was known as the Remonstrant Synod. In 1910 the General Synod of the Non-Subscribing Presbyterian Church was created following a union of the Presbytery of Antrim and the Remonstrant Synod. In 1935 this body was joined by the Synod of Munster. Today there are around 34 congregations, mainly in counties Antrim and Down.

Some of the early Non-Subscribing Presbyterian Church records, created before the split, are in fact Presbyterian records. For example, the early records of Scarva Street Presbyterian Church in Banbridge are to be found in Banbridge Non-Subscribing Presbyterian Church records. In a number of instances a Non-Subscribing Presbyterian Church will be known as the First (Old) Presbyterian Church. Rosemary Street Non-Subscribing Presbyterian Church in Belfast, for example, is generally known as First Presbyterian Church. This can give rise to confusion if there is a Presbyterian Church in a town with the designation First.

For a brief background to this denomination see *A Short History of the Non-Subscribing Presbyterian Church of Ireland* by John Campbell (Belfast: 1914). The denomination's website - www.nspresbyterian.org - includes a map showing the location of all congregations.

The Reformed Presbyterian (Covenanter) Church

The Covenanter or Reformed Presbyterian Church was composed of those who adhered most strongly to the Covenants of 1638 and 1643 and who rejected the Revolution Settlement of 1691 in Scotland. The National Covenant of 1638 was a reaction against the attempts by Charles I to bring the Scottish Church into closer conformity with the episcopal Church of England and to introduce greater ritual and a prescribed liturgy to services. It firmly established the Presbyterian form of church government in Scotland, and bound the people to uphold the principles of the Reformation. The Solemn League and Covenant of 1643 was composed on similar lines and affected England and Ireland as well as Scotland. During the reigns of Charles II (1660 – 85) and James II (1685 – 8) there was considerable persecution of Covenanters, and many were executed or banished. This ended with the accession of William III. In 1691 Covenanters refused to accept the Revolution Settlement as it gave the government a role in the running of the Church of Scotland. Covenanters, therefore, stood apart from mainstream Presbyterianism in Scotland.

Of the early history of the Covenanters in Ireland very little is known, save that the denomination was small and scattered. It was not until the latter part of the eighteenth century that congregations began to be organised and ministers were ordained. Very few Reformed Presbyterian records have survived from the eighteenth century. This can be partly explained by the paucity of ministers at this time; many baptisms and marriages were performed by visiting ministers from Scotland and there is little evidence of proper records being kept of these events. Congregations were divided into societies, composed of several families living within a short distance of each other. From the middle of the eighteenth century Covenanters in Ireland became much more organised with the creation of an Irish Reformed Presbytery in 1763. In 1811 a Synod of the Reformed Presbyterian Church was established. Today there are around 35 congregations.

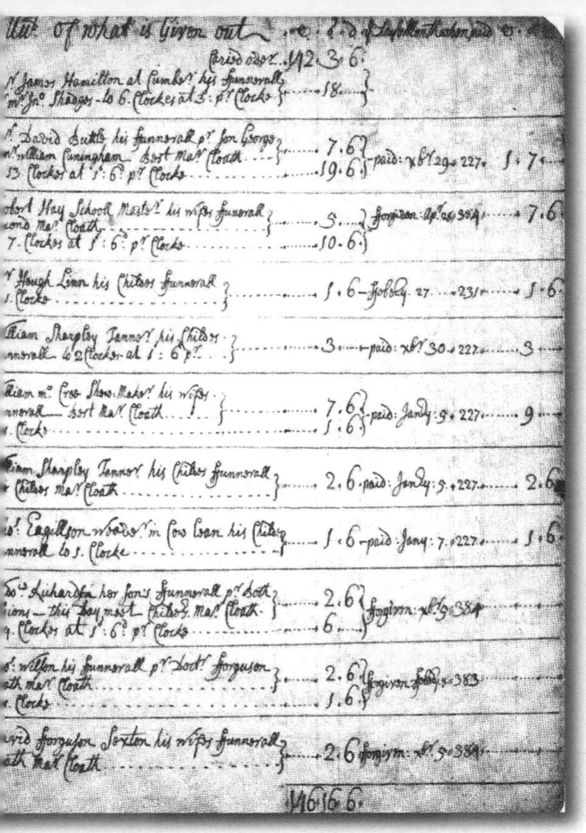

For background information on this denomination see The Covenanters in Ireland: A History of the Reformed Presbyterian Church of Ireland by Adam Loughridge (Belfast, 1984). For information on ministers in the Reformed Presbyterian Church see Fasti of the Reformed Presbyterian Church of Ireland compiled and edited by Adam Loughridge (Belfast, 1970). An updated fasti with short historical sketches of each Reformed Presbyterian congregation was published in 2010. A recent article on researching Covenanter ancestors is *'The Origins of the Reformed Presbyterian Church of Ireland with some comments on its records'* by William Roulston, published in Familia: Ulster Genealogical Review (2008), pages 86-110. The website of this denomination is www.rpc.org. This includes a map showing the location of congregations.

Documentary Records

There is little difference in the types of record generated by the three historic Presbyterian denominations, though there may be occasional differences in emphasis. Therefore, the different categories of Presbyterian records can be considered together. One point I would make at this stage is that it is always worth looking at Church of Ireland registers for baptisms, marriages and burials involving Presbyterians. This is because until 1870 the Church of Ireland was the established or state church in Ireland and because of its status many people who ordinarily belonged to another denomination can turn up in the pages of its registers. Even Catholic records should not be discounted for there was much more intermarriage in Irish society than is often supposed.

Registers of Baptisms, Marriages & Burials

Baptismal Registers

Presbyterians practise infant baptism, and the registers of these baptisms form one of the most useful categories of record when looking for Irish ancestors, especially in the period prior to the introduction of civil registration of births in 1864. The basic information provided in a baptismal register is the name of the child, the name of the father and the date of baptism. The mother's name will usually be given as will a specific location. The occupation of the father and the date of birth of the child may also be provided. Although there are a number of very early Presbyterian registers of baptism, including Drumbo 1692, Killyleagh 1693, Lisburn 1692, and Portaferry 1699, in the majority of cases, baptismal records do not pre-date the nineteenth century. This may be for the very simple reason that the congregation was not established until the 1800s. Less systematic record keeping was also a factor.

Many Presbyterian baptismal registers begin in 1819 or shortly thereafter for at the Synod of 1819 the following instructions were issued:

'That every minister of and Baptism the Synod be enjoined to register, or cause to be registered, in a book to be kept for that purpose, the names of all children baptised by him; the dates of their birth and baptism; the names of their parents, and the places of residence. This book shall be carefully preserved, and considered as the property of the congregation – to remain with them on the death, resignation, or removal of the Minister, and to be handed to his Successor, for the purpose of continuing the registry.'

Even with the ruling of 1819 some Presbyterian congregations do not have

Limerick

complete sets of nineteenth-century registers of baptisms. Some records were accidentally destroyed as the following extract from the baptismal register of West Church, Ballymena records:

'I preached at Churchtown on the 5th of November 1848 according to appointment by Presbytery and the list of children baptised on that day having been accidentally destroyed in my absence, I am necessitated to leave blank in the register at the same time noting its cause.'

Due to the *'negligence and disobedience of a female servant'* the records of Bready Reformed Presbyterian Church were lost in a fire in the home of the clerk of session in September 1868. Other records were destroyed deliberately. One nineteenth-century Reformed Presbyterian minister became convinced that infant baptism was contrary to Scripture and left his congregation, but not before he had destroyed many of the baptismal registers. The baptismal records of Rosemary Street Presbyterian Church, 1868 - 1941, were destroyed as a result of the *'Belfast Blitz'* during the 2nd World War.

On other occasions record-keeping was simply lax. A visitation of 1st Donagheady Presbyterian Church in County Tyrone in 1865 found that there was no baptismal register, no communicants' roll, and no session or committee minute books. In 1876 it was noted that no minutes of any committee meeting had been kept since 1871. It was not until 1878 that a baptismal register was provided. Frequently registers disappeared around the time that a minister died or moved to a new congregation.

For the most part baptismal registers will follow a fairly routine format. Occasionally, however, an entry of some interest might appear. One such entry appears in the baptismal register of Crossgar Presbyterian Church in County Londonderry. Following a record of the baptism on 4th May 1888 of David Campbell at the age of 46 the entry continues:

'This D. Campbell spent 21 years and 43 days in the Army (4 years in England, 1 in Scotland, 3 in Ireland, 12 years and 27 days in India) before his baptism. While in the Army he was an Episcopalian, having gone over from the Presbyterian Church like a great many others; when he got off he attended the Episcopal Church in Macosquin for some time, but he wrote on a letter asking me to baptise him which I did on sincere profession of his faith.'

Marriage Registers

One of the main grievances of Presbyterians in the early eighteenth century concerned the right of their ministers to conduct marriages. In 1737 an act of parliament was passed which, with certain caveats, permitted two Presbyterians to marry. At last in 1782 marriages performed by a Presbyterian minister were legally recognised as being *'as good in law'* as those performed by a minister of the Church of Ireland. However, it was not until the passing of another act of parliament in 1844 that Presbyterians ministers were permitted to marry a Presbyterian and a member of the Church of Ireland.

Prior to the standardisation of marriage registers from 1st April 1845, when all non-Catholic marriages were to be officially registered, these will give in their simplest form the date of the marriage and the names of the bride and groom. The residence and the name of the father of each party are occasionally provided. The names of the witnesses may also be given. At the same Synod of 1819 that exhorted ministers to keep registers of baptisms, similar directions were given for the keeping of marriage registers:

'Overtured and unanimously agreed to – That every Minister of this Synod shall keep, or cause to be kept, a regular registry of all marriages

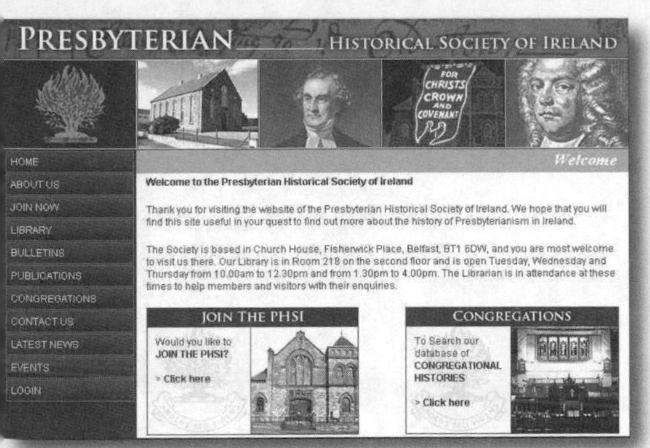

celebrated by him; stating the date of each marriage, the names of the parties, the Congregations or Parishes in which they reside, and the names of at least two of the witnesses present at the celebration of the ceremony.'

*It was also agreed that every min*ister would be required to submit annually to his respective presbytery an accurate list of the marriages he had conducted in the previous year. These marriages would then be copied by the clerk of presbytery into a separate volume. Relatively few of these presbytery marriage books seem to have survived, or at least are in the public domain. One that does relates to the Tyrone Presbytery and covers marriages in the following congregations:

Cookstown (possibly 1st), 1820-8, Loughgall, 1819-22, Tobermore, 1819-22, Vinecash, 1825-8, Carland, 1826-8, Magherafelt, 1819-28, Dungannon (possibly 1st), 1819-28, Benburb, 1827-8, Cloveneden, 1826-8, Richhill, 1826-8, Stewartstown (possibly 1st), 1820-7, Coagh, 1820-2 and Minterburn, 1819-22 (PRONI, MIC/1P/460).

From 1st April 1845, with the introduction of civil registration of non-Catholic marriages, the information on the individuals getting married includes their name, age, status, and occupation. The names and occupations of their fathers are also given. The church, the officiating minister and the witnesses to the ceremony are named. In most cases the exact age of the parties is not given, and the entry will simply read *'full age'* (i.e. over 21) or *'minor'* (i.e. under 21). If the father of one of the parties was no longer living, this may be indicated in the marriage certificate by the word *'deceased'* or by leaving the space blank, but in many cases it is not.

Burial Registers

Few Presbyterian congregations have very old burial registers. Part of the reason for this, as will be discussed presently, is the fact that not every Presbyterian meeting house has an adjoining graveyard. Those burial registers that do exist were mainly started in the late nineteenth or even the early twentieth century. Burial registers can be fairly uninformative, with the name of the deceased, the date of burial and occasionally the occupation and age at death given.

One very interesting early eighteenth-century document relating to the burial of Presbyterians survives among the records of Rosemary Street Non-Subscribing Presbyterian Church in Belfast. It is a register of the hiring of funeral gear – palls, cloaks and hats – for about 2,000 funerals which took place in Belfast between 1712 and 1736. It has been published as ***Funeral register of Rosemary Street Non-Subscribing Presbyterian Church (known as the First Presbyterian Church of Belfast), 1712-36,*** edited by Jean Agnew (Belfast: Ulster Historical Foundation, 1995).

Other Congregational Records

Few denominations generated as many records as the various strands of Presbyterianism with the result that a variety of other items may be found among the records kept by individual Presbyterian congregations. Some of these are discussed below.

Minutes of Session Meetings

The session was the ruling body in each congregation and was composed of the minister, designated the moderator at meetings of session, and elders in a particular congregation. One of the elders served as *'clerk of session'* and was responsible for recording the minutes of the meetings. Session records cover a range of matters, many of which relate to the internal discipline of members of the congregation for a variety of transgressions. Occasionally they may contain baptisms and marriages that are not recorded elsewhere.

Family Records and Congregational Censuses

A real boon to any researcher seeking information on the families that belonged to a particular congregation will be a congregational census. These can take different forms. At their simplest they may be a list of members of the congregation. More detailed census returns will provide the townland and will include the names of all members of the family. For example, the records of Rademon Non-Subscribing Presbyterian Church, County Down, include a census of families arranged by townland, 1836-7, with notes added at a later date indicating those who died or got married, those who left the congregation and those who had emigrated. For Carrigallen Presbyterian Church in County Leitrim there is a visitation book with details of each family by townland and dates of baptisms of children, 1837-92.

A remarkable volume is Rev. Robert Magill's family record book for the congregation of 1st Antrim (Millrow). This includes detailed information on the families that belonged to the congregation in the early nineteenth century and includes baptisms, marriages and deaths. On a number of occasions Magill even went so far as to sketch out family trees, with figure drawings of the various family members. This volume is available for inspection at the Presbyterian Historical Society Library.

Lists of Communicants

These are similar to congregational census, but they only list the names of communicant members of a particular congregation. Sometimes there may be a separate list of the names of new communicants. Occasionally lists of communicants are annotated with additional information, such as when a communicant married, emigrated or died.

Transfer Certificates

Members of one congregation who wished to transfer their congregation to another would be issued with a certificate testifying to their good standing in the church. Frequently a transfer certificate would be issued to those who were emigrating. For example, the transfer certificate given to David Carson by the Rev. Hugh Hamill of 1st Donagheady in 1784 certified that Carson *was 'born and bred of honest Protestant dissenting parents and brought up in that faith, and has lived a sober, regular life which we hope will recommend him to our brethren in America, whom he may chance to associate with.'* Carson took no chances and also sought and received a similar testimonial from a local Reformed Presbyterian Church. For a number of congregations there are lists of people who left the congregation to emigrate abroad.

Financial Records

The financial records of a congregation should not be overlooked when searching for a Presbyterian ancestor. Occasionally they will survive for a period for which registers of baptisms and marriages are absent. These records range from stipend lists (the stipend being the minister's salary), pew rent books, and account books. For 1st Lisburn Presbyterian Church there is a subscription list for the new meeting house from 1764 - 5.

Pew rent books can be particularly interesting documents. Formerly, the greater part of the minister's stipend was derived from pew rents, that is, from the letting of pews or seats within the meeting house for a fixed annual sum. In some congregations there were different classes of pew-sitters, reflecting a certain social stratification. For example, in Glendermott Presbyterian Church pew-sitters were divided into gentlemen, farmers, and artisans/cottiers. Some pew rent books survive from the early eighteenth century. For instance, for Rosemary Street Presbyterian Church in Belfast there are surviving pew rent books, 1726-73, 1788-96, 1816-56 and 1866-73.

Calls to Ministers

When a congregation had settled on their

choice for a new minister a *'call'* was issued to him, signed by the members. It was then up to the individual to whom the call was issued to decide whether or not he wished to accept that call. Some of these calls can incorporate fairly extensive lists of names of members of individual congregations. For example, the call issued to Thomas Clark by the Presbyterians of Ballyalbany, County Monaghan, in 1751 contains the names of over 160 individuals. It was published in S. Lyle Orr and Alex Haslett, *Historical Sketch of Ballyalbany Presbyterian Church (1940)*.

Education Records

Within Presbyterianism there was a strong emphasis on education, especially on literacy and the ability to read the Bible for oneself. Many ministers conducted classes in their home or in the session room of their meeting house. Providing a Classical education, these schools were often used to prepare young men for the ministry. Few records relating to these establishments survive.

Education records that do survive among congregational records relate principally to the Sunday schools that were established in their hundreds in the early nineteenth century. For example, among the records of 2nd Portglenone Presbyterian Church, County Antrim, is a Sunday school roll book, 1821-67. The records for Antrim (Millrow) Presbyterian Church include a Sabbath School library loan book, 1870, and a Sabbath School receipt and expenditure book, 1835-62, incorporating a weekly roll of teachers and salaries, 1840-41.

Administrative Records: Minutes of Meetings of Presbytery and Synod

The Presbytery was the middle layer of government in the Presbyterian Church, above session and below Synod. It comprised the ministers and ruling elders of the congregations affiliated to the Presbytery. It dealt with matters that could not be settled at the level of session, either because there was a dispute of a nature that could not be resolved without recourse to a higher authority or because the issues related to more than one congregation. Presbytery meetings were held on a regular basis. Presbyteries were frequently reorganised. In addition, individual congregations could change presbytery if it meant that a dispute would be resolved.

The surviving minute book for the Presbytery of Strabane, covering the period 1717–40, reveals that the Presbytery dealt with a variety of matters relating to the members of the congregations within its bounds. For instance, in December 1718 John Alison came before Strabane presbytery desiring a certificate testifying to his credentials as a good Presbyterian as he was preparing to emigrate. Presbytery decided not to issue him with one until just before he was ready to leave, and then only conditional on his continued good behaviour.

The Synod of Ulster was the highest authority in the Presbyterian Church in Ulster. It met once a year, usually in June, and was composed of representatives from every congregation in each of the presbyteries. The records of the Synod of Ulster meetings for the period 1690–1820 were published in three volumes by the Presbyterian Church in 1891 (available to read online at www.archive.org). Much of the minutes deal with matters of a fairly routine nature. Occasionally, however, an item of real value will be recorded. From 1840, when the Synod of Ulster and the Secession

Queen's Bridge, Belfast

Synod United, there are the printed minutes of the General Assembly, a set of which is in the library of the Presbyterian Historical Society.

Presbyterian Graveyards and Gravestone Inscriptions

Many, but by no means, all Presbyterian meeting houses have adjoining burial grounds. Few of the inscriptions in graveyards surrounding Presbyterian churches pre-date 1800 and in fact the practise of burying within the grounds of Presbyterian churches does not seem to have happened until the late eighteenth century. The burial ground attached to Castlereagh Presbyterian Church is unusual in having several memorials dating from the late eighteenth century. An exception to this generalisation is the graveyard at Drumbo Presbyterian Church, which includes memorials from the late seventeenth century. However, in the case of Drumbo the meeting house is unique, so far as the present writer knows, in that it stands on the site of a medieval parish church.

If looking for the burial places of Presbyterian ancestors prior to the nineteenth century, the most obvious place to check will be the old parish graveyard, probably dating from the medieval period, and which may or may not have a functioning Church of Ireland church within its bounds. Even after burial grounds began to be laid out around Presbyterian meeting houses, the practise of interment in these older graveyards continued for some families.

It was not until the second half of the nineteenth century that Presbyterians were legally entitled to open a burial ground that did not adjoin one of their own meeting houses. The background to the opening of Balmoral Cemetery in 1855 was an incident in which a Church of Ireland minister obstructed a funeral being conducted by two Presbyterian ministers. One of the ministers involved, Rev. Joseph Mackenzie, secured the ground for the cemetery, and remained its owner, though it was managed by a board of trustees. Though the cemetery was never exclusively Presbyterian, it was predominantly so and was the only burial place of its kind in nineteenth-century Ulster.

The inscriptions from many Presbyterian churchyards have been published in one form or another. The Ulster Historical Foundation has published the inscriptions from more than 50 Presbyterian churchyards in County Down as well as several more in County Antrim. A number of local historical societies have also been involved in transcribing and publishing gravestone inscriptions. Many inscriptions have been made available on the internet.

Locating Records

Over the years the Public Record Office of Northern Ireland (PRONI) has done a tremendous job in acquiring originals or copies

Glenoe Village, County Antrim

of records kept by individual Presbyterian congregations. Most of the Presbyterian records in its custody are on microfilm. The coverage is so extensive that there are relatively few congregations whose records have not been deposited in some form in PRONI - www.proni.gov.uk The majority of these records are available on microfilm, though there are also some original documents, as well as photocopies.

The Presbyterian Historical Society, about which more will be said presently, has copies of most of the microfilms of Presbyterian registers held by PRONI and can be viewed on a microfilm reader at the Society's office in Church House, Belfast. A small number of Presbyterian records are only available at the Presbyterian Historical Society. These include some very early session books, including those of Dundonald and Aghadowey, as well as some registers of baptisms and marriages. A few pre-1900 Presbyterian registers are still in local custody.

With the advent of the internet, the indexing and digitisation of church records has gathered pace. Many of the centres affiliated to the Irish Family History Foundation have indexed Presbyterian registers for their respective counties and made these available online on a pay-per-view arrangement - www.rootsireland.ie - though coverage is far from complete. Local endeavour has also resulted in many registers being made available online free.

The Presbyterian Historical Society

The Presbyterian Historical Society was founded in 1906 to promote public awareness of the history of the various strands of Presbyterianism in Ireland. Once described as a *'Treasure House of Ulster's History,'* the Society's library possesses some 12,000 books and pamphlets. These are mainly concerned with ecclesiastical history and in particular Presbyterian history. The collection includes a large number of congregational histories. A set of *The Witness*, a Presbyterian newspaper, covering the period 1874-1941, is also available for consultation as are the printed minutes of the General Assembly beginning in 1840.

Manuscript material includes session minutes, baptisms and marriages from individual churches as well as some presbytery minutes. These include session accounts for Armagh Presbyterian Church for 1707-32, session minutes for Aghadowey Presbyterian Church for 1702-61 and baptisms from Cullybackey (Cunningham Memorial) Presbyterian Church covering the period 1726-1815. In addition the records of a number of now defunct congregations in the Republic of Ireland have been deposited for safekeeping in its Library. The Society also has a duplicate set of the microfilm copies of Presbyterian Church registers held by PRONI covering the vast majority of Presbyterian congregations in Ireland.

Of particular interest is the large amount of biographical data available on Presbyterian ministers. This material can be accessed through a card index, while there are also handwritten and printed *'fasti'* providing information on clergymen. A small collection of private papers of Presbyterian ministers is also available. These include some of the papers of the most distinguished Presbyterian minister in the nineteenth century, the Reverend Henry Cooke.

The Society's library has been built up gradually over many years through donations, bequests and purchases. The Society is funded through donations and fees, together with a valuable financial contribution each year from the Incidental Fund of the General Assembly of the Presbyterian Church in Ireland. Queries on membership are welcomed and should be addressed to the Society's Librarian, Valerie Adams.

The Society now has its own website - www.presbyterianhistoryireland.com which contains information on upcoming events, membership, and other news. Members of the Society can access a digitised version of the History of Congregations, as well as past editions of the Society's annual publication, The Bulletin. A history of the Society has been published – *Times Passing: The Story of the Presbyterian Historical Society of Ireland from 1907-2007* by Dr Joe Thompson. In 2010 the Presbyterian Historical Society moved to new premises at 26 College Green, Belfast.

Conclusion

Researching Irish Presbyterian ancestors can be as fulfilling or frustrating as investigating forebears from any one of the many other denominations on this island. Among the chief frustrations is the fact that relatively few congregations have registers of baptisms and marriages prior to the 1800s. On the other hand, the large number of administrative and other records that were generated by individual congregations means that it can be possible to put real flesh on the bones of Presbyterian ancestors and so understand more about their social and religious worlds.

The Presbyterian Historical Society of Ireland Library and Archive

Valerie Adams

The Presbyterian Historical Society Library and Archive has been in existence since 1907 and until the autumn 2010 based at Church House in the centre of Belfast. It has now re-located to 26 College Green near to Queen's University and Union Theological College. The Society was formed to preserve books, pamphlets, archives, documents and artefacts in connection with the history of the churches of the Presbyterian Order in Ireland, and to encourage a greater awareness of the history of these churches. From the very beginning the Society has been a library, an archive and a museum.

Published Material

The extensive library of books relates to Presbyterianism in Ireland, Scotland and America and therefore reflects the close links between these three countries. Included are congregational histories (of interest to both family and local historians), biographies and autobiographies. The library also contains a very important pamphlet collection, over 500 of which date from before the mid 19th century. They cover a wide range of theological, political, social and economic issues and are indicative of an age when the production of a pamphlet was the only means of getting your message or your opinion across. A particular strength of the published material is the presence of a large number of Presbyterian magazines dating from the mid 19th century and in some cases even earlier. These are of interest not only from a theological point of view but are also a valuable source of information about churches and Presbyterian ministers.

Another very important resource held by the Society is ***'The Witness'*** - a Presbyterian newspaper which ran weekly from 1874 to 1941. As the original volumes had become too fragile to handle they had to be microfilmed - the films which can be consulted in the Society's library are regularly used by academics and by local and family historians. As well as details about Presbyterian churches and ministers the newspaper is also a rich source of information on community life and events (eg reports of court cases and inquests, lists of student examination successes at Queen's University and schools, subscription lists etc) while the birth, marriages and death notices are of obvious interest to the family historian.

The Presbyterian Historical Society Library and Archive College Green, Belfast

The published material in the Society's library also includes the minutes and reports of the General

Assembly of the Presbyterian Church in Ireland from 1830 and the minutes of its predecessor, the Synod of Ulster from 1691 as well as the minutes of the Reformed Presbyterian Synod of Ireland from 1811.

Archives

The Society holds many congregational records, particularly of churches that are now closed both in Northern Ireland and in the Republic of Ireland. Complementing some unique congregational records only to be found in the Society's library are microfilm copies of the records of Presbyterian churches filmed by the Public Record Office of Northern Ireland. Among the archives held are those of missionaries, of individual Presbyterian ministers, and of Presbyteries, in addition to a large collection of individual manuscripts such as the Adair Narrative which is a 17th century account of the rise and growth of Presbyterianism in Ireland.

Compiled Resources

One of the most frequently consulted resources held by the Society is a set of index cards containing biographical information on Presbyterian ministers. Some of this *'Fasti'* information has been published by the Society but there is frequently additional information on the cards not to be found in the published version. The information recorded includes dates of birth and death and often also of marriage, the name of the father and place of birth, education, and the names of the churches where the minister served and when.

The Society also holds information folders on individual churches and can include newspaper cutting, unpublished histories, photographs of ministers and churches, orders of service for ordinations and for the opening of churches, financial reports and other material.

Publications

The Society has an active publications programme. *The Society's Bulletin*, published annually, contains articles on a wide range of interesting subjects relating to Irish Presbyterianism. A series of small booklets is available on topics such as *The 1625 Six Mile Water Revival, The 1798 Rebellion*, Presbyterianism and Orangeism and Presbyterian Communion Tokens as well as biographical studies on people like the Rev Sinclair Kelburn who was involved in the 1798 Rebellion, and Francis Makemie who is regarded as the father of American Presbyterianism. A full list of the publications is available on the Society's website. The most important publication produced by the Society is the *'History of Presbyterian Congregations from 1610'* which, although now out of print, is accessible on the Society's website and has been brought right up to date.

A typical marriage notice for 3rd July 1874 reads:

BODEL - LEGATE—July 2, at the Imperial Hotel, by special licence, by the Rev. J. D. Martin, uncle of the bride, assisted by her brothers, Rev. E. M. Legate, Ballyclare, and Rev. G. W. Legate, Dungannon, James Bodel, Esq., Katesbridge, to Helena, third daughter of Rev. G. Legate, Edengreen, Kilkinamurry, Co. Down.

Use of the Library

Although anyone can use the library and its resources and we do give free advice and help to enquirers we cannot provide a full genealogical research service and users are encouraged to join the Society – annual membership is £15.00, life membership is £75.00, student membership is £5.00. Becoming an Associate member gives access to the restricted part of the website that includes the *'History of Presbyterian Congregations'* and some issues of the Bulletin.

Presbyterian Historical Society of Ireland
26 College Green, Belfast BT7 1LN
T: +44 (0) 28 9072 7330 E:
phsilibrarian@pcinet.org
W: www.presbyterianhistoryireland.com
Opening Hours:
Tuesday & Wednesday
9.30.a.m. - 1.00.p.m. & 1.30.p.m. - 4.30.p.m.
Thursday 9.30.a.m. - 1.00.p.m.

Online Irish Resources

Chris Paton

Not everyone can make it to the relevant archive or library when it comes to carrying out Irish family history research, but increasingly more and more resources are being made available online to help with the task. In this article I'll outline some of the most useful resources available to help you get to grips with the basics.

Vital Records

Civil registration of births, marriages and deaths commenced in 1864 in Ireland, with the exception of non-Catholic marriages, which started earlier in 1845. Each record was indexed locally and then copies sent to the General Register Office in Dublin, where a

national register was then compiled. From 1922 a separate GRO was set up in Belfast for Northern Ireland. GRO records from 1864-1958 are indexed online for free at **www.familysearch.org** and include records for the Republic throughout this period, and for the counties of Northern Ireland up to 1922 (though there are some later entries). These indexes are also available via the subscription based site **www.ancestry.co.uk/ireland,** the added bonus here being that when you perform a marriage search the returned results will list all those spouses mentioned on a particular register page, including the spouse of the person you are looking for. This can help to confirm the right entry, something which FamilySearch does not allow you to do.

There are three main sites where you can then order copies of the original birth, marriage and death records. For the Republic, the General Register Office of Ireland is the cheapest at **www.groireland.ie**, as you can order photocopies of original records for just €4, though you need to download an application form and then fax or post it through. You can purchase many of the same records online through a separate site, the Health Service Executive at **www.hse.ie/eng/services/Find_a_Service/bdm/Certificates_ie/**, but here you can only buy original certified extracts at €10 each, as well as €1 postage. On the plus side, this site takes credit card payments, though the coverage is a bit more restricted, with marriage records available only from 1920 and deaths from 1924. For Northern Ireland, up to Partition the best bet is to use the GRO Ireland site, though after 1922 you will need to use the Northern Irish GRO at **www.nidirect.gov.uk/gro**, which sadly charges the highest rate for certificates in the United Kingdom, at £14 per record, plus postage.

The Irish Family History Foundation's pay per view based Roots Ireland website at **www.rootsireland.ie** hosts many records for most counties in Ireland, ranging from church and civil registration based records to census

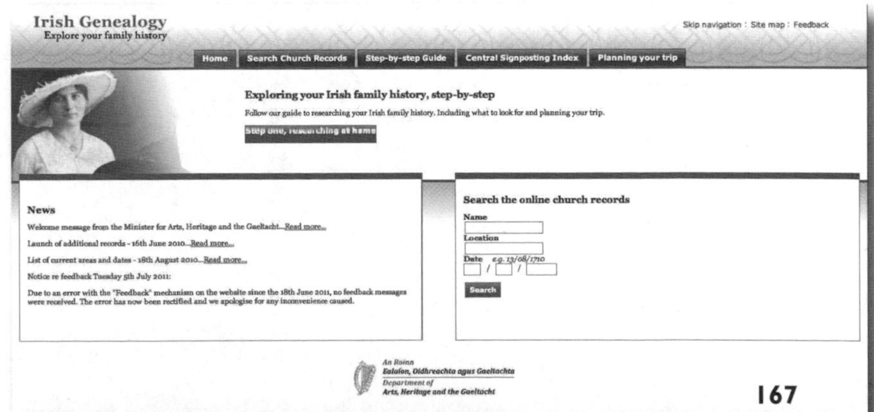

and other records. The offerings for each county vary, so do check the sources information for each collection. Do be advised, however, that the site is expensive to use and has recently introduced a somewhat bizarre credit based payment scheme which only permits discounts with bulk purchases of credits in advance, which you may not necessarily need. If you have ancestors from Kerry, Carlow, Cork or Dublin, try the alternative Irish genealogy website at **www.irishgenealogy.ie**, as hosted by the Irish Government, where you will find free transcriptions of mainly Roman Catholic and Church of Ireland records. FindmyPast Ireland (**www.findmypast.ie**) is also worth looking at, with various miscellaneous collections, and

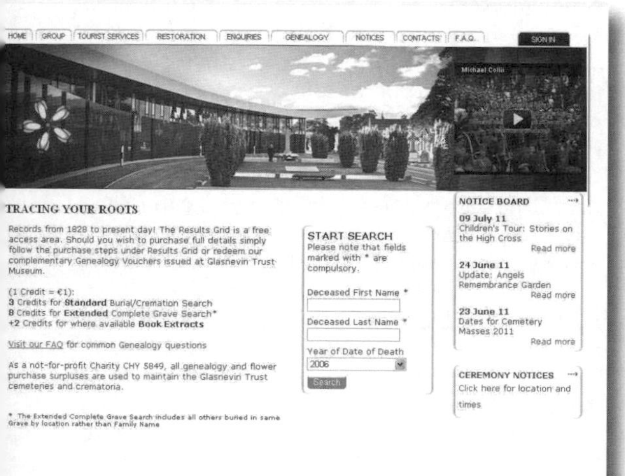

for Northern Ireland another option is the Emerald Ancestors site at **www.emeraldancestors.com**, hosting detailed indexes for many records, for a basic subscription of £10 a month.

Don't forget Ireland's connection to the United Kingdom, as your ancestors may well have been born, married or died in Britain. The UK version of FindmyPast (**www.findmypast.co.uk**) hosts birth, marriage and death indexes from 1837, as well as various British overseas indexes which include Irish entries within army chaplaincy records, consular returns etc. Digitised Scottish BMD records can be accessed at **www.scotlandspeople.gov.uk**, which also includes the Bishopric of the Forces Roman Catholic records, for members of the British army, navy and air force stationed around the world.

Burials

The Irish Genealogy Project Archives pages at **www.igp-web.com** include photos of many cemeteries, such as Mount Jerome in Dublin, whilst the pay per view Glasnevin Cemetery site at **www.glasnevintrust.ie/genealogy** lists burials from 1828 to present day. The impressive Irish Graveyards (**www.irishgraveyards.ie**) is rapidly photographing graveyards across the island. In the north, History from Headstones (**www.historyfromheadstones.com**) offers a pricey way to search for Ulster based inscriptions at £4 each, but Belfast City Council's new site at **www.belfastcity.gov.uk/burialrecords/search.asp** offers free access to burial records transcriptions for the city's three council run burial grounds, City Cemetery, Dundonald and Roselawn, with entries as far back as 1868. There is also now an option to pay for buy copies of the original records at just £1.50 each – it's worth doing as you will find the lairs' owners names recorded, which can be helpful in confirming the right burial as well as listing the cause of death.

Censuses

The 1901 and 1911 censuses for Ireland can be freely accessed at www.census.nationalarchives.ie whilst some surviving pre-1901 census fragments have survived, with many accessible via **www.censusfinder.com/ireland.htm** and Roots Ireland (see above). A slightly less well known resource is the set of copies from the 1841 and 1851 censuses which were created to back up pension applications after 1908, when

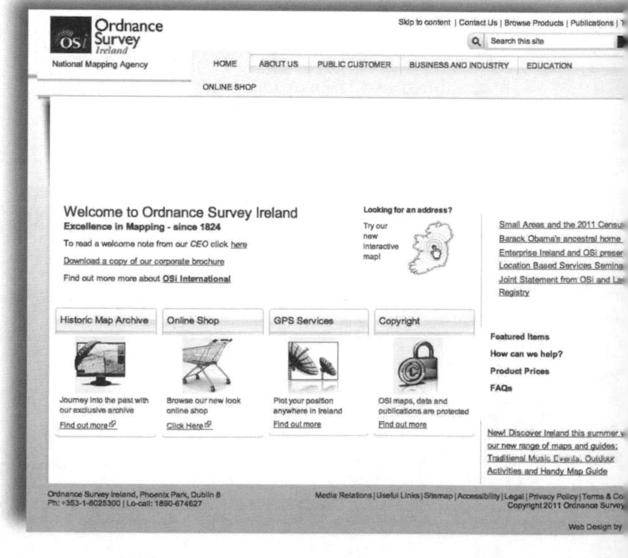

those over 70 could claim a state pension for the first time. It's a bit hit and miss, but if you find an entry, the whole household may well be included in addition to the applicant. The best place to search for these is **www.ireland-genealogy.com** and also through Ancestry.co.uk's Irish pages. Don't forget many Irish labourers were extremely mobile and you may well find them in earlier periods within the censuses in Britain, particularly if they were miners or shipbuilders.

Although most census records from 1821-1891 were destroyed, there are many census substitutes, such as Griffith's Valuation at **www.askaboutireland.ie/griffith-valuation/index.xml**, which lists the heads of households as well as the rateable value of land across the island at one point between 1847 and 1864. Additional land based records, such as tithes records and the *Landed Estates Court Rentals 1850-1885* collection can also be found on FindmyPast Ireland.

Maps and Gazetteers

Establishing the geography of your ancestral homeland can certainly help in your research. The Ordnance Survey of Northern Ireland at **https://maps.osni.gov.uk** carries both historic and current maps for the country (though you will need to register), and the modern Irish Ordnance Survey for the south is available at **www.osi.ie**. The principle land division in Ireland was the townland, and Historic Irish townland maps are online at **www.pasthomes.com**, with the locations of various townlands listed on databases at both **www.seanruad.com** and **www.ulsterancestry.com**. Further old maps for Ulster can be found at **www.ulsterancestry.com/free-ulster-maps.html**, and others at **www.failteromhat.com**, including a map of the Irish Free State, and a road map of the island from 1877. For Irish poor law union maps visit **www.movinghere.org.uk/deliveryfiles/PRO/MFQ1_925/0/1.pdf** (and **/2.pdf** and **/3.pdf**).

To understand the history of a place on the island, try the *Parliamentary Gazetteer of Ireland* from 1844-45 on Google Books (**http://tinyurl.com/ykrzc8h**), or the various e-book and other resources at Ask About Ireland (**www.askaboutireland.ie**). If you need to switch between the Irish and English equivalents of place names, or are just unsure how to pronounce the name of a place, visit the Placenames Database of Ireland site at **www.logainm.ie**.

Archives

The Public Record Office of Northern Ireland (**www.proni.gov.uk**) offers many free records collections, including half a million signatures to the 1912 Ulster Covenant, freeholders records, street directories from the north (also check **www.lennonwylie.co.uk** for more from 1805-1913), wills calendars entries and more. If you are planning to visit PRONI in Belfast, two

other useful sections on the site are the online guides (such as the downloadable *PRONI Guide to Church Listings*), and the catalogue with some one and a half million entries for items held at the archive.

With the exception of the 1901 and 1911 census site described earlier, the National Archives of Ireland site is not quite so well developed at **www.nationalarchives.ie** in terms of online databases. The site has several records that used to exist as standalone databases, such as *Famine Relief Commission Papers* from 1845-47, and records from the first Dáil from 1919-24, but these have recently been integrated into a new and difficult to use catalogue. A new addition is a collection of digitised *Calendars of grants of probate of wills and letters of administration* from 1923-1982, but to save you the pain of accessing these through the catalogue, you can find direct links available to the documents at

http://britishgenes.blogspot.co.uk/p/ireland-probate-calendars.html. A similar and earlier collection from 1858 will in due course be made available on FamilySearch (**www.familysearch.org**).

The National Library of Ireland (**www.nli.ie**) has the impressive *Sources* catalogue from its manuscripts collections and periodicals, as well as a major photography database. The *eResources* page is particularly worthy of notes, listing items which can be accessed within the building, such as various newspaper collections and more, and which is

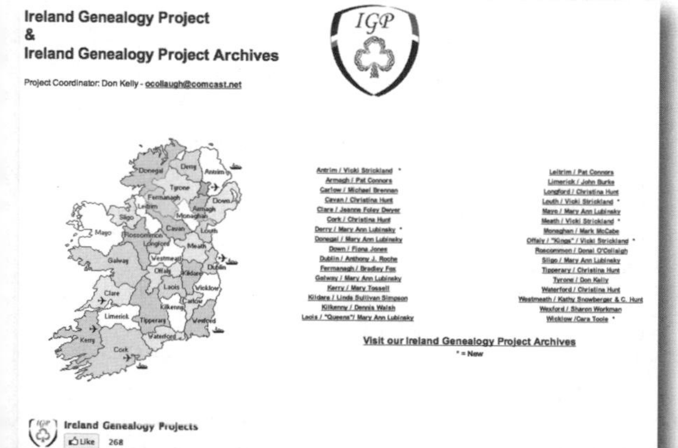

Ulster Ancestry
www.ulsterancestry.com
Ancestral and family history research in Northern Ireland

Free Maps of Ulster

Ulster Ancestry now provide free on-line versions of Ulster maps for Antrim, Armagh, Donegal, Down Fermanagh, Londonderry, Tyrone. Details of the counties major towns and cities are listed below - you can download the Free Maps in 2 different formats.

Map	Major Towns Include	Download Full Map	View Small Map
Antrim	Belfast, Ballymena, Ballymoney, Larne, Carrickfergus, Bushmills	Zip - JPG	View Map
Armagh	Armagh City, Portadown, Lurgan, The Moy, Newry	Zip - JPG	View Map
Donegal	Letterkenny, Donegal Town, Raphoe, Stranorlar, Lifford, Carndonagh	Zip - JPG	View Map
Down	Downpatrick, Saintfield, Lisburn, Ballynahinch, Comber, Newtownards	Zip - JPG	View Map
Fermanagh	Enniskillen Town, Lisnaskea, Belleek, Irvinestown, Lisbellaw, Tempo	Zip - JPG	View Map
Londonderry	City of Londonderry, Coleraine, Maghera, Magherafelt, Limavady, Dungiven	Zip - JPG	View Map
Tyrone	Strabane, Omagh, Clogher, Fintona, Blackwater Town, Newtownstewart	Zip - JPG	View Map

More Detailed Maps of Northern Ireland can be found at MultiMap
Click Here to Visit Northern Ireland maps on Multimap

Download Formats Explained

ZIP : This is a file which has been compressed using a program such as WinZip. You need to then uncompress to view the image.

JPG : One type of internet viewable image - use this option if you do not have WinZip. File is viewable in Internet Explorer.

If you have enjoyed this website why not recommend it to others

also hoped to be made available remotely to registered users in due course. The Family History section is also a vital area to consult at **www.nli.ie/en/intro/family-history-introduction.aspx**, particularly the *What We Have* section where you will find lists of Roman Catholic parish registers as held at the library in microfilm format. A list of newspapers held at the facility can also be found at **www.nli.ie/en/catalogues-and-databases-printed-newspapers.aspx**

Don't forget to check out your local county libraries and archives for holdings also. A good example is Waterford County Archive at **www.waterfordcoco.ie/en/services/archives/archivecollections/** which contains a range of finding aids for local based collections, whilst Waterford County Library has many digitised family history resources at **www.waterfordcountylibrary.ie/en/familyhistory/**, such as digitised copies of newspapers such as the *Dungarvan Leader*. For archival holdings at a local level in libraries, museums and archives, the Research and Special Collections Available Locally database, or 'RASCAL', may help at **www.rascal.ac.uk**.

Newspapers

There are many online newspaper archives site which can help with your research, such as the subscription based Irish Times - **www.irishtimes.com/search** and Irish Newspaper Archives - **www.irishnewsarchives.com** which holds digitised copies mainly of titles from the south. The 19th Century British Library Newspaper Archive at **http://newspapers.bl.uk/blcs** contains copies of the *Belfast Newsletter* and *The Freeman's Journal* , and keep an eye on the new British Newspaper Archive at **www.britishnewspaperarchive.co.uk**, which will soon be adding more content from Ireland.

Also available for the north is Eddie Connolly's amazing newspaper intimations site at **http://freepages.genealogy.rootsweb.ancestry.com/~econnolly/**, whilst free to access copies of the state based title *The Belfast Gazette* from 1922 can be found at **www.belfast-gazette.co.uk**. Although the earlier *Dublin Gazette* is not yet online, its replacement of *Iris Oifigiúil* partially is at **www.irisoifigiuil.ie**, although with an archive from 2002 only at present.

Commercial Vendors

The previously mentioned FindmyPast website hosts much material which was originally available through sites such as Irish Origins at **www.origins.net/iowelcome.aspx** and on CD from Eneclann. It is now substantially enhancing its portfolio with many new collections digitised in partnership with the National Archives of Ireland, such as the *Irish Prison Registers 1790-1924* and *Petty Session Order Books 1850-1910* collections. If your ancestors don't turn up in these, they were clearly saints! The site's sister site, FindmyPast.co.uk, also has useful digitised records collections, particularly for the military from 1760-1913 in the form of Chelsea Pension records and records of British militias, with additional discharge records from Kilmainham Hospital coming soon.

Other sources

There is of course a great deal more available online. To try to find more targeted resources for your particular area try the free to access *'gateway'* sites such as the multilayered GENUKI - **www.genuki.com** - Cyndi's List - **www.cyndislist.com**
Fianna - **www.rootsweb.ancestry.com/~fianna/county/index1.html**
Irish Ancestors - **www.irishtimes.com/ancestor/browse/counties**
From Ireland **www.from-ireland.net** and the Irish Genealogical Project **www.igp-web.com**

Scottish based family historian Chris Paton is the author of ***Tracing Your Family History on the Internet*** Published 2011 Pen and Sword ***www.pen-and-sword.co.uk/?product_id=2974***

The Irish in British India
Emma Jolly

The first British base in India emerged after 1600, when the East India Company (EIC) received permission to trade there from Queen Elizabeth I. The Company's initial trading post (or 'factory') was at Surat in the Gujurat region. Here the EIC traded spices and fought to protect their interests from the dominant Dutch East India Company (VOC). Matters intensified, resulting in the Anglo-Dutch Wars of 1652 and 1674. The heart of the conflict was over sea routes out of Western Europe but grew to impact on other areas: the English lost their trading posts in West Africa as a consequence.

This sets the scene for British involvement in India: trade, conflict and diplomacy. For all of these tasks the EIC needed men. Some of these men came from Ireland. The earliest records of the Irish in India are held with other EIC material in the India Office Records (IOR) in the Asian and African Studies (AAS) reading room of the British Library in London. Particularly useful documents for the 17th century are the factory records in reference IOR/G, Minutes of the EIC's Directors and Proprietors (IOR: B), and EIC General Correspondence (IOR: E). Some of these are indexed and can be identified by searching with an individual's name on the British Library's Explore portal: http://explore.bl.uk/ Many of the original records are not online and can only be seen in the Library.

For those who cannot visit, the British Library has an enquiries service. The team can be contacted at Asian and African Studies enquiries, The British Library, 96 Euston Road, London NW1 2DB U.K. T: +44 (0)20 7412 7873. Online enquiries can be made online: www.questionpoint.org/crs/servlet/org.oclc.admin.BuildForm?&institution=13430&type=1&language=1

Throughout the 17th century, the British established factories at their three main centres of trade. These were:

- Fort St George (the city that later became Madras, the seat of the Madras Presidency) was built by the British in 1640.
- Bombay (acquired from Portugal as part of the dowry of Catherine of Braganza on her marriage to Charles II), which replaced Surat as the trade centre of western India in 1668.
- Fort at Sutanuti on the River Hooghly (now Hugli), at the mouth of the Bay of Bengal, which was controlled by the EIC from 1690. After merging with two other villages, this fort became known as Calcutta.

From these came the three main areas of administration of British India, also known as the *'presidencies.'* These presidencies were Madras, Bombay and Bengal. All EIC and IOR material is arranged by presidency. When researching for Irish ancestors in British India, it is important to establish in which presidency they were based. This can be confusing, as a soldier in the Bengal Army, for example, may have been sent to serve in Madras. However, his recruitment and service papers would be found in the records of Bengal.

East India Dock London

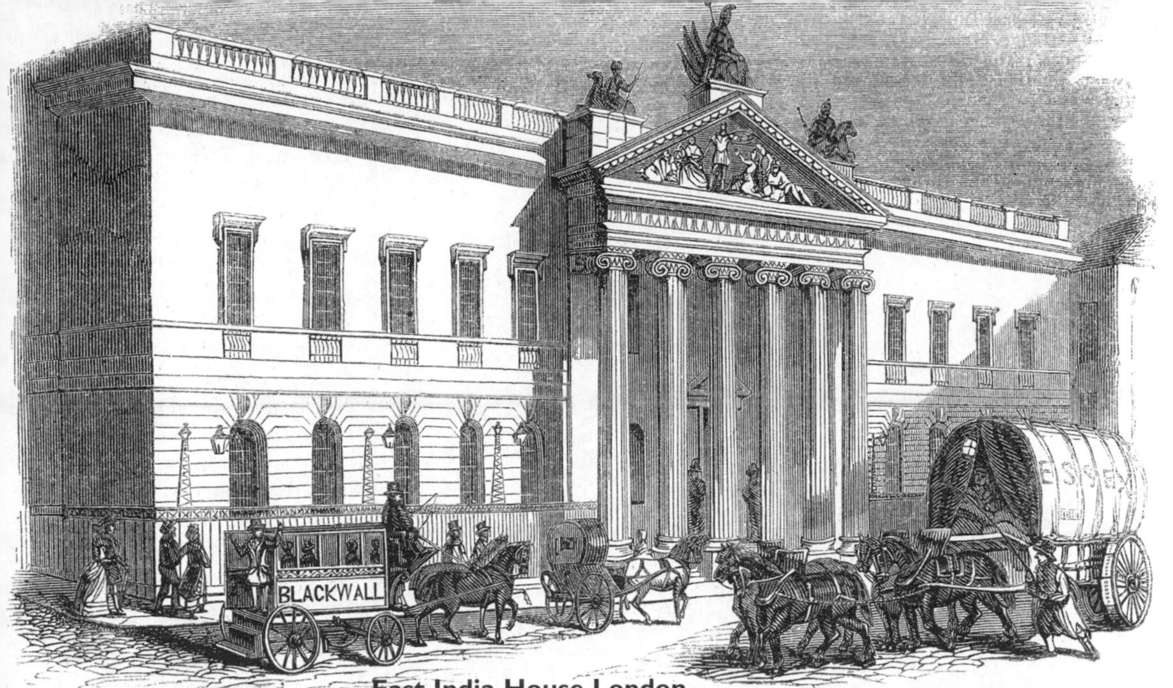

East India House London

The main birth, marriage and death records of Europeans in British India are found in the British Library in the Ecclesiastical Returns (IOR: N). These largely consist of baptism, marriage and burial records from Christian churches. The series is not complete. Estimates are that only 60% of all such records survive here. Copies of these records have been made and are available to search via LDS microfilms and were uploaded in 2012 to www.findmypast.co.uk (FindMyPast). Many of the names in these records have been indexed at www.familysearch.org (FamilySearch). Other useful online indexes for vital events are the British Library's Family History Search http://indiafamily.bl.uk/UI/ and the database of the Families in British India Society (FIBIS) www.new.fibis.org/

Records of the EIC's Marine Department (IOR: L/MAR) also date from the early 17th century. Mariners in the Mercantile Marine, Military Marine or river Pilot Services were essential to the Company's trade, travelling across the seas with precious cargo. Some Irish mariners began their career when they were engaged by the EIC in England. However, Irish merchant seamen may have been engaged at ports across the world and worked for private traders and ship owners in Indian waters. The main set of surviving records are held at The National Archives (TNA). Further details of TNA records can be found via its Discovery portal http://discovery.nationalarchives.gov.uk/SearchUI/Home

Many of TNA's merchant seaman records have been digitised on FindMyPast. Although some Irish mariners had set off to sea in search

Governor General's Palace, Calcutta

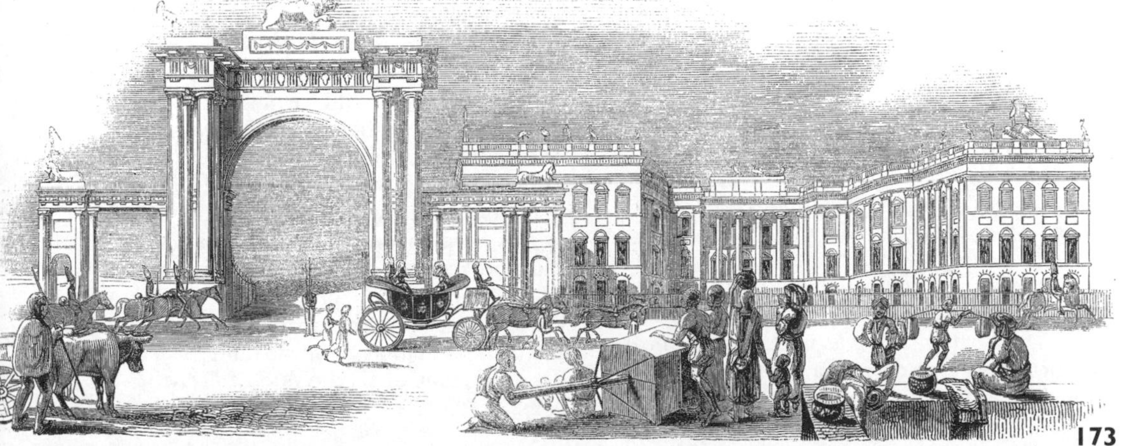

SEPOYS OF BOMBAY, MADRAS, AND BENGAL PRESIDENCIES—IN BACK GROUND A MEMBER OF THE DROMEDARY CORPS.

of work, adventure or fortune, others were escaped criminals and may be harder to trace due to the use of pseudonyms. It may only be through family rumour that the criminal connection is discovered. Other mariners may have had short-lived career, working their passage home. In the 17th century, the journey from Calcutta to the EIC headquarters in London took six months but this was later to be reduced by technological advances and the construction of the Suez Canal.

Irish men also enlisted as sailors or officers in the British Royal Navy. Battles fought by the EIC to establish themselves in India relied heavily on naval support for their success. The EIC's Bengal Marine also had a military function, and combined with the Bombay Marine in 1877 to become Her Majesty's Indian Marine (Royal Indian Marine from 1892) and the Royal Indian Navy in 1935. Useful genealogical sources for marine ancestors can be found at http://www.barnettmaritime.co.uk Other passages to India can be traced through names in published directories or passenger lists. Copies of pre-1833 passenger permits can be found in the Court Minutes (IOR: B) and Despatches (IOR: E). TNA holds later passenger lists, many of which have been digitized on Ancestry and FindMyPast.

Others seeking their fortunes in India were the men who became known as *'nabobs.'* Nabob is a corruption of the princely title *Nawab*. The term nabob was first used to mean 'governor' but later defined a deputy. However, in popular terminology it was used to describe EIC men who achieved great wealth and prominence. The riches of the EIC grew enormously as the

Company profited from the textile trade at the expense of skilled Indian workers. Of those senior Company officers who survived the climate and illnesses of the distant land, many nabobs returned home with vast fortunes. Many Irishmen were amongst those keen to risk the dangerous sea travel and unfamiliar climate in the hope of making their fortune.

One of these men was James Alexander, who was born in 1730, the son of a Derry Alderman. Beginning as a civil servant in Madras. Alexander worked his way through the EIC ranks, becoming Resident at Murshidabad and Patna, and gradually saving a fortune that enabled him to buy 9,000 acres in Ulster in 1776. When he returned to India in 1766, he was appointed Sixth Member of the Bengal Council. In a letter of introduction to a correspondent in Madras in 1767, a referee wrote *'I make no doubt that you have given him every curry that ever was invented at Mdras. He deserves it . . .'* Alexander left India forever in 1772 and retired to a prosperous land-owning lifestyle in Ireland as the 1st Lord Caldeon. The Caledon Papers (including the Caledon East India Company Papers) can be explored at the Public Record Office of Northern Ireland (PRONI) in reference D/2431.

Several governors were drawn from the Irish nobility. Amongst them was the brother of the Duke of Wellington, Richard, Lord Wellesley, who later served as Lord Lieutenant of Ireland. He was born in 1760 at Dangan Castle in County Meath to Lord Mornington, an Anglo-Irish peer and member of the Ascendancy. Before leaving for India, Wellesley had served in both Irish Houses of Parliament. Wellesley was one of the most significant governors of India, ruling as he did from 1798-1805, an era of expansion and British imperial domination. Under his command came the defeat of the Mysore empire and the death of its powerful leader, Tipu Sultan at Seringapatam in 1799, and most important of all, the end of French

A Meeting of The Commanders in Chief of the Army in India 1884

influence in India. After Wellesley, the British were no longer a mere trading power: they were rulers.

The Honourable East India Company's (Civil) Service (HEICS) became better organised under Wellesley. Civil servants were employed by the EIC in ranks varying from the lowly Writer, through to Factor and Junior Merchant, to Senior Merchant. Training schools emerged at Fort William and at Haileybury in England. Haileybury College Archives holds records of the former East India College and its pupils – the future civil servants of India. The college trained civil servants between 1806 and 1858. More information can be found on the website www.haileybury.com/the-school/a-briefhistory/archives

Over time another class of civil servants emerged, some of whom were Irish. They were the uncovenanted civil service, meaning they had not signed a covenant to join. Usually drawn from lower ranks of society, often within India, these administrators worked in government areas such as public works, railways, and telegraphs. They are often more difficult to trace, but records of them can be found in the L/F/10 series. A guide to this has been written by Lawrie Butler (FIBIS Fact File 7).

By far the largest group of Irish in India at this time were those serving as soldiers. It has been estimated that up to half the men in the EIC's Armies (1708-1861) had been born in Ireland. The armies comprised those of the three presidencies: Bengal, Madras and Bombay.

However, these were not the only soldiers in India. Before a standing army was formed, the EIC had drawn from local and European mercenaries. There are records of mercenaries at TNA, but many were not recorded. There were also the men of the British Army, which included many Irish troops and officers. British Army records are held at TNA, although many surviving service records for soldiers have been digitised on FindMyPast. Some of those for the First World War can be found on Ancestry.

References to early officers were made in the Minutes of the Court of Directors (IOR: B). From 1789 to 1860, useful genealogical details of officers of the EIC armies were noted on their recruitment documents, or Cadet Papers. These are held in IOR: L/MIL/9/107-253 and have been filmed by the LDS. These records are due to be uploaded to FindMyPast. Other useful records at the British Library in IOR: L/MIL are officers' service records, casualty returns and pension fund details. Officers' careers can be traced through the Presidency Army Lists.

The father of Godfrey Evan Baker had served as Mayor of the city of Cork in 1769. As a teenager, Godfrey Evan Baker, a member of the

Irish gentry, enlisted as a Cadet in the 3rd European Regiment of the Bengal Army in 1769. The FIBIS database includes a mention to Godfrey Evan Baker in the *List of Officers of the Bengal Army, 1754-1834* 0 Cadet, 1769 (p.77). He was promoted to Captain on 18 November 1779. During his time as an officer, Baker had a servant, camp follower, Dean Mahomed. The two served together for fourteen years. Baker's career ended in disgrace, but whilst packing for a return to Ireland, Mahomed also resigned, even though, by this time, he had reached the prestigious appointment as *subadar.* For Mahomed it appears there was no question that he would stay in the Army as Baker sailed away. In an alleged letter to Baker, Mahomed wrote, *'that I should suffer much uneasiness of mind, in the absence of my best friend.'* This letter and the experiences of Baker and Mahomed were reproduced by the latter in his book, *The Travels of Dean Mahomed* (Cork, 1794). Baker is believed to have died in 1786, not long after his return to Cork. His loyal friend went on to found Britain's first curry house: Dean Mahomed is remembered by a Green Plaque on the front of the *'Site of Hindoostane Coffee House 1810 London's First Indian Restaurant'* at the present 102 George Street, London W1 8NT.

After the Indian Mutiny of 1857, the EIC's dominance came to an end and the Crown began direct rule from the India Office in London. This impacted on the EIC's armies which were renamed the Presidency Armies, but were known informally as the Indian Army. From 1895, the Indian Army became the official army of the government of India. Records for this period are also held in the IOR at the British Library.

Dean Mahomed

For soldiers and NCOs, the Army Registers of Recruits, Embarkation Lists, and Depot Description Lists (IOR: L/MIL/9), often provide the most reliable method of tracing where in Ireland your ancestor originated by naming the parish of birth as well as the place of enlistment. Sadly not all entries are fully completed and not all documents survive. Other useful records in the IOR for soldiers include service records, muster rolls, casualty returns and discharge records. These can be difficult to use as not all are indexed but this should be remedied when they are uploaded to FindMyPast (due 2013).

As most soldiers of other ranks in the Company's armies were not allowed to marry, many cohabited with native women instead. Irish soldiers were amongst those who settled in India, after their service ended, with some marrying local Indian or Anglo-Indian women. Anglo-Indians of Portuguese, Italian and French descent were Catholic, and religion or religious practice often provided a point of introduction. Soldiers' sons often enlisted also, and further research into their children can provide useful clues. Of those who left the Army, many turned to the growing railway industry for work. Several of today's Anglo-Indians, in India and across the world, have Irish ancestors as a consequence of these marriages and relationships.

For Irish Catholics, worship was difficult. The EIC only employed Anglicans, but were forced to be flexible with Irish soldiers when mercenaries became difficult to obtain at the onset of the French Wars. The officers needed recruits and large numbers of the Irish were willing to enlist. This led to a more relaxed approach towards Irish Catholic soldiers. Nonetheless, early ecclesiastical returns are all Anglican, and finding records of Catholics or nonconformists up to the late eighteenth century can thus be difficult. Roman Catholic records can be found in larger numbers from the 1830s as a consequence of the 1829 Catholic Emancipation in England and Wales, as were the many Irish soldiers who supported the British and Indian Armies of the period. Although the records were created separately, they are indexed with Anglican events in the Ecclesiastical Records. Before Emancipation, many Irish Catholic soldiers used the nonconformist missionary chapels.

Disarming Indian Troops 1857

Unfortunately, several nonconformist churches refused to send copies of records to London and they can be difficult to trace today.

Details of Catholic clergy, some of whom were Irish, can be found in directories, such as those of Madras and Thacker's (1885-1942). Original copies of these directories are held on the open access shelves of AAS, although there may be copies in larger libraries.

Not all the Irish in British India were Catholic. The missionary movement became prominent in India in the 18th century. Amongst their number were several Protestant Irish. Amy Wilson-Carmichael was born in County Down in 1867. The daughter of the founder of the Welcome Evangelist Church in Belfast, Wilson-Carmichael joined the Church Missionary Society. After initial service in Japan, she settled into work with children and young women in India, in Tamil Nadu. A prolific writer, Wilson-Carmichael's *Things as They Are: Mission Work in Southern India* can be read online at www.archive.org/stream/thingsastheyarem00wilsuoft#page/n7/mode/2up

The Mundus online gateway to missionary collections at http://www.mundus.ac.uk can be searched by person and also by place. The Adam Matthew digital database www.amdigital.co.uk has many digitized records from East and South Asia, including some concerning missionaries. One of the most comprehensive collections of missionary records can be found at the School of Oriental and African Studies (SOAS) Library in London. These include the Archives of the Conference of British Missionary Societies (1872–1973), records of the Commonwealth Missionary Society (formerly Congregational or Colonial) 1836–1966, the Methodist Missionary Society Library, and the London Missionary Society.

Non-religious birth, marriage and death material also survives. Some can be found via the announcements column of newspapers or early directories. Civil registration records for the Indian States births and deaths survive in the GRO Overseas indexes. These may be particularly relevant for the Irish army families, as they include records of the Army, as well as those of consuls and others from 1761 - 2005 All indexes can be searched at FindMyPast. Copies of the original certificates can be ordered from www.gro.gov.uk

As mentioned above, the details of thousands of births, marriages and deaths have been recorded in the FIBIS database. FIBIS is the family history society for all those researching ancestors in British India. The society's website www.new.fibis.org/ includes an extensive database, blog and FIBIwiki information sources. Members are well supported and they can connect with others through an exclusive social network. A talk by FIBIS Chairman, Peter Bailey, *'The Irish in India, 1790-1920'* can be seen on YouTube at www.youtube.com/watch?v=PQDd0NH1NXg

Useful Websites

SOAS www.soas.ac.uk/
Cambridge South Asian Archive www.s-asian.cam.ac.uk/archome.html
Colonial Film Archive www.colonialfilm.org.uk/
British Association for Cemeteries in South Asia (BACSA) http://indian-cemeteries.org/bacsa/html/cemetery_records.html
Google Books http://books.google.com/ – contains digitised copies of memoirs of Irish people who lived in India, or those who knew them
Historical Maps of India http://homepages.rootsweb.ancestry.com/~poyntz/India/maps.html

Theobald Wolfe Tone
Irish Nationalist & Rebel
Brian Parnaby

In the annals of Irish History there have been countless incidents of patriotism, loyalty, bravery and treachery. In the late Eighteenth Century, one person in particular stands out as an Irish patriot, Theobald Wolfe Tone. He was determined to have a united Ireland and to separate from British rule.

Wolf Tone was born in Dublin in 1763 and studied, firstly, at Trinity College in the city, furthered his studies at Middle Temple, London, and qualified as a Barrister in Dublin in 1789. By religion he was an Episcopalian (belonging to a Church governed by Bishops), but, unusually, supported Roman Catholic emancipation, Catholics in Ireland being at that time an oppressed majority. Tone did not endear himself to the ruling minority in this respect, especially so when he published a document arguing in favour of this emancipation. His crusade, as indeed it became, was further strengthened by his conviction that British power throughout Ireland was inextricably bound up over the privileges enjoyed by this minority. The only solution he envisaged was separation of the Irish from the yoke of the English. Tone, acting as Secretary of an organisation known as the *'Catholic Committee,'* became one of the founding members of the league of *'United Irishmen'* in 1791, dedicated to this cause.

In this connection, Tone began secret discussions in Dublin, with certain French agents (at that time France was Britain's traditional sworn enemy) but, when this was discovered, Tone was forced to flee the country, travelling firstly to America. In Philadelphia the French contingent there were welcoming, as were the Americans.

As a result of new friendships made and confidences exchanged – because of mutual detestation of the British - Tone then travelled to France and, with the support of Napoleon Bonaparte's Government, organised a small army, to travel to Ireland and invade the country; the aim, at best was to drive out the British, but, at worst, to achieve a rapprochement with the British, guaranteeing full rights for the native Irish Catholic population.

Wolfe Tone

The invading force consisted of 15,000 troops to be carried on 43 French vessels – an impressive Armada to be set against the British occupying forces, then much fewer in number than in the days when Oliver Cromwell exercised his harsh rule during the British interregnum, where the Irish were harried at every end and turn and almost totally subjugated.

The Armada duly departed in December 1795, under the joint command of the extremely competent French General Louis-Lazare Hoche, and (General) Wolf Tone. They headed for Bantry Bay on the South West tip of County Cork but, this Armada, as in Elizabeth I's day, came to grief because of the vile weather conditions, and, being unable to make a landing, had to retire back to Normandy.

Had Hoche and Tone been able to affect a successful landing, they would have enjoyed numerical superiority of about six to one over any British Forces they would have encountered. Tone knew this and had pointed out this fact to his associates in Paris, when planning the invasion. At the time there were only about 13,000 regular British troops stationed throughout the whole of Ireland and these would have had to be supported by (mainly Irish) militias, whose loyalty was suspect and whose turnout would be nowhere near the 60,000 militiamen resident throughout Ireland.

The failure of the invasion was propitious for the British Government under William Pitt the Younger; he had disregarded his own instincts over the increasingly volatile situation prevalent throughout Ireland; where a considerable and well educated nucleus of both Catholic and Protestant citizens had begun to flex their political muscles against the narrow minded Protestant rulers who controlled Ireland from Dublin Castle. Political unrest over this problem of autocratic rule began to threaten

Bantry Bay

the whole structure of Government, both in Britain and in Ireland, when it finally dawned on the powers that be that some form of rapprochement between the politically subservient and down-trodden Catholics and the ruling Protestant elite had to be obtained.

There was a great deal of annoyance expressed in British circles, at the realisation that Wolf Tone, an Episcopalian Protestant, could not only support Catholic emancipation, but serve as the Secretary of the Catholic Committee; and, overtly, wear the uniform of a French General, Britain's enemy. A League of United Irishmen was eventually broken up by the British but this was somewhat a pyrrhic victory, as many of the members travelled across the water to Scotland and England and formed alliances with their radical counterparts. In the meantime, Irish agents reported to the French Army, now encamped on the coast of Normandy, that, whilst an invasion of the British mainland was not at all feasible, this was not at all the case as regards Ireland. Still indecision ruled, whilst neither side could decide on what form of action could be taken. Eventually, in 1798, the remnants of the United Irishmen staged an unsuccessful uprising which was ruthlessly suppressed. Not quite simultaneously, the French made a half-hearted invasion attempt, but in the West of Ireland, far away from where the United Irishmen were battling unsuccessfully.

Wolfe Tone's Statue
Bantry Bay

In the meantime Tone had headed a small and totally inadequate invasion fleet bound for Ireland which, whilst it narrowly evaded a British blockade at Brest was quickly intercepted by British ships near the coast of Donegal. Tone was captured and detained in Dublin Castle, before being tried in a military court on a charge of Treason. He was quickly found Guilty and sentenced to death by hanging, but cheated his executioners by committing suicide in 1798, before his execution. Not once did Tone deny his wish and stated aim of achieving emancipation; he continued to make public statements which defined Britain as being the oppressor of the Catholic Irish.

Some time after his death at the early age of 35, Tone's widow published his private papers which supported his public actions in every detail. His reputation as a highly articulate and persuasive person, possessed of a charming manner, remained unsullied; though he was viewed by many, correctly, as somewhat of an adventurer. Nevertheless, to many Irishmen of the time – and since – he was, and is, viewed as the ultimate Irish nationalist. It is interesting to conjecture what benefits he could have brought to Ireland had he lived.

Theobald Wolf Tone lies buried at Bodenstown, County Kildare and the site is a popular place of pilgrimage for aspiring Republicans of various shades of nationalism. There are few Irishmen of his ilk who can aspire to his lofty aims; futile though they were at the time, they eventually bore fruit.

The 1901 and 1911 Census
Beyond Form A
Chris Paton

Whenever we consult the 1901 and 1911 census forms we predominantly do so to discover who was related to whom, what occupations they had, which religious denominations were followed and where and when people were born. Thankfully in Ireland the original household schedules survived, often written in our ancestors' own handwriting, and are freely available to consult online in a digitised format at **www.census.nationalarchives.ie**.

Each census record return starts with a *'primary'* return. For most of us this will be Form A, which provides the basic genealogical information as outlined above. If your ancestor was in an institution, however, they may be found on a different form, such as those for shipping returns (Form B3), workhouses (Form E), hospitals (Form F), academic bodies (Form G), barracks (Form H), asylums (Form I), prisons (Form K), the sick at home (Form C) and *'lunatics'* or *'idiots'* at home (Form D). As well as the key primary form, however, there are many other additional pages present which may be foolish to ignore.

In this article I will look at how these pages can help to tell a further story for domestic residents listed in Form A returns. On the page there is a number given at the top right hand side of the page besides the heading *'Number on Form B,'* which should be noted in order to locate the relevant additional information for your household within the subsequent pages.

Form N is the Enumerator's Extract. From a genealogical perspective, it initially appears to offer little beyond that which can already be deduced from the main Form A, with the page apparently summarising the information found there. It lists how many houses were inhabited, how many people were in each household, and how many people there were of each sex and religion. It also usefully pinpoints the various boundaries within which your ancestor's home existed, with information such as the poor law union, district electoral division, townland, parish and more.

Don't be too hasty in skipping past this form though, particularly for 1901. In particular check the 'Families' column, which asks how many families were present in each house. You may find that on your Form A there is only one family

CENSUS OF IRELAND, 1901.

(Two Examples of the mode of filling up this Table are given on the other side.)

FORM A.

No. on Form B. 8

RETURN of the MEMBERS of this FAMILY and their VISITORS, BOARDERS, SERVANTS, &c., who slept or abode in this House on the night of SUNDAY, the 31st of MARCH, 1901.

NAME and SURNAME. No Persons ABSENT on the night of Sunday, March 31st, to be entered here; EXCEPT those (not enumerated elsewhere) who may be out at WORK or TRAVELLING, &c., during that Night, and who RETURN HOME ON MONDAY, APRIL 1st. Subject to the above instruction, the Name of the Head of the Family should be written first; then the names of his Wife, Children, and other Relatives; then those of Visitors, Boarders, Servants, &c.		RELATION to Head of Family.	RELIGIOUS PROFESSION.	EDUCATION.	AGE.		SEX.	RANK, PROFESSION, OR OCCUPATION.	MARRIAGE.	WHERE BORN.	IRISH LANGUAGE.	If Deaf and Dumb; Dumb only; Blind; Imbecile or Idiot; or Lunatic.
Christian Name.	Surname.	State whether "Head of Family," or "Wife," "Son," "Daughter," or other relative; "Visitor," "Boarder," "Servant," &c.	State here the particular Religion, or Religious Denomination, to which each person belongs. [Members of Protestant Denominations are requested not to describe themselves by the vague term "Protestant," but to enter the name of the Particular Church, Denomination, or Body, to which they belong.]	State here whether he or she can "Read and Write," can "Read" only, or "Cannot Read."	Years on last Birthday.	Months for Infants under one Year.	Write "M" for Males and "F" for Females.	State the Particular Rank, Profession, Trade, or other Employment of each person. Children or young persons attending a School, or receiving regular instruction at home, should be returned as *Scholars*. [Before filling this column you are requested to read the Instructions on the other side.]	Whether "Married," "Widower," "Widow," or "Not Married."	If in Ireland, state in what County or City; if elsewhere, state the name of the Country.	Write the word "IRISH" in this column opposite the name of each person who speaks IRISH only, and the words "IRISH & ENGLISH" opposite the names of those who can speak both languages. In other cases no entry should be made in this column.	Write the respective infirmities opposite the name of the afflicted person.
Thomas	Prendergast	Head of Family	Cateholice	Read and rite	42		m	Farmer	married	Co. Kilkenny	English	
Mary	Prendergast	wife	Cateholice	Read and rite	37		F		married	Co Kilkenny	English	
Thomas	Prendergast	son	Cateholice	Read and rite	9		m	Scholar	Not married	Co Kilkenny	English	
Daniel	Prendergast	son	Cateholice	Read and rite	9		m	Scholar	Not married	Co Kilkenny	English	
Bridget	Prendergast	Daughter	Cateholice	Read and rite	8		F	Scholar	Not married	Co Waterford	English	
Paul	Prendergast	Son	Cateholice	Read and rite	6		m	Scholar	Not married	Co Waterford	English	
Alice	Prendergast	Daughter	Cateholice	Cannot read	3		F		Not married	Co Kilkenny	English	
Mary	Prendergast	Daughter	Cateholice	Cannot read	1		F		Not married	Co Kilkenny		
Bridget	Houlahan	Servant	Cateholice	Read and rite	13		F	Scholar	Not married	Co Waterford	English	

I hereby certify, as required by the Act 63 Vic., cap. 6, s. 6 (1), that the foregoing Return is correct, according to the best of my knowledge and belief.

Patrick [illegible] (*Signature of Enumerator.*)

I believe the foregoing to be a true Return.

Thomas Prendergast Killonerry (*Signature of Head of Family*).

listed, but *'head of household'* does not necessarily mean the *'head of the entire house'* – there may well be other families living in the property, constituting a separate household but still resident within the same property. Both Forms N and B1 can help to flesh out your own family's domestic situation considerably.

A good example lies with my wife's great grandfather's house in County Kilkenny. In 1901 Thomas Prendergast is found listed as a farmer at Killonerry, in the south of the county. He was the head of the household, living with his wife Mary, six children (including six year old Paul, my wife's grandfather), and one servant, Bridget Houlahan. Killonerry was both the farm name and the townland, though the poor law union to which it belonged was in fact Carrick-on-Suir, located just over the county line in Tipperary. The Form A schedule was given the number 8 in the top right hand corner. Upon first inspection this page seems to provide the entire list of occupants for the house, complete with servants, and yet if we then look at Form N, a slightly different story begins to emerge. Under the column *'Families,'* the number '2' is listed. It might be tempting to think this refers to the Prendergasts and the sole member of the Houlahan family, but a check of Form B1 provides a different explanation.

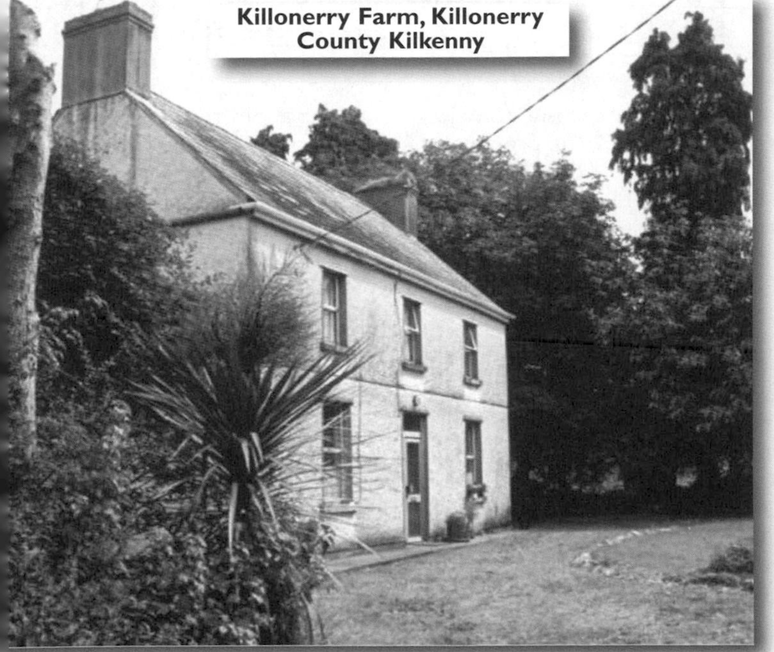

Killonerry Farm, Killonerry County Kilkenny

Form B1 is the *'House and Building Return.'* At the top it again provides a list of the various administrative divisions within which a property is

CENSUS OF IRELAND, 1901.

FORM B. 1.—HOUSE AND BUILDING RETURN.

County, Kilkenny Parliamentary Division, South Kilkenny Poor Law Union, Carrick-on-Suir District Electoral Division, Whitechurch Townland, Killonerry

Parliamentary Borough, — City, — Urban District, — Town or Village, — Street, — Barony, Iverk Parish, Whitechurch

NOTE A.—When a Townland or Street is situated in two Parliamentary Divisions, or in more than one District Electoral Division or Parish, or is partly within and partly without a Parliamentary Borough, City, Urban District, Town, or Village, a *separate Return* should be made for each portion.

HOUSES.					PARTICULARS OF INHABITED HOUSES.						FAMILIES, &c.							
No. of House or Building (Col. 1)	Whether Built or Building (Col. 2)	State whether Private Dwelling, Public Building, School, Manufactory, Hotel, Public-house, Lodging-house, or Shop, &c. (Col. 3)	Number of Out-Offices and Farm-steadings as returned on Form B. 2. (Col. 4)	Is House Inhabited — Yes or No, as the case may be. (Col. 5)	WALLS. If Walls are of Stone, Brick, or Concrete, enter the figure 1 in this column; if they are of Mud, Wood, or other perishable material, enter the figure 0. (Col. 6)	ROOF. If Roof is of Slate, Iron, or Tiles, enter the figure 1 in this column; if it is of Thatch, Wood, or other perishable material, enter the figure 0. (Col. 7)	ROOMS. Enter in this column:— For each House with 1 Room only the figure 1; For Houses with 2, 3, or 4 rooms 2; 5 or 6 3; 7, 8, or 9 4; 10, 11, or 12 5; 13 or more 6 (Col. 8)	Windows in Front. State in this column the exact Number of Windows in Front of House. (Col. 9)	Tot the Figures you have entered in columns 6, 7, 8, & 9, and enter the Total for each House in this column. (Col. 10)	CLASS OF HOUSE. When Total in Col. 10 is:— 1 or 2, enter "4th"; 3, 4, or 5 "3rd"; 6, 7, 8, 9, 10, or 11 "2nd"; 12 or over "1st" (Col. 11)	No. of distinct Families in each House. (Col. 12)	Name of the Head of each Family residing in the House. (Col. 13)	No. of Rooms occupied by each Family. (See Note B at foot.) (Col. 14)	Total Number of Persons in each Family. (Col. 15)	Date on which Form A was collected. (Col. 16)	Number of Persons in each Family who were sick on 31st March, 1901. (Col. 17)	Name of the Landholder (if any) on whose Holding the House is situated, whether that name appears in column 13 or not. (Col. 18)	No. on Form M. 1 if House is on the Holding of a Landholder. (Col. 19)
1	Built	Private dwelling	2	yes	0	0	2	3	5	3rd	1	James Keefe	4	4	1901 April 4th	–	James Keefe	12
2	Built	Private dwelling	8	yes	1	1	3	6	11	2nd	1	Anne Burke	6	5	do	–	Anne Burke	2
3	Built	Private dwelling	5	yes	0	0	2	3	5	3rd	1	William McNamara	3	8	do	–	William McNamara	10
4	Built	Private dwelling	6	yes	1	1	2	2	6	2nd	1	James Norris	4	5	do	–	James Norris	8
5	Built	Private dwelling	9	yes	1	1	3	7	12	1st	1	William O'Donnell	6	7	do	–	William O'Donnell	6
6	Built	Private dwelling	6	yes	1	0	2	3	6	2nd	1	Richard Maher	3	10	do	–	Richard Maher	3
7	Built	Private dwelling	3	yes	0	0	2	3	5	3rd	1	Michael Phelan	3	11	do	–	Michael Phelan	9
8	Built	Private dwelling	11	yes	1	1	5	7	14	1st	2	Patrick Prendergast	6	8	do	–	Patrick Prendergast	1
–	–	–	–	–	–	–	–	–	–	–	–	Thomas Prendergast	5	9	do	–	Patrick Prendergast	"
9	Built	Private dwelling	8	yes	1	1	4	3	9	2nd	1	John O'Dwyer	5	9	do	–	John O'Dwyer	5
10	Built	Private dwelling	9	yes	1	1	2	3	7	2nd	1	Thomas Holden	4	3	do	–	Thomas Holden	7
11	Built	Private dwelling	11	no	–	–	–	–	–	–	–	–	–	–	–	–	Thomas Walsh	4

NOTE B.—If one Room is occupied by more than one Family, the Names of the Heads of Families so occupying it should be bracketted together in Col. 13, thus:— John Jones, Peter Murray, } and the figure 1 entered in Col. 14, opposite the middle of the bracket. See pattern Table in Instructions, page 8. [OVER.

1901 Census Detail Form B1

3rd	1	Michael Phelan	3	11	do	–	Michael Phelan	9
1st	2	Patrick Prendergast	6	8	do	–	Patrick Prendergast	1
	–	Thomas Prendergast	5	9	do	–	Patrick Prendergast	"
2nd	1	John O'Dwyer	5	9	do	–	John O'Dwyer	5
2nd	1	Thomas Holden	4	3	do	–	Thomas Holden	7

located, with a series of detailed questions then answered beneath on the nature of the houses and occupants found there. These are divided into four key sections, with each line relating to a different household. The first section provides the number corresponding to the returns on Form A, allowing you to look for the right household, followed by a series of more detailed questions on the building occupied – whether built or being built; whether a private dwelling, public building, school, factory hotel etc; the number of out offices and farm steadings attached to the property; and whether inhabited. The second section asks for particulars on the building, including details on the fabrication of the house (walls, roofs, rooms), how many windows at the front, and the *'class'* of the house. Whilst these are all useful to help gain an idea about the nature of the property, the third section is really the gold dust here. Under *'Families'* it again asks for the number of families in each building, as well as how many rooms are occupied by each, the total number of people in each family and the numbers who may have been sick on census night. Crucially, it also provides the names of the heads of the households in the building, and the name of the landholder. The fourth section relates to landowners only, noting a further form (M1) filled in by them but not available online. For some households there is a also a Form B2 which provides further details about the numbers of out offices and farm steadings attached to each property.

There are in fact details of two heads of household given on Form B1 for property

(Col. 11.)	(Col. 12.)	(Col. 13.)	(Col. 14.)	(Col. 15.)	(Col. 16.)	(Col. 17.)	(Col. 18.)	(Col. 19.)
1st	1	William O'Donnell	6	8	1911. April 7th		William O'Donnell	
2nd	1	Thomas Pendergast	6	9	do		Thomas Pendergast	
1st	1	Patrick Pendergast	9	9	do		Patrick Pendergast	
2nd	1	John Dwyer	6	5	do		John Dwyer	
2nd	1	Philip Kelly	4	6	do		Mrs Walsh	5

1911 Census Detail Form B1

number 8 in Killonerry. Thomas turns out to be the second name, the first being Patrick Prendergast, who was Thomas' older brother. Both families shared the same farm building in 1901, with Patrick and his family occupying six rooms, and Thomas and his family the other five. Patrick was also noted as the landholder, and a subsequent search reveals an entirely different Form A household return for him, his family and his own servants.

Family lore had it that the brothers did indeed live together, but at some point the farmland was divided between them. If we now skip forward ten years and check the census for both families, this is in fact documented. In 1911, each brother is again listed as the head of a household at Killonerry, and both listed as farmers, however on this occasion Patrick's schedule is noted as number 1 whilst Thomas's is given as number 3. Form B1 develops the story further. Thomas is noted as the landholder of his property, with his family of nine, whilst Patrick is the landholder of his, with a family of nine. Clearly the brothers parted way in between the two census years. Note that for Form N in 1911, the number of families per building is not asked, only the number of occupants in each house.

As can be seen, consulting the subsequent forms should be just as important as Form A (or its institutional counterpart). As well as offering further information about the house itself, in many cases they may also help to tell another story in their own right. The list of heads of households in Form B1 also allows you to check for the names of neighbouring families, some of whom may well be related. If you choose to ignore these additional documents, you may well only end up with half of the story waiting to be discovered!

About the author
Chris Paton is a professional genealogist who runs the Scotland's Greatest Story research service **www.ScotlandsGreatestStory.co.uk** and the British GENES genealogical news blog **www.britishgenes.blogspot.co.uk**
He is the author of Tracing Your Family History on the Internet, Discover Scottish Church Records, Discover Scottish Land Records, Irish Family History Resources Online, and Researching Scottish Family History.

This article was first published in Irish Roots magazine. It has been revised and updated by the Author

My Ancestor and The Sudan War 1884

Robert Blatchford

Everyone can have a '*wow*' or '*Eureka*' moment when researching their family history. The adrenalin rush from the discovery when these moments happen is far greater when they are unexpected!

When Genes Reunited - www.genesreunited.co.uk - announced on 20th December 2011 that the British Newspaper Archive could be accessed through their website I little realized that one search I would make would result in giving me a first hand account of a decisive battle in British history.

In their blog Genes Reunited said, *'This is unlike any other data set available online, and will give you an insight into what was going on in the world whilst your ancestors were alive. View articles written at the time of key events in history . . .'*

I went to the Genes Reunited British Newspaper Archive Search Page and entered the barest of details – my surname, the county (South Glamorgan, Wales) and the year range (1850 to 1900). The final entry field is a choice of file types and I chose *'All Types.'*

Within seconds I received thirty three matches and scrolling down I found an entry from The Western Mail, Glamorgan for 7th April 1884. My attention was drawn to this particular entry is because it referred to a William Blatchford of Quaker's Yard. My great grandfather was William Blatchford and lived in Quaker's Yard, Glamorgan, South Wales.

The newspaper report said the letter was from a South Wales Marine, which had been received a few days previously by Mr Wm Blatchford, mason, Quaker's Yard, from his nephew, who was serving with the Royal Marines in Egypt.

Royal Marines landing in Sudan

Western Mail Monday April 7 1884

Letter from a South Wales Marine

The following letter was received a few days ago by Mr Wm Blatchford, mason, Quaker's Yard, from his nephew, who is now serving with the Royal Marines in Egypt:

Continued Page 186 ...

General Graham's Force Landing

Continued from Page 185 . . .

Royal Marines Battalion, Suakim
16th March 1884

My dear Uncle

I thank God I am spared to write once more to inform you of our great victory on the 13th inst. We left on 11th inst at five o'clock in the evening for a place called Zareba, about ten miles from here, and we arrived there about midnight. We stayed there until one o'clock on the following day (12th inst), when we left for Tamai, where we arrived about half past five that evening, and formed square, piled arms, and laid down for the night. Everything went well until twelve o'clock that night, when the enemy commenced firing upon us, and they continued firing all night until five o'clock the following morning, when we fired a few shells on them. Their firing was very high, and only two of our men got killed during the night, and one man wounded. That was considered very lucky. However, the 13th of the month was now at hand and this was the day we were to defeat or be defeated.

At 5.30.a.m. we had a little breakfast, and each man served out with one half pint of water and 100 rounds of ammunition. At 7 o'clock we commenced to march towards the enemy. We thought we would have to march a mile or two before we should meet them, but to our surprise they attacked us before we were 200 yards from where we lay all night. They arose in thousands all around, and opened fire on us; of course we retaliated, and for an hour or more the air was thick with bullets, which whizzed in all directions. When the enemy charged the 42nd Highlanders and the 65th fell back, and we were the right face and part rear face of the square, so we turned about and took the front face and poured volleys into the enemy with excellent effect. Then the General said we should be the battalion of direction. During the time the 42nd and 65th Regiments fell back the enemy captured three guns which the blue jackets had, and the 42nd Regiment covered them. As soon as the enemy got up they took the guns but could not use them; but they killed two naval officers and seven sailors. As soon as we advanced a little we recaptured the guns, so that the sailors had them for action once more.

We fought hard for four hours and twenty minutes. It was constant firing each way until what was left of the enemy commenced to retire to the hills. We followed them up and shot them as they lifted their heads above the ground; we had part of it in a hand to hand fight, where we used our bayonets freely. At about half past twelve we arrived at and took possession of Tamai Wells. Then the battle was over, and we went to the Wells and drank, and filled our water bottles. I never knew the exact want of water until then, and I assure you we prized it; and everyman I saw was thanking God, for our tongues were hanging out of our mouths with thirst.

The General and the other remaining old officers said they never witnessed such an engagement before. I do not know the exact number we killed of the enemy, but I am sure there were thousands killed, for the next day we saw the ground thick with them when we were going out reconnoitring. I believe we killed over 5,000. Our loss, I am sorry to say, was over 100 killed and about the same number wounded, and those who were killed were hacked to pieces. They were beyond identification. We buried them that night just outside the place where we stopped for the night, and I assure you it was a painful sight. We went out reconnoitring on the 14th, but we only met a few. They fired some stray shots, and we soon had them down, and as we got amongst the hills we found the rebels' magazines. We set fire to their ammunition and stores. It was over an hour blowing up, and it was the prettiest sight I ever witnessed to see the powder blaze and the shells burst by thousands amongst the hills. It was said that Osman Digna, the chief rebel, was over eighteen years collecting the ammunition, &c, which we destroyed. We stopped at the hills until half past two o'clock that afternoon.

We saw no more rebels, so we marched off for Suakim, a distance of about eighteen miles, and reached here at about eleven o'clock that night – viz, the 14th. The next day we rested, and I took the first opportunity of letting you know of our victory.

It is impossible for me to describe the scene by letter, but I shall be able to give you a personal account some day. I cannot say whether it is all over yet, but I hope it is. I am glad to say I escaped without a scratch. So I conclude, with fondest love to all many times.

From your affectionate nephew,
James Blatchford
Corporal R.M.B.

The flank of a Square marching up in fours

The Sudan War 1883 - 1884

Sudan, in the 19th Century was the ruled by the Khedive (King) of Egypt under the Ottoman Turkish Empire. In 1881 a young Muslim boat builder's apprentice named Muhammad Ahmad Ibn Seyyid Abdullah began a Jihadist revolt against the Khedive and proclaimed himself the '*Mahdi*' (Saviour). In the East of the Sudan the revolt was led by Osman Digna, the Mahdi's lieutenant. Osman Digna , who real name was Uthman abu Bakr Diqna, was born in Suakin but lived in Alexandria in Egypt where he worked in the slave trade. However, after the British suppressed the slave trade he joined the revolt of Arabi Pasha, an Egyptian army officer opposed to foreign rule. With the failure of that revolt at the Battle of Tel el Kebir in September 1882, Osman Digna joined the cause of the Mahdi.

On 29th April 1883 the Mahdi's army annihilated an Egyptian force at Kashgate, commanded by Colonel Hicks, a retired Bombay Army officer. The remaining Egyptian garrisons were scattered all over the Sudan and were vulnerable to attack by the Mahdi and his tribesmen. In January 1884 an Egyptian force under the command of a British officer arrived at Suakin to provide cover for a withdrawal of the Egyptian garrisons in the eastern part of Sudan but was annihilated by the Mahdists at El Teb a few miles inland from a port called Trinkitat.

After pressure from the British Government, the Khedive subsequently appointed General Charles Gordon to oversee the evacuation of the Egyptian forces from the Sudan. General Gordon had had been a very effective governor of the Sudan in the 1870s and arrived at Khartoum, the capital of the Sudan, on 18th February 1884.

A British army, commanded by Major General Graham, was dispatched from Egypt by ship to land at Suakin and relieve the Egyptian garrison at Tokar which was fifty miles south of Suakin. Graham's force arrived at Suakin on 20th February 1884 and other Royal Navy ships arrived later with the remaining regiments. Once assembled, the force moved down the coast by ship to Trinkitat to march and relieve Tokar. However the Governor of Tokar surrendered to the Mahdi's forces with his troops joining the rebels to avoid a massacre.

General Graham abandoned his plan to withdraw the British force to Egypt so moved from Suakin to attack Osman Digna's camp at Tamai. It is from this point that it is relevant to read James Blatchford's letter again because it fully describes the events and battle that day.

A Critical Moment - The Enemy Attacking The Brigade Square

Casualties

All battles between the British and the Mahdists were very ferocious. The Mahdi ordered that all non Muslims in the Sudan faced death but the Muslim Egyptian and Turkish soldiers in the Sudan faced a similar fate. Any British infantryman who was wounded did not survive the battle nor did any cavalryman, who fell from his horse, unless they were immediately rescued. Likewise British troops took few prisoners. No wonder James begins his letter *'I thank God I am spared to write once more to inform you of our great victory on the 13th inst . . .'*

Official figures for British casualties were six officers and 105 non-commissioned ranks killed with a further eight officers and 103 non-commissioned ranks wounded. British estimates put the Mahdist Sudanese dead at around 2,500 with the number of wounded being unknown.

Intrigued by the letter and the history of the Sudan Campaign I wanted to find out more information about my cousin James.

I visited The National Archives website and discovered that the *Royal Marines Registers of Service* could be searched and the service registers of around 110,000 men who joined the Royal Marines between 1842 and 1925 could be downloaded. - https://www.nationalarchives.gov.uk/documentsonline/royalmarines.asp?WT.hp=Royal%20Marines%20Service%20Records

I entered the criteria requested at https://www.nationalarchives.gov.uk/documentsonline/browse-refine.asp?CatID=36&searchType=browserefine&pagenumber=1&query=*&queryType=1

Within seconds the result https://www.nationalarchives.gov.uk/documentsonline/details-result.asp?Edoc_Id=8092906&queryType=1&resultcount=1 came up.

I downloaded James Blatchford's service record. It is a fascinating document. James was enlisted in the Royal Marines on 17th July 1880 in Liverpool and engaged by a Captain Parker. The record shows that he was born on 17th July 1859 at Bandon, County Cork. His religion was Roman Catholic and he was a labourer before enlisting.

At the time of the Sudan War James was onboard H.M.S. Euryalus. On 14th September 1883 James was awarded The Egypt Medal & Star whilst serving on H.M.S. Euryalus and on 16th April 1885 he had the Suakim & Tamai clasps added to his decoration. Reading James' service record

shows that he served with distinction for over 21 years being discharged on 31st July 1901. He height was described as 5 feet 8¾ inches, he had a fresh complexion and had brown hair and blue eyes. The Service Record description was unchanged on his discharge.

James was living in the Royal Marine Barracks, Eastry, Kent when the 1881 census took place. In the 1901 England Census Private James Blatchford was living in The Royal Marine Barracks, East Stonehouse, Devon aged 42. James was *'Found Drowned'* in the Docks at Milford Haven, Pembrokeshire, Wales on 26th August 1911. A Coroner's Inquest into his death took place on 28th August 1911

The National Archives | DocumentsOnline | Image Details

www.nationalarchives.gov.uk/documentsonline/details-result.asp?Edoc_Id=8092906&queryType=1&resultcount=1

The National Archives

Search the archives | Search | Advanced search | Cookie policy

About us | Education | Records | Information management | Archives sector | Shop online

here: Home > DocumentsOnline > Image details

DocumentsOnline — Download *your* history...

Image details

Description	Name	Blatchford, James
	Register Number:	1886
	Division:	Royal Marine Light Infantry: Plymouth Division
	When Enlisted/Date of Enlistment:	17 July 1880
Date	17 July 1859	
Catalogue reference	ADM 159/63	
Dept	Records of the Admiralty, Naval Forces, Royal Marines, Coastguard, and related bodies	
Series	Admiralty: Royal Marines: Registers of Service	
Piece	1349 - 1950	
Image contains	1 document of many for this catalogue reference.	

Number of image files: 1

Image Reference	Format and Version	Part Number	Size (KB)	Number of Pages	Price (£)
537 / 518	PDF 1.2	1	183	1	3.36
Total Price (£)					**3.36**

Refine search > | + Add to shopping

The National Archives, Kew, Richmond, Surrey, TW9 4DU. Tel: +44 (0) 20 8876 3444. Contact us

The whole of the campaign was covered by the newspapers of the time. There is a treasure trove of illustrations in *The Graphic* and *Illustrated London News* for 1884. These images bring to life a military campaign which occurred nearly 130 years ago.

There is more to find out about James Blatchford my first cousin twice removed. However on the basis of my discovery I have not only had a Eureka moment but I have also had my hand on history.

Further Research

British Newspaper Archive - www.genesreunited.co.uk

The National Archives - www.nationalarchives.gov.uk

Royal Marines Museum, Eastney Esplanade, Southsea, Portsmouth, Hampshire, PO4 9PX T: 023 9281 9385 E: info@royalmarinesmuseum.co.uk

Tracing Your Royal Marine Ancestors Richard Brooks & Matthew Little : Pen & Sword Books : ISBN 978 1 844158690

HMS Euryalus
Robert Blatchford

H.M.S. Euryalus

Six ships have been named *Euryalus.* James Blatchford served on the third Euryalus -1877-1897. This was a screw cruiser (sometimes designated a corvette) built at Chatham and launched on 31st January 1877. The ship was 280 feet long, was 4140 tons in weight, and had a maximum speed of 14.7 knots. Armaments on the ship were 14 7 inch muzzle loading rifled guns and two 84 pounder guns. Unlike her predecessor a wooden sailing ship with an engine the third *Euryalus* was a wooden clad iron steamship with auxiliary masts and sails. In1878 it was the flagship of the East Indies Station and was based in Trincomalee, Sri Lanka (Ceylon). Together with other ships based in the east the *Euryalus* was used in the Sudan War. On the long voyages the *Euryalus* used it's sails to preserve coal. In 1885 *H.M.S. Euryalus* ceased being a flagship and returned to Britain and went into the reserve at Chatham Naval Base. The *Euryalus* was sold for scrap in May 1897 for £4,736. The sixth and last *Euryalus* was decommissioned on the 31st March 1989 and sold in 1990 for scrap. A history of all six ships is at www.euryalus.org.uk

Further Information
HMS Euryalus Association - www.euryalus.org.uk

H.M.S. Euryalus in Sudan

The Work of The Commonwealth War Graves Commission in Ireland

Ireland and the two world wars

At the outbreak of the First World War in 1914, Ireland was part of the United Kingdom. Both Nationalist and Unionist leaders initially supported the war and men from north and south, from both Catholic and Protestant backgrounds, enlisted.

It is believed that 210,000 Irishmen served in the British forces during the First World War, while many others of Irish descent served with the forces of other Commonwealth nations or those of America.

Estimates for the number of Irishmen killed during the war vary considerably, but it is believed that as many as 50,000 died.

During the Second World War Ireland, apart from the six counties of Northern Ireland, remained neutral and it is estimated that in the British army alone, as many as 100,000 people from Ireland served, and at least 10,000 of them were killed. Again many more of Irish descent served with the Allied forces of other nations.

In addition to serving personnel, some 1,000 Irish civilians were killed during the Second World War in air raids on Belfast and Dublin.

Dugort Church of Ireland Churchyard, County Mayo

War Graves in Ireland

The majority of those Irishmen and women who died in service, lie buried or commemorated in the countries where they died – their graves and memorials looked after in perpetuity by the Commonwealth War Graves Commission.

Less well known is the fact that there are more than 5,500 Commonwealth war dead buried or commemorated at more than a 1,000 burial grounds or churchyards throughout Ireland.

The majority of the war burials in Ireland are Irish casualties who died in the United Kingdom during both world wars and whose bodies were taken home for burial by their families in their local cemetery or churchyard. Some were buried in family graves marked with private memorials but others are commemorated either by Commission headstones erected on their graves or by commemorative memorials where it was not possible to mark the actual place of burial.

Most of the burials on the west coast of Ireland are those of men who lost their lives in the many ships which were torpedoed and sunk by German U-boats in the first years of the Second World War and whose bodies were washed ashore or recovered from the sea; a great many of them could not be identified.

The largest concentrations of graves will be found in Belfast and Dublin. The cemeteries with the most war burials are Grangegorman Military Cemetery with over 600 and Glasnevin (or Prospect) Cemetery with over 200 (both in Dublin) and Belfast City Cemetery with almost 600.

Grangegorman Military Cemetery, Dublin

Caring for war graves in Ireland

For the maintenance of all but a few of the Commonwealth War Graves in the Republic of Ireland, the Commission has an arrangement with the Office of Public Works. The war graves in Northern Ireland are maintained by local auhorities, church authorities and individuals. These arrangements are administered by the Commission's United Kingdom Area office at the address given at the end of this article. The Commission has a Regional Supervisor responsible for inspecting war graves throughout Ireland and ensuring that the war casualties continue to be adequately commemorated.

The Island of Ireland Peace Park
Messines, Belgium
is dedicated to the soldiers of Ireland,
of all political and religious beliefs, who died,
were wounded or missing in
the Great War of 1914 - 1918

Among the war burials in Grangegorman Military Cemetery are 145 officers and men whose bodies were recovered following the sinking of the mail-boat Leinster which had been struck by a torpedo from a German submarine after leaving Dun Laoghaire for Holyhead on 10 October 1918. Also in the cemetery is a memorial to 72 casualties whose graves elsewhere in Ireland could no longer be maintained and memorial headstones to some 83 casualties buried in Cork Military Cemetery whose graves could not be maintained there.

At Glasnevin Cemetery, the Commission and the Glasnevin Trust (who oversee the maintenance of the cemetery) have been working together on a project to identify war graves within the cemetery and to erect the familiar Commission headstone on many graves that until now have been unmarked.

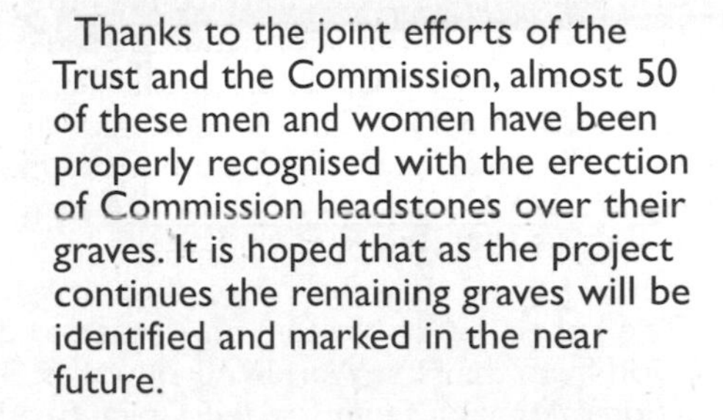

Thanks to the joint efforts of the Trust and the Commission, almost 50 of these men and women have been properly recognised with the erection of Commission headstones over their graves. It is hoped that as the project continues the remaining graves will be identified and marked in the near future.

The Commonwealth War Graves Commission is responsible for the commemoration of almost 1,700,000 members of the Commonwealth forces who gave their lives in the two world wars. The Commission operates in 23,000 locations, in 153 countries.

The graves and memorials of these men and women, who came from all parts of the Commonwealth and who were of many faiths and none, are found around the world in some 150 countries.

CWGC Head Office 2 Marlow Road, Maidenhead, Berkshire SL6 7DX U.K. T: +44 (0) 1628 634221 E: casualty.enq@cwgc.org

CWGC UK Office Jenton Road, Sydenham, Leamington Spa, Warwickshire CV31 1XS U.K. T: +44 (0) 1926 330137

The Ulster Memorial Tower Somme France

Tracing Army Ancestry at The Imperial War Museum

Sarah Paterson MA DipLib

Where to Find Army Service Records

The key piece of information you need to know is the unit that an individual served with (it is a sad fact that those who died during the world wars will be easier to trace than those who survived, and this information is readily obtainable from the Commonwealth War Graves Commission). The personal service record should be your starting point, but many First World War files were lost or damaged by bombing in 1940. Records are located according to an individual's date of discharge.

The Imperial War Museum only covers the period from the First World War onwards. The National Army Museum, Royal Hospital Road, Chelsea, London SW3 4HT (Tel: 020 7730 0717; W: www.national-army-museum.ac.uk) has information on military history from 1485 to date. Pre-1914 service records are held at The National Archives, Ruskin Avenue, Kew, Richmond, Surrey TW9 4DU (Tel: 020 8876 3444; Website: www.nationalarchives.gov.uk). The National Archives (TNA), formerly Public Record Office, also holds all surviving First World War service records for officers who left the Army before 1922. These are held in record classes *WO 339* and *WO 374*, and you can now check the index to these online. Surviving First World War service records for other ranks who ceased service before 1920 are now held at TNA (unfortunately large numbers of these were destroyed by bombing in the Second World War). These can now be accessed online through the subscription based

website www.ancestry.co.uk The publication *First World War Army Service Records* by William Spencer (4th Edition Pub The National Archives 2008) is essential reading for those interested in First World War records, and you can find many useful research guides on the website.

The records of any First World War soldier who saw service after the cut-off dates detailed above or who rejoined the Army, and those who served in the Second World War, are held by the Ministry of Defence. These can be applied for by post from the Army Personnel Centre, Disclosures 4, MP 555, Kentigern House, 65 Brown Street, Glasgow G2 8EX. Initial contact with the Army Personnel Centre (APC) can be made by telephone (0845 600 9663) or email – please include your postal address (disc4@apc.army.mod.uk). Records will be released to proven next of kin (currently there is a £30 fee) and there is likely to be a lengthy wait for this service. You can find a copy of the application form on the Veterans UK website at: www.veterans-uk.info/service_records/service_records.html

Home Guard records are also available through the APC (although not all have survived, and they are usually brief with very little information).

The Brigade of Guards form an exception as records are held by the Regimental Headquarters: Grenadier / Coldstream / Scots / Irish / Welsh Guards, Wellington Barracks, Birdcage Walk, London SW1E 6HQ. First World War officers' records are held by TNA.

The careers of Army officers can be traced using the regular official publication the *Army List*, and the Imperial War Museum (IWM) holds an almost complete set of these from 1914 to 2007, when it ceased to be published in hard copy.

Casualty Records

The Commonwealth War Graves Commission, 2 Marlow Road, Maidenhead, Berkshire SL6 7DX (Tel: 01628 507200) has details of all service personnel who died between the dates 4 August 1914-31 August 1921 and 3 September 1939-31 December 1947. The Commonwealth War Graves Commission (CWGC) may charge a fee for postal enquiries, but the website containing their computerised database, *Debt of Honour*, can be consulted at www.cwgc.org

The new Armed Forces Memorial website has a roll of honour that allows you to search for Army personnel who died after 1948. This can be found at www.veterans-uk.info/amf2/index.php

Details of service personnel buried in 'non-World War' graves are available from the JCCC (Joint Casualty and Compassionate Centre), SPVA (Service Personnel and Veterans Agency), Innsworth House, Imjin Barracks, Innsworth, Gloucester GL3 1HW. Please mark your enquiry *'Graves Casework.'*

Sources held by the IWM include a complete set of the CWGC's memorial and cemetery registers and the 80 volume *Soldiers Died in the Great War, 1914-19*. This was originally published in 1921 by HMSO but was republished by JB Hayward in 1989. This and the less

detailed *Officers Died in the Great War, 1914-19* (published in 1919) are available on a CD-ROM produced by Naval and Military Press, and also on a pay per view basis on the website www.military-genealogy.com (this can also be accessed via the family history pages at www.iwm.org.uk).

A CD-ROM for Army personnel who died in the Second World War has also been produced by Naval and Military Press, and the information is available through www.military-genealogy.com Rolls of honour for other later conflicts are also held, and in addition the IWM has a large collection of published rolls of honour for localities, schools, institutions, etc. Regimental histories and magazines often contain rolls of honour. Some rolls of honour can be found online at www.roll-of-honour.com

The soldiers' own home area should not be forgotten when researching an individual's service - there may be local war memorial records, a local account of war service may have been published, and contemporary local newspapers can prove very helpful. It is also possible that school, church or workplace records may still exist.

The United Kingdom National Inventory of War Memorials is recording details of all war memorials in the country. More information about this project can be found at www.ukniwm.org.uk

Medal Records

Campaign medals are those given to soldiers who are eligible for them because they were in a particular theatre of war within given dates. The First World War Medal Roll which provides a listing of all those who qualified for the 1914 Star, 1914/15 Star, British War Medal, Victory Medal, Territorial Force War Medal and/or the Silver War Badge is held at TNA. If a First World War record was destroyed some basic information about a soldier's service may be found in this. The index cards can now be accessed on the internet at www.nationalarchives.gov.uk/documentsonline These cards are an index to the medal rolls – these can be consulted at TNA, and may yield additional information.

You can also access these cards online at www.ancestry.co.uk – this shows both the front and back of the cards (the reverse may contain additional details).

Post First World War medal claims or enquiries can be addressed to: Ministry of Defence Medal Office, Innsworth House, Imjin Barracks, Innsworth, Gloucester GL3 1HW.

Gallantry medals are those medals awarded for an especially heroic deed or action. Records for these are held at TNA, but may not be very detailed. Notifications and citations

(if published, which was not the case for awards such as the Military Medal and Mentions in Despatches) appeared in the official journal *London Gazette*. A complete set of this, and the all important indexes, is held at TNA. The *London Gazette Online Archive* at www.london-gazette.co.uk provides access to First and Second World War entries. The IWM has some

published listings of medal awards for decorations such as the Victoria Cross and Distinguished Conduct Medal. Usually you will need to go either to the official unit war diary (held at TNA) or to a published unit history to see whether you can find out more about the action for which the decoration was awarded. Local newspapers may also have reported medal awards. Recommendations for Honours and Awards, 1935-1990, are now available online at www.nationalarchives.gov.uk/documentsonline

Regimental Histories

The IWM has an excellent collection of regimental histories. For those unable to visit in person, *A Bibliography of Regimental Histories of the British Army* compiled by Arthur S White (London: London Stamp Exchange, 1988) provides details of published histories that may be available through your local library's inter-library loan scheme. Regimental magazines and forces newspapers should not be overlooked. *Soldier* magazine was first published in 1945, and continues to be an excellent source of information about military life. Some articles from past and present issues can be found on the website at www.soldiermagazine.co.uk

TNA has copies of the official unit war diaries – some of these for the First World War and Army of Occupation are now available online at www.nationalarchives.gov.uk/documentsonline

A useful title for locating regimental museums (although these are unlikely to hold information about individuals) is *The AMOT Guide to Military Museums in the UK* produced by the Army Museums Ogilby Trust *(Third Millennium Publishing, 2010)*. You can also find contact details at www.armymuseums.org.uk

The IWM Collections Enquiry Service can also advise on the addresses of Old Comrades Associations. The internet has made it easier to establish contact with people who may have served in the Forces, or who may be conducting research similar to your own. The Royal British Legion website at www.britishlegion.org.uk is a good place to start. The Army website at www.army.mod.uk is also useful. An excellent site for First World War Orders of Battle and Army information is www.1914-1918.net The Western Front Association at www.westernfrontassociation.com is also recommended. The Second World War is not as well covered on the internet, but one useful site is www.unithistories.com

Further Reading

More detailed information can be found in our

publication *Tracing Your Family History: Army* – this is currently out of print, but copies can be viewed in the Explore History Centre. The Museum does not hold any personal service records or official documentation, but can help the enquirer as long as some basic facts are known. The Collections Division welcomes visitors by appointment and is able to provide useful reading material and advice for finding out more about those who served. Other types of material - art, documents, three-dimensional objects, film, photographs and sound recordings - may also be able to assist.

Contact
Collections Enquiry Service
Imperial War Museum
Lambeth Road, London SE1 6HZ
T: (+44) 020 7416 5342
F: (+44) 020 7416 5246
E: collections@iwm.org.uk
W: www.iwm.org.uk

Michael O'Leary V.C.

MICHAEL O'LEARY V.C. AT HOME
Characteristic photograph of the gallant Irish Guardsman taken near his home in Co. Cork when he was in the Old Country on leave.

Irish Family History Research at The Imperial War Museum

Sarah Paterson MA DipLib

An Irish visitor to the Explore History Centre at the Imperial War Museum was very surprised to hear that we would be able to help him with the history of three First World War relatives, each of whom had a typical Irish experience. The first had served at the Battle of the Somme with the Royal Munster Fusiliers as part of the British Army, the second had served with the IRA in the immediate post-war period, and the third, who had emigrated to the United States of America, had served in France with an American regiment.

One third of the regular British Army was Irish on the outbreak of the First World War. This was a huge contribution, and many of these men will have joined up in peacetime because the military provided a roof over their head, food on the table and a regular income. The Army also offered the possibility of improving their lives through promotion and education opportunities, as well as offering a chance to see the world and fulfil a young man's yearning for adventure. With the coming of the war many more Irishmen enlisted, with both patriotism and the desire for home rule being added to the economic attractions of army life. There was never conscription in Ireland (introduced elsewhere in the British Isles from 1916) and all Irishmen who enlisted in Ireland were volunteers.

Those who fell were recorded in one of the most visually attractive of the many rolls of honour produced after the conflict: *Ireland's Memorial Records, 1914 - 1918: Being the Names of Irishmen who fell in the Great European War, 1914-1918.* This eight-volume work was compiled by the *Committee of the Irish National War Memorial,* under the direction of the Earl of Ypres, and published in very limited numbers in 1923. One hundred copies were printed *'for distribution through the principal libraries of the country.'* of the eight-volume set were printed. The printing; decoration and binding of the volumes was carried out by Irish artists and workers of the highest reputation and efficiency.

There are eight different page border designs by the artist Harry Clarke, best known for his work in stained glass. These repay close examination since they are filled with intricately worked cap badges, medals, and silhouettes, many taken from iconic photographs of the conflict. Over 49,000 names are listed – men serving

A page from Ireland's Memorial Records 1914 - 1918 showing the entry for John (Jack) Kipling son of Rudyard Kipling - Author & Poet

IRELAND'S MEMORIAL RECORDS 1914-1918

KINSLEY, MICHAEL. Reg. No. 5572. Rank, Corporal, Royal Munster Fusiliers, 2nd Batt.; killed in action, France, May 9, 1915; born Fothera, Co. Clare.

KINSLEY, PERCY. Reg. No. 7223. Rank, Private, Royal Irish Regiment, 2nd Batt.; killed in action, France, September 3, 1916; born High Barnet, Middlesex.

KIPLING, JOHN. Rank, Lieutenant, Irish Guards; killed in action, September 27, 1915.

KIRBY, JOHN. Reg. No. 22751. Rank, Corporal, King's Liverpool Regiment, 13th Batt.; killed in action, France, May 3, 1917; born Listowel, Ireland.

KIRBY, JOHN. Reg. No. WR/313219. Rank, Sapper, Royal Engineers (Inland Water Transport); died, home, August 6, 1918; born Cork.

KIRBY, MICHAEL. Reg. No. 6382. Rank, Private, Royal Irish Regiment, 2nd Batt.; died of wounds, France, January 22, 1915; born Trinity Without, Waterford.

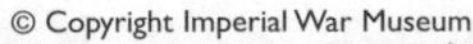

with Irish regiments, or those in other units, including commonwealth forces, who had Irish connections. It is not totally comprehensive – these rolls of honour seldom are – and gathering the names together must have been hampered by the political situation that had developed since the end of the First World War.

The actual details recorded vary from record to record. Name, Rank, Regiment and Regimental Number, and in most cases Place of Birth/County are recorded. In many cases Place of Death is also recorded.

Over 30,986 declared Ireland as their country of birth. For 741 individuals just Ireland was listed. 11,299 were from the six counties of Northern Ireland while 18,946 came from the remaining twenty-six counties. 7,405 had no place of birth recorded. The remaining 11,000 plus had Places of Birth spread throughout Britain, continental Europe, the United States of America, Canada and the rest of the World. These men and women considered themselves to be Irish, of Irish Heritage or fought with an Irish Regiment.

Many of the Irish infantry regiments disbanded in 1922 – The Connaught Rangers, The Royal Dublin Fusiliers, The Royal Irish Regiment, The Leinster Regiment and The Royal Munster Fusiliers - and although the Imperial War Museum has always been able to provide regimental histories, photographs and some personal letters and diaries, we have felt the lack of regimental museums and other places to which people can be referred. It has been wonderful to see the interest in the Great War that has been reawakening in Ireland over the last decade – the publications that are pouring out, the stamp commemorating the 90th anniversary of the Battle of the Somme in 2006, and the regimental associations that are now flourishing.

Relating to our visitor's second strand of interest, although the Imperial War Museum does not have an extensive collection of material on the Irish Republican Army, there is certainly some. There will also be collections relating to the British Army stationed in Ireland – and anybody wanting to look at IRA actions in the early 1920s would presumably be interested in looking at what the forces they were campaigning against were doing.

Finally, the Imperial War Museum is able to help with regard to Irish émigrés who may have ended up in the American Army – or that of Commonwealth countries such as Australia, Canada or New Zealand. We have an extensive collection of regimental histories from all of these countries which can be consulted by making an appointment to visit our Research Room. This is open Monday-Friday between 10.00.a.m. and 5.00.p.m. We also have the drop in Explore History Centre open every day of the week, where you can look at basic reference works, watch selected film footage and listen to interviews with veterans, as well as consult our catalogues and view selected websites.

Ireland has an immensely rich and varied history, which will make genealogical research interesting. The First World War played a huge part in the history of the country, and whatever your political stance, all those who served were individuals who deserve to be remembered.

Although the Imperial War Museum does not have personal service records or official documentation, we do have a wealth of material that can help you find out about what their unit did, and provide information about what the experience was like – at home and overseas, in both peace and war.

Contact

Collections Enquiry Service, Imperial War Museum, Lambeth Road, London SE1 6HZ
T: 020 7416 5346 E: collections@iwm.org.uk
W: www.iwm.org.uk

Useful Websites

www.findmypast.ie/search-records/Military-and-rebellion
www.findmypast.ie/content/irelands-memorial-record-world-war-1-1914-1918
www.findmypast.co.uk/irelands-memorial-records-search-start.action?product=IMR

Further Reading

Ireland's Memorial Records: World War 1 1914-1918 - CD-Rom ENEC011 Pub: Eneclann Ltd, Unit 1 Trinity College Enterprise Centre, Pearse Street, Dublin 2 (www.eneclann.ie/acatalog/ENEC011.html) ISBN: 1 905118 01 5

The Irish Genealogical Services Directory

Archives, Record Offices & Repositories

national

An tSeirbhís um Chlárú Sibhialta - The General Register Office Convent Road , Roscommon, Co Roscommon T: +353 9 0663 2900 E: gro.groireland.ie W: www.groireland.ie

Church of Ireland Representative Church Body - Library Representative Church Body Library, Braemor Park, Churchtown, Dublin 14, T: +353 1 492 3979 E: library@ireland.anglican.org W: www.library@ireland.anglican.org/

Commonwealth War Graves Commission 2 Marlow Road, Maidenhead, Berkshire SL6 7DX T: 01628 634221 E: casualty.enq@cwgc.org W: www.cwgc.org

Garda Historical Society - www.policehistory.com 8 Aisling Close, Ballincollig, County Cork T: +353 86 806 0385 E: pressoffice@garda.ie W: www.policehistory.com

Garda Siochana Museum & Archives The Records Tower, Dublin, 2 T: +353 1 6719 597 E: j_herlihy@esatclear.ie W: www.esatclear.ie/~garda/museum.html

General Register Office of Northern Ireland Oxford House, 49 - 55 Chichester Street, Belfast, BT1 4HL T: (028) 90 252000 E: gro.nisra@dfpni.gov.uk W: www.nidirect.gov.uk

Grand Lodge of Freemasons of Ireland Freemasons' Hall, 17 Molesworth Street, Dublin 2 T: + 353 01 6761337 E: office@freemason.ie W: www.irish-freemasons.org/

Irish World Heritage Centre 51 Dungannon Road, Coalisland, BT71 4HP T: 028 877 46055 E: info@irish-world.com W: www.irish-world.com/

Irish World Heritage Centre 51 Dungannon Road, Coalisland, BT71 4HP T: 028 877 46055 E: info@irish-world.com W: www.irish-world.com/

National Archives of Ireland Bishop Street, Dublin 8, T: +353 1 407 2300 E: mail@nationalarchives.ie W: www..nationalarchives.ie

Office of the Chief Herald of Ireland Kildare Street, Dublin 2, County Dublin T: +353 1 603 0200 E: herald@nli.ie W: www.nli.ie

Óglaigh na hÉireann - The Defence Forces Military Archives Officer in Charge - Military Archives, Cathal Brugha Barracks, Rathmines, Dublin, Dublin 6 T: + 353 1 8046457 E: archives@military.ie W: www.militaryarchives.ie

Presbyterian Historical Society of Ireland 26 College Green, Belfast, BT7 1LN T: 028 9072 7330 E: phsilibrarian@pcinet.org W: www.presbyterianhistoryireland.com

Public Record Office of Northern Ireland 2 Titanic Boulevard Belfast, BT3 9HQ T: 028 90 534800 E: proni@dcalni.gov.uk W: www.proni.gov.uk

Registry of Deeds Henrietta Street, Dublin 1, T: +353 1 8716518 E: daire.guidera@prai.ie W: www.landregistry.ie

Religious Society of Friends (Quakers) in Ireland Quaker House, Stocking Lane, Dublin, 16 T: +353 1 4998003 F: +353 1 4998005 E: office@quakers-in-ireland.ie W: www quakers.ie

The National Archives Kew, Richmond, Surrey TW9 4DU T: 020 8876 3444 E: Online contact Form W: www.nationalarchives.gov.uk/

Valuation Office Irish Life Centre, Lower abbey Street, Dublin 1, T: +353 1 817 1000 E: info@valoff.ie W: www.valoff.ie

Imperial War Museum Lambeth Road, London, SE1 6HZ T: 020 7416 5342 E: collections@iwm.org.uk W: www.iwm.org.uk

National Army Museum Royal Hospital Road, Chelsea, London, SW3 4HT T: 020 7730 0717 E: info@nam.ac.uk W: www.nam.ac.uk

Probate Principal Registry of the Family Division First Avenue House, 42 - 49 High Holborn, London, WC1V 6NP T: (020) 7947 6939 W: www.courtservice.gov.uk

Probate Service The Postal Searches & Copies Department, Leeds District Probate Registry, York House, York Place, Leeds LS1 2BA T: +44 (113) 389 6133 W: www.justice.gov.uk/courts/probate/family-history

Royal Air Force Museum Grahame Park Way, Hendon, London, NW9 5LL T: (020) 8200 1763 E: research@rafmuseum.org W: www.rafmuseum.org.uk

Royal Marines Museum Eastney, Southsea, Hampshire PO4 9PX T: (023) 9281 9385 Exts 224 E: info@royalmarinesmuseum.co.uk W: www.royalmarinesmuseum.co.uk

The Australian Irish Heritage Association PO Box1583 , Subiaco , 6904 T: (08) 9345 3530 E: aiha@irishheritage.net

U.K. National Inventory of War Memorials Imperial War Museum, Lambeth Road, London SE1 6HZ T: 020 7207 9863/9851 E: memorials@iwm.org.uk W: www.ukniwm.org.uk

Email and Internet or Web Addresses

Email and Web addresses shown in this book have been notified to us by the Organisation or advertiser. Unlike a normal postal address these addresses are subject to frequent change. In the case of businesses Email forwarding and Website transfer are usually provided by links to the original address. This does not always happen and the only solution is to use the various search engines available on the internet. However because of the increasing amount of spam many organisations are using website based emailers and scripts to avoid the harvesting of email addresses by spammers. In instances where an email is not listed or if listed is rejected please visit the organisations website for contact details.

Regional

Belfast

Belfast Central Library Belfast Ulster Irish Studies, Royal Avenue, Belfast, BT1 1EA T: (028) 9024 3233 E: sheila.mcclean@librariesni.org.uk W: www.librariesni.org.uk

Belfast Family History & Cultural Heritage Centre 64 Wellington Place, Belfast, BT1 6GE T: (028) 9023 5392 E: office@iwhc.com

County Antrim

Belfast Central Library Belfast Ulster Irish Studies, Royal Avenue, Belfast, BT1 1EA T: (028) 9024 3233 E: sheila.mcclean@librariesni.org.uk W: www.librariesni.org.uk

County Armagh

Armagh Public Library 43 Abbey Street, Armagh, County Armagh BT61 7DY T: 028 37 523 142 E: admin@armaghpubliclibrary.co.uk W: armaghpubliclibrary.arm.ac.uk

County Carlow

Carlow County Library Tullow Street, Carlow, County Carlow T: +353 0 59 917 0094 E: library@carlowcoco.ie

County Cavan

Cavan County Library & Archives Farnham Centre, Farnham Street, Cavan, County Cavan T: +3530 49 437 8500 E: library@cavancoco.ie archives@cavancoco.ie

County Clare

Clare County Archives Clare County Council - Áras Contae an Chláir, New Road, Ennis, Co Clare T: +353 65 684 6414 E: archivesrecords@clarecoco.ie W: www.clarelibrary.ie/eolas/archives/archives_index.htm

Clare Heritage & Genealogical Centre Church Street, Corofin, County Clare T: + 353 65 683 7955 E: clareheritage@eircom.net W: www.clareroots.com

County Cork

Cork City & County Archives The Seamus Murphy Building, 33a Great William O'Brien Street, Blackpool, Cork City, County Cork T: + 353 (0) 21 450 5876 E: archivist@corkcity.ie W: www.corkarchives.ie

Cork City Ancestral Project c/o Cork County Library, Carrigrohane Road, Cork, County Cork T: +353 21 428 5648 E: corkancestry@corkcoco.ie

Mallow Heritage Centre 27-28 Bank Place, Mallow, County Cork T: +353 22 50302 E: mallowheritagecentre@gmail.com W: www.rootsireland.ie/

Skibbereen Heritage Centre Old Gas Works Building, Upper Bridge Street, Skibbereen, County Cork T: +353 28 40900 E: skibbheritage1@gmail.com W: www.skibbheritage.com

County Donegal

Donegal Ancestry Centre c/o John Coyle, Killycreen, Ramleton, County Donegal T: +353 74 915 1111 T: +353 9158285 : T: +353 868206714 E: info@donegalancestry.com W: www.donegalancestry.com

Donegal County Archives Cultural Services, 3 Rivers Centre, Lifford, County Donegal T: + 00353 74 72490 E: archivist@donegalcoco.ie W: www.donegal.ie

Donegal Local Studies Centre Central Library & Arts Centre, Oliver Plunkett Road, Letterkenny, County Donegal T: 00353 74 24950 E: Portal@donegalcoco.ie W: www.donegal.ie/library

County Down

Banbridge Genealogy Services Tourist Information Centre, F E McWilliam Gallery & Studio, 200 Newry Road, Banbridge, County Down BT32 3NB T: +44 (0)28 4062 3322 F: +44 (0)28 4062 5933 E: info@banbridgegenealogy.com W: www.banbridgegenealogy.com/

Belfast Central Library - see Belfast

County Dublin

Dun Laoghaire Heritage & Genealogy Centre Craft Courtyard, Marlay Park, Rathfarnham, County Dublin T: +353 1 204 7264 E: cmalone@dlrcoco.ie W: www.dlrcoco.ie/library/lhistory.htm

Fingal Genealogy / North Dublin - Swords Historical Society Ltd Carnegie Library, North Street, Swords, County Dublin T: +353 1 8400080 E: swordsheritage@eircom.net : fingalgenealogy@gmail.com W: www.rootsireland.ie

Dublin

Dublin City Library & Archives 138 - 144 Pearse Street, Dublin, 2 T: + 353 1 674 4800 E: cityarchives@dublincity.ie W: www.dublincitypubliclibraries.ie www.dublincitypubliclibraries.com www.dublinheritage.ie

County Kildare

Kildare Heritage & Genealogy Riverbank, Main Street, Newbridge, County Kildare T: +353 45 448350 E: kildaregenealogy@iol.ie W: http://kildare.rootsireland.ie

County Limerick

Limerick City Archives Limerick City Council, Merchant's Quay, Limerick, County Limerick T: +353 61 407293 E: archives@limerickcity.ie W: www.limerickcity.ie/

Limerick Genealogy Lissanalta House, Dooradoyle Road, Limerick, County Limerick T: +353 61 496 542 E: research@limerickgenealogy.com W: www.limerickgenealogy.com

Limerick Studies Lissanalta House, Dooradoyle Road, Limerick, T: +353 61 496 526 E: limerickstudies@limerickcoco.ie W: www.limerickcoco.ie

County Londonderry

Derry City Council Heritage & Museum Service Archive & Genealogical Service, Foyle Valley Railway Museum, Foyle Road, Derry BT48 6SQ T: 028 7136 5151 Ext 8250 E: bernadette.walsh@derrycity.gov.uk W: www.derrycity.gov.uk/museums W: www.derry.rootsireland.ie

County Longford

Longford Genealogy 17 Dublin Street, Longford, County Longford T: +353 43 334 1235 E: longroot@iol.ie

County Louth
Louth County Archive Service Old Gaol, Ardee Road, Dundalk, Co Louth T: + 353 (0)42 933 9387 E: archive@louthcoco.ie W: www.louthnewryarchives.ie W: www.louthcoco.ie
Louth County Library Roden Place, Dundalk, County Louth T: +353 42 935 3190 E: libraryhelpdesk@louthcoco.ie W: www.louthcoco.ie
Louth County Reference Library Roden Place, Dundalk, County Louth T: +353 42 933 5457 E: referencelibary@louthcoco.ie

County Mayo
Local Record Offices The Registration Office, New Antrim Street, Castlebar, County Mayo T: + 353 964 3024
Mayo North Family History Research Centre Enniscoe, Castlehill, Ballina, County Mayo T: + 353 96 31809 E: normayo@iol.ie W: www.mayo.irish-roots.net
South Mayo Family Research Centre Main Street, Ballinrobe, County Mayo T: +353 94 954 1214 F: +353 94 954 1103 E: soumayo@iol.ie W: http://mayo.irishroots.net/

County Meath
Meath Heritage Centre Town Hall, Castle Street, Trim, County Meath T: +353 46 943 6633 or +353 86 805 3293 E: meathhc@iol.ie

County Offaly
Irish Midlands Ancestry Bury Quay, Tullamore, County Offaly T: +353 506 21421 E: info@irishmidlandsancestry.com W: www.irishmidlandsancestry.com

County Roscommon
Roscommon Heritage & Genealogical Centre Church Street, Strokestown, County Roscommon T: +353 71 963 3380 E: info@roscommonroots.com W: www.roscommonroots.com

County Sligo
County Sligo Heritage & Genealogy Society Aras Reddan, Temple Street, Sligo, County Sligo T: +353 71 914 3728 E: heritagesligo@eircom.net

County Tipperary
Tipperary Excel Heritage Co. Ltd Mitchell Street, Tipperary Town, County Tipperary T: + 353 62380520 E: manager@tipperary-excel.com W: www.tipperary-excel.com
Tipperary Family History Research Centre Mitchell Street, Tipperary Town, County Tipperary T: + 353 62 80555 E: research@tfhr.org W: www.tfhr.org
Tipperary North Genealogy Centre The Governor's House, Kickham Street, Nenagh, County Tipperary T: +353 673 3850 E: tipperarynorthgenealogy@eircom.net W: www.tipperarynorth.ie/genealogy W: www.rootsireland.ie W: www.facebook.com/GenealogyinNorthTipperary
Tipperary South - Bru Boru Cultural Centre Rock of Cashel, Cashel, County Tipperary T: +353 62 61122 E: eolas@bruboru.ie

County Waterford
Waterford Archives & Local Records St Joseph's Hospital, Dungarvan, County Waterford T: 058-42199 E: dungarvanlibrary@waterfordcoco.ie
Waterford Heritage Services St Patrick's Church, Jenkin's Lane, Waterford, County Waterford T: +353 51 876 123 E: mnoc@iol.ie

County Westmeath
Athlone - Westmeath County Library - Local Studies Athlone Civic offices, Church Avenue, Athlone, County Westmeath T: +353 90 644 2157 E: athlib@westmeathcoco.ie W: www.westmeathcoco.i
Dun na Si Heritage Centre Knockdomney, Moate, County Westmeath T: +353 90 648 1183 E: dunnasimoate@eircom.net W: www.dunnasi.ie
Mullingar - Westmeath County Library - Local Studies County Buildings, Mount Street, Mullingar, County Westmeath T: +353 44 933 2161 E: mgarlib@westmeathcoco.ie

County Wicklow
Wicklow Family History Centre Wicklow County Archives, County Buildings, Station Road, Wicklow, County Wicklow T: +353 404 20126 E: wfh@eircom.net W: www.wicklow.ie/familyhistorycentre

Military
Óglaigh na hÉireann - The Defence Forces
Military Archives Officer in Charge - Military Archives, Cathal Brugha Barracks, Rathmines, Dublin, Dublin 6 T: + 353 1 8046457 E: archives@military.ie W: www.militaryarchives.ie

Police
Garda Historical Society - www.policehistory.com 8 Aisling Close, Ballincollig, County Cork T: +353 86 806 0385 E: pressoffice@garda.ie W: www.policehistory.com
Garda Siochana Museum & Archives The Records Tower, Dublin, 2 T: +353 1 6719 597 E: j_herlihy@esatclear.ie W: www.esatclear.ie/~garda/museum.html

County Genealogy Centres

Belfast
Ulster Historical Foundation 49 Malone Road, Belfast, BT9 6RY T: 028 9066 1988 F: 028 9066 1977 E: enquiry@uhf.org.uk W: www.ancestryireland.com

County Antrim
Ulster Historical Foundation 49 Malone Road, Belfast, BT9 6RY T: 028 9066 1988 F: 028 9066 1977 E: enquiry@uhf.org.uk W: www.ancestryireland.com

County Armagh
Armagh Ancestry 40 English Street, Armagh, County Armagh BT61 7BA T: 028 3752 1800 E: researcher@armagh.gov.uk W: www.armagh.co.uk

County Carlow - No Service

County Cavan
Cavan Genealogy Johnston Central Library, Farnham Street, Cavan, County Cavan T: +353 49 436 1094 E: cavangenealogy@eircom.net

County Clare
Clare Heritage & Genealogical Centre Church Street, Corofin, County Clare T: + 353 65 683 7955 E: clareheritage@eircom.net W: www.clareroots.com

County Cork
Cork City Ancestral Project c/o Cork County Library, Carrigrohane Road, Cork, County Cork T: +353 21 428 5648 E: corkancestry@corkcoco.ie
Mallow Heritage Centre 27-28 Bank Place, Mallow, County Cork T: +353 22 50302 E: mallowheritagecentre@gmail.com W: www.rootsireland.ie/
Skibbereen Heritage Centre Old Gas Works Building, Upper Bridge Street, Skibbereen, Co Cork T: +353 28 40900 E: skibbheritage1@gmail.com W: www.skibbheritage.com

County Donegal
Donegal Ancestry Centre c/o John Coyle, Killycreen, Ramleton, County Donegal T: +353 74 915 1111 : +353 9158285 : +353 868206714 E: info@donegalancestry.com W: www.donegalancestry.com

County Down
Ulster Historical Foundation 49 Malone Road, Belfast, BT9 6RY T: 028 9066 1988 F: 028 9066 1977 E: enquiry@uhf.org.uk W: www.ancestryireland.com

County Dublin
Dublin North
Fingal Genealogy / North Dublin - Swords Historical Society Ltd Carnegie Library, North Street, Swords, County Dublin T: +353 1 8400080 E: swordsheritage@eircom.net fingalgenealogy@gmail.com W: www.rootsireland.ie
Dublin South
Dun Laoghaire Heritage & Genealogy Centre Craft Courtyard, Marlay Park, Rathfarnham, County Dublin T: +353 1 204 7264 E: cmalone@dlrcoco.ie W: www.dlrcoco.ie/library/lhistory.htm

County Fermanagh
Irish World Heritage Centre 51 Dungannon Road, Coalisland, BT71 4HP T: 028 87 746065 E: info@irish-world.com W: www.irish-world.com/

County Galway
East Galway Family History Society Company Ltd Woodford Heritage Centre, Woodford, Loughrea, County Galway T: +353 90 974 9309 F: +353 90 974 9546 E: galwayroots@eircom.net E: galwayroots@gmail.com W: www.galwaysroots.com W: www.rootsireland.ie
Galway Family History Society (West) Ltd St. Joseph's Community Centre, Ashe Road, Shantalla, County Galway T: +353 91 860464 F: +353 91 860432 E: galwaywestroots@eircom.net W: www.rootsireland.ie

County Kerry - No Service

County Kildare
Kildare Heritage & Genealogy Riverbank, Main Street, Newbridge, County Kildare T: +353 45 448350 E: kildaregenealogy@iol.ie W: http://kildare.rootsireland.ie

County Kilkenny
Rothe House Family History Rothe House, Kilkenny, County Kilkenny T: +353 56 7722893 E: kilkennyfamilyhistory@rothehouse.com W: www.rothehouse.com

County Leitrim
Leitrim Genealogy Centre Main Street, Ballinamore, Co Leitrim T: +353 71 964 4012 E: leitrimgenealogy@eircom.net W: www.leitrimroots.com

County Limerick
Limerick Genealogy Lissanalta House, Dooradoyle Road, Limerick, Co Limerick T: +353 61 496 542 E: research@limerickgenealogy.com W: www.limerickgenealogy.com

County Londonderry
Derry Genealogy Centre Foyle Valley Railway Museum, Foyle Road, Londonderry, BT48 6SQ, Northern Ireland T: (028) 7136 5151 ext. 8254 E: genealogy@derrycity.gov.uk W: www.derry.rootsireland.ie

County Longford
Longford Genealogy 17 Dublin Street, Longford, Co Longford T: +353 43 334 1235 E: longroot@iol.ie

County Louth
Louth County Library Roden Place, Dundalk, County Louth T: +353 42 935 3190 E: libraryhelpdesk@louthcoco.ie W: www.louthcoco.ie

County Mayo
Mayo North Family History Research Centre Enniscoe, Castlehill, Ballina, County Mayo T: + 353 96 31809 E: normayo@iol.ie W: www.mayo.irish-roots.net
South Mayo Family Research Centre Main Street, Ballinrobe, County Mayo T: +353 94 954 1214 F: +353 94 954 1103 E: soumayo@iol.ie W: http://mayo.irishroots.net/

County Meath
Meath Heritage Centre Town Hall, Castle Street, Trim, County Meath T: +353 46 943 6633 or +353 86 805 3293 E: meathhc@iol.ie

County Monaghan
Monaghan Genealogy 6 Tully, Monaghan, County Monaghan T: +353 4 783 469
E: theomcmahon@eircom.net
Over 14,000 new records covering Kilmore & Drumsnat Catholic Marriages; Monaghan Catholic Parish marriages; Clontibret Parish Catholic marriages, Aghabog Catholic Marriages, Ematris Catholic marriages, Muckno (Castleblayney) Catholic marriages; Tullycorbet (Ballybay) Catholic marriages; Drumully (Currin) Catholic marriages are available on the County Monaghan Genealogy website. Additional baptismal records for Monaghan parish and Aghabog are nearing completion. Over 8,000 Clones COI baptismal records will also be available

County Offaly
Irish Midlands Ancestry Bury Quay, Tullamore, County Offaly T: +353 506 21421
E: info@irishmidlandsancestry.com
W: www.irishmidlandsancestry.com

County Roscommon
Roscommon Heritage & Genealogical Centre
Church Street, Strokestown, County Roscommon
T: +353 71 963 3380 E: info@roscommonroots.com
W: www.roscommonroots.com

County Sligo
County Sligo Heritage & Genealogy Society
Aras Reddan, Temple Street, Sligo, County Sligo
T: +353 71 914 3728 E: heritagesligo@eircom.net

County Tipperary
Tipperary North Genealogy Centre The Governor's House, Kickham Street, Nenagh, County Tipperary T: +353 673 3850
E: tipperarynorthgenealogy@eircom.net
W: www.tipperarynorth.ie/genealogy www.rootsireland.ie
W: www.facebook.com/GenealogyNorthTipperary

Tipperary South - Bru Boru Cultural Centre
Rock of Cashel, Cashel, County Tipperary
T: +353 62 61122 E: eolas@bruboru.ie

County Tyrone
Centre for Migration Studies Ulster American Folk Park, Mellon Road, Castletown, Omagh, County Tyrone BT78 5QY T: 028 82 256315
E: cms@librariesni.org.uk W: www.qub.ac.uk/cms
Irish World Heritage Centre 51 Dungannon Road, Coalisland, BT71 4HP T: 028 87 746065
E: info@irish-world.com W: www.irish-world.com/

County Waterford
Waterford Heritage Services St Patrick's Church, Jenkin's Lane, Waterford, County Waterford
T: +353 51 876 123 E: mnoc@iol.ie

County Westmeath
Dun na Si Heritage Centre Knockdomney, Moate, County Westmeath T: +353 90 648 1183
E: dunnasimoate@eircom.net W: www.dunnasi.ie

County Wexford - E: info@ifhf.ie

County Wicklow
Wicklow Family History Centre Wicklow County Archives, County Buildings, Station Road, Wicklow, County Wicklow T: +353 404 20126
E: wfh@eircom.net
W: www.wicklow.ie/familyhistorycentre

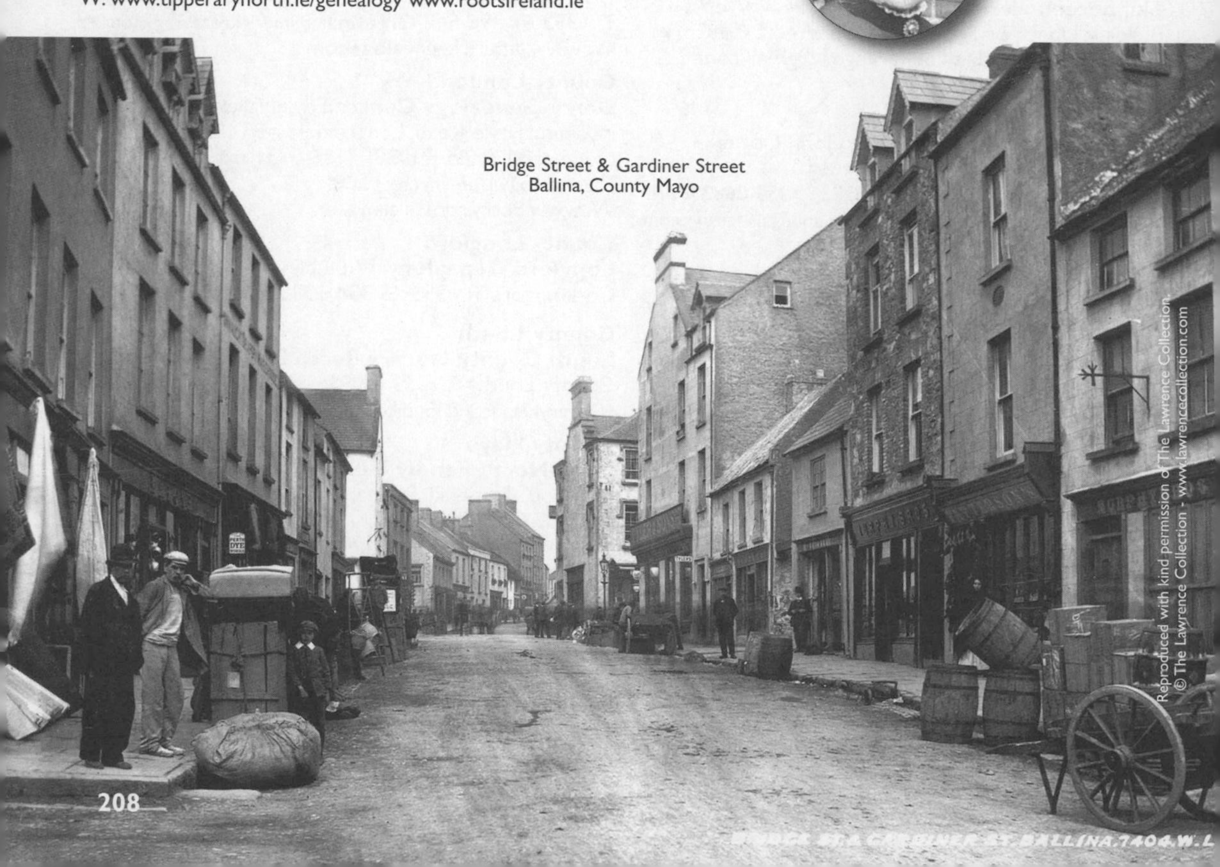

Bridge Street & Gardiner Street
Ballina, County Mayo

National

Mellon Centre for Migration Studies Ulster American Folk Park, Mellon Road, Castletown, Omagh, County Tyrone BT78 5QY T: 028 82 256315 E: mcms@librariesni.org.uk W: www.qub.ac.uk/cms
Linen Hall Library 17 Donegall Square North, Belfast, BT1 5GB T: 028 9032 1707 E: info@linenhall.com W: www.discovernorthernireland.com/The-Linen-Hall-Library-Belfast-P3057
National Library of Ireland Kildare Street, Dublin, 2 T: +353 1 6030 200 E: info@nli.ie W: www.nli.ie
Religious Society of Friends (Quakers) in Ireland Quaker House, Stocking Lane, Dublin, 16 T: +353 1 4998003 F: +353 1 4998005 E: office@quakers-in-ireland.ie W: www quakers.ie

Regional

Belfast
Belfast Central Library Belfast Ulster Irish Studies, Royal Avenue, Belfast, BT1 1EA T: (028) 9024 3233 E: sheila.mcclean@librariesni.org.uk W: www.librariesni.org.uk

Derry
Derry Central Library 35 Foyle Street, Derry, BT48 6AL T: 028 7127 2300 E: derrycentrallibrary@librariesni.org.uk

Dublin
Dublin City Library & Archive 138 - 144 Pearse Street, Dublin, 2 T: + 353 1 674 4999 E: dublinstudies@dublincity.ie cityarchives@dublincity.ie W: www.dublincitypubliclibraries.ie (Heritage & History) www.dublincitypubliclibraries.com www.dublinheritage.ie

County Antrim
NEELB Local Studies Service Ballymena Central Library, 5 Pat's Brae, Ballymena, County Antrim BT43 5AX T: (028) 2563 3960 E: localstudies.neelb@ni-libraries.net W: www.neelb.org.uk
North Eastern Library Board & Local Studies Area Reference Library, Demesne Avenue, Ballymena, Antrim BT43 7BG T: (028) 25 6641212 E: yvonne_hirst@hotmail.com W: www.neelb.org.uk

South Antrim
South Eastern Library Board & Local Studies Library HQ, Windmill Hill, Ballynahinch, County Down BT24 8DH T: (028) 9756 6400 E: ballynahinchlibrary@librariesni.org.uk

County Armagh
Armagh Public Library 43 Abbey Street, Armagh, County Armagh BT61 7DY T: 028 37 523 142 E: admin@armaghpubliclibrary.co.uk W: armaghpubliclibrary.arm.ac.uk

County Carlow
Carlow County Library Tullow Street, Carlow, County Carlow T: +353 0 59 917 0094 E: library@carlowcoco.ie

County Cavan
Cavan County Library & Archives Farnham Centre, Farnham Street, Cavan, County Cavan T: +3530 49 437 8500 E: library@cavancoco.ie archives@cavancoco.ie

County Clare
Clare County Library The Manse, Harmony Row, Ennis, County Clare T: +353 65 684 6271 E: mailbox@clarelibrary.ie W: www.clarelibrary.ie

County Cork
Cork City Library 57 - 61 Grand Parade, Cork, County Cork T: +353 21 492 4900 E: libraries@corkcity.ie W: www.corkcitylibraries.ie/
Cork County Library and Arts Service County Libary Building, Carrigrohane Road, Cork, Co Cork T: +353 21 454 6499 E: corkcountylibrary@corkcoco.ie W: www.corkcoco.ie/library : twitter.com/corkcolibrary
Mallow Heritage Centre 27-28 Bank Place, Mallow, County Cork T: +353 22 50302 E: mallowheritagecentre@gmail.com W: www.rootsireland.ie/

County Donegal
Donegal Central Library Oliver Plunkett Road, Letterkenny, County Donegal T: +353 74 912 4950 E: central@donegallibrary.ie
Donegal Local Studies Centre Central Library & Arts Centre, Oliver Plunkett Road, Letterkenny, County Donegal T: 00353 74 24950 E: Portal@donegalcoco.ie W: www.donegal.ie/library

County Down
South Eastern Library Board & Local Studies Library HQ, Windmill Hill, Ballynahinch, County Down BT24 8DH T: (028) 9756 6400 E: ballynahinchlibrary@librariesni.org.uk

County Dublin
Ballyfermot Public Library Ballyfermot Road, Dublin, 10 T: +353 1 626 9324 E: ballyfermotlibrary@dublincity.ie W: www.dublincity.ie
Dun Laoghaire Library Lower George's Street, Dun Laoghaire, County Dublin T: 2801147 E: localhistory@dlrcoco.ie W: www.dlrcoco.ie/library/lhistory.htm
Fingal Local Studies & Archives Clonmel House, Forster Way, Swords, County Dublin T: +353 1 870 4495 E: local.studies@fingalcoco.ie

County Fermanagh
Enniskillen Library Irish and Local Studies, Halls Lane, Enniskillen, County Fermanagh BT74 7DR T: 028 6632 2886 E: enniskillenlibrary@librariesni.org.uk
Enniskillen Library Halls Lane, Enniskillen, County Fermanagh T74 7DR T: 028 6632 2886 E: enniskillenlibrary@librariesni.org.uk

County Galway
Galway County Library Island House, Cathedral Square, Galway, County Galway T: +353 91 562 471 E: info@galwaylibrary.ie W: www.galwaylibrary.ie

County Kerry
Kerry Library Moyderwell, Tralee, County Kerry T: +353 66 712 1200 E: localhistory@kerrylibrary.ie E: archivist@kerrylibrary.ie W: www.kerrylibrary.ie

County Kildare
Kidare Library & Arts Services Kildare Collections & Research Services, Riverbank Arts Centre, Main Street, Newbridge, County Kildare T: +353 45 448351/448352 E: localhistory@kildarecoco.ie W: www.kildare.ie/library
Kildare County Library Newbridge, County Kildare T: +353 45 431109 E: Kildarelib@kildarecoco.ie W: www.kildare.ie/countycouncil/
Kildare Heritage & Genealogy Riverbank, Main Street, Newbridge, County Kildare T: +353 45 448350 E: kildaregenealogy@iol.ie W: http://kildare.rootsireland.ie

County Kilkenny
Kilkenny County Library John Green's House, John's Green, Kilkenny, County Kilkenny T: +353 56 779 4160 E: info@kilkennylibrary.ie

County Laois
Laois County Library J.F.L. Avenue, Portlaoise, County Laois T: +353 57 867 4315 E: laoislibrary@laoiscoco.ie

County Leitrim
Leitrim County Library Main Street, Ballinamore, County Leitrim T: +353 71 964 5582 E: leitrimlibrary@leitrimcoco.ie W:www.leitrimlibrary.ie

County Limerick
Limerick City Archives Limerick City Council, Merchant's Quay, Limerick T: +353 61 407293 E: archives@limerickcity.ie W: www.limerickcity.ie/
Limerick County Library Lissanalta House, Dooradoyle Road, Limerick County Limerick T: +353 61 496 526 E: libinfo@limerickcoco.ie
Longford County Library Town Centre, Longford, County Longford T: +353 43 334 1124 E: library@longfordcoco.ie

County Londonderry
Central and Reference Library 35 Foyle Street, Londonderry BT24 6AL T: (028) 71272300 E: derrycentrallibrary@librariesni.org.uk
Irish Room Coleraine County Hall, Castlerock Road, Ballymena, County Londonderry BT1 3HP T: 028 705 1026 E: educationlibraryservice@librariesni.org.uk W: www.neelb.org.uk

County Louth
Louth County Library Roden Place, Dundalk, Co Louth T: +353 42 935 319 E: libraryhelpdesk@louthcoco.ie W: www.louthcoco.ie
Louth County Reference Library Roden Place, Dundalk, County Louth T: +353 42 933 5457 E: referencelibary@louthcoco.ie

County Mayo
Central Library John Moore Road, Castlebar, County Mayo T: + 353 94 904793 E: plmccart@mayococo.ie W: www.mayococo.ie
Mayo County Library John Moore Road, Castlebar, County Mayo T: +353 94 9047921 E: librarymayo@mayococo.ie W: www.mayolibrary.ie

County Meath
Meath County Library Railway Street, Navan, County Meath T: +353 46 902 1134 E: localstudies@meathcoco.ie W: www.meath.ie/library

County Offaly
Offaly County Library O'Connor Square, Tullamore, County Offaly T: +353 57 934 6832 E: libraryhq@offalycoco.ie

County Roscommon
Roscommon County Library Abbey Street, Roscommon, County Roscommon T: +353 90 663 7275 E: roslib@roscommoncoco.ie

County Sligo
Sligo County Library Stephen Street, Sligo, County Sligo T: +353 71 9111 1850 E: sligolib@sligococo.ie W: www.sligococo.ie/
Sligo Reference & Local Studies Library Westward Town Centre, Bridge Street, Sligo, County Sligo T: +353 71 911 1858 E: sligolib@sligococo.ie W: www.sligolibrary.ie

County Tipperary
Tipperary County Libary Local Studies Department Castle Avenue, Thurles, County Tipperary T: +353 504 21555 E: studies@tipplibs.iol.ie W: www.iol.ie/~TIPPLIBS
Tipperary Excel Heritage Co. Ltd Mitchell Street, Tipperary Town, County Tipperary T: + 353 62380520 E: manager@tipperary-excel.com W: www.tipperary-excel.com
Tipperary Family History Research Centre Mitchell Street, Tipperary Town, County Tipperary T: + 353 62 80555 E: research@tfhr.org W: www.tfhr.org
Tipperary Studies Source Library, Cathedral Street, Thurles, County Tipperary T: +353 504 292 78 E: studies@tipperarylibraries.ie

County Tyrone
Omagh Library 1 Spillars Place, Omagh, County Tyrone BT78 1HL T: 028 8224 4821 E: omaghlibrary@librariesni.org.uk W: www.librariesni.org.uk

County Waterford
Waterford County Library Dungarvan Central Library, Davitt's Quay, Dungarvan, County Waterford T: +353 58 412 31 E: dungarvanlibrary@waterfordcoco.ie W: www.waterfordcoco.ie/

County Westmeath
Athlone - Westmeath County Library - Local Studies Athlone Civic offices, Church Avenue, Athlone, County Westmeath T: +353 90 644 2157 E: athlib@westmeathcoco.ie W: www.westmeathcoco.ie
Mullingar - Westmeath County Library - Local Studies County Buildings, Mount Street, Mullingar, County Westmeath T: +353 44 933 2161 E: mgarlib@westmeathcoco.ie

County Wexford
Enniscorthy Branch Library Lymington Road, Enniscorthy, County Wexford T: +353 53 923 6055
E: enniscorthylib@wexfordcoco.ie
W: www.wexford.ie/library
New Ross Branch Library Barrack Lane, New Ross, County Wexford T: +353 51 21877
E: newrosslib@wexfordcoco.ie W: www.wexford.ie/
Wexford Library McCauley's Car Park, Off Redmond Square, Wexford, County Wexford
T: +353 53 912 1637 E: wexfordlib@wexfordcoco.ie
W: www.wexford.ie/

County Wicklow
Wicklow County Library Boghall Road, Bray, County Wicklow T: +353 1 286 6566
E: library@wicklowcoco.ie W: www.wicklow.ie

Couny Monaghan
Monaghan County Library 98 Avenue, Clones, Couny Monaghan
T: +353 47 74712 or +353 47 74713
E: clennon@monaghancoco.ie

Museums

National

The National Museum of Ireland The National Museum of Ireland - Archaeology, Kildare Street, Dublin 2 next door to Leinster House (Government Buildings).
The National Museum of Ireland - Decorative Arts & History, Collins Barracks, Dublin 7
The National Museum of Ireland - Natural History, Merrion Street, Dublin 2 is centrally located on Merrion Street, Dublin 2, next door to the National Gallery.
The National Museum of Ireland - Country Life, Turlough Park, Castlebar, Co. Mayo has modern exhibition galleries in the spectacular grounds of Turlough Park House with its magnificent gardens and lake.
T: +353 1 6777444 W: www.museum.ie
Opening Times: (All four museums)
Tuesday to Saturday 10.00.a.m – 5.00.p.m.; Sunday 2.00.p.m. – 5.00.p.m. Closed Mondays (including Bank Holidays), Christmas Day and Good Friday
Admission is free to all four museums.
Garda Siochana Museum & Archives The Records Tower, Dublin, 2 T: +353 1 6719 597
E: j_herlihy@esatclear.ie W: www.esatclear.ie/~garda/museum.html
Police Museum - Police Service of Northern Ireland Brooklyn, 65 Knock Road, Belfast BT5 6LE
T: 0845 600 8000 Ext: 22499
E: museum@psni.police.uk
W: www.psni.police.uk/index/about-us/police_museum.htm
The Police Museum holds microfilm copies of the Royal Irish Constabulary service records 1822-1922, the originals of which are held at the Public Record Office at Kew in London

Regional

Belfast
Royal Ulster Rifles Regimental Museum 5 Waring Street, Belfast, BT1 2EW T: (028) 9023 2086
E: rurmuseum@yahoo.co.uk
W: www.armymuseums.org.uk/museums/0000000121-Royal-Ulster-Rifles-Museum.htm
http://news.bbc.co.uk/1/hi/northern_ireland/8175481.stm
Ulster Museum Botanic Gardens Botanic Gardens, Stranmillis Road, Belfast, BT9 5AB T: (028) 90381251 E: info@nmni.com W: www.nmni.com/

County Antrim
Ballymoney Museum Ballymoney Town Hall, 1 Townhead Street, Ballymoney, Co Antrim BT53 6BE
T: 028 2766 0230 E: museum@ballymoney.gov.uk
W: www.ballymoneyancestry.com
Friends of the Ulster Museum 12 Malone Road, Belfast, County Antrim BT9 5BN T: (028) 90681606
E: info@nmni.com
Irish Linen Centre & Lisburn Museum Market Square, Lisburn, County Antrim BT28 1AG
T: 028 9266 3377 E: irishlinencentre@lisburn.gov.uk
W: www.lisburncity.gov.uk
NI Museums Council 66 Donegall Pass, Belfast, County Antrim BT7 1BU T: (028) 90550215
E: info@nmni.com W: www.nimc.co.uk
The Braid Ballymena Town Hall Museum & Arts Centre, 1 - 29 Bridge Street, Ballymena, County Antrim BT43 5EJ T: 028 2565 716
F: 028 2563 5941 E: braid.enquiries@ballymena.gov.uk
The Museum Of The Royal Irish Regiment Royal Irish Fusiliers Museum, Sovereign's House, The Mall, Armagh, County Armagh BT61 9DL T: (028) 3752 2911 E: fusiliersmuseum@yahoo.co.uk
W: http://www.army.mod.uk/infantry/regiments/royalirish
Ulster American Folk Park Project Team Belfast 4 The Mount Albert Bridge Rd, Belfast, County Antrim BT5 4NA T: (028) 90452250
E: info@nmni.com
Ulster Aviation Society Heritage Centre, The Maze Regeneration Site, Halftown Road, Lisburn, County Antrim BT27 5RF
E: info@ulsteraviationsociety.org
W: www.ulsteraviationsociety.org/

County Armagh
Armagh County Museum The Mall East, Armagh, County Armagh BT61 9BE T: (028) 37523070
E: info@nics.gov.uk W: www.nmni.com/acm
Royal Irish Fusilers Museum Sovereign's House, Mall East, Armagh, BT61 9DL T: (028) 3752 2911
E: fusiliersmuseum@yahoo.co.uk
W: www.armymuseums.org.uk/museums/0000000103-Royal-Irish-Fusiliers-Regimental-Museum.htm

County Down
Down County Museum The Mall, Downpatrick, County Down BT30 6AH T: (028) 44615218
E: madeleine.mcallister@downdc.gov.uk
W: www.downcountymuseum.com

Downpatrick Railway Museum Railway Station, Market St, Downpatrick, County Down BT30 6LZ
T: (028) 44615779 E: downtrains@yahoo.co.uk
W: www.downrail.co.uk/

The Ferguson Linen Centre 54 Scarva Road, Banbridge, County Down BT32 3QD
T: 028 4062 3491 E: info@fergusonsirishlinen.com
W: www.fergusonsirishlinen.com

The Somme Heritage Centre 233 Bangor Road, Newtownards, County Down BT23 7PH
T: 028 9182 3202 E: enquiry.shc@hotmail.co.uk
W: www.irishsoldier.org

Ulster Folk and Transport Museum Cultra, Holywood, County Down BT18 0EU
T: 028 9042 8428 E: info@nmni.com
W: www.nmni.com/uftm

County Dublin

Dublin Civic Museum 58 South William Street, Dublin, 2 T: +353 679 4260
E: customerservices@dublincity.ie W: www.dublincity.ie/RecreationandCulture/MuseumsGalleriesandTheatres/Pages/Museums.aspx

County Fermanagh

Fermanagh County Museum Enniskillen Castle Castle Barracks, Enniskillen, Co Fermanagh BT74 7HL
T: 028 66 32 5000 E: castle@fermanagh.gov.uk
W: www.enniskillencastle.co.uk

Roslea Heritage Centre Monaghan Road, Rosslea, Enniskillen, County Fermanagh BT92 7DF
T: 028 6775 1750 E: clairybums@o2.co.uk
W: www.claires-rosleaancestry.co.uk/

Royal Inniskilling Fusiliers Regimental Museum The Castle, Enniskillen, County Fermanagh BT74 7HL T: (028) 66323142
E: info@inniskillingsmuseum.com
W: www.inniskillingsmuseum.com

County Londonderry

Foyle Valley Railway Museum Foyle Rd, Londonderry, County Londonderry BT48 6SQ
T: (028) 71265234 E: museums@derrycity.gov.uk
W: www.derrycity.gov.uk/museums

Garvagh Museum 142a Main St, Garvagh, County Londonderry BT51 5AE T: (028) 2955 7924
E: info@garvaghmuseum.com
W: www.garvaghmuseum.com

Londonderry Harbour Museum Harbour Square, Londonderry, County Londonderry BT48 6AF T: 028 7137 7331
E: museums@derrycity.gov.uk
W: www.derrycity.gov.uk

County Tyrone

The Ulster History Park Cullion, Lislap, County Tyrone BT79 7SU T: (028) 8164 8188
E: mail@sperrincottages.com
W: www.omagh.gov.uk/historypark.htm

Ulster American Folk Park Mellon Centre for Migration Studies, Mellon Rd, Castletown, Omagh, County Tyrone BT78 5QY T: (028) 8225 6315
E: info@nmni.com W: www.nmni.com

Other Museums

Imperial War Museum Lambeth Road, London, SE1 6HZ T: 020 7416 5342
E: collections@iwm.org.uk W: www.iwm.org.uk

Irish Jewish Museum 3 - 4 Walworth Road, South Circular Road, Dublin, 8 T: +353 857 067 357
E: museum@jewishireland.org
W: www.jewishmuseum.ie

Irish World Heritage Centre & Irish Diaspora Museum 10 Queens Road, Cheetham Hill, Manchester, M8 8UF T: 0161 205 4007
E: office@iwhc.com W: www.iwhc.com

London Irish Rifles Regimental Museum Connaught House, Flodden Road,, Camberwell, London, SE5 9LL T: 020 7820 4040
E: nwilkinson@googlemail.com
W: www.londonirishrifles.com

Sussex Combined Services Museum (Royal Sussex Regiment and Queen's Royal Irish Hussars) Redoubt Fortress, Royal Parade, Eastbourne, Sussex BN22 7AQ T: 01323 410300
E: redoubtmuseum@eastbourne.gov.uk
W: www.eastbournemuseums.co.uk

Bandon
County Cork

Registration Records for Births, Marriages & Deaths

The General Register Office
An tSeirbhís um Chláru Sibhialta
Government Offices,, Convent Road, Roscommon
T: +353 (0) 90 663 2900 W: www.groireland.ie/
The General Register Office also maintains a family history research facility at 3rd Floor, Block 7, Irish Life Centre, Lower Abbey Street, Dublin
This is the central repository for all records relating to life events (Births, Deaths, Marriages, Legal Domestic Adoptions, Stillbirths) in the Irish State. The General Register Office (An tSeirbhís um Chláru Sibhialta) maintains a genealogical / family history research facility at 3rd Floor, Block 7, Irish Life Centre, Lower Abbey Street, Dublin 1.
The Research facility is open Monday to Friday, (excluding public holidays) from 9.30 a.m. to 4.30 p.m. for the purpose of searching indexes to birth, death and marriage records and for obtaining photocopies of records identified from the indexes.
The indexes in relation to the following records of life events are available for inspection at the Research Facility:

1. Births registered in the island of Ireland between 1st January, 1864 and 31st December, 1921 inclusive, and in Ireland (excluding the six north-eastern counties of Derry, Antrim, Down, Armagh, Fermanagh and Tyrone known as Northern Ireland) from 1922 onwards.
2. Deaths registered in the island of Ireland between 1st January, 1864 and 31st December, 1921 inclusive and in Ireland (excluding Northern Ireland) from 1922 onwards.
3. Non-Roman Catholic Marriages registered in the island of Ireland between 1st April, 1845 and 31st December, 1863 inclusive.
4. Marriages registered in the island of Ireland between 1st January, 1864 and 31st December, 1921 inclusive and in Ireland (excluding Northern Ireland) from 1922 onwards.
5. Legal Domestic Adoptions registered in Ireland from 10th July, 1953 onwards.

Searches & Fees
Two types of searches may be undertaken at the Research Facility's Reading Room:
a specific search covering a maximum of 5 years
Fee: €2.00
a general search covering any number of years
Fee: €20.00 per day
A photocopy of an entry in the records (where the search has been carried out and the entry identified) can be purchased for €4.00.
Photocopies which cannot be provided immediately on request can be posted to applicants or may be collected by them at a later
All communications should be addressed to Government Offices, Convent Road, Roscommon, County Roscommon, Ireland. It is the central repository for all records relating to life events (Births, Deaths, Marriages, Legal Domestic Adoptions, Stillbirths) in the State. In addition to the records maintained at the genealogical/family history research facility, indexes to following registers of life events are maintained solely at GRO:

- Births at Sea of children, one of whose parents was born on the island of Ireland between 1st January, 1864 and 31st December, 1921. Births at Sea of Children, one of whose parents was born in Ireland after 1921.
- Deaths at Sea of persons born on the island of Ireland between 1st January, 1864 and 31st December, 1921 and of persons born in Ireland after 1921.
- Births of children of Irish parents, certified by British Consuls abroad, between 1st January, 1864 and 31st December, 1921.
- Deaths of Irish-born persons, certified by British Consuls abroad, between 1st January, 1864 and 31 December, 1921.
- Marriages celebrated in Dublin by the late Rev. J F G Schulze, Minister of the German Protestant Church , Poolbeg Street , Dublin , from 1806 to 1837 inclusive.
- Births, Deaths & Marriages registered under The (Army) Act, 1879.
- Births & Deaths registered under The Defence (Amendment) (No. 2) Act, 1960.
- Certain births and deaths occurring outside the State (under The Births, Deaths and Marriages Registration Act, 1972, Sec. 4).
- Certain Lourdes Marriages (under the Marriages Act, 1972, Sec.2).
- Stillbirths registered in Ireland from 1st January 1995 (certified copies available to parents only).
- Deaths of Irish officers and enlisted persons killed in action or who died while serving abroad in The Great War (WW1) 1914 - 1919.
- Death returns relating to the South African War (1899 – 1902) in so far as they relate to Irish subjects.

General Register Office of Northern Ireland, Oxford House, 49 - 55 Chichester Street, Belfast, BT1 4HL T: 03002007890 from U.K. + 44 28 9151 3101 E: gro.nisra@dfpni.gov.uk W: www.groni.gov.uk
GRONI holds civil birth, adoption, death, marriage and civil partnership records. It also maintains a public search room where you can search computerised indexes. The index provides name, date and place of event.
Registration indexes held by GRONI:
Births registered in Northern Ireland from 1st January 1864
Adoptions recorded in the Adopted Children Register Northern Ireland from 1st January 1931
Deaths registered in Northern Ireland from 1st January 1864

Registered Non-Roman Catholic marriages from 1st April 1845 and all registered marriages from 1st January 1864
Civil Partnerships registered in Northern Ireland from 5th December 2005
World War II death indexes from 1939 to 1945

Scotland
General Register Office for Scotland New Register House, Edinburgh, EH1 3YT
T: 0131 314 4300
E: enquiries@scotlandspeoplehub.gov.uk
E: records@gro-scotland.gsi.gov.uk
W: www.gro-scotland.gov.uk W: www.scotlandpeople.gov.uk

England & Wales
The General Register Office Room E201, Trafalgar Road, Birkdale, Southport, PR8 2HH T: 0845 603 7788 W: www.direct.gov.uk/gro

Isle of Man
Civil Registry Registries Building, Deemster's Walk, Bucks Road, Douglas IM1 3AR T: 01624 687039 E: civil@registry.gov.im W: www.gov.im/registries/general/civilregistry/birth.xml

Channel Islands
Guernsey
HM Greffier Royal Court House, St Peter Port, Guernsey GY1 2PB T: 01481 725277 W: www.gov.gg/ccm/portal/

Jersey
Judicial Greffe Morier House, Halkett Place, St Helier, Jersey JE1 1DD T: 01534-502300 E: jgreffe@super.net.uk W: www.gov.je/
Jersey 10 Royal Square, St Helier, Jersey JE2 4WA T: 01534 502335

Family History Societies

National

Cumann Geinealais na hÉireann : Genealogical Society of Ireland Archive: An Daonchartlann, Carlisle Pier, Dún Laoghaire Harbour, Co. Dublin, Ireland Secretary: 11 Desmond Avenue, Dún Laoghaire, Co Dublin, Ireland T: 353 1 284 2711
E: eolas@familyhistory.ie W: www.familyhistory.ie: www.facebook.com/familyhistory.ie
Twitter: @GenSocIreland

FamilySearch - (Genealogical Society of Utah) 185 Penns Lane, Sutton Coldfield, West Midlands B76 1JU T: 0121 384 9921 E: withingtonk@familysearch.org W: www.familysearch.org

Hugenot Society of Great Britain & Ireland - Irish Section Echo Hall, Spa, County Down BT24 8PT E: secretary@huguenotsociety.org.uk W: http://huguenotsociety.org.uk/

The Huguenot Society of Great Britain & Ireland PO Box 3067, Warlingham, CR6 0AN T: 020 7679 5199 E: secretary@huguenotsociety.org.uk W: www.huguenotsociety.org.uk

Irish Ancestry Group Irish Ancestry Group, Manchester & Lancashire FHS, 3rd Floor Clayton House, 59 Piccadilly, Manchester M1 2AQ T: 0161 236 9750 E: office@mlfhs.org.uk Web site www.mlfhs.org.uk

Irish Family History Forum PO Box 67, Plainview, New York 11803-0067 E: Web Form W: www.ifhf.org

Irish Family History Foundation c/o Riverbank, Newbridge, County Kildare T: 00 353 45 448 350 E: enquiries@rootsireland.ie W: www.rootsireland.ie

Irish Family History Society P0 Box 36, Naas, Co Kildare E: ifhs@eircom.net W: www.ifhs.ie

Irish Genealogical Society International 1185 Concord Street North, Suite 218, South St Paul, Minnesota 55075 E: Membership@IrishGenealogical.org W: www.irishgenealogical.org/

Irish Genealogical Research Society 18 Stratford Avenue, Rainham, Gillingham, Kent ME8 0EP E: info@igrsoc.org W: www.igrsoc.org

Irish Heritage Association PO Box 1583, Subiaco, 6904 T: 028 90455325 E: aiha@irishheritage.net W: www.irishheritage.net/

Irish Jewish Genealogical Society (A Division of the Irish Jewish Museum) Jasonia Centre, 76 Dame Street, Dublin, 2 T: +353 1 677 3808 E: srosenblatt@irishjewishroots.com for **Baltic Research** Len Yodaiken - shoshly@kfar-hanassi.org.il

Jewish Irish Group -ShalomIreland@yahoogroups.com for **Lithuanian research:** http://litvaksig.org/

Irish Jewish Community W: www.jewishireland.org/genealogy

Irish Palatine Association Old Railway Buildings, Rathkeale, County Limerick T: +353 (0)69 63511 E: info@irishpalatines.org W: www.irishpalatines.org

Irish Genealogical Research Society 18 Stratford Avenue, Rainham, Gillingham, Kent ME8 0EP E: info@igrsoc.org W: www.igrsoc.org

North of Ireland Family History Society Graduate School of Education, Queen's University of Belfast, 69 University Street, Belfast, BT7 1HL E: web@nifhs.org W: www.nifhs.org

Society of Genealogists Enterprises Ltd 14 Charterhouse Buildings, Goswell Road, London, EC1M 7BA T: 020 7251 8799 E: genealogy@sog.org.uk W: www.sog.org.uk

The Clans of Ireland - Finte na hÉireann 3 Cherry Park, Quinsboro Road, Newcastle, County Galway Ireland T: +353 91 524 811 E: info@clansofireland.ie W: www.clansofireland.ie

Ulster Historical Foundation 49 Malone Road, Belfast, BT9 6RY T: 028 9066 1988 F: 028 9066 1977 E: enquiry@uhf.org.uk W: www.ancestryireland.com

Regional

Belfast
Belfast Family & Community History 39 Rugby Road, Belfast, BT7 1PT W: www.belfasthistory.com

County Armagh
Armagh Ancestry 40 English Street, Armagh, County Armagh BT61 7BA T: 028 3752 1800 E: researcher@armagh.gov.uk W: www.armagh.co.uk

County Cavan
Cavan Genealogy Johnston Central Library, Farnham Street, Cavan, County Cavan
T: +353 49 436 1094 E: cavangenealogy@eircom.net

County Cork
Bandon Genealogy Group Kilbrogan House, Kilbrogan Hill, Bandon, County Cork
T: 00 353 23 88 44935 E: bandon.genealogy@gmail.com
W: www.kilbrogan.com www.bandon-genealogy.com
Cork Genealogical Society 22 Elm Drive, Shamrock Lawn, Douglas, County Cork
T: 086 8198359 W: www.corkgenealogicalsociety.com

County Dublin
Cumann Geinealais na hÉireann : Genealogical Society of Ireland Archive: An Daonchartlann, Carlisle Pier, Dún Laoghaire Harbour, Co. Dublin Secretary: 11 Desmond Avenue, Dún Laoghaire, Co Dublin T: 353 1 284 2711
E: eolas@familyhistory.ie W: www.familyhistory.ie

County Galway
East Galway Family History Society Company Ltd Woodford Heritage Centre, Woodford, Loughrea, Co Galway T: +353 90 974 9309
E: galwayroots@eircom.net E: galwayroots@gmail.com
W: www.galwaysroots.com www.rootsireland.ie
Galway Family History Society (West) Ltd St. Joseph's Community Centre, Ashe Road, Shantalla, County Galway T: +353 (0)91 860464
E: galwaywestroots@eircom.net
W: www.rootsireland.ie

County Kikenny
Rothe House Family History Rothe House, Kilkenny, County Kilkenny T: +353 56 7722893
E: kilkennyfamilyhistory@rothehouse.com
W: www.rothehouse.com

County Wexford
County Wexford Heritage and Genealogy Society County Wexford Heritage and Genealogy Society, Yola Farmstead, Folk Park, Tagoat, Rosslare, Co Wexford T: +353 53 9132610
E: wexgen@eircom.net W: http://homepage.eircom.net/~yolawexford/contactyola.htm
Wexford Family History Society 24 Parklands, Wexford, Co Wexford T: +353 53 22973
E: murphyh@tinet.ie

County Wicklow
Wicklow County Genealogical Society
1 Summerhill, Wicklow, County Wicklow

Dublin
Ballinteer Family History Society 29 The View, Woodpark, Ballinteer, Dundrum, Dublin 16
T: +353 1 298 8082 E: ryanct@eircom.net
Council of Irish Genealogical Organisations
31a All Saints Road, Raheny, Dublin 5
T: +353 1 406 3542 E: info@cigo.ie W: www.cigo.ie/
Flannery Clan / Clann Fhlannabhra 81 Woodford Drive, Clondalkin, Dublin, 22
E: oflannery@eircom.net W: www.flanneryclan.ie
Raheny Heritage Society 101 Collins Park, Donnycarney, Dublin 9, Dublin T: + 353 8 6160 5099
E: bjwray@eircom.net W: www.rahenyheritage.ie

One Name Studies

Guild of One Name Studies Box G, 14 Charterhouse Buildings, Goswell Road, London, EC1M 7BA T: 0800 011 2182 : E: guild@one-name.org
W: www.one-name.org
Clan Davidson Association 58 Chandos Avenue, Whetstone, London, N20 9DX T: +44 2084 452 787
E: contactus@clandavidson.org.uk
W: www.clandavidson.org.uk/

Overseas

The Australian Irish Heritage Association PO Box1583 , Subiaco , 6904 T: (08) 9345 3530
E: aiha@irishheritage.net
The Irish Ancestral Research Association Dept W, 2120 Commonwealth Avenue, Auburndale, Massachusetts 02466-1909 E: president@tiara.ie
W: www.tiara.ie

Local History Societies

Archives & Records Association (UK & Ireland) Prioryfield House, 20 Canon Street, Taunton, Somerset TA1 1SW T: 01823 327030
E: ara@archives.org.uk W: www.archives.org.uk
British Association for Local History PO Box 6549, Somersal Herbert, Ashbourne, Derbyshire DE6 5WH T: 01283 585947 E: mail@balh.co.uk
W: www.balh.co.uk
Federation of Local History Societies - Ireland Winter's Hill, Kinsale, County Cork
E: historyfed@eircom.net
W: http://homepage.eircom.net/~localhist/index.html
Federation for Ulster Local Studies 18 Ardmore Avenue, Downpatrick , County Down BT30 6JU T: +44(0)28 4461 2986 E: info@fuls.org.uk
W: www.fuls.org
Hugenot Society of Great Britain & Ireland Hugenot Library University College, Gower Street, London, WC1E 6BT T: 020 7679 5199
E: secretary@huguenotsociety.org.uk
W: www.hugenotsociety.org.uk
Hugenot Society - Irish Section Echo Hall, Spa, County Down BT24 8PT
E: secretary@huguenotsociety.org.uk
W: http://huguenotsociety.org.uk/
Irish Georgian Society 74 Merrion Square, Dublin, 2 T: +353 1 676 7053 E: info@igs.ie
W: www.igs.ie
Methodist Historical Society of Ireland, Methodist Study Centre, Edgehill College, 9 Lennoxvale, Belfast, BT9 5BY, Northern Ireland T: 028 9068 6934 E: archives@irishmethodist.org
W: www.edgehillcollege.org/library
Presbyterian Historical Society of Ireland 26 College Green, Belfast, BT7 1LN T: 028 9072 7330
E: phsilibrarian@pcinet.org
W: www.presbyterianhistoryireland.com

Regional

County Carlow

Carlow Historical & Archaeological Society 38 Kennedy Street, Carlow, County Carlow

County Cork

Bandon Genealogy Group Kilbrogan House, Kilbrogan Hill, Bandon, County Cork T: 00 353 23 88 44935 E: bandon.genealogy@gmail.com W: www.kilbrogan.com www.bandon-genealogy.com

County Dublin

Ballyfermot Heritage Group c/o Ballyfermot Library, Ballyfermot Road, Dublin, 10 E: Ballyfermotheritagegroup@gmail.com

Raheny Heritage Society 101 Collins Park, Donnycarney, Dublin 9, Dublin T: + 353 8 6160 5099 E: bjwray@eircom.net

County Londonderry

Roe Valley Historical Society 36 Drumachose Park, Limavady, County Londonderry BT49 0NZ E: r.w-guthrie@tiscali.co.uk

County Mayo

Mayo North Family History Research Centre Enniscoe, Castlehill, Ballina, County Mayo T: + 353 96 31809 E: normayo@iol.ie W: www.mayo.irish-roots.net

South Mayo Family Research Centre Main Street, Ballinrobe, County Mayo T: +353 94 954 1214 F: +353 94 954 1103 E: soumayo@iol.ie W: http://mayo.irishroots.net/

County Offaly

Offaly Historical & Archaeological Society Offaly Research & Exhibition Centre, Bury Quay, Tullamore, County Offaly T: + 353 5 062 1421 W: www.offalyhistory.com/

County Tyrone

Centre for Migratlon Studies Ulster American Folk Park, Mellon Road, Castletown, Omagh, County Tyrone BT78 5QY T: 028 82 256315 E: cms@librariesni.org.uk W: www.qub.ac.uk/cms

County Wexford

Wexford Historical Society c/o Melford House, Ballyhealy, Kilmore, County Wexford E: chair@wexfordhistoricalsociety.com W: www.wexfordhistoricalsociety.com

Police

Garda Historical Society www.policehistory.com 8 Aisling Close, Ballincollig, County Cork T: +353 86 806 0385 E: pressoffice@garda.ie W: www.policehistory.com

Cemeteries & Crematoria

County Antrim

Ballymena Cemetery Cushendall Rd, Ballymena, County Antrim BT43 6QE T: 01266 656026 E: council.reception@ballymena.gov.uk

Ballymoney Cemetery 44 Knock Rd, Ballymoney, County Antrim BT53 6LX T: 012656 66364 E: info@ballymoney.gov.uk

Blaris New Cemetery 25 Blaris Rd, Lisburn, County Antrim BT27 5RA T: 01846 607143 E: council@downdc.gov.uk

Carnmoney Cemetery 10 Prince Charles Way, Newtownabbey, County Antrim BT36 7LG T: 01232 832428 E: gmcburney@newtownabbey.gov.uk

City Cemetery 511 Falls Rd, Belfast, Co Antrim BT12 6DE T: 028 9032 3112 E: generalenquiries@belfastcity.gov.uk W: www.belfastcity.gov.uk/citycemetery

Greenland Cemetery Upper Cairncastle Road, Larne, County Antrim BT40 2EG T: 01574 272543 E: admin@larne.gov.uk

Milltown Cemetery Office 546 Falls Rd, Belfast, County Antrim BT12 6EQ T: 01232 613972 E: cemeteries@antrim.gov.uk

County Armagh

Kernan Cemetery Kernan Hill Rd, Portadown, Craigavon, County Armagh BT63 5YB T: 028 38339059 E: info@armagh.gov.uk

Lurgan Cemetery 57 Tandragee Rd, Lurgan, Craigavon, Co Armagh BT66 8TL T: 028 38342853 E: Info@armagh.gov.uk

County Down

Ballyvestry Cemetery 6 Edgewater Millisle, Millisle, Donaghadee, County Down BT21 0EF T: 01247 882657 E: council@downdc.gov.uk

Banbridge Public Cemetery Newry Rd, Banbridge, County Down BT32 3NB T: 018206 62623 E: council@downdc.gov.uk

Bangor Cemetery 62 Newtownards Rd, Bangor, County Down BT20 4DN T: 028 91271909 E: council@downdc.gov.uk

City of Belfast Crematorium 129 Ballgowan Road, Crossacreevy, Belfast, County Down BT5 7TZ T: 028 9044 8342 E: crematorium@belfastcity.gov.uk W: www.belfastcity.gov.uk/crematorium

Clandeboye Cemetery 300 Old Belfast Rd, Bangor, County Down BT19 1RH T: 028 91853246 E: council@downdc.gov.uk W: www.downdc.gov.uk

Comber Cemetery 31 Newtownards Rd, Comber, Newtownards, County Down BT23 5AZ T: 01247 872529 E: council@downdc.gov.uk W: www.downdc.gov.uk

Struell Cemetery, Old Course Rd, Downpatrick, County Down BT30 8AQ T: 01396 613086 E: council@downdc.gov.uk W: www.downdc.gov.uk

Down District Council - Lough Inch Cemetery Lough Inch Cemetery, Riverside Rd, Ballynahinch, County Down BT24 8JB T: 01238 562987 E: council@downdc.gov.uk W: www.downdc.gov.uk

Kirkistown Cemetery Main Rd, Portavogie, Newtownards, County Down BT22 1EL T: 012477 71773 E: council@downdc.gov.uk

Movilla Cemetary Movilla Rd, Newtownards, County Down BT23 8EY T: 01247 812276
E: council@downdc.gov.uk
Redburn Cemetery Old Holywood Rd, Holywood, County Down BT18 9QH
T: 01232 425547 E: council@downdc.gov.uk
Roselawn Cemetery 127 Ballygowan Rd, Crossnacreevy, Belfast, County Down BT5 7TZ
T: 01232 448288
E: generalenquiries@belfastcity.gov.uk
Whitechurch Cemetary 19 Dunover Rd, Newtownards, County Down BT22 2LE
T: 012477 58659 E: council@downdc.gov.uk

Dublin & County Dublin
Glasnevin Trust, Finglas Road Dublin 11
T: + 353 (0) 1 8826500, E: info@glasnevintrust.ie
W: www.glasnevintrust.ie
Dardistown Cemetery, Collinstown Cross, Old Airport Road, Cloghran, Co. Dublin
T: + 353 (0) 1 8424677 F: + 353 (0) 1 8424294
E: dardistowncemetery@glasnevintrust.ie
Glasnevin Cemetery & Crematorium, Finglas Road, Dublin 11 T: + 353 (0) 1 882 6500
F: + 353 (0) 1 830 1594 E: info@glasnevintrust.ie
Goldenbridge Cemetery, St. Vincents Street, Inchicore, Dublin 8 T: + 353 (0) 1 8301133
F: + 353 (0) 1 8301594 E: info@glasnevintrust.ie
Newlands Cemetery & Crematorium, Ballymount Road, Dublin 24 T: + 353 (0) 1 4592288
F: + 353 (0) 1 4592423
E: newlandscemetery@glasnevintrust.ie
Palmerstown Cemetery, Kennelsfort Road, Palmerstown Dublin 20T: + 353 (0) 1 4592288
F: + 353 (0) 1 4592423
E: palmerstowncemetery@glasnevintrust.ie
Dublin City Archives Dublin City Library & Archive, 138 - 144 Pearse Street, Dublin, 2
T: + 353 1 674 4800 E: cityarchives@dublincity.ie
The archives hold the *Registers of Mount Jerome Cemetery,* Dublin 1836 - 1972; *Registers of Deansgrange Cemetery,* Dublin 1865 - 1972;
The archives also hold a copy of *Memorials of the Dead* which is a series of volumes which list gravestone inscriptions in cemeteries in Dublin, Wicklow and Wexford. They are not published but are available in bound typescripts.

Dublin City Council is responsible for the following cemeteries: St. Canice's Cemetery, Killester Cemetery, Raheny Cemetery, Clontarf Cemetery, Bluebell Cemetery, Donnybrook Cemetery, Merrion Cemetery.

County Londonderry
Altnagelvin Cemetery Church Brae, Altnagelvin, Londonderry, County Londonderry BT47 3QG
T: 01504 343351 E: willie.burke@derrycity.gov.uk
City Cemetery Lone Moor Road, Londonderry, County Londonderry BT48 9LA T: 028 7136 2615
E: info@derrycity.gov.uk W: www.derrycity.gov.uk

County Tyrone
Cookstown Cemetery Westland Rd, Cookstown, County Tyrone BT80 8BX T: 028 8676 6087
E: info@cookstown.gov.uk W: www.cookstown.gov.uk
Greenhill Cemetery Mountjoy Road, Omagh, County Tyrone BT79 7BL T: 028 8224 4918
E: info@omagh.gov.uk W: www.omagh.gov.uk/

DeceasedOnline.com is the a central database of statutory burial and cremation registers for the UK and Republic of Ireland. In the past in order to search cemetery records it was necessary to contact one of nearly 3,250 burial authorities and crematoria. Each holding their own registers, mostly as old fragile books. DeceasedOnline.com are making it possible for burial and cremation authorities around the country to convert their register records, maps and photographs into digital form and bring them together into a central searchable collection.

It is a growing database, holding records mainly from the 1850s onwards which can provide invaluable information for researching family trees, and can reveal previously unknown family links from other interments recorded in the same grave.

The aim is to build a substantial database of tens of millions of burial and cremation records. Data is continually being added from all over the UK and Ireland.

www.interment.net is a publisher of cemetery transcriptions with online FREE listings and many of the transcriptions are of cemeteries that no longer exist. Cemeteries listed include the Counties of Antrim, Armagh, Carlow, Cavan, Clare, Cork, Derry (Londonderry), Donegal, Down, Dublin, Fermanagh, Galway, Kerry, Kildare, Kilkenny, Laois, Leitrim, Limerick, Longford, Louth, Mayo, Meath, Monaghan, Offaly, Roscommon, Sligo, Tipperary, Tyrone, Waterford, Westmeath, Wexford, Wicklow

Professional Genealogists & Researchers

Ancestor Network Limited Hyde Bank, 1 Hyde Park Avenue, Blackrock, County Dublin
T: +353 (0)1 219 5799 E: info@.ancestor.ie W:www.ancestor.ie
Deirdre Bryan - Bradan Research Services 91 Beech House, Sussex Road, Dublin, 4
T: + 353 86 047 7609 E: info@bradanresearch.com W: www.bradanresearch.com
Carmel Gilbride 49 Fitzwilliam Square, Dublin 4 E: carmel@itsyourhistory.ie
W: www.itsyouririshhistory.com
Kiara Gregory 47 Highfield Grove, Cathersless, Tralee, County Kerry E: gregoryk@eircom.net
John Hamrock Hyde Bank, 1 Hyde Park Avenue, Blackrock, County Dublin
T: +353 (0)1 219 5799 E: john.hamrock@ancestor.ie W: www.ancestor.ie
Historical Research Associates Glen Cottage, Glenmachan Road, Belfast BT4 2NP
T: 028 9076 1490 E: joan@historicalresearchassociates.com W: www.historicalresearchassociates.com
Historical Research Associates 40 Carrickburn Road, Carrickfergus, BT38 7ND
T: 028 93 368 50 E: jennifer@historicalresearchassociates.com W: www.historicalresearchassociates.com
Historical Research Associates offer a friendly, efficient and professional research service. All enquiries are answered promtly and all reports are well documented.
William Noel Jenkins Dublin, 18 T: + 353 129 597 15 E: wnoel@eircom.net
W: www.family-tree-research.com
Peter Kenny APG - Irish Family Ancestry Sligo, E: info@irishfamilyancestry.com
W: www.irishfamilyancestry.com
MC Research APG Seabank, Castlebellingham, Dundalk, County Louth T: +353 42 937 2046
E: mcres@iol.ie W: www.mc-research.com
Brendan O'Donoghue 47 Kerrymount Rise, Foxrock, Dublin, 18 T: +353 1 289 4462
E: brendan@researchireland.com W: www.researchireland.com
Gillian Weir Scully - Gillian's Genealogy Service Tivoli Mews, 7 Tivoli Terrace South, Dun Laoghaire, County Dublin T: + 353 1663 6668 E: help@gilliansgenealogy.ie
W: www.gilliansgenealogy.ie

Society of Genealogists Northern Ireland - SGNI

Society of Genealogists Northern Ireland (SGNI) 280 Castlereagh Road, Belfast , BT5 6AD
E: secretary@sgni.net W: www.sgni.net The Society of Genealogists Northern Ireland (SGNI) is a professional association comprising genealogists based in the six counties of Northern Ireland (Antrim, Armagh, Down, Fermanagh, Londonderry (Derry) and Tyrone). Members adhere to a Code of Practice and aim to promote genealogy at all levels and to provide a high quality of genealogical research. SGNI's website is www.sgni.net and the Secretary can be contacted at secretary@sgni.net To commission research contact Members direct.

Brookhill Ancestry - Kathleen McClure B.Sc. (Hons) 20 Croft Park, Holywood, County Down
BT18 0PF E: kmcc953041@aol.com Specialises in tracing living relatives
O D Cresswell 54 Rosscoole Park, Belfast, BT14 8JX E: ulsterfamilies@btinternet.com
Sylvia Cresswell 54 Rosscoole Park, Belfast, BT14 8JX E: ulsterfamilies@btinternet.com
Family Ulster - Brian Watson B.Sc. (Hons) 24 Moyne Park, Belfast, BT5 7QT
T: 028 90798551 E: info@familyulster.com W: www.familyulster.com
Ulster Ancestors - Heather Flanders 280 Castlereagh Road, Belfast BT5 6AD
E: heather.flanders@ntlworld.com W: www.ballynagarrick.net/ulsterancestors
Ulster Ancestree - Janet Abernethy 23 Larch Hill, Craigavad, Holywood, County Down
BT18 0JN E: janet@ulsterancestree.com W: www.ulsterancestree.com

Professional Genealogists and Researchers - Disclaimer

The Editors and Publishers of **The Irish Family & Local History Handbook 2** do not sponsor nor do they endorse the individuals or organisations listed here. We verify all information published with each of the professional genealogists listed. Professional qualifications and membership of accrediting organisations are as declared by the organisation or individual. Listing in this section is provided *FREE* of charge.

This list of researchers - private individuals and organisations - have indicated their willingness to carry out family history and other research on a professional, fee-paying basis.

The professional genealogists listed are expected to provide a high standard of service to our readers. If there is a failure to provide such a service the Editor and Publishers reserve the right to refuse to accept the inclusion of their details in future issues or reprints. We cannot accept responsibilty for research arrangements, payments or results or for any errors or omissions or for any losses however they may arise.

The Editors and Publishers cannot be held responsible for the errors, omissions or non performance by these individuals or organisations and where their performance falls below an acceptable level readers are asked to notify the Editors and Publishers in writing.

Professional Genealogists & Researchers

The Association of Professional Genealogists in Ireland

The Association of Professional Genealogists in Ireland E: info@apgi.ie W: www.apgi.ie
The Association of Professional Genealogists in Ireland (APGI) is the accrediting body for Irish genealogists. It was founded in 1986 and acts as a regulating body to maintain high standards amongst its members and to protect the interests of clients.

Mary Beglan FCII - Beglan Research Service, 13 St Assam's Drive,, Raheny,, Dublin 5
T: + 353 1 831 0848 E mbeglan@eircom.net
Pamela Bradley MAPGI - Research Ireland Blue Rock, Killough, Kilmacanogue, County Wicklow
T: + 353 1 286 9645 E: pamelabradley52@gmail.com W: www.apgi.ie/members-bradley.html
Susan Chadwick MAPGI - Clonymohan, Dunkerrin, Birr, County Offaly T: + 353 87 6419514
E: susan@ofirishdescent.com W: www.ofirishdescent.com W: www.apgi.ie/members-chadwick.html
Linda Clayton SRN MAPGI - 28 Marlfield, Cabinteely, Dublin 18 T: +353 1 285 6360
E: LindaClayton@iol.ie W: www.apgi.ie/members-clayton.html
Robert C Davison MAPGI - Enquireland, Ballynester House, 1a Cardy Road, Greyabbey, Newtownards, County Down BT22 2LS T: 028 4278 8386 E: enquireland@tiscali.co.uk
W: www.apgi.ie/members-davison.html
Aiden Feerick MAPGI - 17 Brooklawn Avenue, Blackrock, County Dublin T: + 353 1 2887882
T + 353 8 77916533 E: aidenfeerick@gmail.com W: www.ancestor.ie W: www.ancestor.ie
Steven C ffeary-Smyrl FIGRS MAPGI - Massey and King Ltd, 6 Brighton Road, Rathgar, Dublin, 6
T: + 353 1 406 3542 E: steven@masseyandking.com W: www.masseyandking.com
Fiona Fitzsimons - Eneclann Ltd, Unit 18 Trinity College Enterprise Centre, Pearse Street, Dublin, 2
T: + 353 1 671 0338 F: + 353 1 671 0281 E: info@eneclann.ie W: www.eneclann.ie
Paul Gorry FSG FIGRS MAPGI - 84 Ardglass, Baltinglass, County Wicklow E: gorry@indigo.ie
W: www.apgi.ie/members-gorry.html
John Grenham MA MAPGI FIGRS 7 Windele Road, Drumcondra, Dublin 9 W: www.johngrenham.com
Helen Kelly MAPGI 30 Harlech Crescent, Clonskeagh, Dublin, 14
T: + 353 1 278 4040 E: helen@helenkelly.com W: www.helenkelly.com
Gerry Kennedy MA BSc - Cloonmoney, Crusheen, County Clare T: +353 87 755 3304
E: jamesgkennedy@gmail.com W: www.apgi.ie/members-gkennedy.html
Máire Mac Conghail BA FIGRS MAPGI - 14 Ascaill Ghairbhile, Ráth Garbh, Baile Átha Cliath, 6
T: + 353 1 497 4621 E: : mairemacconghail@eircom.net W: www.apgi.ie/members-MacConghail.html
Henry McDowell FIGRS MAPGI - Celbridge Lodge, Celbridge, Co Kildare T: + 353 628 8347
W: www.apgi.ie/members-McDowell.html
David McElroy MAPGI - IGS Ltd, 94 University Avenue, Belfast, BT17 1GY T: 028 9066 7274 F: 028 9066 1277 E: research@igslimited.com W: www.igslimited.com W: www.apgi.ie/members-McElroy.html
Hilda McGauley MSc MAPGI - Records Ireland 13 The Glade, Woodfarm Acres, Palmerstown, Dublin 20
T: 0353 1 626 0189 E: research@recordsireland.ie W: www.recordsireland.ie
Justin Homan Martin MAPGI - 9 Fortfield Gardens, Rathmines, Dublin 6 T: +353 1 496 2617
E: jhomanmartin@gmail.com W: www.apgi.ie/members-Martin.html
Brian Mitchell MAPGI - Foyle Valley Railway Museum, Foyle Road, Derry BT48 6SQ
T: (44-28) 7136 5151 ext. 8254 E: genealogy@derrycity.gov.uk W: www.derry.rootsireland.ie
Nicola Morris MAPGI - Timeline Research Ltd 146 Tritonville Road, Sandymount, Dublin, 4
T: +353 87 632 5673 E: research@timeline.ie W: www.timeline.ie
Eileen Ó Dúill MA CG MAPGI - 47 Delwood Road, Castleknock, Dublin, 15 T: + 353 1 821 7272
E: info@heirsireland.com W: www.heirsireland.com
Joan Sharkey MAPGI - 68 Raheny Park, Raheny, Dublin, 5 T: + 353 1 831 4729 E: joan.sharkey@gmail.com
Robert Somerville-Woodward PhD MAPGI - Timeline Research Ltd 146 Tritonville Road, Sandymount, Dublin, 4 T: +353 87 632 5673 E: research@timeline.ie W: www.timeline.ie
Rosaleen Underwood MAPGI - 15 Whitechurch Drive, Ballyboden, Dublin, 16
E: underwor.rmc@gmail.com W: www.apgi.ie/members-underwood.html
Michael Walsh BSc (Econ) MAPGI - Carrowkeel, Murrisk, Westport, Co. Mayo T: +353 98 64746
E: michael9walsh@gmail.com W: www.myirishconnections.com

Please mention
The Irish Family and Local History Handbook
when contacting any of these listed Professional Genealogists and Researchers

Index to Advertisers

A

Ancestor Network Ltd 24
Archives
- Public Record Office of Northern Ireland 105
- Imperial War Museum 196
- National Library of Ireland 32
- National Library of Wales 65

B

Booklet Printers
- Charlesworth Press Ltd 221

C

Cassini Maps 48
Chapman on Football, Herbert 223
Charlesworth Press Ltd 221
Chart Printing - Family Trees My History 223
Christopher Paton 102 : 108
Computer Software My History 223
Cumann Geinealais na hÉireann
- Genealogical Society of Ireland 41

D

Data Disks
- Family and Local History Handbook 171

E

Eneclann 131

F

Family and Local History Handbook
- Omnibus 1-13 Data Disks 171

Family History Societies
- Cumann Geinealais na hÉireann
  - Genealogical Society of Ireland 41
- Irish Family History Society 30 : 58
- Ulster Historical Foundation 272

Family Tree Printing My History 223
Football - Herbert Chapman on Football 223
Find My Past Ireland Inside Front Cover

G

Genealogical Society of Ireland
- Cumann Geinealais na hÉireann 41

Genealogy Solutions, Irish 94

H

Herbert Chapman on Football 223
Historical Research Associates 35 : 166

I

Imperial War Museum 194
Ireland, Historical Research Associates 35 : 166
Irish Family History Societies
- Cumann Geinealais na hÉireann
  - Genealogical Society of Ireland 41
- Irish Family History Society 30 : 58
- Ulster Historical Foundation 20

Irish Family History Foundation IBC : 6 : 24
Irish Family History Society 30 : 58
Irish Genealogy Solutions 94
Irish Lives Remembered 166
Irish Research
- Ancestor Network Ltd 24
- Christopher Paton 102 : 108
- Eneclann 131
- Irish Family History Foundationl IBC : 6 : 24
- National Library of Ireland 32
- Historical Research Associates 35 : 166
- MC Research Services - M P McConnon M.A 58 : 139

Irish Roots Magazine 48 : 183

L

Lawrence Collection, The 48
Libraries
- National Library of Ireland 32
- National Library of Wales 65

M

Magazines - Irish Roots Magazine 48 : 183
Magazine Printing - Charlesworth Press Ltd 221
Maps Cassini Maps 48
Memorial s Irish Lives Remembered 166
MC Research Services
- M P McConnon M.A 58 : 139

Museums Imperial War Museum 196
My History 223

N

National Libary of Ireland 32

O

Omnibus - Family and Local History Handbooks
- 1-13 Data Disks 171

P

Paton B.A, Christopher 138
Photographic Collections
- The Lawrence Collection 48

Printing -
- Charlesworthworth Press Ltd 221
- My History 223

Professional Genealogists
- Ancestor Network Ltd 24
- Christopher Paton 102 : 108
- Eneclann 131
- Irish Family History Foundationl BC : 6 : 24
- National Library of Ireland 32
- Historical Research Associates 35 : 166
- MC Research Services - M P McConnon M.A 58 : 139

Public Record Office of Northern Ireland 105

R

Research
- Ancestor Network Ltd 24
- Christopher Paton 102 : 108
- Eneclann 131
- Irish Family History Foundationl BC : 6 : 24
- National Library of Ireland 32
- Historical Research Associates 35 : 166
- MC Research Services - M P McConnon M.A 58 : 139

Roots Ireland
- Irish Family History Foundation IBC : 6 : 24

S

Scotland's Greatest Story 102 : 108
Scottish GENES 102
Scottish Research :
Christopher Paton B.A. 102 : 108
Societies, Irish Family History
Cumann Geinealais na hÉireann
Genealogical Society of Ireland 41
Ulster Historical Foundation 20

T

The Family and Local History
Omnibus 1-13 Data Disk 171
The Irish Family and Local History Handbook 152
The Lawrence Collection 48
The National Library of Ireland 32
The Public Record Office of Northern Ireland 105
Tracing Your Ancestors in Ireland :
MC Research Services 58 : 139
TWR Computing 223

U

Ulster Historical Foundation 20

W

Wales, National Library of 65
www.ancestor.ie 24
www.cassinimaps.com 48
www.charlesworth.com 221
www.eneclann.ie 131
www.familyhistory.ie 41
www.findmypast.ie IFC
www.genealogical.co.uk 152 : 171
www.genealogical.ie 152 : 171
www.herbertchapman.com 223
www.historialresearchassociates.com 35 : 166
www.irishgenealogysolutions.com 94
www.irishlivesremembered.com 166
www.irishrootsmagazine.com 48 : 183
www.lawrencecollection.com 48
www.llgc.org.uk 65
www.mc-research.com 58 : 139
www.my-history.co.uk 223
www.nli.ie 32
www.proni.gov.uk 105
www.rootsireland.ie IBC : 6 : 24
www.ScotlandsGreatestStory.co.uk 102 : 108
www.ScottishAncestry.blogspot.com 108
www.uhf.org.uk 20

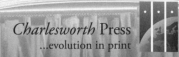

Index to Articles

A
Abduction, Attempt at Tipperary 117
Abductions in Eighteenth Century Ireland 113
Archives
- Dublin City Archives 70
- Public Record Office of Northern Ireland 103
- The National Library of Ireland 32
- The National Archives of Ireland 66
- The National Archives, Kew 145
- The National Library of Wales 62

Archives, Record Offices & Repositories – National 204
Archives, Record Offices & Repositories – Regional 205
Army: Tracing Army Ancestry 196

B
Beginners - Researching Irish Ancestors 8
Bram Stoker 125
British Parliamentary Papers relating to Ireland 85

C
Cemeteries & Crematoria 216
Commonwealth War Graves Commission 191
Census - The 1901 and 1911 Irish Censuses 180
Certificate of Irish Heritage 21
County Genealogy Centres 207
Church Records
- Presbyterians in Ireland: 153
- Presbyterian Historical Society of Ireland 164
- Representative Church Body Library 140
- Roman Catholic Parish Registers. 132

County Genealogy Centres 207
Cemeteries & Crematoria 216

D
Dublin City Archives 70

E
Editorial 7
Emigration
- Seeking Irish Ancestors in South Africa 118
- The Sad Side 42

F
Family History Societies
- Family History Societies – National 214
- Family History Societies – Regional 215
- One Name Studies - Overseas 215

From Gibraltar to Belfast 99
From the Mixer to the Modem- Irish Navvy 109

G
Genealogy Advisory Service 73
Genealogists & Researchers 218
Genealogy Centres 207

H
Harry Furniss : Illustrator 123
HMS Euryalus 190

I
Imperial War Museum 196 & 201
Index to Advertisers 220
Index to Articles 222
Internet - Online Irish Resources 167
Ireland's Memorial Records, 1914 - 1918 201
The Irish Family History Foundation 25
Irish Marriage and Death Certificates 213

J
John (Count) McCormack (The Peerless Irish Tenor) 59

L
Libraries 209
- Ask About Ireland 150
- Representative Church Body Library 140
- The National Library of Wales 62
- The National Library of Ireland 32

Local History Societies – National & Regional 215

M
McCormack, John (Count) (The Peerless Irish Tenor) 59
Military History
- Commonwealth War Graves 191
- My Ancestor and The Sudan War 184
- Tracing Army Ancestry 196

Military Museums 211
Miscellaneous Information 2
Museums 211
Museums
- The Imperial War Museum 196
- The National Museum of Ireland 69

Museum - Listings 211

N
Navy & Royal Marines :
- HMS Euryalus 190
- The Sudan War 184

The National Archives of Ireland 66
National Archives, Kew 145
The National Library of Ireland 32
The National Museum of Ireland 69

O
Online Irish Resources 167

P
Parliamentary Papers relating to Ireland 85
Professional Genealogists & Researchers 2
Presbyterians in Ireland: 153
Presbyterian Historical Society of Ireland 164
Professional Genealogists & Researchers 218
PRONI - Public Record Office of Northern Ireland 103
Publishing Information 2

R
Researchers, Professional Genealogists & 218
Researching
- Researching Irish Ancestors 8
- Seeking Irish Ancestors in South Africa 118

Record Offices & Archives 204
Registration Records for Births, Marriages & Deaths 213
Representative Church Body Library 140
Roman Catholic Parish Registers. 132

S
Societies, Family History Societies 214 : 215
South Africa - Seeking Irish Ancestors 118
Starting Out Researching Irish Ancestors 8

T
The Irish Genealogical Services Directory 203
in Ireland 191
Theobald Wolfe Tone - Irish Nationalist & Rebel 178
Tracing Army Ancestry at The Imperial War Museum 196

U
Upon Your Honour Sir! Duelling in Ireland 1750-1820 44

W
Wales, The Irish in 62
Wolfe Tone, Theobald - Irish Nationalist & Rebel 178